STREET FIGHTER ANNIVERSARY COLLECTION
OFFICIAL FIGHTER'S GUIDE

BY JOEY CUELLAR, MARK ROGOYSKI, ADAM DEATS, KEN SCHMIDT, CHRIS HAUSERMANN

D1242605

Before beginners can use the strategies, combos, and tactics presented in this guide, it's important to learn the common vocabulary of the *Street Fighter II* community. This language consists of not only official terms, but also naming conventions coined by various players as new techniques were created and explained. Learning these basic terms also provides a solid understanding of the core strategic concepts to construct effective gameplans.

BASIC ABILITIES

Despite the diversity found in the *Street Fighter* cast, each fighter shares the same control configuration and, therefore, the same basic move set. These moves are divided amongst several categories, each with distinct properties separating them.

NORMAL MOVES

Normal moves are attacks that require no control pad input. For example, when you press HP your character responds with a Hard Punch. Normal moves are great for stopping special normals or special moves. Normal moves come in four basic groups, including: crouching normals (hold ↓ on the control pad), close normals (close to an opponent), far normals (at a distance from an opponent), or jumping normals (in the air, pressing a punch or kick button).

SPECIAL NORMALS

Special normals are moves that require one controller motion plus a button. As an example, try Chun Li's → + HK. This makes her perform a Knee Flip Kick high into the air over opponents. These moves aren't part of the four basic groups of normal moves that each character has in common. Almost every character has one (or more) of these moves, so learn to utilize them.

SPECIAL MOVES

Special moves are moves that require multiple controller inputs plus a punch or kick at the end of the last input. These are powerful attacks

that inflict a lot of damage to an opponent. Almost all special moves can be used at the end of a combo for a big finish. Special moves also cause block damage, so be wary of blocking an opponent's special moves when your character is low on health.

SUPER COMBO

Super combos only exist in *Super Street Fighter II Turbo*. These attacks have special properties that usually consist of one (or more) special moves that are modified to have shadows behind them. Almost all sof these attacks can be used in a combo, and some can be followed up with normal or special moves. All super combos have invincibility frames at the beginning, so they cannot be stopped before they reach their attack phase. Also, all super combo attacks require a full Super Meter, and the attack drains the entire meter upon execution.

THROWS

Throws are performed by pressing → or ← along with a medium punch, hard punch, medium kick, or hard kick (depending on the character). Throws are instantaneous and unblockable, but they cannot be used while an opponent is reeling from an attack or stuck in a block animation following a blocked attack. Ground throws cannot be used against airborne opponents. Therefore, it's possible to escape every throw attempt by using a properly timed counter-attack with invincibility frames (such as Guile's Somersault Kick or M. Bison's Knee Press Nightmare). Any throw with multiple hits is not techable, and only *Super Turbo* characters have the ability to tech a throw.

BLOCK DAMAGE

Block damage is a term used to describe the damage dealt by a blocked special move. An attack's block damage is usually a small fraction of its actual damage (the damage that would normally be dealt if the attack were not blocked). However, a cornered opponent forced to block multiple special moves without a safe means of escape will quickly lose a significant portion of life. Super combos also deal block damage when they are blocked.

INVINCIBILITY FRAMES

Some special moves and super combos have invincibility frames, usually at the beginning of the attack. During this short period of time, the character becomes invulnerable to all attacks. A great example of this is Chun-Li's super combo (Senretsukyaku) where she unleashes six kicks in a row. She can pass through projectiles by performing this super combo at the last moment, and proceed to pummel her surprised opponent. Special moves such as Ryu's Tatsumaki Senpukyaku (from *Street Fighter II Turbo*) also have invincibility frames. In this case, the short invincibility period begins when Ryu leaves the ground and lasts until he starts to spin around in the air. With proper timing, this move can be used to pass through projectiles or escape any throw setup.

BASIC COMBO THEORY

In its simplest terms, a combo is a series of attacks that cannot be blocked or escaped from once the initial attack connects. Standard ground combos end when an opponent is allowed enough time between hits to recover (and block), or when the opponent is pushed out of attack range. With the exception of a special set of moves available in *Super Street Fighter II Turbo*, no attack can hit the opponent following a knockdown. The challenge of constructing powerful combos lies in avoiding these limitations for as long as possible. Although it's impossible to catalogue every possible combo, most combos are composed using a relatively small set of simple techniques. Understanding these principles is the first step in creating new and interesting combos.

RAPID-FIRE WEAK ATTACK COMBOS

Most characters have at least one standing or crouching light attack that can be chained into another, known as a rapid-fire weak attack. A "chain" is the interruption of one normal move by using another normal move. The only characters without any rapid-fire weak attacks are E. Honda, Blanka, Dhalsim, Vega, and Sagat.

 PRESSING THE CROUCHING LP BUTTON REPEATEDLY WITH ZANGIEF YIELDS A FOUR- OR FIVE-HIT RAPID-FIRE WEAK ATTACK COMBO BEFORE AN OPPONENT IS PUSHED OUT OF RANGE.

LINK COMBOS

Many attacks cause such a long hit stun and recover so quickly that an opponent is left reeling long after the attack animation finishes. You can follow the natural end of one move with another move, so that the two register as a combo. This is known as a "link."

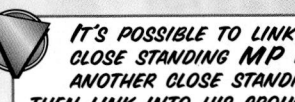

 IT'S POSSIBLE TO LINK BLANKA'S CLOSE STANDING MP WITH ANOTHER CLOSE STANDING MP, THEN LINK INTO HIS CROUCHING HK.

CANCEL COMBOS

One of the groundbreaking features of the *Street Fighter II* game engine is the ability to "cancel" normal attacks. A cancel is the interruption of a normal attack into a special move. Not all normal moves can be cancelled, and some characters have different sets of normal moves that cancel from one version to the next.

 AFTER LANDING KEN'S CROUCHING MK, YOU SIMPLY NEED TO COMPLETE THE HADOKEN MOTION TO TRUNCATE THE CROUCHING MK RECOVERY ANIMATION AND SCORE A TWO-HIT CANCEL COMBO.

JUMP ATTACK COMBOS

Jump attacks make excellent combo openers for a number of reasons, including: they cause a lengthy hit stun; they don't push an opponent back very far; and they permit another attack almost immediately upon landing. A common misconception is that it's always necessary to perform a "deep jump-in" attack (an air attack performed as late as possible). While this method allows for more time to follow up with a ground attack, it also pushes the opponent further away from the attacker. On the other hand, a "high jump-in" (an air attack performed as early as possible) leaves the attacker some air time to land closer to the opponent, but tightens the timing on the follow-up ground attack.

IT'S EASY TO FOLLOW ANY OF RYU'S JUMPING HPS WITH HIS CLOSE STANDING HP. HOWEVER, IT'S WISE TO ONLY FINISH WITH HIS LP SHORYUKEN IF THE COMBO IS STARTED WITH A HIGH JUMP-IN HP.

ADVANCED COMBO TECHNIQUES

An "illegal cancel" is something like crouching LK, crouching LK, crouching LK, or Flash Kick. Normally, the game doesn't allow rapid-fire weak attacks to be canceled after they have been chained together. However, you can utilize the Renda Kara technique to circumvent this rule. Although it's not necessary to master these techniques to be successful against most opponents, many players find them interesting intricacies of the game engine.

CROSS-UP JUMP ATTACK COMBOS

Some jump attacks can hit an opponent from in front of and behind an opponent. Jumping over an opponent and connecting with this type of air attack while facing the wrong way is known as performing a "cross-up" jump attack. Since cross-ups are performed while facing away from an opponent, they pull the opponent toward the attacker instead of pushing them away. This creates opportunities for longer combos than normal compared with frontal jump-in attacks.

YOU CAN CANCEL T. HAWK'S STANDING MK INTO HIS 2-HIT HP THUNDERSTRIKE FOR A 3-HIT COMBO. ADDING A FRONTAL JUMP-IN MK TO THE BEGINNING OF THIS COMBO CAUSES THE SECOND HP THUNDERSTRIKE HIT TO WHIFF. ON THE OTHER HAND, PERFORMING A CROSS-UP JUMP-IN MK RESULTS IN A GUARANTEED 4-HIT COMBO.

CORNER COMBOS

Attacks performed mid-screen push an opponent away from the attacker. Similarly, attacks performed against a cornered opponent push the attacker away. The main advantage of "corner combos" stems from a rule regarding projectile attacks (such as Guile's Sonic Boom or Sagat's Tiger Shot).

Although projectiles typically push an opponent back, performing them against cornered opponents does

not push the attacker away. Characters with quick projectile recovery can use this convention to follow the projectile up with another attack against cornered opponents. Furthermore, the corner provides a boundary necessary for several important juggle combos.

WITH THE PROPER SPACING, YOU CAN CANCEL CHUN-LI'S STANDING HP INTO HER MP KIKOKEN AND STILL HAVE ENOUGH TIME TO LINK A CROUCHING MK FOR AN IMPRESSIVE CORNER DIZZY COMBO.

JUGGLE COMBOS

Super Street Fighter II Turbo was the first *Street Fighter* game in which opponents could legitimately get hit multiple times while in the air or after a knockdown attack. This "juggle combo" system follows very strict, well-defined rules. Certain moves are assigned specific constant juggle potentials, which limit the number of juggle hits they can perform.

Most super moves have a juggle potential equal to the number of times they hit, and this property even extends to an exclusive group of special and normal attacks. To start a juggle combo, you must knock your opponent into the air by a move with non-zero juggle potential. After doing so, the opponent may be juggled for a maximum number of hits equal to the juggle potential of the attack used.

M. Bison's Knee Press Nightmare is a 4-hit super move with a juggle potential of four. Connecting this attack against a grounded opponent causes a knockdown on the final hit, creating a juggle setup. M. Bison's jumping MP has a juggle potential of two. Following his Knee Press Nightmare, use two jumping MP attacks to juggle the opponent for a total of six hits. Upon reaching the two juggle-hit limit, any further jumping MP attacks will fail to connect against the falling opponent.

As a counter-example, it's impossible to juggle after M. Bison's Double Knee Press special because it has zero juggle potential. Therefore, it does not qualify as a valid juggle setup, even though it knocks the opponent just as high into the air as his Knee Press Nightmare.

SUPER CANCEL COMBOS

Since super combos require such lengthy input sequences, it's nearly impossible to perform "super cancels" in the same way that a special move cancels. The timing is simply too difficult to be practical. Therefore, it's necessary to incorporate the desired normal attack halfway into the super move command. The specific methods vary greatly from super combo to super combo and with each normal that is canceled. With a little experimentation, it's easy to find the best method for performing any desired super cancel.

TO CANCEL SAGAT'S CROUCHING MK INTO THE TIGER GENOCIDE SUPER COMBO, YOU MUST PERFORM A QUICK ↓, ↘, → MOTION FOLLOWED BY A SHORT PAUSE TO AVOID EXECUTING AN ACCIDENTAL GROUND TIGER SHOT AND FINISH WITH ↓ + MK, ↘ + K.

RENDA KARA CANCEL COMBOS

In general, the *Street Fighter II* game engine does not allow a rapid-fire weak attack to be canceled into special moves or super combos if it has been used in a chain combo. The easiest way to overcome this obstacle is to alternate between crouching and standing light attacks on the hit before the cancel. This isn't a viable option, however, against crouching opponents because the necessary standing light attack will miss.

The advanced solution, called "Renda Kara" canceling, is to perform the desired number of rapid-fire weak attacks, then chain them into one more weak attack but can-

cel it into the target special or super combo before it animates. Although mastering this method requires extensive practice, it's a powerful and versatile technique. Since the final light attack is not meant to connect, this method can even use light attacks that are not normally cancelable.

CPS1 CHAIN COMBOS

Of the five games contained within *Hyper Street Fighter II Anniversary Collection*, the first three games were produced for Capcom's CPS1 hardware and the final two for Capcom's CPS2 hardware. *Street Fighter II*, *Street Fighter II Champion Edition*, and *Street Fighter II Turbo* all shared a peculiar glitch known as the "CPS1 chain," whereby rapid-fire light kick attacks could be chained into medium and hard punch attacks.

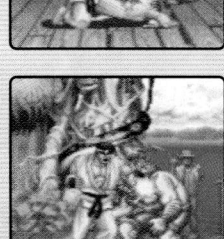

Following any crouching rapid-fire light kick attack, you could press standing LK + MP or LK + HP to cause a chain into that attack. The timing is the same as chaining rapid-fire light attacks. Oddly enough, standing light attacks can only be chained into crouching medium and hard attacks, while crouching light attacks can only be chained into standing medium and hard attacks. Those characters who do not have rapid-fire light kick attacks do not have this ability.

This glitch was removed during the transition to CPS2, and therefore making it absent from the *Super Street Fighter II* and *Super Street Fighter II Turbo* characters in the *Hyper Street Fighter II Anniversary Collection*.

> AFTER CONNECTING WITH RYU'S CROUCHING LK, IT'S POSSIBLE TO CPS1 CHAIN INTO HIS STANDING HP BY USING THE LK + HP INPUT. THIS CAN FURTHER CANCEL INTO AN HP HADOKEN! THIS POWERFUL 3-HIT COMBO USUALLY DIZZIES ANY OPPONENT.

> AFTER CHAINING THREE CROUCHING LK ATTACKS, TAP LK ONE MORE TIME AND ALMOST SIMULTANEOUSLY PRESS ↑ + HK TO RENDA KARA CANCEL INTO GUILE'S HK SOMERSAULT KICK FOR A 4-HIT COMBO. WHAT MAKES THIS COMBO EVEN MORE INTERESTING IS THE FACT THAT GUILE'S CROUCHING LK ISN'T A CANCELABLE NORMAL MOVE.

DEFENSIVE ABILITIES

The decision to block high, low, or the opposite direction is a huge factor in every match. Most standing attacks are blocked high by holding ← or low by holding ↙. Most crouching kicks hit low, so hold ↙ to block them. To block jumping attacks, hold ←.

CROSS-UP DEFENSE

If an opponent jumps over your character and attempts a cross-up attack, the correct block direction depends on the opponent's position when the hit occurs. If the cross-up connects before the attacker makes it to the other side, hold ← to block it, just like a frontal jump-in attack. If the cross-up connects after the defender turns around, it must be blocked high in the opposite direction.

BLOCK STUN

Following any blocked attack, the defending character is stuck in block animation for a fixed period of time. This condition, known as "block stun," varies in duration based upon the strength of the blocked attack.

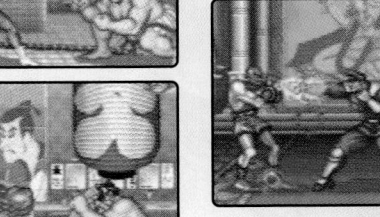

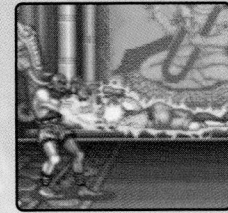

TURTLING

A player who does too much blocking is sometimes referred to as a "turtle." This term refers to a defensive style of play that relies on positioning, patience, and safe moves to slow down the pace of the game.

> M. BISON FROM STREET FIGHTER II CHAMPION EDITION HAS A SET ORDER OF MOVES THAT CAN KEEP AN OPPONENT IN BLOCK STUN FOR THE ENTIRE GAME. PERFORM A SCISSOR KICK, CROUCHING MK, LK, LP PSYCHO CRUSHER, LK, LK, SCISSOR KICK (OVER AND OVER). YOUR OPPONENT WILL HAVE FEW OPTIONS TO ESCAPE A SLOW DEATH BY BLOCK DAMAGE.

TICK-THROW

While keeping an opponent in block stun, follow up any attack by immediately throwing them. This is known as "tick-throwing." This usually involves using an LP or LK attack to put the character in block stun, then moving forward to throw them. This is one of the harder attack sequences to escape.

THROW ESCAPE

To combat an over-reliance on throwing, a throw escape system was added that reduced throw damage in half. This is known as "teching." To perform it, input a throw command immediately after being thrown. This enables the defender to escape the throw and fly into the air halfway, only taking half damage. It takes time to master the timing for this technique, but it is a great skill to learn.

WALKING UNDER JUMP-INS

When using a character with excellent walking speed (such as Chun-Li or Vega), walking under jump-in attacks becomes a very effective air defense tactic. This technique enables you to avoid the opponent's attack and gives you the initiative. Use it to set up big damage by tricking an opponent into blocking the wrong way at the last moment. Most characters can walk under a character with an extremely slow jump (such as M.Bison or Chun-Li).

SACRIFICE THROW

Another great technique is the "sacrifice throw," otherwise known as "taking the hit." In some instances, getting hit by an opponent's attack early enough enables you to recover first—and throw them—before they can follow up with another attack. This is great when an opponent performs an early jumping HK in an attempt to counter your character's anti-air options. By walking directly into the attack without blocking, you will be free to throw them first as they land. This tactic is also extremely useful in getting out of cross-up situations.

REVERSAL

A "reversal" occurs when a special move or a super combo is performed in the first instant following hit stun, block stun, knock down, air reel animation, or throw tech. Air reel animation is simply when a character gets hit in the air by a non-knockdown attack. The character basically does a backflip and becomes invincible until he or she lands. Each time a reversal is performed, the game notes it with a congratulatory message and bonus points. Performing a reversal attack with invincibility frames is the only guaranteed counter to a tick-throw.

WAKE-UP SITUATIONS

Each time your character gets knocked down, your opponent gains the opportunity to establish perfect spacing for an attack. In each case, you must get your character to stand up without getting hit by properly defending him or her. This situational guessing game is often referred to as "wake-up."

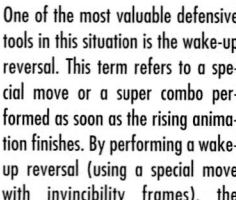

One of the most valuable defensive tools in this situation is the wake-up reversal. This term refers to a special move or a super combo performed as soon as the rising animation finishes. By performing a wake-up reversal (using a special move with invincibility frames), the defending player is guaranteed priority against any throw attempts or normal attacks. Characters from *Super Street Fighter II Turbo* can perform a reversal super combo on wake-up. This is extremely useful in corner situations, when both players are low on health.

Apart from performing a reversal, another wake-up option is to block patiently. Wake-up reversals are good for countering an opponent's attacks, but they leave you vulnerable if your opponent chooses to wait for them instead of attacking. Blocking will defend against any normal attacks, gradually pushing you away from the attacking character. As long as the attacker does not attempt a throw, you will be safe.

TRAPS

Character's like Ryu and Ken have Hadoken "traps." A trap is any repeatable pattern of attack that limits an opponent's options, leaving the defending player at a strategic disadvantage by rewarding the attacking player with sustained initiative.

Predicting the attacker's next move—and taking the safest course of action to avoid it—is the only way to escape good traps. Sometimes the best option is to give up the block damage and wait until the attacker becomes repetitive and predictable.

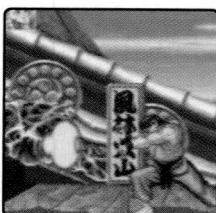

CONSIDER THIS EXAMPLE: RYU KNOCKS DOWN YOUR CHARACTER IN THE CORNER AND THROWS A HADOKEN THAT HITS YOUR CHARACTER ON WAKE-UP. YOUR OPTIONS ARE: BLOCK, GET HIT, OR JUMP. IF YOU BLOCK, RYU CAN THROW ANOTHER HADOKEN UNTIL YOU JUMP. IF YOU GET HIT, RYU STILL HAS AN ADVANTAGE (HE CAN THROW MORE HADOKENS). IF YOU JUMP, RYU CAN UNLEASH HIS SHORYUKEN. USE A SUPER COMBO ON WAKE-UP, HOWEVER, AND ITS INVINCIBILITY FRAMES WILL ALLOW YOU TO GO THROUGH HIS HADOKEN AND PUT HIM ON THE DEFENSIVE.

ADVANCED TACTICS

Although a solid knowledge of the basic offensive and defensive tools will enable you to defeat most beginners, it won't be enough to take on intermediate and expert players. This final section is dedicated to advanced tactics to help you defeat any opponent and, more importantly, to help you understand why you lost.

POKING

Advanced gameplay involves several tactics to win. Most players will use a barrage of normal moves instead of just doing special moves. Using safe mid-range or long range attacks is known as "poking." Many special moves take much longer to recover than normal moves. As such, they are more risky against experienced players who know the proper counter-attacks for them. Since poking is rather easy and safe to do, it is more common than a lot of the other techniques.

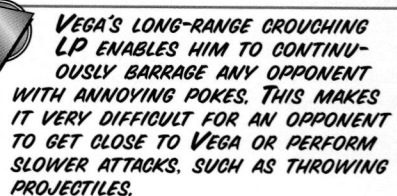

VEGA'S LONG-RANGE CROUCHING LP ENABLES HIM TO CONTINUOUSLY BARRAGE ANY OPPONENT WITH ANNOYING POKES. THIS MAKES IT VERY DIFFICULT FOR AN OPPONENT TO GET CLOSE TO VEGA OR PERFORM SLOWER ATTACKS, SUCH AS THROWING PROJECTILES.

ZONING

While poking requires knowledge of attack speeds and recovery rates, "zoning" focuses on attack ranges and positioning. The primary goal here is to acquire and maintain certain positions on-screen that are favorable to your character's arsenal, but unfavorable to your opponent's character. A character's best zoning distance is often equal to the range of that character's longest poke.

 *WHILE CHUN-LI'S MOST EFFECTIVE ZONING RANGE IS WITHIN STRIKING DISTANCE OF HER STANDING MP, DHALSIM HAS A ZONING ADVANTAGE OF ALMOST THREE-QUARTERS SCREEN DISTANCE FROM AN OPPONENT. IN FACT, DHALSIM'S LONG-RANGE LIMBS ENABLE HIM TO THREATEN AN OPPONENT FROM SUCH A LONG DISTANCE THAT IT'S DIFFICULT TO ZONE AGAINST HIM.*

FOOTSIES

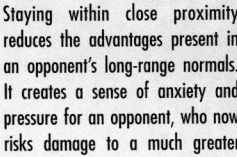

It's difficult to mount an effective long-range zoning gameplan against characters who have a strong attack range advantage. In such cases, it becomes necessary to play "footsies." The term footsies is basically a subset of zoning that is focused primarily on close-range normals, where the most common goals are to knock the opponent down and set up cross-up opportunities.

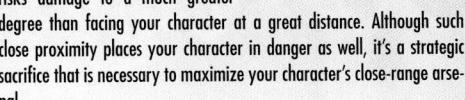

Staying within close proximity reduces the advantages present in an opponent's long-range normals. It creates a sense of anxiety and pressure for an opponent, who now risks damage to a much greater degree than facing your character at a great distance. Although such close proximity places your character in danger as well, it's a strategic sacrifice that is necessary to maximize your character's close-range arsenal.

If an opponent attempts a slow, long-range attack to push you away and force you to block, attempt a cross-up to force the opponent into a difficult guessing game. If an opponent attempts a quick short-range attack instead, stay just outside of the attack's range and use a crouching HK to counter attack when it whiffs, or fails to make contact. Knocking down an opponent in this way creates an advantage for the offensive player by allowing for a guaranteed cross-up or a tick-throw attempt.

 *SINCE GUILE'S NORMALS HAVE A GREATER RANGE THAN RYU'S, IT'S IMPORTANT FOR RYU TO STAY CLOSE TO GUILE AND PLAY FOOTSIES. IF GUILE TRIES TO PUSH RYU AWAY WITH HIS CROUCHING MK, RYU SHOULD WALK BACK TO FORCE IT TO WHIFF AND PUNISH IT USING HIS CROUCHING HK SWEEP. IF GUILE TRIES TO THROW A SONIC BOOM, RYU CAN JUMP OVER IT AND GO FOR A CROSS-UP ATTACK. IF GUILE BECOMES RELUCTANT TO ATTACK, RYU CAN SIMPLY INCH FORWARD AND THROW HIM. THIS ENTIRELY CLOSE-RANGE GUESSING GAME IS KNOWN AS FOOTSIES.*

MIND GAMES

"Mind games" are the most important part of *Street Fighter II*. By taking this approach, it's possible to make an opponent think that you will do a certain move, or series of moves, but instead do something different. By making an opponent do what you want them to do, you will be in control of the entire match. Keep track of your opponent's habits and patterns. Along the same lines, break free from your own patterns.

 *FIRST, ESTABLISH A SIMPLE PATTERN USING KEN AS AN EXAMPLE (SUCH AS JUMP IN HK, CROUCHING LK, CROUCHING MK, HADOKEN) BY PERFORMING THIS SERIES OF MOVES TWO OR THREE TIMES. WHEN YOUR OPPONENT GROWS ACCUSTOMED TO THIS PATTERN, BREAK IT BY DOING JUMP-IN HK, CROUCHING LK, THEN WALK UP AND PERFORM A THROW. NOW IT BECOMES VERY DIFFICULT FOR YOUR OPPONENT TO PREDICT YOUR INTENTIONS AFTER A JUMP-IN. THE NEXT TIME YOU ATTEMPT THE SAME PATTERN, YOUR OPPONENT MAY ATTEMPT A THROW ESCAPE AND INSTEAD GET HIT BY THE CROUCHING MK, HADOKEN COMBO.*

OVERALL GAME-PLAN

While the tactics explained in this chapter provide answers to several common situations, they are far from an overall "gameplan." A gameplan is a general outline of strategy and tactics for achieving victory, typically stemming from knowledge of character match-ups and player abilities. Hopefully after reading all these strategies, you will understand the game much better and construct effective gameplans for all situations on the fly.

OLD CHARACTERS AND NOT SO OLD CHARACTERS

There is a unique mode for *Hyper Street Fighter: Anniversary Collection* that lurks in the programming. It was originally intended for the arcade version of *Super Street Fighter II Turbo* where people could select the *Super Street Fighter II* versions of their character in the arcade. But when the programmers reprogrammed the code for the game, they made some errors and caused three characters to have some new properties. To access this secret mode, before picking your character version, hold down the Start button, select "Super" mode of play. Now release Start, and move to the character of your choice and select them. Now below your character, you should see the *Super Street Fighter II Turbo* logo (with Super in blue) with no super meter bar. This means you have successfully selected the "old" version of a *Super Street Fighter II Turbo* character. Of the 17 characters in the game, three had differences from their Super Street Fighter II counterparts. Chun Li has a special normal (→ + MK) that can now be done by doing (← + MK). This enables her to include it in combos. Fei Long can buffer his ↓ + LK, ↓ + MK, and ↓ + MP all into Rekka Ken's. Sagat has the ability to throw extremely fast Tiger Shot's without any recovery time, and the ability to use LK or MK to hit your opponent twice and follow it up with any special move.

SUPER STORING

Three characters in *Super Street Fighter II Turbo* have the ability to store special moves and super moves via a code. This was also a glitch, but made these characters extremely good in tournament play with this option. Chun Li, E. Honda, and Vega all have the ability to "store". To access this storing mode, before picking your character version, hold down the Start button, select "SuperT" mode of play. Now release Start, and move to the character of your choice and select any character. There will be no physical change of the super meter and logo of your character, but you will have moves that you can "store". Chun Li can store her Senretsukyaku by doing the super motion partially (Charge ← for 2 seconds, →, ←, and hold → without pressing a kick button. The Senretsukyaku is now stored. This means whenever you hit the next kick button, the Senretsukyaku will automatically come out. E. Honda can do the same with his super combo (Charge ← for 2 seconds, →, ←, and hold → without pressing a punch button. He can also "store" his Ohicho Throw. If you do → ↘ ↓ ↙ ←, and hold ←, whenever you hit the next punch button and are next to your opponent, the Ohicho Throw will come out. This can be stored in the air also. Lastly, Vega can store a flip kick. By charging ↙, and then holding ←, and pressing kick when you want the flip kick to come out.

Blanka

STANDING

One of the best anti-air moves in *Street Fighter II* for Blanka is the standing HK. This move is a modified flip kick, and it's a great anti-air move for any adversary who jumps in.

STANDING CLOSE

The close-range HK is one of the Blanka's coolest in-close normals. Without having to crouch, Blanka can sweep an opponent from a standing position. This is a huge maneuver in terms of the "high-low" game. In *Champion Edition*, Blanka's standing close HP changed from the rolling two-hit to a one-hit attack.

CROUCHING

Blanka's crouching HP is the second-best crouching move in the game. Only Guile can top him in this department. His crouching HP has great range and it stops an adversary from jumping most of the time because it connects even if the opponent is in the air.

THROWS

Blanka has one of the best throwing ranges in the game. He can grab an adversary from insane distances, and it isn't susceptible to the tech throw escape by *Super Street Fighter II Turbo* characters. You can add more hits to the throw by rapidly pressing all three punch buttons.

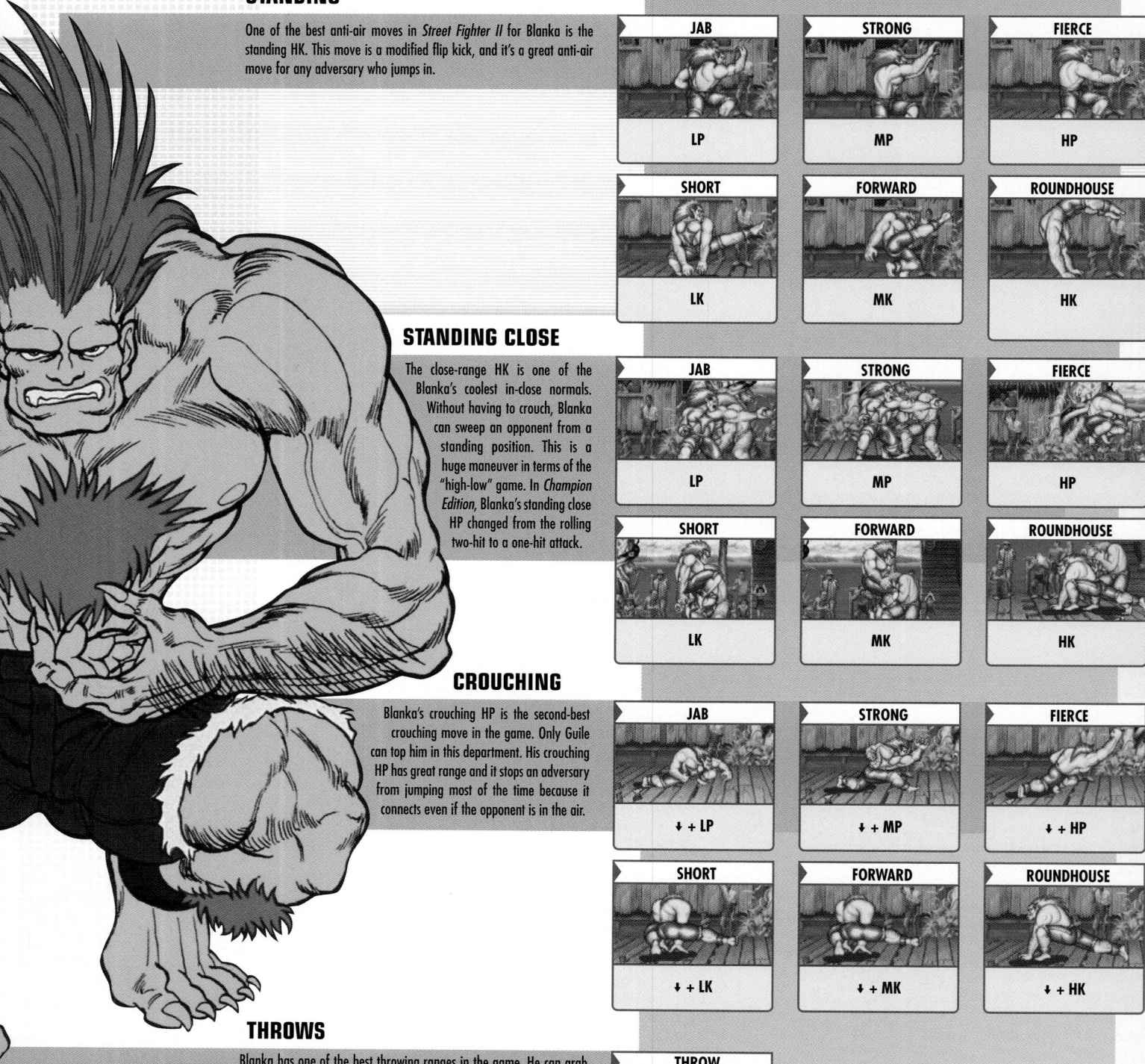

JAB	STRONG	FIERCE
LP	MP	HP
SHORT	FORWARD	ROUNDHOUSE
LK	MK	HK
JAB	STRONG	FIERCE
LP	MP	HP
SHORT	FORWARD	ROUNDHOUSE
LK	MK	HK
JAB	STRONG	FIERCE
↓ + LP	↓ + MP	↓ + HP
SHORT	FORWARD	ROUNDHOUSE
↓ + LK	↓ + MK	↓ + HK

THROW
→ / ← + HP

JUMPING

One of the best strategies for Blanka is to get in front of the opponent and jump straight up and down with HK. The jumping HK has a lot of range, and it can hit an opponent out of almost every move, *except* the Shoryuken.

JAB	STRONG

↑ + LP	↑ + MP

FIERCE	FIERCE

↑ + HP	↘ / ↗ + HP

SHORT	FORWARD

↑ + LK	↑ + MK

ROUNDHOUSE	ROUNDHOUSE

↑ + HK	↗ / ↖ + HK

SPECIAL NORMALS

→ + MP   **Headbutt**

The Headbutt is a great move for pressuring an opponent. While putting your opponent in Block Stun, it hits twice and leaves you in an advantageous situation.

SPECIAL MOVES

Press P rapidly   **Electric Thunder**

Electric Thunder is one of Blanka's greatest moves, even one of the best anti-air specials. If an opponent jumps in at you while Blanka is performing it, they will get hit. You may get hit in the process, but it hits your opponent every time. Electricity can also be used in a combo at any time.

Charge ←, → + P   **Rolling Attack**

The Rolling Attack has two practical uses. One is to use it in a combo, while the other use is for positioning. By using different buttons for the Rolling Attack, you can go across the screen and get next to an opponent within seconds. If you stop in front of your opponent, use a throw for maximum effectiveness and damage.

Charge ↓, ↑ + K   **Vertical Rolling Attack**

The Vertical Rolling Attack provides a huge advantage. Not only does this move hit on the way up, but if it misses on the way up, it will hit on the way down. This move is best used to hit an opponent on the way down and put them in Block Stun. In this manner, it's possible to walk up and throw them.

COSTUMES

STREET FIGHTER II

COSTUME

STREET FIGHTER II

ALTERNATE COSTUME

CHAMPIONSHIP

COSTUME

TURBO

COSTUME

STREET FIGHTER II

Blanka's Rolling Attack is weaker than the other versions and, if it doesn't hit the opponent, it still goes into the air. Also, if you get hit out of the Rolling Attack, you will take four times the damage. Stay away at all costs!

STREET FIGHTER II CHAMPION EDITION

This version of Blanka lost the up-close normal HP. This move was a somewhat weak, two-hit punch. Other than that, there were no major changes to this version of Blanka.

STREET FIGHTER II TURBO

Arguably the second-best Blanka in this series of games. His Rolling Attack trap into throw, and his overall speed make him a force to be reckoned with. His throw range is the best in the game, so use it to your advantage. Knock your opponent down in the corner with a crouching HK, use the Vertical Rolling Attack to land on your opponent's head as he gets up, then go for the throw. This is a really difficult pattern to get out of.

COMBOS

STREET FIGHTER II

Jump in HK, MP, HK

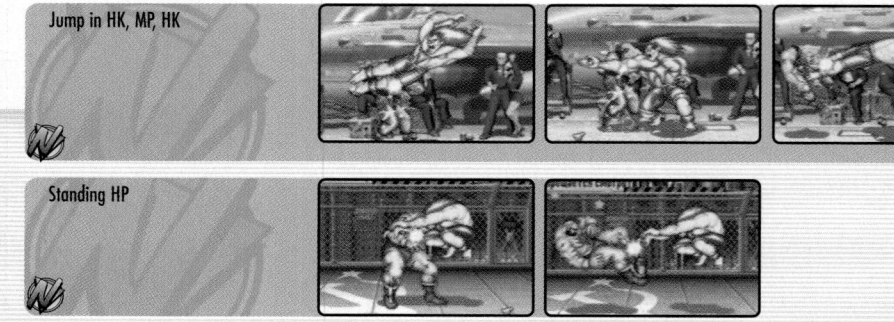

Standing HP

STREET FIGHTER II CHAMPION EDITION

Cross-up MP, MP, MP Electric Thunder

Jump in HK, MP, ↓ + HP

STREET FIGHTER II TURBO

HK Vertical Rolling Attack, MP, HK Vertical Rolling Attack

Cross-up MK, MP, MP, ↓ + HP

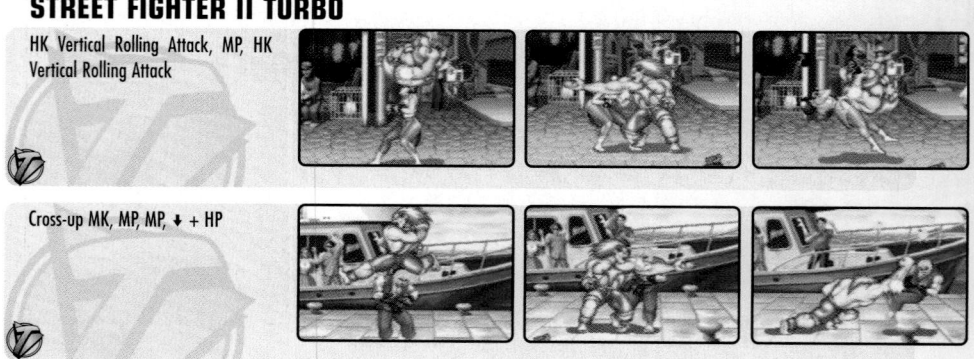

GOOD MATCH-UP

VS GUILE

Although Guile can counter Blanka's attacks from across the screen, Blanka controls the flow of this match-up very well from up close. Start the match with Blanka at a good range, but even if you get pushed away, it shouldn't be too difficult to get back in if you're patient. When fighting up close, Blanka's poking normal moves beat almost all of Guile's effective pokes, plus they inflict more damage. In particular, crouching MK is fast and hits with ease. Guile needs to set up his attacks by throwing Sonic Booms, but it's easy to respond to these attacks. From up close, use a crouching MK, crouching HK, or crouching HP to either trade damage with the projectile, or hit Guile to trade (and do more damage) after the Sonic Boom is already out, but before Guile has recovered. Blanka can also use the ↘ + HP Slide, which moves cleanly underneath the Sonic Boom, hits Guile, and knocks him down to setup a cross-up with jumping LK into a combo or a throw attempt. This move is also safe if blocked, but don't become too obvious with it or your opponent may Somersault Kick or sweep you out of it. Blanka can also jump over the Sonic Boom from close range and trade with, or beat, Guile's anti-air normal moves. If Guile blocks any of these attacks, go for a throw after landing; Blanka's huge range gives him the advantage here. Blanka also has a number of effective anti-air options. Moves like standing MK, standing HK, standing MP, standing HP, and the Vertical Rolling Attack (if charged) can all effectively prevent Guile from jumping at Blanka.

SUPER STREET FIGHTER II

There are a couple of new upgrades worth noting in this version. Blanka received the Backstep Rolling Attack and the ability to go past an opponent with the traditional Rolling Attack. The Backstep Rolling Attack is great for going over projectiles, or just trying to cross-up an opponent. The new placement of the end time on the Rolling Attack is an interesting addition, because you can knock down your opponent, roll past his or her body, and be on the other side when you get up. This is a big advantage when you're playing mind games with your opponent.

SUPER STREET FIGHTER II TURBO

This is definitely the best version of Blanka in this game, and his two new upgrades do a great job of balancing his attacks. The first big improvement is a new Slide attack (↘ + HP). This move slithers under projectiles and makes an opponent think twice about relying on a distance projectile approach. The other improvement is the Hop. This move does a couple of things. First, it helps Blanka charge the Super Meter faster than normal moves. You can actually charge the Super Meter to full in about seven or eight Hops. Second, this move can also put you in throwing range in a matter of seconds. Since Blanka has one of the best throws in the game, this move creates perfect opportunities to set up throws.

COMBOS

SUPER STREET FIGHTER II

Crossup MP, ← + HP, MP Electric Thunder

Jump In HK, ↓ + MK, MK Vertical Rolling Attack

SUPER STREET FIGHTER II TURBO

Jump In MK, ↓ + MK, ↓ + MK, HP Rolling Attack

  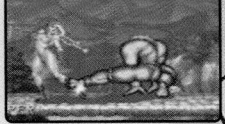

↓ + HK Knockdown, Ground Shave Rolling On Getup (Cross-up), ↓ + MK, HK Vertical Rolling Attack

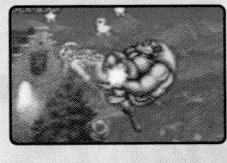 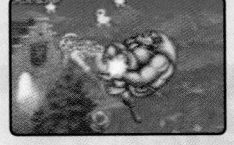 

BAD MATCH-UP

VS E. HONDA

E. Honda can win this match for a simple reason: He has some safe attack options and Blanka doesn't. Without a projectile, Blanka must use normal attacks. Unfortunately, E. Honda can just turtle up and use random Headbutts to counter the pokes. If Blanka attempts to turtle against Honda, Honda's pokes become more difficult to counter and he must also face E. Honda's Hundred Hand Slap. This move is relatively safe against Blanka, and can do enough block damage to force you to respond. Use Blanka's quick jump straight up and down in E. Honda's face, where his high priority MK and HK can stuff almost anything Honda can unleash. This may also bait Honda into doing a FP Headbutt. If this occurs, it will pass harmlessly underneath Blanka, and he can land and counter with a crouching HK before Honda recovers. This technique provides some extra time to try a setup with a cross-up LK. You can even misdirect E. Honda with Hopping or Electric Thunder attacks. Unfortunately, none of these options are particularly safe or effective, and defeating E. Honda usually requires some mistakes on the part of your opponent.

COSTUMES

LP

MP

HP

START

Hold any button

LK

MK

HK

NORMAL MOVES

STANDING

Blanka's standing moves are all extremely good for knocking your opponent out of the air. He has great speed and range, so all of his normals are great. His HK is a flip in place that works well at the end of a combo or for an anti-air move.

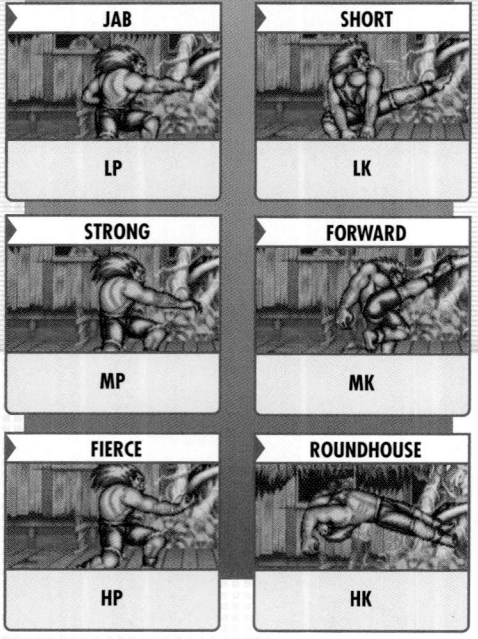

JAB — LP	SHORT — LK
STRONG — MP	FORWARD — MK
FIERCE — HP	ROUNDHOUSE — HK

STANDING CLOSE

Blanka's standing close moves are extremely good for following up with a throw. His LK and MK moves leave your opponent extremely vulnerable for a throw afterwards. His HP and HK moves are identical up-close as to their standing counterparts.

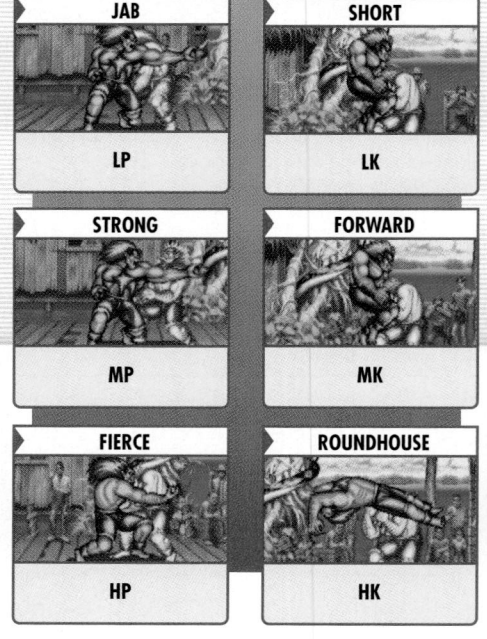

JAB — LP	SHORT — LK
STRONG — MP	FORWARD — MK
FIERCE — HP	ROUNDHOUSE — HK

CROUCHING

Blanka's crouching moves are great asset to him. His HP has incredible range and can hit your opponent before they leave the ground if they are jumping. His HK move is great for knocking your opponent off his feet and setting up a cross-up.

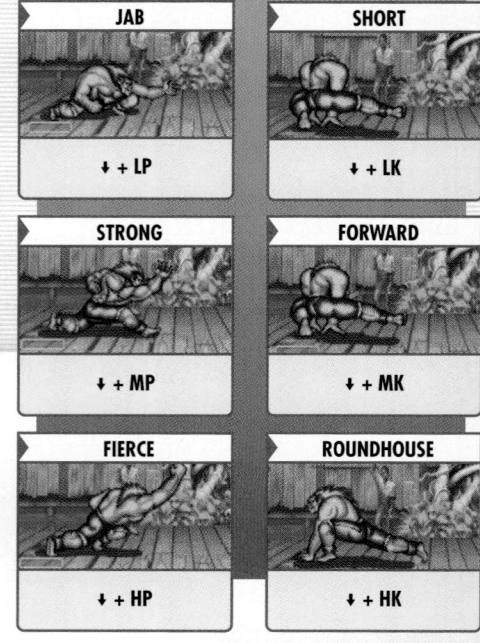

JAB — ↓ + LP	SHORT — ↓ + LK
STRONG — ↓ + MP	FORWARD — ↓ + MK
FIERCE — ↓ + HP	ROUNDHOUSE — ↓ + HK

SPECIAL NORMALS

→ + MP **Headbutt**

Blanka's Headbutt is a great weapon for last second combos when you don't have time to charge a special move. It strikes lightning quick, and does decent damage. You are also able to cancel out of the first part of it and combo it into a special move.

THROWS

Use the throw in conjunction with the Hop manuver and you're good to go! You can Hop multiple times in a row to get close to an opponent to throw them.

THROW

→ / ← + HP

↘ + HP **Slide**

Three of the best new moves are here. The Slide goes under every projectile, including the Ground Tiger Shot by Sagat! This move is extremely safe to use.

→ + 3K **Hop**

This is a great move for advancing forward in a short period of time. You can go across the screen within a few seconds. The Hop is also useful for adding to your Super Meter in a quick amount of time. It just takes a few Hops back and forth to fill up the bar.

← + 3K **Hop**

The Hopping moves can be used to charge the Super Meter or to get somewhere fast. It can also be used to get out of difficult situations when they arise.

JUMPING

Against a lot of projectile characters, Blanka has to utilize his jumping attacks. His main game is jumping straight up and down over projectiles and hitting opponents. His HK has incredible reach, and will stop a lot of moves from coming out. His MK is great for crossing up and starting a huge combo. Blanka also has great priority in the air with his jumping straight up punches.

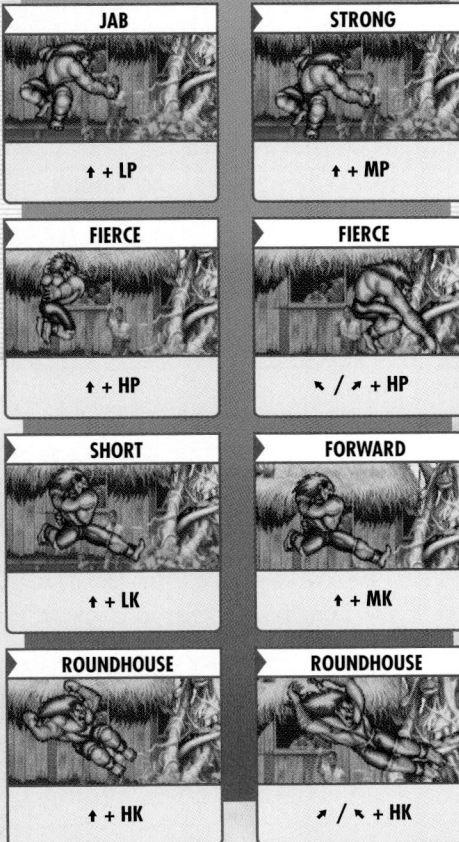

JAB	STRONG
↑ + LP	↑ + MP

FIERCE	FIERCE
↑ + HP	↘ / ↗ + HP

SHORT	FORWARD
↑ + LK	↑ + MK

ROUNDHOUSE	ROUNDHOUSE
↑ + HK	↗ / ↖ + HK

SUPER COMBO

Charge ←, → ← → + P   **Ground Shave Rolling**

Since this super combo has start-up invincibility frames, use it to go through projectiles. If you perform this move at the exact moment that the projectile is about to hit Blanka, he will go through it and hit your opponent since, the opponent's projectile isn't on-screen yet. You can also buffer and hold this move by holding a punch button while inputting the command for the super combo.

SPECIAL MOVES

Press P rapidly   **Electric Thunder**

Electric Thunder hasn't gotten any better or any worse over the years.

Charge ←, → + P   **Rolling Attack**

This is where it gets good. This attack is amazing to use for placement or with combos. In this version, it's possible to two-in-one this move. This move also enables you to place Blanka anywhere on the screen at any time—for any reason! This is big for setting up throws and combos on the other side of an opponent. When your adversary gets knocked down, use an MP Rolling Attack to get next to them and mix it up from there.

Charge ←, → + K   **Backstep Rolling Attack**

This move is great for going over projectiles and setting up throws. To do so, use it just short of opponents when it looks like it is going to hit them, it will land short of them, then you can throw them immediately after. It is best if you completely miss with this move and set up another attack to create serious mind games.

Charge ↓, ↑ + K   **Vertical Rolling Attack**

This move is extremely good for taking an opponent out of the air. Since it no longer comes down in a "ball-like" animation, this is the only purpose for this special move.

Chun-Li

STANDING

Chun-Li's high-priority normal moves are often faster than any special move. When used at the correct time, they can stuff almost any opponent's attack. They also link well into one another for easy combos.

JAB	STRONG	FIERCE
LP	MP	HP

SHORT	FORWARD	ROUNDHOUSE
LK	MK	HK

STANDING CLOSE

Chun-Li's standing close normals are great for setting up throws, or forcing your opponent to stay in block stun for a while. After landing one of these moves, you will be at a substantial frame and recovery advantage. Her standing LP is a great example of a quick move that can put opponents in block stun to create a throw opportunity.

JAB	STRONG	FIERCE
LP	MP	HP

SHORT	FORWARD	ROUNDHOUSE
LK	MK	HK

CROUCHING

Crouching normals are key for long-distance attacks. Most of her crouching moves go longer and farther than her standing moves, which makes them ideal for poking from afar.

JAB	STRONG	FIERCE
↓ + LP	↓ + MP	↓ + HP

SHORT	FORWARD	ROUNDHOUSE
↓ + LK	↓ + MK	↓ + HK

THROWS

Throws are a key part of any player's game in high-level play, and Chun-Li's excellent foot speed, high-pressure style, and big damage throws are a staple. Her standing LP is the best way to set up her tick-throw. Put your opponents in a block stun, then when they come out of it, throw them! Chun-Li's air throw is also one of the best in the game.

THROW	AIR THROW
→ / ← + MP / HP	→ / ← / ↓ + MP / HP

JUMPING

Many of these air moves can be used to cross-up opponents and start combos (Chun-Li's MK is a good choice in almost every version) that lead to big damage.

JAB

↑ + LP

JAB

↖ / ↗ + LP

STRONG

↑ + MP

STRONG

↖ / ↗ + MP

FIERCE

↑ + HP

FIERCE

↖ / ↗ + HP

SHORT

↑ + LK

SHORT

↖ / ↗ + LK

FORWARD

↑ + MK

FORWARD

↖ / ↗ + MK

ROUNDHOUSE

↑ + HK

ROUNDHOUSE

↖ / ↗ + HK

SPECIAL NORMALS

While jumping, ↓ + MK — **Heel Stomp**

Her Heel Stomp, one of the most unique moves in the game, results in a double-jump in the air off your opponent's head. This move carries with it the potential for many interesting set-ups.

→ / ← + MK — **Backflip Kick**

The Backflip Kick now hits twice on hit or block, and is great for combos where you don't have to have a charge stored to hit an opponent for damage.

→ / ← + HK — **Knee Flip Kick**

Chun-Li's Knee Flipkick is arguably the best special normal move in the game. It is used for going over the top of projectiles, or crossing up an opponent on wake-up. There are three different ways to time it, which will keep your opponent guessing.

SPECIAL MOVES

Press K rapidly — **Hyakuretsu Kyaku**

The Hyakuretsu Kyaku is one of Chun-Li's best moves. Use it as a surprise attack or for block damage. In *Champion Edition* and beyond, you can put the Hyakuretsu Kyaku at the end of certain combos for heavy damage.

Charge ↓ ↑ + K — **Spinning Bird Kick**

The Spinning Bird Kick is great for going through projectiles. It's also her only reversal until *Super Street Fighter II Turbo*. Sometimes this move is the best option for escaping from tough spots. When it connects, expect big damage!

← ↙ ↓ ↘ → + P — **Kikoken**

The Kikoken is a great addition to Chun-Li's *Street Fighter II Turbo* arsenal. This projectile can only be used in a combo when it is used in conjunction with a standing HP two-in-one. Use this move as a shield for setting up regular moves and throws.

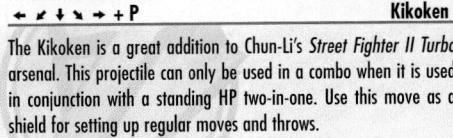

CHUN-LI

COSTUMES

STREET FIGHTER II

COSTUME

STREET FIGHTER II

ALTERNATE COSTUME

CHAMPIONSHIP

COSTUME

TURBO

COSTUME

COMBOS

STREET FIGHTER II

Jump in MK, standing MP, standing HP

Jump in HP, ↓ + MK, ↓ + HK

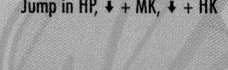   

STREET FIGHTER II CHAMPION EDITION

Cross-up HP, standing MP, → + MK

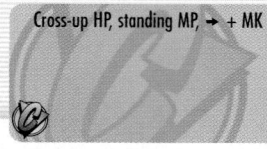   

In air, ↓ + MK, 4 times

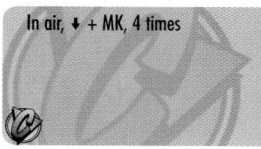   

STREET FIGHTER II TURBO

Jump in HP, HP, HP Kikoken

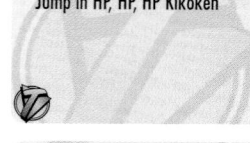   

Jump in HP, HP, HK Hyakuretsu Kyaku

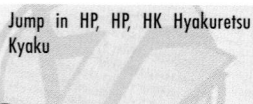   

STREET FIGHTER II AND CHAMPION EDITION

Chun-Li's lightning-fast speed and her ability to throw for heavy damage (nearly 25% damage per throw) should be the focus for her game. She has the ability to bounce off walls and stay on top of her opponent like no other character. Use her speed to barrage an opponent with normal moves and throws. If an opponent jumps in at you, hit them with a crouching HK, standing MP, standing MK, or even a jumping move to knock them down. Then, counter attack with the fury of Chun-Li's normal moves. Chun-Li's crouching MK is her most effective move against opponents who throw projectiles. Oftentimes, this move will hit before the projectile animation of her opponent is finished, thus stopping the projectile from ever launching. Standing MK is another possibility for this technique. If you are a full screen away against a projectile-throwing opponent, either jump off the wall to trick them or use Chun-Li's Knee Flipkick (*Champion Edition*) to get over them.

STREET FIGHTER II TURBO

The addition of the Kikoken to Chun-Li's arsenal changes her strategy quite a bit. While this move is too slow to use in a combo, it's quite possible to follow behind it and use it as a shield. You can also use this projectile to pressure an opponent into a mistake. Don't use the Kikoken up close, because its lack of speed is an issue. Although slow, the move can be used defensively against other characters who use projectiles. Another useful move is her jumping LK, which has major priority in the air. It can be performed early in a jump to freeze an opponent in place (your opponent can't walk backward if you have an attack on-screen). This tactic leads to mix-ups with throws once your character returns to the ground.

GOOD MATCH-UP

VS ZANGIEF

The toughest Zangief version is the one from *Super Street Fighter II*. His Banishing Punch can repel projectiles, thus enabling him to move close to Chun-Li. Keep him at bay with her crouching HK when he jumps. During any other moves, use crouching MKs to poke him out of his attacks. If you are playing as a version of Chun-Li that has a Kikoken, use it to make him jump, then take him out of the air with a crouching HK. After knocking Zangief down, stand about half a character's-length away and use a Hyakuretsu Kyaku when he gets up. If you get too close to him, Zangief can his Spinning Piledriver for a lot of damage. When Zangief uses his Spinning Lariat, use the Heel Stomp (↓ + MK) to penetrate his defense. This technique should stop him from using it when you throw a Kikoken. Zangief does have the potential to win this fight by using repeated HP Body Presses in the corner, as Chun-Li has no counter for this attack. Even if you can throw Zangief out of this pattern, he can Tech Escape the throw and reverse it with a Spinning Pile Driver before you can recover.

SUPER STREET FIGHTER II

Super Street Fighter II introduced the charge-motion Kikoken to Chun-Li's repertoire. Now you can insert it into a combo, it executes much faster, and it's safe to use in close combat. With the overall slower game speed in this version, her normals play a crucial role in her strategy. To succeed, mix up your gameplay by using the crouching MK to poke at an opponent from afar. Also, use the standing MP to jab when fighting in close.

SUPER STREET FIGHTER II TURBO

A big addition to everyone's arsenal in this game is the super combo, and Chun-Li's is fantastic! It causes major damage, has decent invincibility at the beginning, and is one of only two super combos in the game that can be "stored" for instant execution. With the addition of the Whirlwind Kick, Chun-Li now has an improved wake-up game without sacrificing any of her old deadly techniques.

COMBOS

SUPER STREET FIGHTER II

Corner only—Jump in HP, HP, HP Kikoken, ⬇+MK

Jump in HP, MP, ⬇ + MK, ⬇ + HK

SUPER STREET FIGHTER II TURBO (OLD)

Jump-in HP, ⬅ + MK, HP Kikoken

SUPER STREET FIGHTER II TURBO

Jump in MK, ⬇+MP, ⬆+HK, Senretsukyaku

Charge ⬅, ➡, ⬅, Hold ➡, Jump in HP, HP, Any K, charge ⬇, ⬆ + HK

BAD MATCH-UP

VS SAGAT

Most of the time, it's difficult to avoid some of Sagat's traps. Sagat has three major attacks: his high projectile, his low projectile, and his Tiger Uppercut. Chun-Li's major weakness is her lack of attacks to counter a full-screen fight. For Chun-Li to be effective, it's important to fight up close. Against Sagat, however, this is a difficult task to complete. Use her Knee Flip Kick to pass over the low projectiles and inch forward. Be patient; if you try to jump in to attack, she may get knocked out of the air by his Tiger Uppercut. If you jump in from full-screen, Sagat can sweep Chun-Li and throw low projectiles to knock her back. When fighting Sagat up close, use a variety of normals, throws, and combos. Stay inside against him at all costs.

COSTUMES

LP

MP

HP

START

Hold any button

LK

MK

HK

CHUN-LI

NORMAL MOVES

STANDING

These normal moves haven't changed since the beginning of the *Street Fighter II* series. Her standing HP and crouching MK are two of her best normal moves. Her standing HP is one of her most useful standing moves. It can be used as an effective poke, and as a limited anti-air attack.

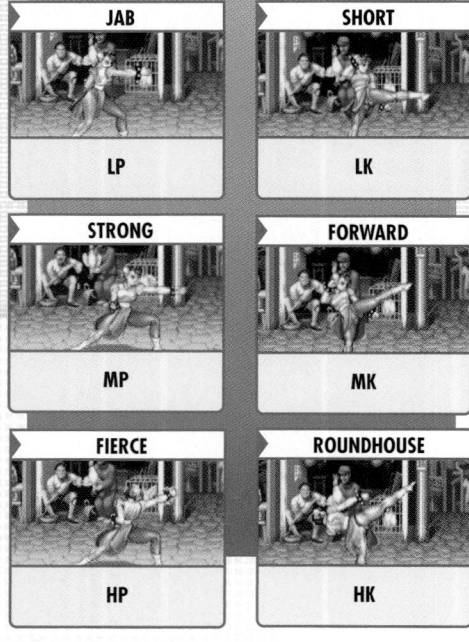

JAB	SHORT
LP	LK
STRONG	FORWARD
MP	MK
FIERCE	ROUNDHOUSE
HP	HK

STANDING CLOSE

The only close-up normal move that changes in *Super Turbo* is the standing HK. This move is extremely good against an opponent who is jumping in. When this occurs, use it at the last moment to stop the attack.

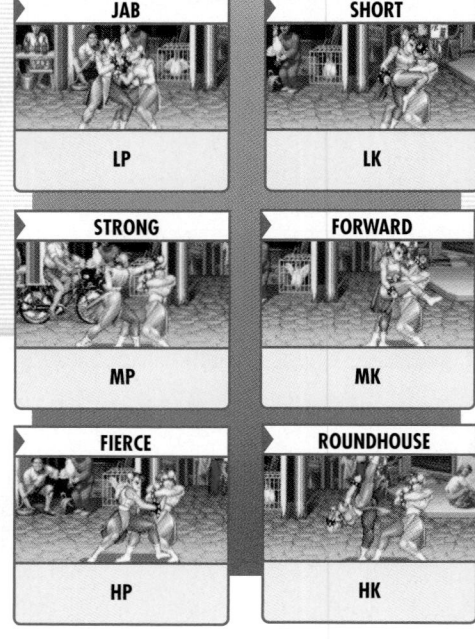

JAB	SHORT
LP	LK
STRONG	FORWARD
MP	MK
FIERCE	ROUNDHOUSE
HP	HK

CROUCHING

Chun-Li's crouching MK may be her most useful attack. Use it to poke at long range.

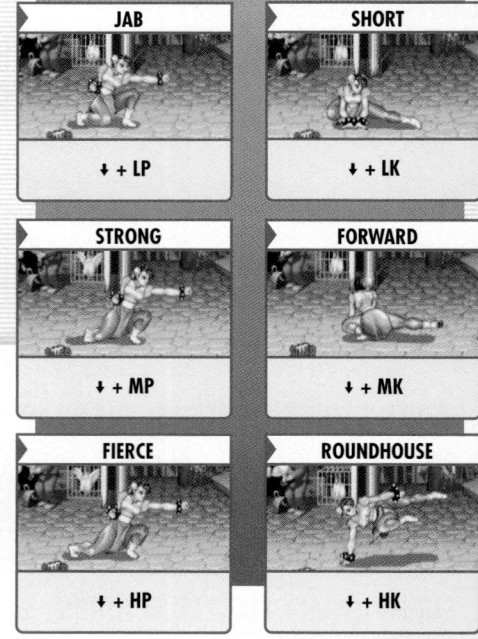

JAB	SHORT
↓ + LP	↓ + LK
STRONG	FORWARD
↓ + MP	↓ + MK
FIERCE	ROUNDHOUSE
↓ + HP	↓ + HK

SPECIAL NORMALS

While jumping, ↓ + MK　　　　　**Heel Stomp**

Chun Li lost the ability to stomp on an opponent's head and then cancel into a Spinning Bird Kick. The Heel Stomp is still great for bouncing over your opponent's head to mess with them. Trick them into thinking you won't cross them up, and then go for it.

In close, → + MK　　　　　**Backflip Kick**

There are two practical uses for this move. One great use is to use it in a combo for style points! The other is to use it to retreat from your opponent. If you like to play the zoning game with Chun Li, this is a great move to use to accomplish that.

In close, → + HK　　　　　**Knee Flip Kick**

The Knee Flip Kick can only be done will close to your opponent. This is an excellent move for going over projectiles, or for tricking your opponent to block the wrong way when it connects. Since she flips high in the air, it is not advised you do this move randomly, but wait until a projectile is coming or they are knocked down.

↖ + MK　　　　　**Backflip Kick**

They have mysteriously changed the command of the Backflip kick again! Now to perform this move you need to hold the joystick ↖ and press MK.

↖ + HK　　　　　**Knee Flip Kick**

Chun-Li's special normals are some of the best in the game. Her ↖ HK Knee Flip Kick is the best for wake-up games. When performed early, you will land without hitting your opponent and enable the throw. If you perform the move when your opponent is getting up, it will cross them up and leave you in an advantageous situation.

JUMPING

JAB	JAB

↑ + LP	↗ / ↖ + LP

STRONG	STRONG

↑ + MP	↗ / ↖ + MP

FIERCE	FIERCE

↑ + HP	↗ / ↖ + HP

SHORT	SHORT
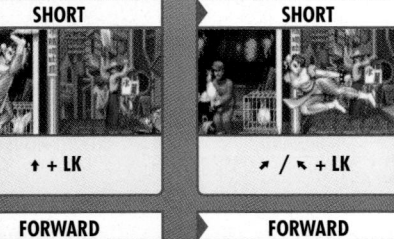	
↑ + LK	↗ / ↖ + LK

FORWARD	FORWARD

↑ + MK	↗ / ↖ + MK

ROUNDHOUSE	ROUNDHOUSE

↑ + HK	↗ / ↖ + HK

THROWS

THROW	AIR THROW
	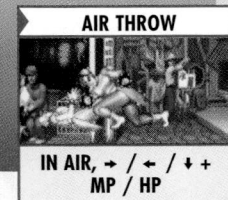
→ / ← + MP / HP	IN AIR, → / ← / ↓ + MP / HP

SPECIAL MOVES

Tap K rapidly — **Hyakuretsu Kyaku**

The Hyakuretsu Kyaku has been revamped in this version, as it can be used in a combo. The best way to use this special move is to poke at your opponent with a crouching MK, then rapidly press the Kick button (after a hit) to use the Hyakuretsu Kyaku in a two-hit combo. This is a very effective way to add damage to your ground game.

Charge ←, → + P — **Kikoken**

Chun-Li's new and improved Kikoken is much faster and more powerful in *Super Street Fighter II* and *Super Turbo*. With this new upgrade, she can hang with Guile and Ryu in projectile-throwing battles. The only downside to her new Kikoken is that it doesn't travel across a full screen.

SUPER COMBO

Charge ← → ← → + K — **Senretsukyaku**

There are two versions of this move. One of them is actually a famous glitch that made Chun-Li one of the game's favorite players. She can store her super combo and use it at her own discretion, rather than use it immediately after the command is entered. If you input the command (←, →, ←) and hold → but don't press a Kick button, the super is stored as long as continue to hold →. After pressing any Kick button, the super combo comes out in all its glory. You can follow the Senretsukyaku with a Whirlwind Kick for maximum damage. You can hold ↘ to hold the charge for the command, but you can't move.

Charge ←, → + K — **Spinning Bird Kick**

This move can be used in the air, which makes this a huge upgrade to Chun-Li's versatility. Use this move to run away after performing a Head Stomp, or use it to avoid projectiles. You can even use it to charge the Super Meter in *Super Turbo*. **NOTE: The command for this move in *Super Street Fighter II* is Charge ↓, ↑ + K.**

Charge ↓, ↑ + K — **Whirlwind Kick**

Her most valuable upgrade in *Super Street Fighter II Turbo* the Whirlwind Kick is one of the best wake-up moves in this game. This move has great range and it causes a lot of damage. With the addition of this move, Chun-Li has an effective tool and a tactic to use on wake-up.

Dhalsim

STANDING

Dhalsim has some awesome standing moves. Since his limbs extend a great distance, he can attack from far away without much fear. His standing LK, which is extremely fast, goes across half of the screen. The advantage here is that it will stop most special moves from connecting. But watch out: His limbs are susceptible at any time from far away, so don't use normal moves at random against a character like Ryu or Ken.

STANDING CLOSE

Dhalsim's close normals are extremely efficient. His LP normal is proficient at knocking opponents out of the air and his HP inflicts massive damage and hits twice when it connects. His LK, MK, and MP moves are all good for "tick-throw" setups.

CROUCHING

Dhalsim gets so low to the ground, that he can actually reach under projectiles and hit the opponent without getting him himself. This will make projectile characters think twice about throwing projectiles Dhalsim's way. Also, all of his crouching kick moves are variations of slides. These can also go under projectiles and place you next to your opponent ready for a throw.

THROWS

Dhalsim's throw works from a distance, and it is extremely easy to loop setup traps with it. With the slide and throw combination, he instantly becomes a force to be reckoned with. By getting your opponent to block while fighting in close, try to attempt a throw whenenever possible. You can even mix up the throw and the in-close slide to trick an opponent for maximum effectiveness.

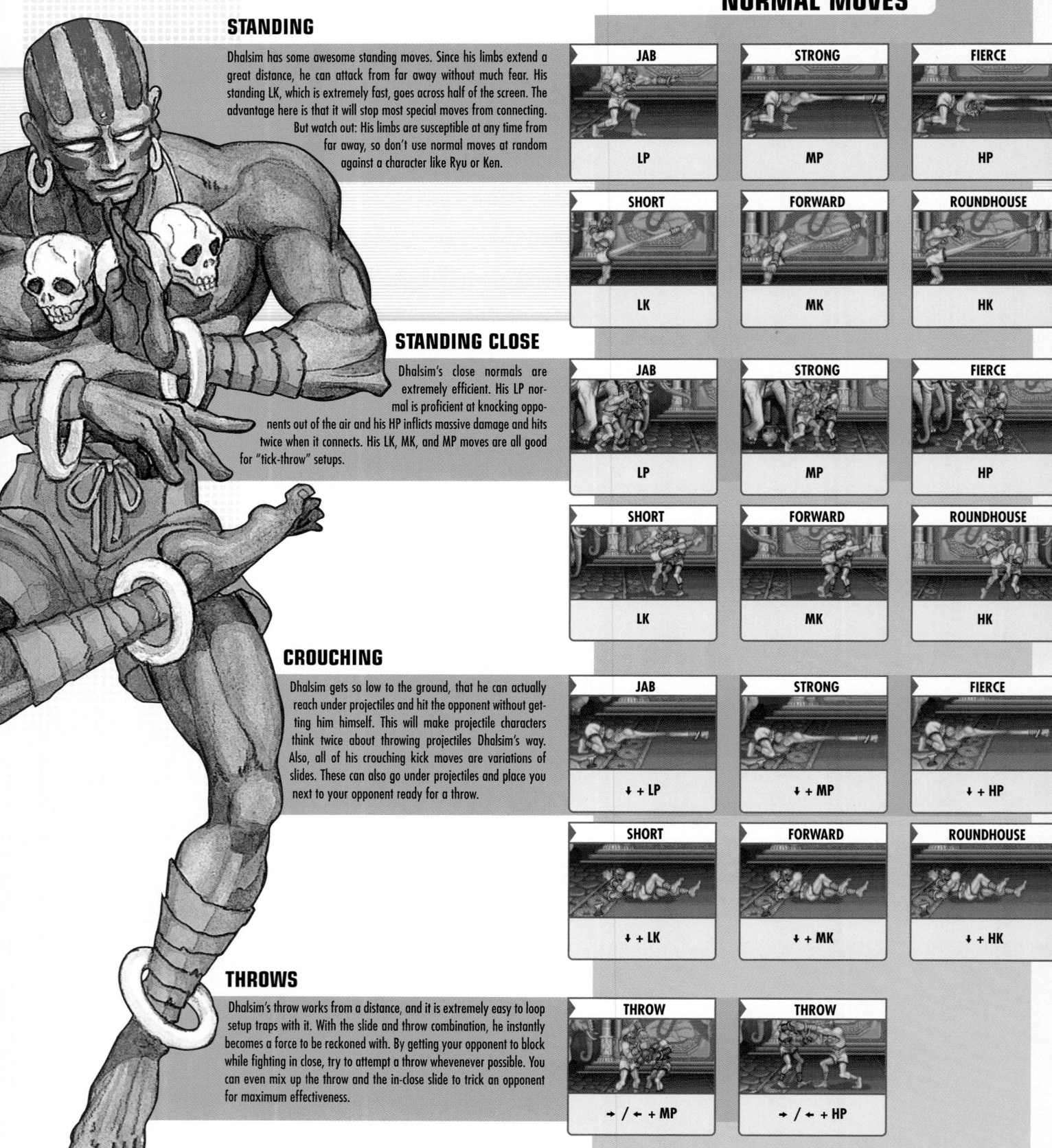

NORMAL MOVES

JAB	STRONG	FIERCE
LP	MP	HP

SHORT	FORWARD	ROUNDHOUSE
LK	MK	HK

JAB	STRONG	FIERCE
LP	MP	HP

SHORT	FORWARD	ROUNDHOUSE
LK	MK	HK

JAB	STRONG	FIERCE
↓ + LP	↓ + MP	↓ + HP

SHORT	FORWARD	ROUNDHOUSE
↓ + LK	↓ + MK	↓ + HK

THROW	THROW
→ / ← + MP	→ / ← + HP

JUMPING

In *Street Fighter II*, Dhalsim's Drills were difficult to use because it required that you input the command at the apex of his jump. This gave your opponent time to counter the attack. In *Street Fighter Champion Edition* and beyond, you could unleash the Drill Headthrust or Drill Kick at any point of the jump. This is a very important change in the gameplay, because it enables you to use this move to go over projectiles at the last second.

SPECIAL MOVES

↓ ↘ → + P — Yoga Fire

Yoga Fire is a fairly standard projectile. The special aspect about this projectile is its ability to burn when it hits. It doesn't cause more damage, but it definitely looks cool! This move prevents Dhalsim from getting locked down in Hadoken traps by Ryu and Ken.

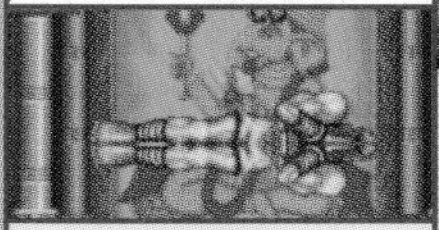

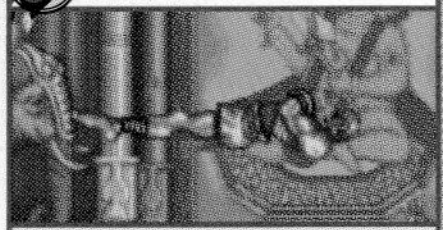

JAB	STRONG
↑ + LP	↑ + MP

FIERCE	DRILL HEADTHRUST
↑ + HP	↗ / ↖ AT APEX OF JUMP, HP

IN CLOSE, CROUCHING

Dhalsim's in-close crouching moves vary compared to his regular crouching moves. From afar, his crouching kicks all result in slides, while they turn into short-range moves from up close. The lone advantage to his crouching close-up moves is the ability to tick-throw into the MP throw. The crouching HK (slide) is a great move for knocking down an opponent from close range and playing wake-up games. Try to lock down your opponent by making them block, then look for a chance to throw.

SHORT	FORWARD
↑ + LK	↑ + MK

ROUNDHOUSE	DRILL KICK
↑ + HK	↗ / ↖ AT APEX OF JUMP, HK

← ↙ ↓ ↘ → + P — Yoga Flame

This is a great wake-up move. When an opponent gets up from the ground, perform a Yoga Flame. Make sure, however, that you're far enough away from your adversary that he or she can't cause damage during wake-up. This technique causes block damage and puts your opponent in block stun. This move is also good for maximum damage.

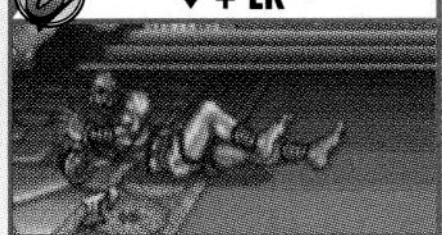

JAB	STRONG
↓ + LP	↓ + MP

SHORT	FORWARD
↓ LK	↓ + MK

DRILL HEADTHRUST	DRILL KICK
WHILE JUMPING, ↓ + HP	WHILE JUMPING, ↓ + HK

In *Street Fighter II Champion Edition*, Dhalsim was given greater control over Drill Headthrust and Drill Kick. This change remains in effect for the rest of the games in the *Street Fighter II* series.

↓ + LK

In *Street Fighter II Champion Edition*, Dhalsim was changed so that his crouching LK was always a slide. This move carried over into *Street Fighter II Turbo*.

→ ↓ ↘ / ← ↓ ↙ + PPP / KKK — Yoga Teleport

In *Street Fighter II Turbo*, Dhalsim was given the ability to teleport. Ever since *Street Fighter II*, in which Dhalsim had a glitch that made him disappear, the *Street Fighter* programmers had a notion to put this into their next revision of the game. Since Dhalsim's is somewhat slow, it's extremely difficult to get out of traps. By giving him the Yoga Teleport, he can escape from any trap in the game. But watch out: When Dhalsim reappears, he becomes vulnerable to attacks.

DHALSIM

COSTUMES

STREET FIGHTER II
COSTUME

STREET FIGHTER II
ALTERNATE COSTUME

CHAMPIONSHIP
COSTUME

TURBO
COSTUME

COMBOS

STREET FIGHTER II

LP Yoga Fire, HK

STREET FIGHTER II CHAMPION EDITION

Crouching MK x 2

STREET FIGHTER II TURBO

Crouching MK, MP Yoga Fire

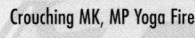

STREET FIGHTER II

Dhalsim is arguably one of the best characters in all five versions of *Street Fighter II*. His long limbs and his Yoga Flame prevent opponents from getting too close, and his high priority throws get him out of trouble at close range. His MP throw is so good that you can repeat it in all versions (MP throw, then crouching LK slide, or Drill Kick, then MP throw again). You can even make him go on the offensive with both of his Drill attacks and his LK slides.

STREET FIGHTER II CHAMPION EDITION

Basic Dhalsim keep-away involves throwing LP Yoga Fire (they're more difficult to jump over than the ones thrown with HP), then doing anti-air attacks against jumping attacks. Standing LK, standing MK, standing MP (close), and standing LP are all good anti-air attacks. Any of his slides are good to use when an opponent lands from a jump-in attack. Other options are to jump back and use HK in the air (a great air-to-air counter), or jump back, then drill (this works particularly well against M. Bison's Psycho Crusher, or Honda's Headbutt).

STREET FIGHTER II TURBO

In *Street Fighter II*, Dhalsim can only use his Drill attacks when he's at the height of his jump. In addition, you can't cancel his crouching MK with a Yoga Fire. From *Street Fighter II Champion Edition* and onward, you can cancel his crouching MK and Drill at any height while in the air, but that is the only major change. In *Street Fighter II Turbo*, he caused less damage and he received Yoga Teleport, which is useful for getting out of trouble. It is a notable move because it's Dhalsim's only "reversal" attack. This is the only frame he can become invulnerable in the instant he does it.

GOOD MATCHUP

VS SAGAT

Super Street Fighter II Turbo Dhalsim is incredibly good against Sagat. When in doubt, stay back and use his Yoga Fire attack to match his Tiger Shots. Watch for when your opponent throws his next Tiger Shot. When this occurs, jump and Drill Kick with LK to hit Sagat's hands. This requires some timing, but it shuts down Sagat's projectile game when executed correctly. Sagat cannot jump in at Dhalsim, since he can beat all of Sagat's air attacks with any of the four following moves: crouching HP, crouching LK slide, crouching MK slide, or crouching HK slide. The crouching HK slide knocks down, the crouching LK slide "combos" into a throw, and the crouching MK slide can combo into a 2-hit HP headbutt for a dizzy, when done properly.

SUPER STREET FIGHTER II/SUPER STREET FIGHTER II TURBO

Dhalsim received no upgrades in *Super Street Fighter II*. On the other hand, he received a good super combo, two new Drill angles (with LK and HK), and the ability to control when he does close/far attacks in *Super Street Fighter II Turbo*. Overall, there are really no changes to his strategy since the first *Street Fighter II* and the tactics used to win with him remain the same.

COMBOS

SUPER STREET FIGHTER II

LP Yoga Fire, HP

CORNER ONLY——LP Yoga Fire, Drill Headthrust

BAD MATCHUP

VS VEGA

The majority of Vega's moves have a better priority than Dhalsim's moves. Vega's Flying Barcelona Attack is tough to reliably counter, but try jumping back and using HK in the air. You can even stay on the ground and use a standing MP or standing LP. If your opponent gets a knockdown on Dhalsim, you can expect some repeated attacks and keep in mind that Dhalsim has no reliable wake-up move. Yoga Teleport is an option, but it is very difficult to execute. To vanquish Vega, you must prevent him from using this attack by using carefully timed standing HKs and Drills. Be careful, though, as Vega can Flip Kick against Dhalsim's Drill. One advantage in this fight is Dhalsim's crouching LK slide used in conjunction with the MP throw. If you can land an MP throw on Vega, you'll take control of the round because it's so difficult to escape the trap (MP throw, crouching MK slide, MP throw, repeat). If Vega blocks a Drill, use an MP throw right away, or crouch LK slide into an MP throw. Develop your skills at executing the throw trap, and press your advantage against Vega with it.

COSTUMES

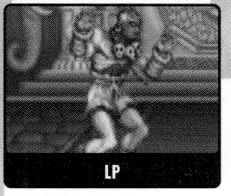
LP

MP

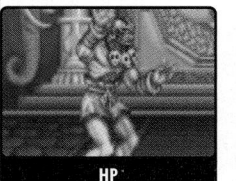
HP

START

Hold any button

LK

MK

HK

DHALSIM

NORMAL MOVES

STANDING

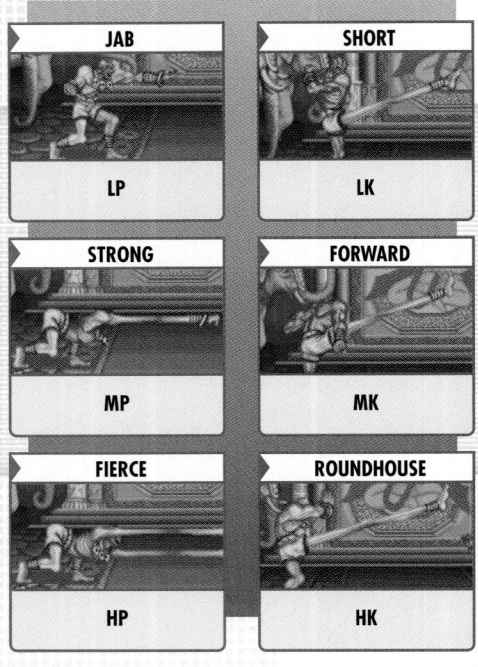

JAB	**SHORT**
LP	LK
STRONG	**FORWARD**
MP	MK
FIERCE	**ROUNDHOUSE**
HP	HK

THROWS

Throws haven't changed much. The MP throw still a has a very generous range, and it is great to use with a slide.

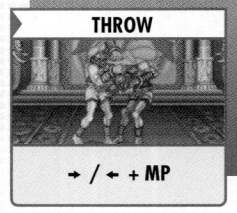 

THROW	**THROW**
→ / ← + MP	→ / ← + HP

STANDING CLOSE

In *Super Street Fighter II*, all the close normals remain the same but in some of the moves change drastically in *Super Street Fighter II Turbo*. LP and LK still are the same, but when you use MP, MK, HP, or HK, these moves pass through an opponent if you're standing close. To make them close normals, hold back while pressing the appropriate button.

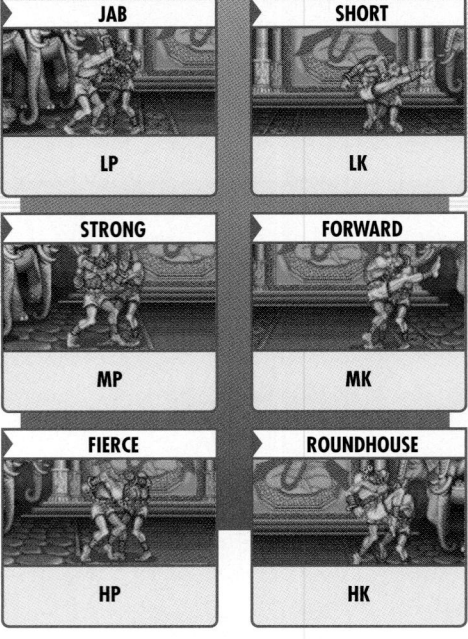

JAB	**SHORT**
LP	LK
STRONG	**FORWARD**
MP	MK
FIERCE	**ROUNDHOUSE**
HP	HK

CROUCHING

This is an excellent change for Dhalsim. All of his crouching moves are controllable, which means that regardless of the situation you have triple the number of options to use to defeat your opponent. By holding certain directions, you can hit your opponent from close and far to control the fight.

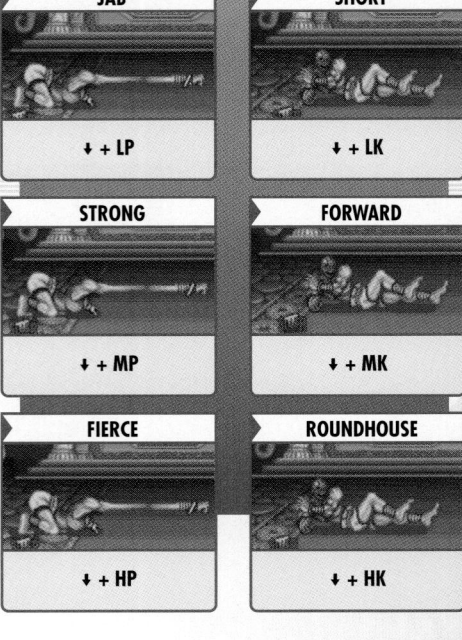

JAB	**SHORT**
↓ + LP	↓ + LK
STRONG	**FORWARD**
↓ + MP	↓ + MK
FIERCE	**ROUNDHOUSE**
↓ + HP	↓ + HK

NORMAL MOVES SUPER TURBO ONLY

JAB	**SHORT**	**JAB**	**SHORT**
← + LP	→ + LK	↙ + LP	↙ + LK
STRONG	**FORWARD**	**STRONG**	**FORWARD**
← + MP	← + MK	↙ + MP	↙ + MK
FIERCE	**ROUNDHOUSE**	**FIERCE**	**ROUNDHOUSE**
← + HP	← + HK	↙ + HP	↙ + HK

JUMPING

Although jumping back and pressing HK in the air is a great deterrent for jumping opponents, the addition of his Drill attacks is huge. At any point during his jump, he can Drill downward over projectiles and get close extremely fast. Since this is where Dhalsim's main game is mainly played, it's in your best interest to get close to your opponent.

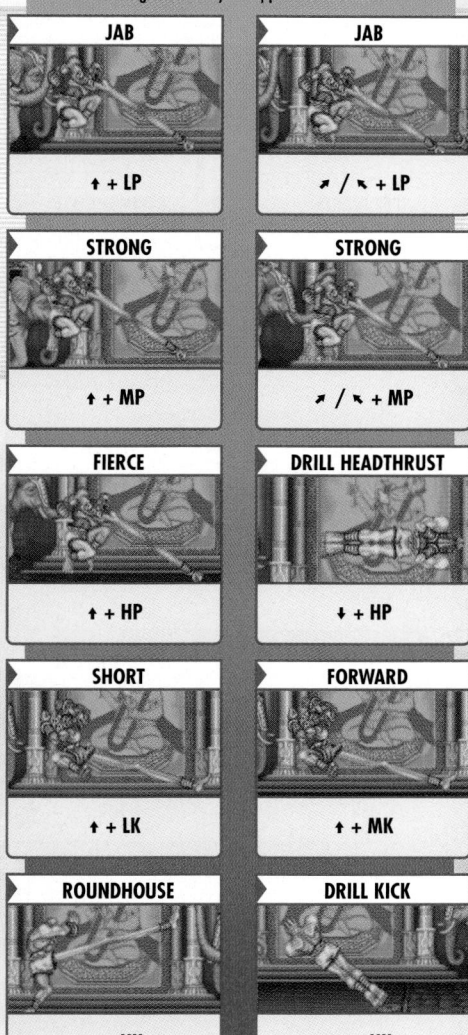

JAB	JAB
↑ + LP	↗ / ↖ + LP
STRONG	**STRONG**
↑ + MP	↗ / ↖ + MP
FIERCE	**DRILL HEADTHRUST**
↑ + HP	↓ + HP
SHORT	**FORWARD**
↑ + LK	↑ + MK
ROUNDHOUSE	**DRILL KICK**
↑ + HK	↓ + HK

SUPER COMBO

← ↙ ↓ ↘ → (x2) + P — Yoga Inferno

This is another great anti-air super combo. If one hit connects while in the air, all of the rest will do the same. It can even be used for chip damage (against a block) on an opponent's wake-up. It's possible to use it in a combo, but it's difficult to do and it's very situational.

SPECIAL MOVES

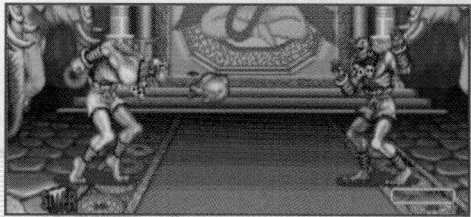

↓ ↘ → + P — Yoga Fire

This move's speed and damage remain the same. One change, however, is that it doesn't knock down your opponent anymore in *Super Street Fighter II Turbo*. This is a very important factor when it comes to combos, because the Yoga Fire can be followed up by a long-range standing HP or HK.

← ↙ ↓ ↘ → + P — Yoga Flame

The Yoga Flame hasn't changed over the versions, it is just as good as it was before.

→ ↓ ↘ / ← ↓ ↙ + PPP / KKK — Yoga Teleport

The Yoga Teleport is more susceptible now, so use it when your opponent doesn't have a super combo ready.

← ↙ ↓ ↘ → + K — Yoga Blast

The Yoga Blast is a new addition at Dhalsim's lineup. It is great for an anti-air attack and it goes away extremely fast, which makes the recovery time quite good.

E. Honda

STANDING

E. Honda's standing HP animation consists of a chopping motion over his head, which makes it an effective anti-air option. His standing jabs are quick, which makes it possible to use tick-throw options for maximum damage.

STANDING CLOSE

E. Honda's standing close attacks are good for linking into other normal moves. They are also effective for tick-throw traps. Close standing LP and MP are both good options for this type of gameplay.

CROUCHING

E. Honda is at his best while crouching, because it's possible to hold the "↙" charge and still throw out attacks. His crouching LP has nice range and speed, making it useful for snuffing out an opponent's pokes. Crouching LK can be buffered, which makes it possible to do some Sumo Splash mix-ups and combos involving the Head Butt. The crouching HP animation starts like an LP attack, but it hits twice.

THROWS

E. Honda's throws are key to his effectiveness. His MP throw tosses an opponent a decent distance and it has average recovery. Use it to get an opponent into the corner where a lot of damage can be unleashed. You can cause extra damage with the Bear Hug throw (→ / ← + HP) by button-mashing. This throw is also useful in the corner, or mid-screen, to set up some walk-under moves as well as cross-up attempts.

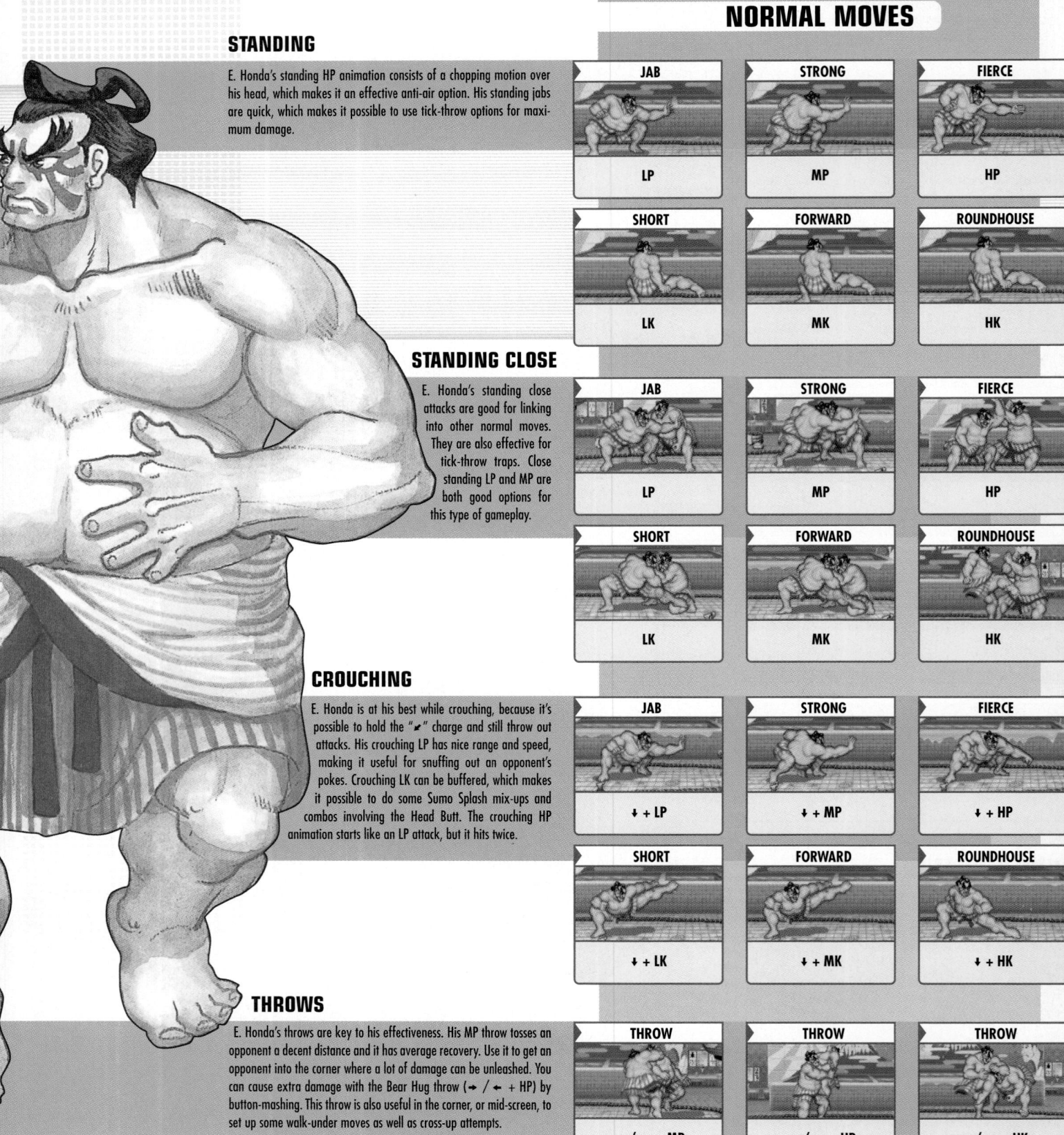

NORMAL MOVES

JAB	STRONG	FIERCE
LP	MP	HP

SHORT	FORWARD	ROUNDHOUSE
LK	MK	HK

JAB	STRONG	FIERCE
LP	MP	HP

SHORT	FORWARD	ROUNDHOUSE
LK	MK	HK

JAB	STRONG	FIERCE
↓ + LP	↓ + MP	↓ + HP

SHORT	FORWARD	ROUNDHOUSE
↓ + LK	↓ + MK	↓ + HK

THROW	THROW	THROW
→ / ← + MP	→ / ← + HP	→ / ← + HK

JUMPING

Honda's jumping attacks complement his ground game with a balance of good range and high priority. The jumping LP animation stays out for a long time and it has great priority. This move is very useful against an opponent who likes to stay in the air, but make sure you press the button early in your jump to hit them before he or she can unleash an attack. Jumping HK unloads fantastic damage and it also has great range. Use it to punish projectiles, but timing is of the essence. When timed improperly, Honda will be vulnerable to a Shoryuken or a similar anti-air attack. Jumping MK, with its decent priority, is effective against opponents who try to make you land on long, ground-based normal attacks (like Guile's Crouching MK). Use this attack to trade hits. Use a jumping MP to start a combo, or force an opponent into blocking a Hundred Hands Slap.

JAB	STRONG
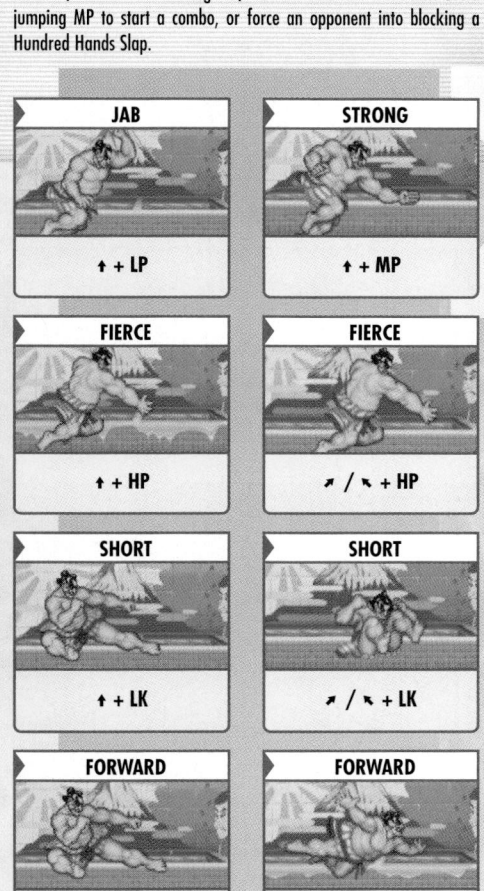	
↑ + LP	↑ + MP
FIERCE	**FIERCE**
↑ + HP	↗ / ↖ + HP
SHORT	**SHORT**
↑ + LK	↗ / ↖ + LK
FORWARD	**FORWARD**
↑ + MK	↗ / ↖ + MK
ROUNDHOUSE	**ROUNDHOUSE**
↑ + HK	↗ / ↖ + HK

SPECIAL MOVES

Charge ←, → + P **Headbutt**

This is one of Honda's signature moves. He rises off the ground and flies through the air toward his opponent. This self-projectile has good speed and causes nice damage. Early versions of this move would not knock down, but that was changed as subsequent versions of the game were released. The LP version of this move is one of the best anti-air attacks in the game. If an opponent jumps in and E. Honda is charged, blast them with a Headbutt.

Rapidly press P **Hundred Hand Slap**

When executed, E. Honda slaps his hands at his opponent with blinding speed. This attack can cause severe damage when used against a cornered opponent. Even if the attack gets blocked, it can pile on a decent amount of damage and keep pressure on an aggressive opponent.

Honda gains the ability to move while performing the Hundred Hand Slap in *Street Fighter II Champion Edition* and *Street Fighter II Turbo*.

Charge ↓, ↑ + K **Sumo Smash**

This move enables Honda to deal with pesky in-your-face projectiles by blowing through them and smacking an opponent on the way up, as well as on the way down.

COSTUMES

STREET FIGHTER II

COSTUME

STREET FIGHTER II

ALTERNATE COSTUME

CHAMPIONSHIP

COSTUME

TURBO

COSTUME

COMBOS

STREET FIGHTER II

Cross-up MK, MP, MK

Cross-up MK, MP, ↓ + HP

STREET FIGHTER II CHAMPION EDITION

Jump in HK, MP, MP Hundred Hand Slap

Jump in HK, HP Headbutt

STREET FIGHTER II TURBO

Cross-up MK, MP, ↓ + HK

Cross-up MK, → + MK, LP

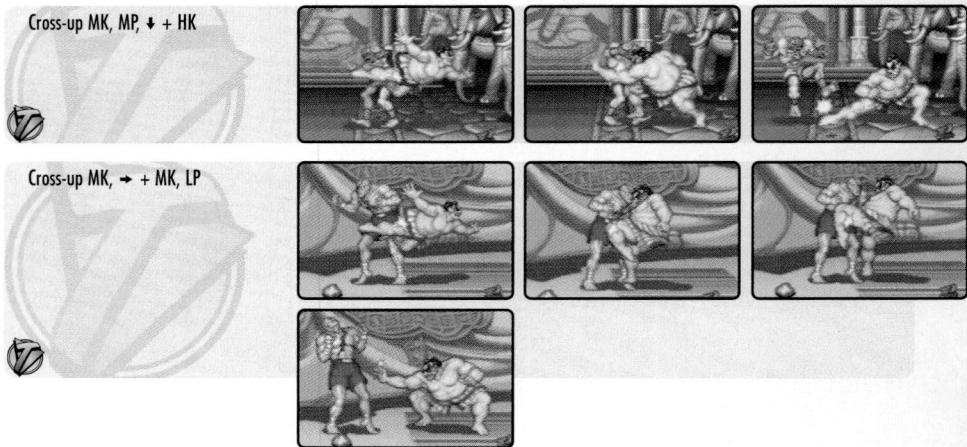

STREET FIGHTER II

E. Honda was certainly *not* a character to get close to in the first version of *Street Fighter II*. His grappling moves (throw with HP or HK) would cause almost 30% damage! Also, his normal moves allowed him to do several chain combos. His arsenal of special moves included his Headbutt, one of the best anti-air special moves. E. Honda's Hundred Hands Slap was also effective when fighting up close. Against characters who had projectiles, though, E. Honda had trouble. Trying to get close was the goal, since his ability to cause damage from a distance was basically non-existent. One you are in close, mix it up with tick-throws and use the Hundred Hands Slap to damage opponents through their block.

STREET FIGHTER II CHAMPION EDITION

Honda gained a unique function during the transition from *Street Fighter II* to *Street Fighter II Champion Edition*. He gained the ability to move forward while performing the Hundred Hands Slap. This is great for pounding an opponent into the corner and trading hits in the air when an opponent jumps in.

STREET FIGHTER II TURBO

With the addition of his Sumo Smash, E. Honda could finally deal with projectiles in *Street Fighter II Turbo*. This move would breeze through projectiles and smack an opponent on the way up, as well as on the way down. E. Honda's LP Headbutt no longer travels the length of the screen and stops short of an opponent in this version. It is still a powerful anti-air tool, and it does retain some invincibility properties against projectiles.

GOOD MATCH-UP

VS. M. BISON

E. Honda is a good match-up against most of the non-projectile characters. He has a particular advantage against M. Bison, because M. Bison's Tick-Throw game is thrown out the window due to E. Honda's Ohicho and normal throws. Plus, M. Bison has no viable reversal move when knocked down (his only reversal is his super combo) to escape a throw trap. Strive for getting a knockdown at mid-screen. Cross-up with his normal (↓ + MK) Splash, throw out a crouching LP, and input the motion for his Ohicho Throw. This tactic works great against the entire *Street Fighter II* cast; it can only be countered by a last-ditch throw with some characters.

SUPER STREET FIGHTER II

The Sumo Smash was upgraded to knock down on the way up, as well as on the way down for *Super Street Fighter II*. His Headbutt was slowed down just a bit in this version, but it is still a great anti-air weapon. E. Honda's usual arsenal of throws remains mostly unchanged in this version, but they are toned down a bit from the *Champion Edition* and *Turbo* versions.

SUPER STREET FIGHTER II TURBO

This is the best version of E. Honda in the *Anniversary Edition*. Several upgrades were made, ranging from new special attacks to new normal attacks. Some close standing normal moves were added, his crouching LK can be buffered into a Headbutt, and the standing HP animation has been changed to a ducking attack. The biggest change is the addition of the Ohicho Throw, which is performed by moving the controller from → to ↙. In "Old " *Super Street Fighter II Turbo* mode (choose the *Super Turbo* version of E. Honda while holding the "Start" button), you can "store" this throw. This means that you can do the motion before actually using it. Input the move and hold ↙, then when the opponent comes close press any punch button to perform the throw. This is only one of two moves in the game that can be stored for later use.

His super combo is useful for going through projectiles. If the first hit doesn't knock out your opponent, he or she can interrupt the super combo in motion after the first hit by doing a reversal attack. It's also useful to store the super combo and walk forward, perhaps tricking an opponent into jumping toward you. Wait until the last moment and press any punch button to start the super combo. Your opponent gets knocked down, and you can begin a cross-up game that includes combos and throws.

COMBOS

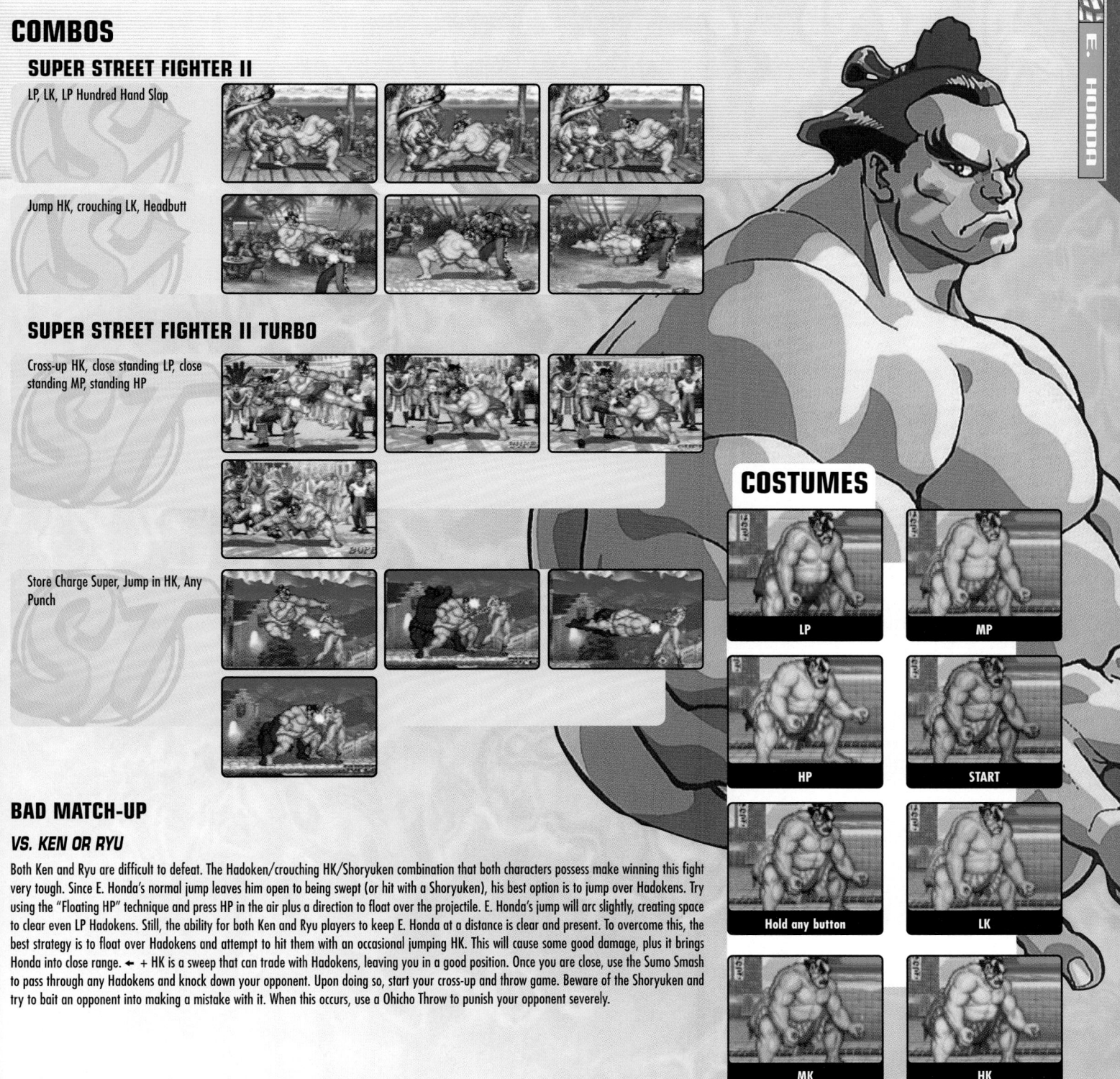

SUPER STREET FIGHTER II

LP, LK, LP Hundred Hand Slap

Jump HK, crouching LK, Headbutt

SUPER STREET FIGHTER II TURBO

Cross-up HK, close standing LP, close standing MP, standing HP

Store Charge Super, Jump in HK, Any Punch

COSTUMES

LP	MP
HP	START
Hold any button	LK
MK	HK

BAD MATCH-UP

VS. KEN OR RYU

Both Ken and Ryu are difficult to defeat. The Hadoken/crouching HK/Shoryuken combination that both characters possess make winning this fight very tough. Since E. Honda's normal jump leaves him open to being swept (or hit with a Shoryuken), his best option is to jump over Hadokens. Try using the "Floating HP" technique and press HP in the air plus a direction to float over the projectile. E. Honda's jump will arc slightly, creating space to clear even LP Hadokens. Still, the ability for both Ken and Ryu players to keep E. Honda at a distance is clear and present. To overcome this, the best strategy is to float over Hadokens and attempt to hit them with an occasional jumping HK. This will cause some good damage, plus it brings Honda into close range. ← + HK is a sweep that can trade with Hadokens, leaving you in a good position. Once you are close, use the Sumo Smash to pass through any Hadokens and knock down your opponent. Upon doing so, start your cross-up and throw game. Beware of the Shoryuken and try to bait an opponent into making a mistake with it. When this occurs, use a Ohicho Throw to punish your opponent severely.

NORMAL MOVES
STANDING

In *Super Street Fighter II*, all three of E. Honda's kick moves are knockdown moves. This is unique only for *Super Street Fighter II*. In *Super Turbo*, he returns to his old normals. His HK sweep is extremely fast and knocks down on contact.

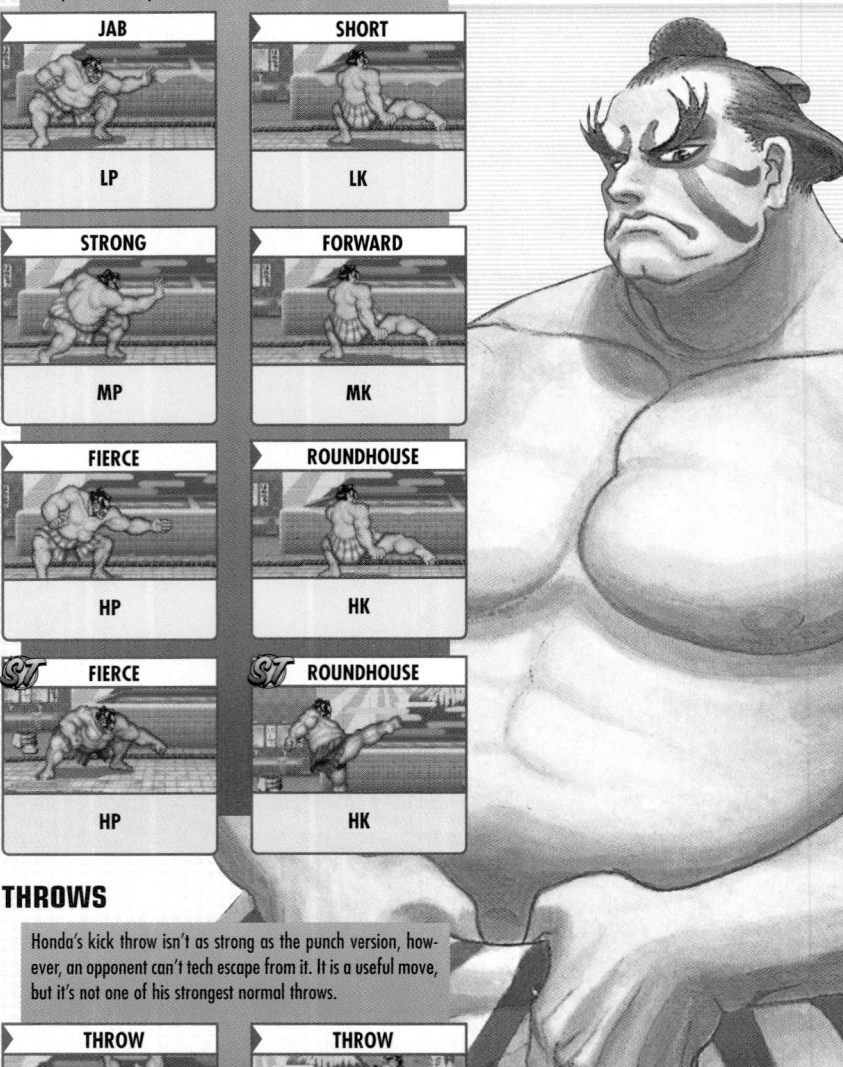

JAB	SHORT
LP	LK

STRONG	FORWARD
MP	MK

FIERCE	ROUNDHOUSE
HP	HK

ST FIERCE	ST ROUNDHOUSE
HP	HK

THROWS

Honda's kick throw isn't as strong as the punch version, however, an opponent can't tech escape from it. It is a useful move, but it's not one of his strongest normal throws.

THROW	THROW
→ / ← + MP	→ / ← + HP

THROW
→ + HK

STANDING CLOSE

If Honda gets in close, these are the best setup moves for throwing an opponent. Since they are lightning quick, the odds will shift in your favor if you use these standing close moves into throws.

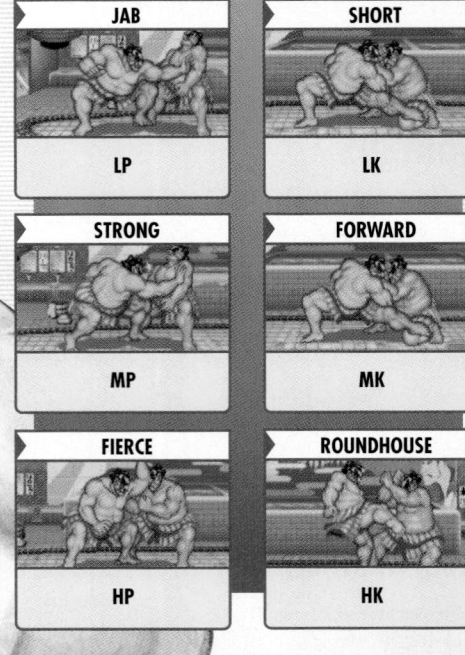

JAB	SHORT
LP	LK

STRONG	FORWARD
MP	MK

FIERCE	ROUNDHOUSE
HP	HK

CROUCHING

His crouching HP hits twice, as does his MK. This is perhaps E. Honda's best set of moves, based on the fact that all of his special moves can be charged from ↙. So, by throwing out these moves, he doesn't lose his charge and he is immediately ready to go into a Sumo Splash or Headbutt.

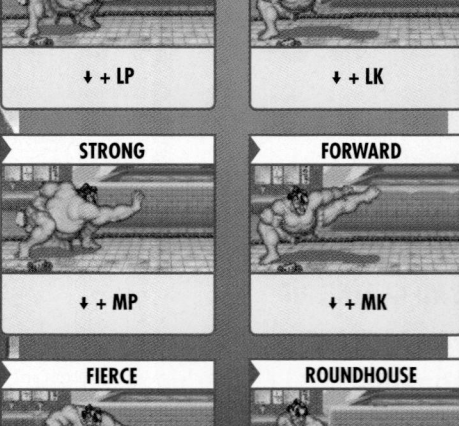

JAB	SHORT
↓ + LP	↓ + LK

STRONG	FORWARD
↓ + MP	↓ + MK

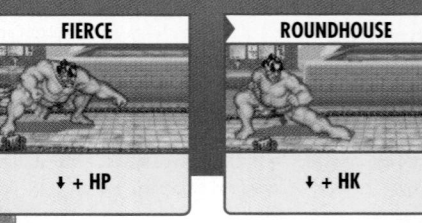

FIERCE	ROUNDHOUSE
↓ + HP	↓ + HK

JUMPING

One of the biggest complaints about the previous versions of E. Honda was the fact that he couldn't effectively jump over projectiles. Jump and press HP to jump straight up; hold → or ← + HP in the air to glide in that direction. With his jump arc changed, you can cover similar distance but he stays much closer to the ground. Use this move to jump in early, because it is difficult to counter attack.

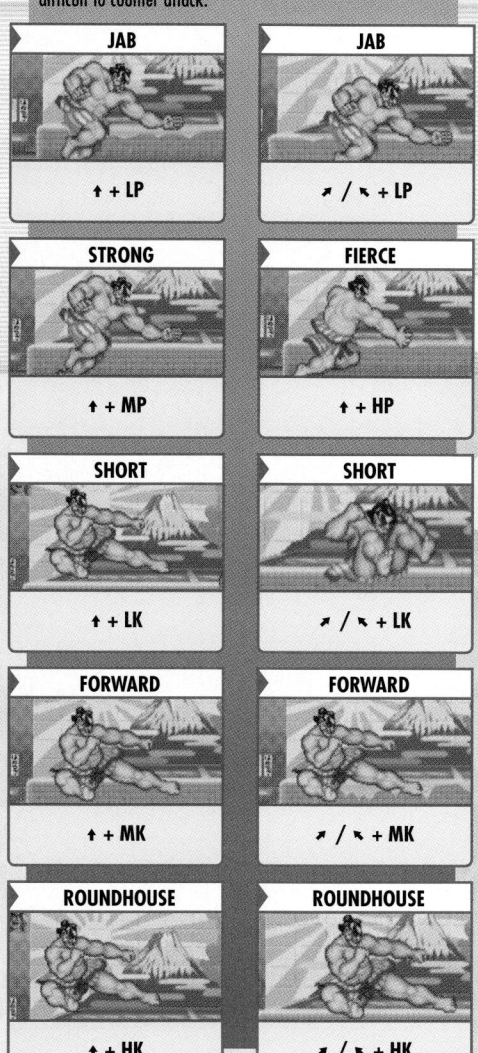

▶ JAB	▶ JAB
↑ + LP	↗ / ↖ + LP

▶ STRONG	▶ FIERCE
↑ + MP	↑ + HP

▶ SHORT	▶ SHORT
↑ + LK	↗ / ↖ + LK

▶ FORWARD	▶ FORWARD
↑ + MK	↗ / ↖ + MK

▶ ROUNDHOUSE	▶ ROUNDHOUSE
↑ + HK	↗ / ↖ + HK

SUPER COMBO

Charge ←, → → → + P — Double Sumo Headbutt

E. Honda's super combo will connect up to four times, depending on the spacing between your character and your opponent. Two Headbutts are performed, each of which hits two times. This super combo isn't at the top of the list, however, it's capable of getting a hit to win a match. This super combo will annihilate any normal projectile once it gets started, plus it enables you to quickly close in on an opponent on the other side of the screen. If you don't knock out your opponent after the first hit, you will be susceptible for a reversal anti-air move (Tiger Uppercut, Shoryuken, etc).

SPECIAL NORMALS

↗ or ↘, ↓ + MK — Splash

The Splash is the best cross-up in the game. It has high priority and it leads into some of his best combos. This move is also effective against attacking players who don't have wake-up moves or reversal attacks with high priority.

← / → + HK — Sweep

E. Honda's sweep move can take out opponents from long distance. It is the replacement for all the normal moves from *Super Street Fighter II*.

SPECIAL MOVES

Charge ←, → + P — Headbutt

This move, which now knocks down, enables you to get close to an opponent and play wake-up games. This is one of E. Honda's biggest assets.

Charge ↓, ↑ + K — Sumo Smash

This move was changed in *Super Street Fighter II* and *Super Street Fighter II Turbo* so you could knock down an opponent on the first hit. When executed close to opponents, it's possible to cross them up and force them to lose their charge. This is a huge advantage when fighting against another charge-based character.

→ ↘ ↓ ↙ ← + P — Ohicho Throw

It's highly recommended to base your gameplay around this move when using the *Super Street Fighter II Turbo* version. The Ohicho Throw is a command grab, similar to Zangief's Spinning Pile Driver. There are some big differences, however. First, the motion is very easy to do (similar to a half-circle). Next, after inputting the move, you can "hold" the controller in the ↙ position. This basically "stores" the motion so all that remains is pressing a punch button when your opponent gets close. This throw has great priority and range and it's fantastic in tick-throw attacks. It is best used after a crouching LP.

This "storing" technique only works for the "Old" Super Street Fighter II Turbo version of E. Honda. To select this version, hold down the START button when choosing Super Street Fighter II Turbo *before selecting a character.*

Guile

STANDING

Guile's most useful standing normal moves are his long-range HP Backfist and his fast HK roundhouse. The HP Backfist is good for discouraging opponents from jumping, and it is difficult to punish. If an opponent manages to avoid the Backfist, Guile's standing HK roundhouse will neutralize almost any frontal air attack. Laslty, Guile's MK is excellent for countering low attacks like crouching foot sweeps.

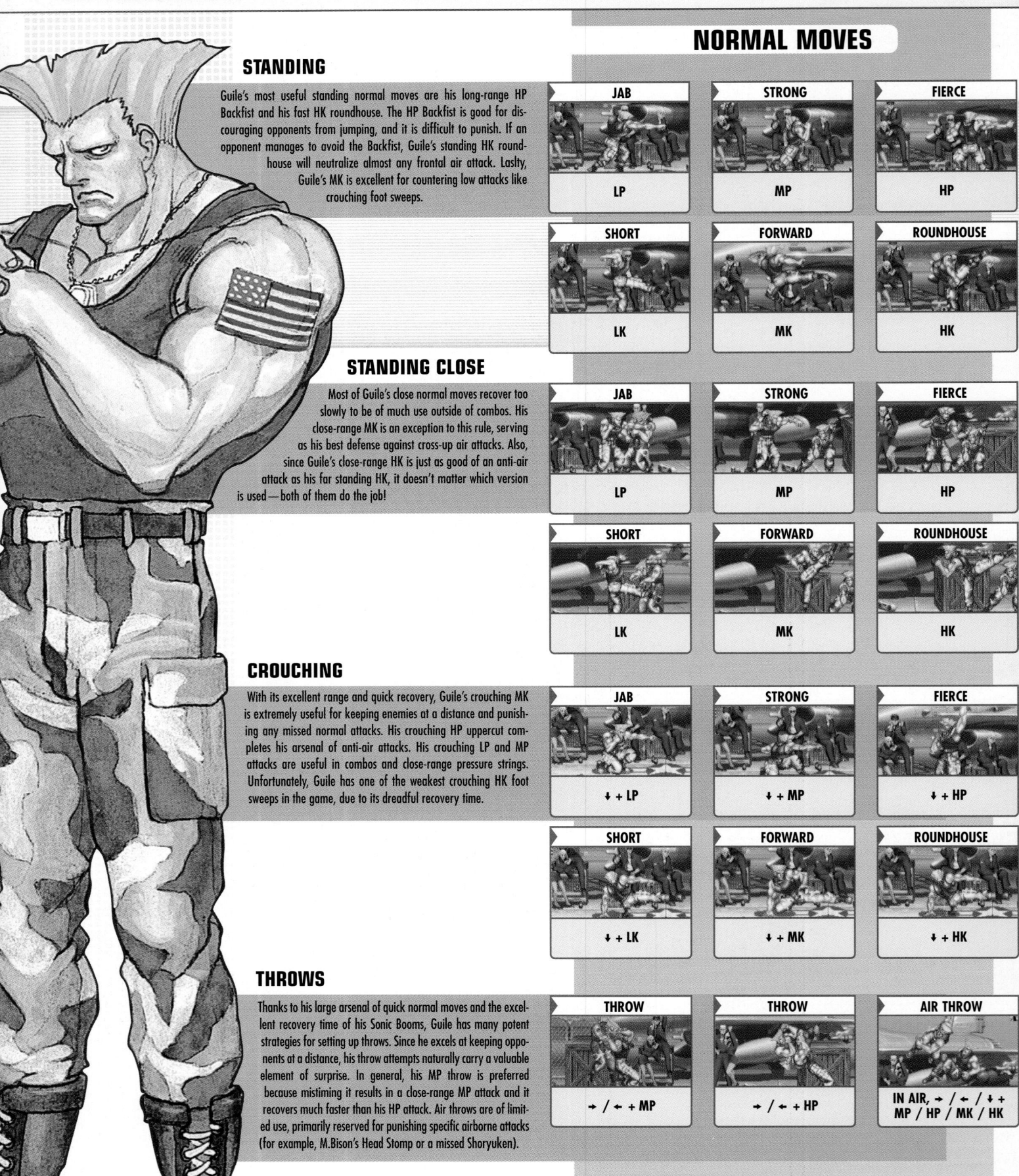

JAB	STRONG	FIERCE
LP	MP	HP

SHORT	FORWARD	ROUNDHOUSE
LK	MK	HK

STANDING CLOSE

Most of Guile's close normal moves recover too slowly to be of much use outside of combos. His close-range MK is an exception to this rule, serving as his best defense against cross-up air attacks. Also, since Guile's close-range HK is just as good of an anti-air attack as his far standing HK, it doesn't matter which version is used—both of them do the job!

JAB	STRONG	FIERCE
LP	MP	HP

SHORT	FORWARD	ROUNDHOUSE
LK	MK	HK

CROUCHING

With its excellent range and quick recovery, Guile's crouching MK is extremely useful for keeping enemies at a distance and punishing any missed normal attacks. His crouching HP uppercut completes his arsenal of anti-air attacks. His crouching LP and MP attacks are useful in combos and close-range pressure strings. Unfortunately, Guile has one of the weakest crouching HK foot sweeps in the game, due to its dreadful recovery time.

JAB	STRONG	FIERCE
↓ + LP	↓ + MP	↓ + HP

SHORT	FORWARD	ROUNDHOUSE
↓ + LK	↓ + MK	↓ + HK

THROWS

Thanks to his large arsenal of quick normal moves and the excellent recovery time of his Sonic Booms, Guile has many potent strategies for setting up throws. Since he excels at keeping opponents at a distance, his throw attempts naturally carry a valuable element of surprise. In general, his MP throw is preferred because mistiming it results in a close-range MP attack and it recovers much faster than his HP attack. Air throws are of limited use, primarily reserved for punishing specific airborne attacks (for example, M.Bison's Head Stomp or a missed Shoryuken).

THROW	THROW	AIR THROW
→ / ← + MP	→ / ← + HP	IN AIR, → / ← / ↓ + MP / HP / MK / HK

JUMPING

Guile's best frontal air attacks against grounded opponents are his jumping MK and jumping HP. Both of these attacks have good priority and a convenient downward angle. His best air attack against airborne opponents is the jumping HK, due to its excellent range. Guile's jumping LK knee is the perfect cross-up attack to use when jumping over an opponent. It's difficult to block this move correctly, and it can be used to set up a combo or a throw.

JAB	JAB
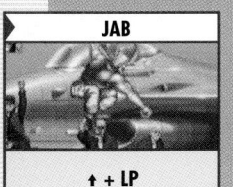	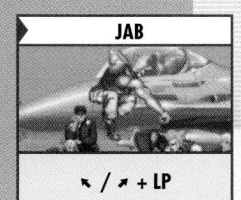
↑ + LP	↖ / ↗ + LP

STRONG	STRONG
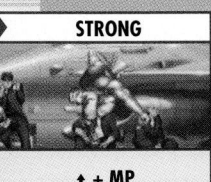	
↑ + MP	↖ / ↗ + MP

FIERCE	FIERCE
	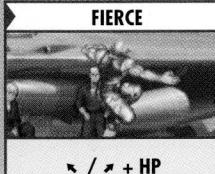
↑ + HP	↖ / ↗ + HP

SHORT	SHORT

↑ + LK	↖ / ↗ + LK

FORWARD	FORWARD

↑ + MK	↖ / ↗ + MK

ROUNDHOUSE	ROUNDHOUSE

↑ + HK	↖ / ↗ + HK

SPECIAL NORMALS

→ / ← + MK	Knee Bazooka

Due to its lengthy recovery period, avoid using the Knee Bazooka as a conventional attack. Instead, its value lies in its mobility. Using the ← + MK command, Guile can move forward without sacrificing his stored charge. When performed after throwing a slow Sonic Boom, the Knee Bazooka creates an opportunity to advance toward an opponent and throw a second Sonic Boom immediately after the first one connects.

In close, → / ← + HK	Reverse Spin Kick

Much like Guile's standing MK Rolling Sobat, the Reverse Spin Kick hovers above most low attacks. Unfortunately, the move is too slow to serve as a primary attack against opponents who have quick reactions. This move is most effective when used sparingly, so as to catch an opponent off-guard.

SPECIAL MOVES

Charge ← → + P	Sonic Boom

Projectile attacks have always been dominant tools in any incarnation of *Street Fighter*. Guile's Sonic Boom has the quickest recovery time of all projectiles, which makes it one of the best special moves in the game. The Sonic Boom can be used to keep opponents away, set up throws, create combos, force opponents to jump, and control space. Guile's entire gameplan revolves around using Sonic Booms to force opponents to commit errors and capitalize on their mistakes.

Charge ↓ ↑ + K	Somersault Kick

Although the Somersault Kick is one of the few near-perfect anti-air special moves in the game, its usefulness is limited by its charge requirement. Since you will need to use Guile's charge to throw Sonic Booms, you will rarely have the luxury of using the charge toward a Somersault Kick. Therefore, it's important to become adept at using Guile's various anti-air normals when his Somersault Kick is unavailable.

However, if you can fool an opponent into jumping while Guile is charged for a Somersault Kick, the opponent will take a powerful knockdown hit. Otherwise, the Somersault Kick is most useful in combos. The damage it inflicts, along with the knockdown it provides, make it difficult to pass up as a finisher for a combo.

COSTUMES

STREET FIGHTER II

COSTUME

STREET FIGHTER II

ALTERNATE COSTUME

CHAMPIONSHIP

COSTUME

TURBO

COSTUME

STREET FIGHTER II

Although Guile was perhaps the best selectable character in *Street Fighter II*, it had more to do with the weaknesses of the rest of the cast than Guile's own strengths. With his various gamebreaking glitches removed, the only unique tools available now are his extended standing LP, and his stationary knee attack. The far-standing LP is arguably the best jab attack in the game. It virtually guarantees victory over a stunned opponent through repeated "re-dizzy" combos. However, his sluggish recovery on normal attacks, painfully slow jumping speed, and the absence of several advancing normal attacks introduced in later revisions leave much to be desired.

STREET FIGHTER II CHAMPION EDITION/TURBO

Champion Edition Guile and *Turbo* Guile are virtually identical. Their movelists consist of the same exact set of normals, throws, and specials. Under this pair of configurations, Guile is best suited for defensive play, with a heavy reliance on Sonic Booms. Use his quick crouching MK to keep opponents at bay while charging for a Sonic Boom. Opponents who attempt to jump over Sonic Booms must face three forms of normal anti-air attacks: Guile's standing HK roundhouse, crouching HP uppercut, and close-range MK Heel Kick. If opponents start to attack early in the air in an attempt to stuff these attacks, forego these attacks in order to crouch under it and leave the opponent open for a throw upon landing. Against opponents who attempt to counter Sonic Booms with projectiles of their own, Guile's superior recovery time often provides the opportunity to follow through with his HP Backfist, while your opponent is stuck in the recovery phase. Since *Champion* and *Turbo* Guile can use the HP Backfist while charging back, the counter attack can be followed immediately by another Sonic Boom. With patience and caution, this play style can whittle down any opponent's patience.

COMBOS

STREET FIGHTER II

A repeated standing LP until stunned

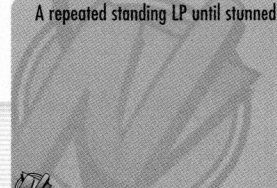

CORNER ONLY — ← + MK, HP, HP
Sonic Boom

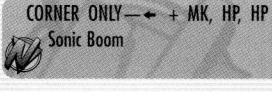

STREET FIGHTER II CHAMPION EDITION

Jumping HP, crouching MP, LK
Somersault Kick

↓ + LK x 4, HP

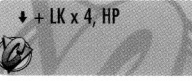

STREET FIGHTER II TURBO

CORNER ONLY — Jumping HP, HP, HP
Sonic Boom, HP Backfist

↓ + LK, MP, HK Somersault Kick

GOOD MATCH-UP

VS CAMMY

Cammy's entire game plan hinges on her ability to get close to an opponent. With her fast speed and extensive inventory of knockdown attacks, it's easy to accomplish that goal. However, she's weak against projectile attacks because they render nearly all of her ground attacks useless, including her Cannon Drill. Against characters with slow projectile animations (such as Ryu), one well-timed jump-in can guarantee victory for Cammy. With the near-instant recovery time of Sonic Boom, it's tough for Cammy to do the same to Guile no matter how well an opponent times her jumps. Therefore, nothing can stop Guile from barraging Cammy with a continuous stream of Sonic Booms, forcing her back against the corner while sustaining significant repeated block damage. If your opponent attempts to jump, Guile's crouching HP uppercut will send her reeling every time, forcing her to land on a Sonic Boom — with more on the way!

SUPER STREET FIGHTER II

The *Super Street Fighter II* variation of Guile is possibly the weakest incarnation of the batch. Without access to the various mobility options his *Super Street Fighter II Turbo* upgrade provides, this version is simply a clone of the *Champion/Turbo* Guile without the advantage of his original chains. His gains are mostly cosmetic, including a sharper-looking Sonic Boom and another victory animation. His vertical jumping MK now looks identical to his standing MK, and provides yet another anti-air option to utilize. His HK Somersault Kick has reverted to its original single-hit form. Although this form is superior to the problematic two-hit version, it provides no advantages over the one-hit LK and MK Somersault Kicks available to *Champion/Turbo* Guile. Defensive players seeking to maximize Guile's Sonic Boom traps and zoning patterns should stick to his *Champion Edition* and *Turbo* versions.

SUPER STREET FIGHTER II TURBO

Although *Super Street Fighter II Turbo* Guile gains exclusive access to a super move and builds his super meter effortlessly, his most valuable upgrades are his modified normal moves. His new standing HK provides a safer method of moving forward while conserving charge than his MK Knee Bazooka. He also gains directional control of his standing MK Rolling Sobat, and can now move forward or backward with it. While the forward variation of this move is a powerful offensive tool in footsies, the backward MK Rolling Sobat provides the rare ability of retreating from an opponent's attack while simultaneously attacking. Backward motion on the ground is impossible without it because the presence of an opponent's attack on-screen triggers Guile's blocking animation.

Unfortunately, Guile's new standing HP Right Hook, which prevents him from retaining charge, makes this version of Guile a bit weaker while performing his HP Backfist. Overall, the *Super Street Fighter Turbo* Guile is the most versatile and best from an offensive-fighting standpoint, and it is recommended for players who enjoy playing footsies.

COMBOS

SUPER STREET FIGHTER II

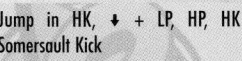
CORNER ONLY— ↓ + MK, HP, HP
SONIC BOOM, HP

Jump in HK, ↓ + LP, HP, HK
Somersault Kick

SUPER STREET FIGHTER II TURBO

HP *Sonic Boom*, ↓ + LP, LP, LP *Sonic Boom*, ↓ + LK, → + MK

Jumping cross-up LK, ↓ + LK, ↓ + LK, standing LK, Double Somersault Kick *super combo*

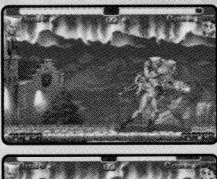  

BAD MATCH-UP

VS VEGA

Vega's attack range, move priority, and jump speed have made him one of Guile's most dangerous opponents since *Champion Edition*. Vega's quick jumps enable him to hop over Guile's Sonic Booms, and his high-priority air attacks enable him to overcome most of Guile's anti-air normal moves. On the ground, Vega's constant barrage of claw pokes makes it difficult to maintain an effective defense. To stand a chance in this fight, use Guile's Sonic Booms sparingly at carefully planned ranges to avoid Vega's ground pokes. Also, stay outside of Vega's best jump ranges. Patience is the key to tricking an opponent into jumping while Guile is charged for a Somersault Kick. Once knocking down Vega, follow through with a tick setup or go for a jumping cross-up attack. Vega lacks a good Reversal, which leaves him susceptible to precisely timed throw attempts. To defeat Vega, follow through on every successful knockdown and pressure Vega into making mistakes. Playing carelessly will give your opponent too many opportunities to take advantage of Guile's weaknesses, but you must must be willing to take some chances. Playing it safe in this match-up may lead to a slow loss.

COSTUMES

LP

MP

HP

START

Hold any button

LK

MK

HK

GUILE

35

NORMAL MOVES

STANDING

Super Street Fighter II Guile retains the same exact set of basic normals since the Champion Edition incarnation. The Super Street Fighter II Turbo upgrade adds two completely new standing normal attacks: his standing HP Right Hook and standing HK Advancing Kick. The gameplay and strategy remains the same with these new changes.

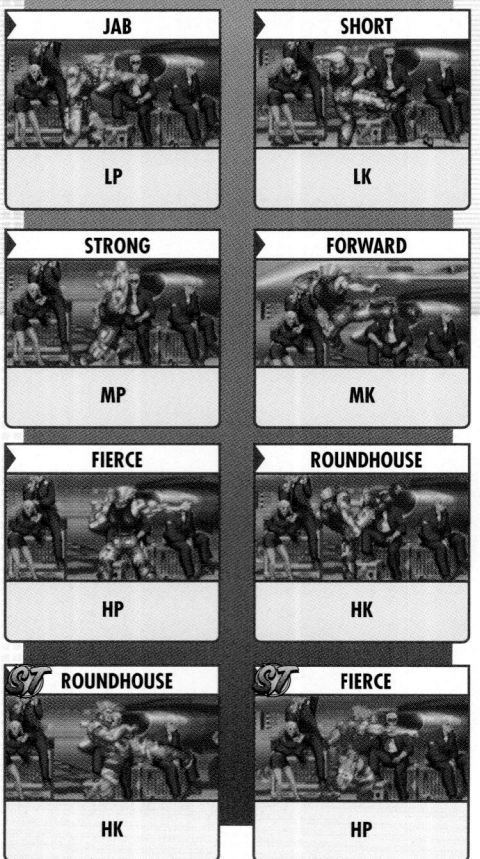

JAB	SHORT
LP	LK

STRONG	FORWARD
MP	MK

FIERCE	ROUNDHOUSE
HP	HK

ST ROUNDHOUSE	ST FIERCE
HK	HP

STANDING CLOSE

Super Street Fighter II Guile retains the exact same set of normal moves since his introduction in Street Fighter II. However, Super Street Fighter II Turbo Guile loses the close-range HK High Kick, restricting his anti-air options in favor of greater mobility.

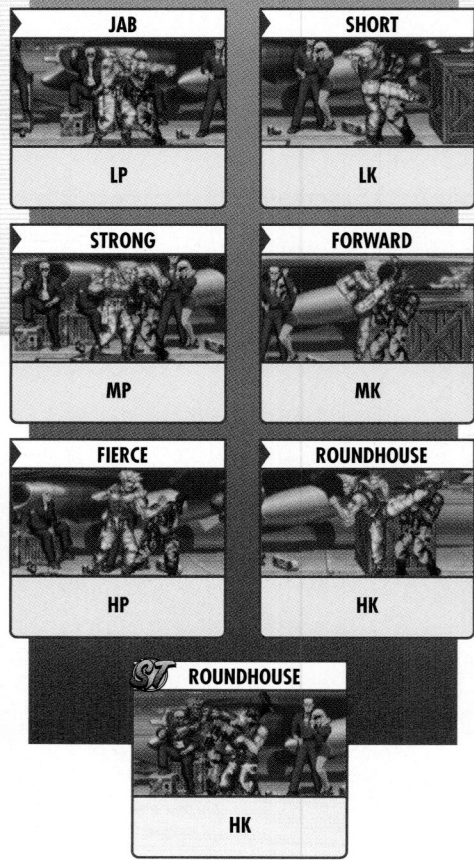

JAB	SHORT
LP	LK

STRONG	FORWARD
MP	MK

FIERCE	ROUNDHOUSE
HP	HK

ST ROUNDHOUSE
HK

CROUCHING

The full set of Guile's crouching attacks remains essentially unchanged throughout all of his versions in the game. His crouching MK is still his best long-range attack, and his crouching HP still functions as a very dependable anti-air attack. Unfortunately, his crouching HK foot sweep is still the slowest attack of its type in the game.

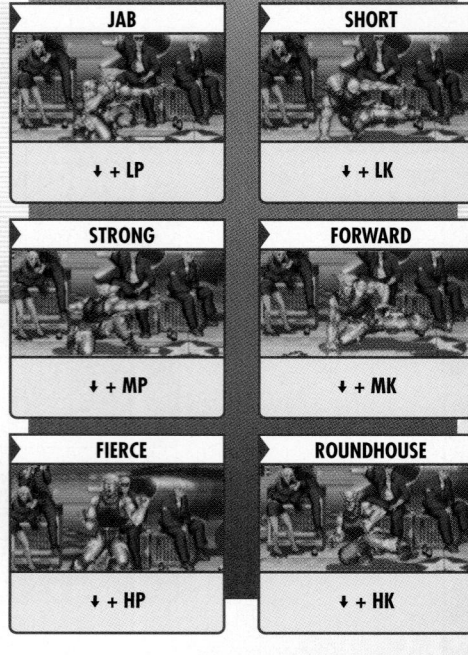

JAB	SHORT
↓ + LP	↓ + LK

STRONG	FORWARD
↓ + MP	↓ + MK

FIERCE	ROUNDHOUSE
↓ + HP	↓ + HK

SPECIAL NORMALS

In close, → / ← + HK	Roundhouse

Guile's → + HK special normal is great for going over most character's crouching attacks. Guile turns himself upside down and kicks the opponent in the head from a far distance. This move is great for a surprise to beat your opponents crouching attacks.

→ / ← + LK	Short

Guile's Knee Bazooka has been moved over to the LK button in Super Street Fighter II Turbo. Interestingly enough, this creates some new combo possibilities for the move by allowing it to be chained from Guile's crouching LK attacks.

→ / ← + MK	Forward

Super Street Fighter II Turbo Guile's moveset has been modified slightly to make room for his new directional MK Rolling Sobats. With the controllable Rolling Sobats taking up the MK button, he has an extremely fast MK move which can move both forward and back.

JUMPING

Apart from the modification of Guile's vertical jumping MK in *Super Street Fighter II* and *Super Street Fighter II Turbo* to use the same animation as his standing MK Rolling Sobat, Guile's entire arsenal of air attacks remains the same . The forward jumping MK is stil his best frontal airborne attack, while his jumping HK remains his best air-to-air attack. Finally, his jumping LK knee is still his only true jumping cross-up attack.

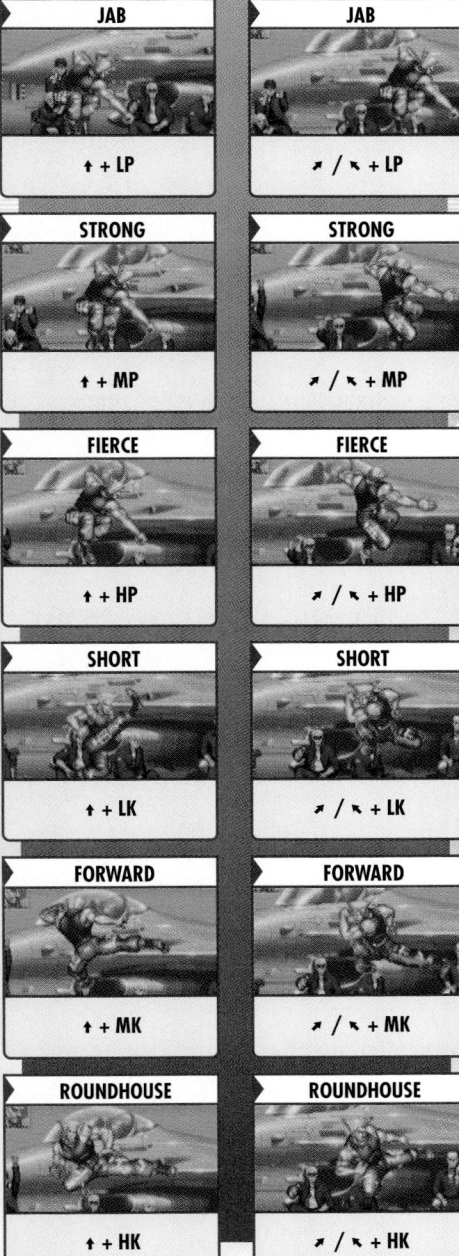

JAB	JAB
↑ + LP	↗ / ↖ + LP
STRONG	**STRONG**
↑ + MP	↗ / ↖ + MP
FIERCE	**FIERCE**
↑ + HP	↗ / ↖ + HP
SHORT	**SHORT**
↑ + LK	↗ / ↖ + LK
FORWARD	**FORWARD**
↑ + MK	↗ / ↖ + MK
ROUNDHOUSE	**ROUNDHOUSE**
↑ + HK	↗ / ↖ + HK

THROWS

Guile's throws remain untouched throughout his transition from *Street Fighter II* all the way to *Super Street Fighter II Turbo*. Like the other characters, only other *Super Street Fighter II Turbo* characters can escape one of *Super Street Fighter II Turbo* Guile's throws. Since Guile isn't overly dependent on throws, and because many of his toughest match-ups arise from *Super Street Fighter II Turbo* characters, this fact favors *Super Street Fighter II Turbo* Guile overall.

THROW	THROW
→ / ← + MP	→ / ← + HP

AIR THROW	AIR THROW
IN AIR, → / ← / ↓ + MP / HP	IN AIR, → / ← / ↓ + MK / HK

SPECIAL MOVES

Charge ← → — **Sonic Boom**

Despite obvious cosmetic alterations in the appearance of Guile's Sonic Boom, the move remains essentially unchanged. It travels along the same horizontal axis as before and recovers just as quickly. It's still the most valuable tool in Guile's arsenal.

Charge ↑ ↓ — **Somersault Kick**

Guile's LK and MK Somersault Kicks remain the same, but his HK Somersault Kick has reverted to the original single-hit knockdown form associated with the normal *Street Fighter II* version. Although the two-hit version (present in *Turbo* and *Champion Edition*) often missed on its second hit, leaving opponents standing and Guile vulnerable to counter attack, players quickly learned to rely on the LK and MK versions instead. Therefore, this change has had little effect overall.

SUPER COMBO

Charge ↙ ↘ ↙ ↗ + K — **Double Somersault Kick**

Because Guile gains so much Super Meter with every Sonic Boom, it's rare for a round to end without gaining access to this move. Unfortunately, the Double Somersault Kick is arguably one of the weakest super moves in the game compared to other characters. It's totally unsafe when it gets blocked. Furthermore, it must be performed at point-blank range to connect with all of its hits. If not, it will fail to knock down the opponent, leaving Guile vulnerable to counter attack.

On the plus side, it can score four powerful hits against airborne opponents when timed properly. The only use for the Double Somersault Kick outside of anti-air situations is to finish off an opponent through multiple hits of block damage. You shouldn't concern yourself with landing this move; getting trigger-happy with super moves is one of the easiest ways to lose track of your overall game plan.

GUILE

Ken

STANDING

Ken and Ryu's normal moves are identical. Ken's standing MP is great at stuffing projectiles before an opponent can finish throwing them. His HK is ideal for stopping jump-in attacks, if there isn't time to complete a Shoryuken.

STANDING CLOSE

Ken's standing close normals are his staple for big damage. In close, Ken has the ability to dizzy you if he connects with anything. If Ken connects any normal move, he can chain it into alot of moves that result in a dizzy. A standing HP up close will combo into any special move that Ken has, and MK will combo into special moves in *Street Fighter II Turbo*.

CROUCHING

All of Ken's crouching kick moves are extremely useful. The crouching LK is great for unleashing multiple hits and, when chained together, they can sometimes dizzy an opponent. His crouching MK can two-in-one into any special move, which makes it a very powerful normal. His crouching HK is great for buffering a Hadoken, whether or not it connects, as the Hadoken will come out after the sweep is complete. This is a great technique to use for trapping opponents in the corner with the Hadoken.

THROWS

Because Ken has a slower projectile, his tick-throw traps are almost inescapable. Using a slow projectile followed by a throw is a ruthless strategy! Ken's kick-throw animation is different than Ryu's, as Ken rolls twice on the ground and throws his opponent, while Ryu only rolls once.

JAB	STRONG	FIERCE
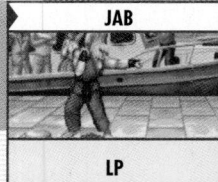		
LP	MP	HP

SHORT	FORWARD	ROUNDHOUSE

LK	MK	HK

JAB	STRONG	FIERCE
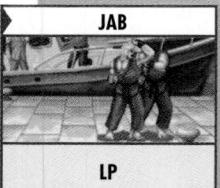		
LP	MP	HP

SHORT	FORWARD	ROUNDHOUSE

LK	MK	HK

JAB	STRONG	FIERCE
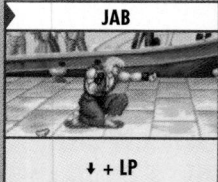		
↓ + LP	↓ + MP	↓ + HP

SHORT	FORWARD	ROUNDHOUSE
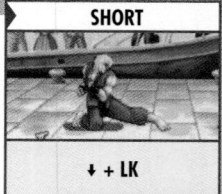		
↓ + LK	↓ + MK	↓ + HK

THROW	THROW
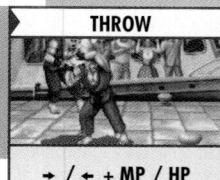	
→ / ← + MP / HP	→ / ← + MK / HK

JUMPING

Ken's air moves are best utilized for jump-in attacks. Some of them can be used to beat your opponent's move in the air. For example, all of Ken's straight-up moves have priority over his jump-forward moves. Use ↑ + HK when an opponent jumps in to knock them out of the air.

JAB

↑ + LP

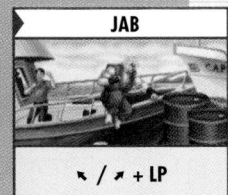

JAB

↙ / ↗ + LP

STRONG

↑ + MP

STRONG

↙ / ↗ + MP

FIERCE

↑ + HP

FIERCE

↙ / ↗ + HP

SHORT

↑ + LK

SHORT

↙ / ↗ + LK

FORWARD

↑ + MK

FORWARD

↙ / ↗ + MK

ROUNDHOUSE

↑ + HK

ROUNDHOUSE

↙ / ↗ + HK

SPECIAL MOVES

↓ ↘ → + Any P   **Hadoken**

This cool projectile, like other projectiles, can be used to pressure opponents, keep them at bay, and force them to jump or make a mistake. Ken's Hadoken is slighty slower then Ryu's, but it can still be used in a combo.

→ ↓ ↘ + P   **Shoryuken**

Ken's Shoryuken is the most recognized move in all of *Street Fighter*. It changes in *Champion Edition*, though, to distinguish the move a bit from Ryu. In this version, it's capable of multiple hits, just like his Tatsumaki Senpukyaku. It also gains an arc that makes it much easier to use as an anti-air defense.

↓ ↙ ← + K   **Tatsumaki Senpukyaku**

Ken's Tatsumaki Senpukyaku is great to use in multi-hit combos, especially if you don't want to knock down your opponent. In *Street Fighter II*, this special move is the exact same as Ryu's. In the *Champion Edition* version, Ken's Tatsumaki Senpukyaku doesn't knock down on the first connected hit, so it can be used in a combo for multiple hits. In the *Street Fighter II Turbo* version, use the Tatsumaki Senpukyaku as a two-in-one in the air for three or more hits.

In Air ↓ ↙ ← + K   **Tatsumaki Senpukyaku**

Instead of knocking down an opponent like Ryu's Tatsumaki, this move continues to hit in the air. This can lead to big damage and oftentimes a dizzy, if it's used in a combo.

COSTUMES

STREET FIGHTER II

COSTUME

STREET FIGHTER II

ALTERNATE COSTUME

CHAMPIONSHIP

COSTUME

TURBO

COSTUME

COMBOS

STREET FIGHTER II

Jump in HK, HP, LP Shoryuken

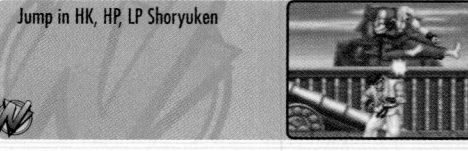

↓ + LK x 3, standing HP

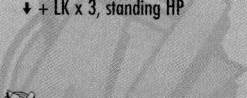

STREET FIGHTER II CHAMPION EDITION

Cross-up HK, HP, HK Tatsumaki Senpukyaku

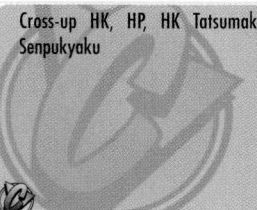

Cross-up HK, HP, HP Shoryuken

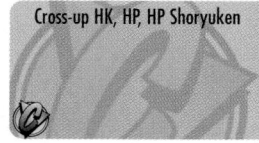

STREET FIGHTER II TURBO

Jump in HK, ↑ + HK, HK Tatsumaki Senpukyaku

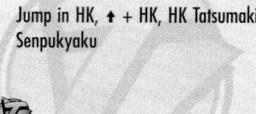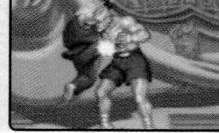

Jump in HP, ↓ + MP, ↓ + HK

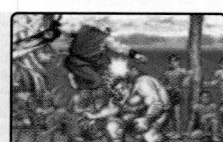

STREET FIGHTER II

Street Fighter II Ken is all about combos. Master the 4-hit combos and you'll most certainly dizzy an opponent every time. Cross-up HK, crouching LK, and LK + HP together (to make the LK cancel into a HP), then finish with a HP Hadoken. Learn this combo and use it each time you dizzy and opponent for an easy victory.

STREET FIGHTER II CHAMPION EDITION

In *Champion Edition* Ken has a faster Hadoken, which is great for Hadoken traps. Since he has a Shoryuken that arcs, use his Shoryuken when an opponent jumps out of the Hadoken trap. This is one of the most difficult traps to escape from in the game, so use this tactic to defeat your opponents.

STREET FIGHTER II TURBO

Here is where the changes really begin. Ken's Tatsumaki Senpukyaku is much faster and adds hits to a combo. If you two-in-one his jumping HK into an air Tatsumaki Senpukyaku, it creates a dizzy almost every time! Ken's Shoryuken is also capable of knocking down, so combo into it to make your opponent drop. You can even take advantage of projectile traps or zoning games.

GOOD MATCH-UP

VS. CHUN-LI

Chun Li's main weakness is that she must be close to be effective. Obviously, the main goal is to keep her away! Mix up the Hadokens with different speeds, then use a Shoryuken when she jumps. After knocking down Chun-Li, throw a LP Hadoken to hit her on the back of her head on her wake up. Follow this Hadoken and throw her after it hits, or continue to barrage her with Hadokens in the corner. It is extremely difficult for Chun-Li to escape this trap without jumping, and Ken's Shoryuken should punish her if she does get airborne.

SUPER STREET FIGHTER II

Super Street Fighter II Ken has gained two new properties for his older moves in this version. He now has the Flaming Shoryuken. This move hits three times for serious damage. It also goes up at more of a angle than Ryu's. Also, since it hits three times at different points in the arc, you will be able to hit opponents from farther away than before. His new and improved Tatsumaki Senpukyaku now has a rainbow pattern (in the air). You can also use it at the end of your jump, to maximize your safety, and still hit your opponent with a Tatsumaki Senpukyaku.

SUPER STREET FIGHTER II TURBO

The differences between Ryu and Ken have been growing steadlily since *Champion Edition*, but these differences are very easy to see in *Super Turbo*. Ken gains an overhead kick move in this version, which hits mid then hits high. Sadly, his best new asset in this version is not a new move, it is his MK throw. Ken now grabs his opponent by the head and knees them in the stomach multiple times. This opens up one of the greatest mix-ups ever. When the throw is complete, it pushes the target into the air while Ken stays on the ground. This prepares you for another throw, or a crouching attack linked into the Shoryureppa. This technique can also be employed to trick your opponent by walking under them to get on the other side. Yet another option is to jump up and use a LP and two-in-one this move into a Tatsumaki Senpukyaku. Ken's HK in this version is also a great asset, since it moves farther than any of his normals. The new special kicks in his arsenal can be used for tricks too, like doing HK (no hold) version while standing directly over someone getting up. Ken "teleports" to the other side and can combo them from behind for a surprise.

COMBOS

SUPER STREET FIGHTER II

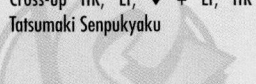
Cross-up HK, LP, ↓ + LP, HK
Tatsumaki Senpukyaku

Cross-up HK, HP, HP Shoryuken

SUPER STREET FIGHTER II TURBO

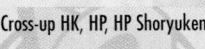
Cross-up MK, ↓ + MK, ↓ ↘ → + MK,
↓ + HK

Jump in HP, (any kick) Air Tatsumaki
Senpukyaku, ↓ + LK, Shoryureppa

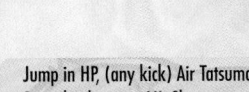

BAD MATCH UP

VS SAGAT

Ken has major problems in this battle. Ken has no reliable ways to get close to Sagat without doing a blind air Tatsumaki Senpukyaku. Fighting Sagat with Hadokens only works for a limited time, so avoid that strategy. Some people like to use Sagat's Ground Tiger Shots in sets of two, so use the LK Tatsumaki Senpukyaku twice in a row to hop over them. This will keep you within range for a quick Shoryuken or close combo. Don't get close with an Air Tatsumaki Senpukyaku, unless you anticipate a Ground Tiger Shot. Or, do one quickly after jumping to create a lower flying arc and get back on the ground sooner. Otherwise, you may get knocked out of the air by a Tiger Uppercut. When Sagat gets knocked down in the corner, use a Hadoken trap to make him jump, or force him to battle it out with Tiger Shots.

COSTUMES

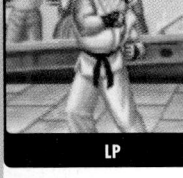
LP

MP

HP

START

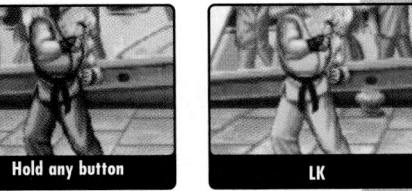
Hold any button

LK

MK

HK

KEN

NORMAL MOVES
STANDING

There are big changes to Ken's HK move in *Super Turbo*. It now goes much further and it can't be used for anti-air attacks. It is great at stuffing attacks and getting close to opponents. If you play against someone who hesitates a lot, use this move to make them react.

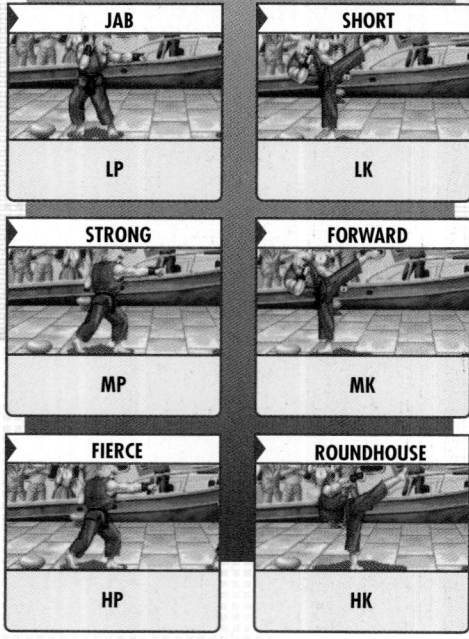

JAB	SHORT
LP	LK

STRONG	FORWARD
MP	MK

FIERCE	ROUNDHOUSE
HP	HK

ST ROUNDHOUSE
HK

STANDING CLOSE

Ken's close MK has been replaced by a one-hit axe kick in *Super Turbo*. The HK axe kick is completely gone, having been replaced by his new HK normal. In many ways, this version of Ken is a complete departure from the early versions of Ken and the *Super Street Fighter II* version.

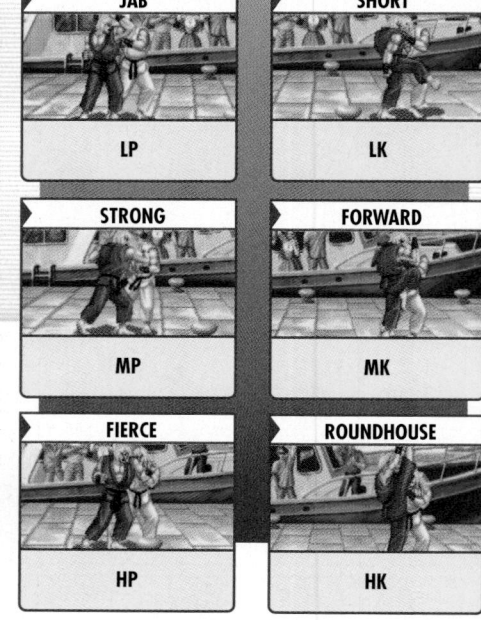

JAB	SHORT
LP	LK

STRONG	FORWARD
MP	MK

FIERCE	ROUNDHOUSE
HP	HK

ST FORWARD
MK

SPECIAL NORMALS
JUMPING

One change in the *Super Turbo* version of Ken is his ↖ / ↑ / ↗ + MK. This is a great move for crossing up an opponent, because it almost always crosses up when you jump in with it. And, unlike Ryu, Ken can follow up a hit with a combo since it doesn't knock down his opponent.

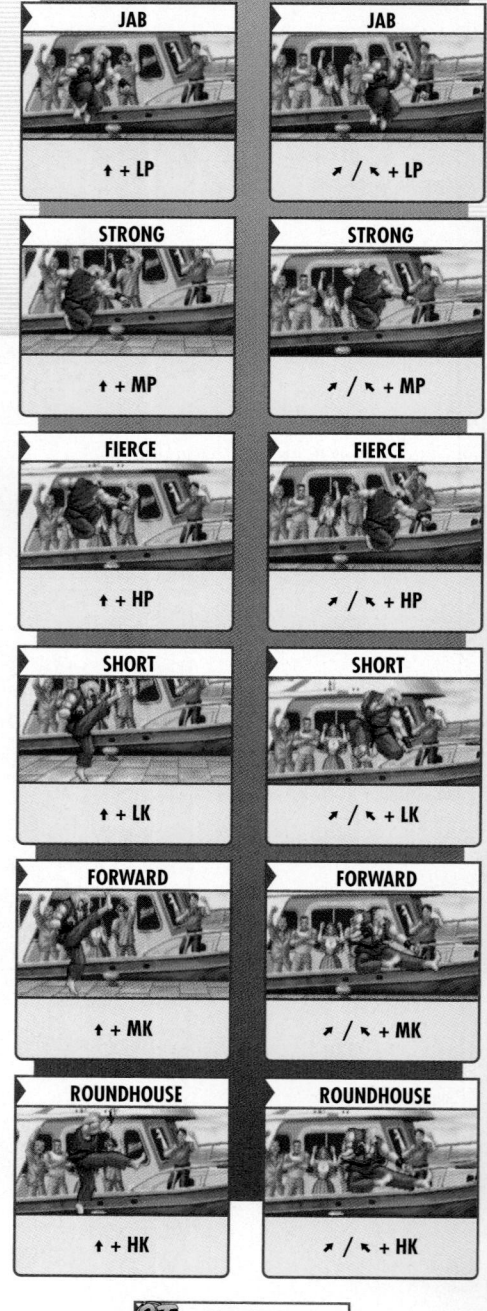

JAB	JAB
↑ + LP	↗ / ↖ + LP

STRONG	STRONG
↑ + MP	↗ / ↖ + MP

FIERCE	FIERCE
↑ + HP	↗ / ↖ + HP

SHORT	SHORT
↑ + LK	↗ / ↖ + LK

FORWARD	FORWARD
↑ + MK	↗ / ↖ + MK

ROUNDHOUSE	ROUNDHOUSE
↑ + HK	↗ / ↖ + HK

ST FORWARD
↗ / ↖ + MK

THROWS

Ken's MK throw, in *Super Turbo*, is one of the best in the game. He grabs his opponent's head and knees him in the stomach. You can mash on the controller for quicker, additional hits. After the knee strike you are clearly at an advantage, because you are on the ground while your opponent has to come down from the air. There are several mixups off this throw. For example, just walk toward your opponent to warp to the other side and perform a combo. Or, you have the ability to go high, low, or overhead.

THROW	THROW
→ / ← + MP / HP	→ / ← + MK / HK

ST THROW	ST AIR THROW
→ / ← + MK	IN AIR, → / ← / ↓ + MK / HK

CROUCHING

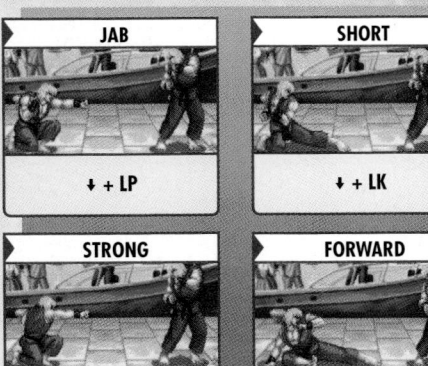

JAB	SHORT
↓ + LP	↓ + LK
STRONG	**FORWARD**
↓ + MP	↓ + MK
FIERCE	**ROUNDHOUSE**
↓ + HP	↓ + HK

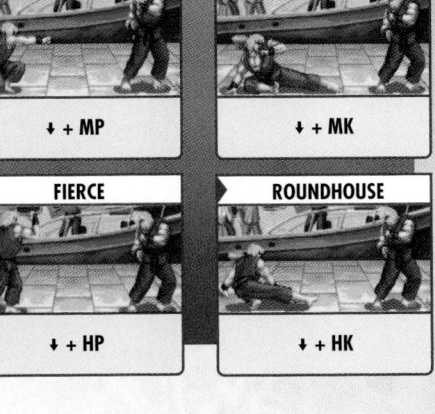

SPECIAL MOVES

↓ ↘ → + Any P — **Hadoken**

This version of the Hadoken is faster than its predecessor, but slower than Ryu's Hadoken. It also has a lot less recovery than before, which makes it a really good projectile. The LP Hadoken is extremely slow so you can walk behind it and follow it up with a normal attack.

↓ ↙ ← + K — **Tatsumaki Senpukyaku**

Ken's Tatsumaki Senpukyaku still hits multiple times, and it has gained a rainbow effect in the air. It can also be perfomed at the last second, while approaching the ground, to minimize the exposure of getting hit. If you perform this move at the last second above an opponent's head, it will connect twice and create a short period of time to follow with a combo. Using the LK Tatsumaki Senpukyaku in the air before landing is a great way to charge the super meter in *Super Street Fighter II Turbo*.

→ ↓ ↘ + P — **Shoryuken**

Ken's Shoryuken uppercut differs immensely from Ryu's in these two versions. When performed with LP, it hits once, MP hits twice, and HP hits three time and includes flames. Also, the Shoryuken extends further from the starting point, making it somewhat more effective.

↓ ↘ → + K, hold for second overhead kick

Although the overhead combos here, it can still be used as an overhead if it gets blocked. Holding down the kick button causes the move to turn into an overhead attack if your opponent blocks low.

SUPER COMBO

↓ ↘ → ↓ ↘ → + P — **Shoryureppa**

The Shoryureppa is a great super combo for anti-air attacks that have good priority. For example, if someone playing as Zangief constantly jumps toward you with the Body Splash multiple times, use this move to gain some space. Because this move starts with invincibility, the Shoryureppa will connect and your opponent's attack won't. You can add this super combo to another combo to produce huge damage.

KEN

Ryu

STANDING

Ryu's normal moves are pretty slow. His standing HP has distance and it can punish opponents when it connects. However, the the opportunity to use it is limited because it is slower than most other attacks in the game. On the other hand, Ryu's standing HK is a great anti-air attack if an opponent is out of range of Ryu's Shoryuken.

STANDING CLOSE

Ryu's close normals are great in a combo because they cause big damage. A close-range HP can be followed by a Hadoken for a two-in-one. Also, Ryu's standing LP can set up a chance for a throw if it is blocked.

CROUCHING

Ryu's crouching normals are great to string together for big combos. You can chain five crouching LKs together or end it with a crouching HK. Sometimes, you can dizzy an adversary by linking five LKs together. You can also "buffer" moves off his crouching HK. For example, do a crouching HK, then buffer a Hadoken to come out during the last few frames of the crouching HK. Although this won't act as a combo, it's a great way to keep the pressure on a blocking opponent. Ryu also has a great crouching MK, which can used for a two-in-one with a Hadoken or a Shoryuken afterward.

THROWS

Throws with Ryu are especially important, because you can follow up a Hadoken to put them in block stun, and throw them while they are still blocking without retaliation. These kinds of tactics are considered "cheap" by some players, so keep that in mind. Throws are also the only known difference between Ryu and Ken in *Street Fighter II*; when Ryu does his kick throw, he rolls only once.

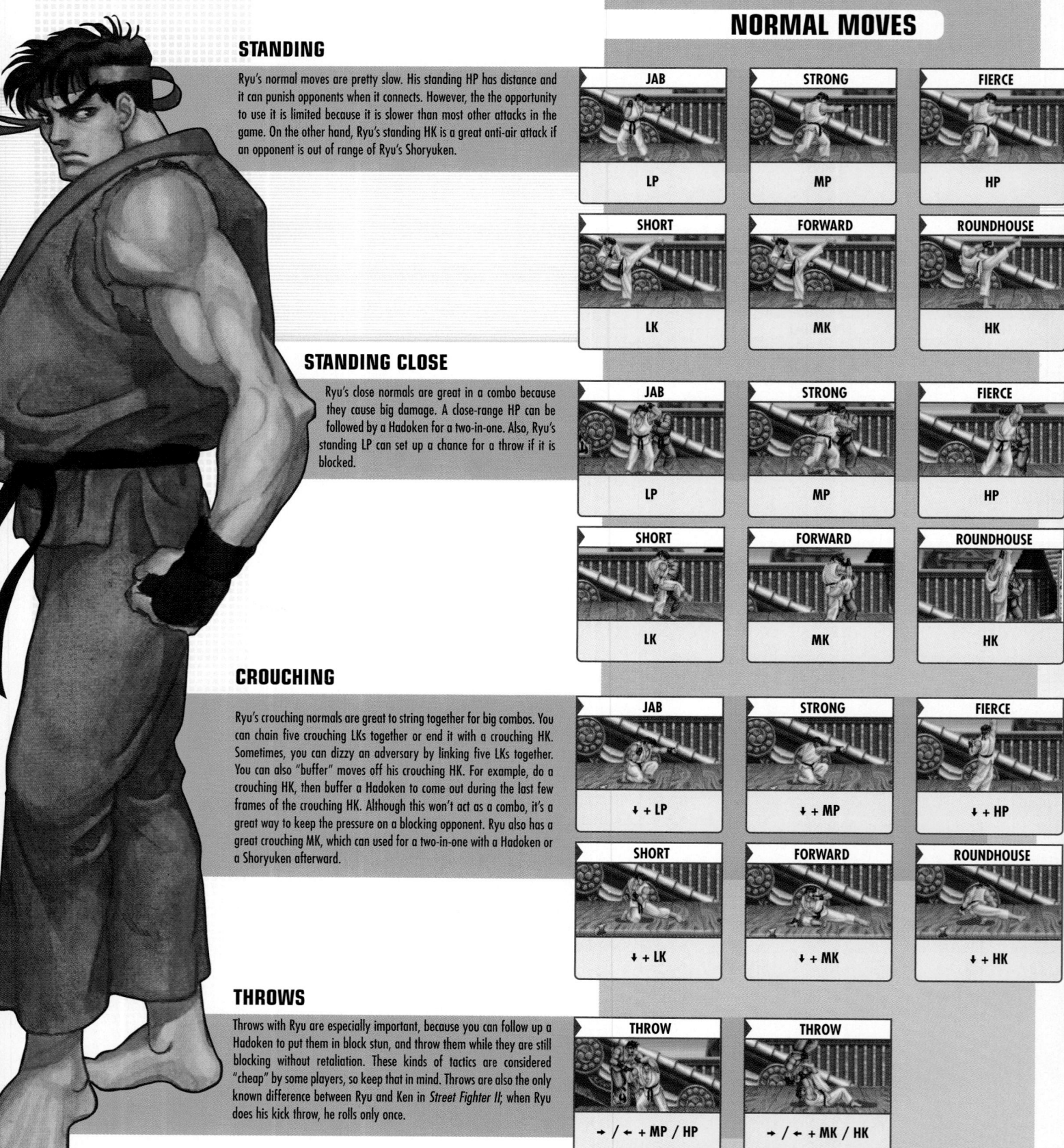

NORMAL MOVES

JAB	STRONG	FIERCE
LP	MP	HP
SHORT	FORWARD	ROUNDHOUSE
LK	MK	HK

JAB	STRONG	FIERCE
LP	MP	HP
SHORT	FORWARD	ROUNDHOUSE
LK	MK	HK

JAB	STRONG	FIERCE
↓ + LP	↓ + MP	↓ + HP
SHORT	FORWARD	ROUNDHOUSE
↓ + LK	↓ + MK	↓ + HK

THROW	THROW
→ / ← + MP / HP	→ / ← + MK / HK

JUMPING

Ryu's air moves are fairly straightforward. His jumping LK in the air has a lot of priority, but it causes almost no damage. If you are looking to get close to an opponent upon landing, it is the best move to use.

JAB	JAB
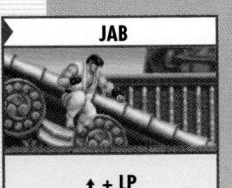	
↑ + LP	↙ / ↗ + LP

STRONG	STRONG

↑ + MP	↙ / ↗ + MP

FIERCE	FIERCE

↑ + HP	↙ / ↗ + HP

SHORT	SHORT

↑ + LK	↙ / ↗ + LK

FORWARD	FORWARD

↑ + MK	↙ / ↗ + MK

ROUNDHOUSE	ROUNDHOUSE

↑ + HK	↙ / ↗ + HK

SPECIAL MOVES

↓ ↘ → + Any P **Hadoken**

The Hadoken, one of the best projectiles ever, is a mighty force. The power of the Hadoken comes from Ryu's own fists and leaves an imprint of his fists inside. The Hadoken has three different speeds and mixing them up will really confuse an opponent.

→ ↓ ↘ + P **Shoryuken**

Ryu's Shoryuken is one of the most powerful moves in all of *Street Fighter*. It inflicts *huge* damage and is effective against anyone who dares to jump in. The Normal version of this move only knocks down your opponent when he or she gets hit out of the air, so beware. This move also hits an opponent twice on the ground if you are fighting in close. This is your most prized asset when fighting opponents. You can also combo the Shoryuken after a crouching MK or a standing HP in close.

In Air ↓ ↙ ← + K **Tatsumaki Senpukyaku**

The air Tatsumaki Senpukyaku is a valuable upgrade for Ryu. Use it to fly across the screen where very few adversaries can reach you, or use it to confuse an opponent by using it on the other side to cross him up. Lastly, unleash it in a combo on bigger characters, such as Sagat and Zangief.

↓ ↙ ← + K **Tatsumaki Senpukyaku**

Ryu's Tatsumaki Senpukyaku is great if you need to travel long distances in a short period of time. It can go over Guile's Sonic Boom and Dhalsim's Yoga Fire, too. Use it in conjunction with a crouching MK to combo for big damage. From *Champion Edition* onward, the Tatsumaki Senpukyaku knocks down an adversary on the first successful hit. In *Street Fighter II Turbo*, you can 2-in-1 the Tatsumaki Senpukyaku in the air and and make it connect for two hits.

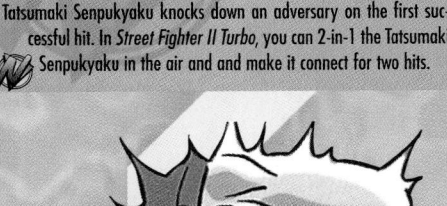

RYU

COSTUMES

STREET FIGHTER II
COSTUME

STREET FIGHTER II
ALTERNATE COSTUME

CHAMPIONSHIP
COSTUME

TURBO
COSTUME

STREET FIGHTER II

Street Fighter II Ryu is all about combos. If you master the 4-hit combos, you can dizzy your opponent almost every time. Ryu also has a "glitched out" combo that utilizes LK + HP. Start with a cross-up HK, then do a crouching LK, link LK + HP together to make the HP combo, then finish with a HP Hadoken. If you master this combo, you can dizzy your opponent almost every time.

STREET FIGHTER II CHAMPION EDITION

In *Champion Edition*, Ryu gained a faster Hadoken that is great for projectile traps. Because he has the fastest projectile in the game, it's possible to lock down characters in the corner with multiple HP Hadokens. If they get out of this trap and jump toward you, take them out of the air with a Shoryuken.

STREET FIGHTER II TURBO

With the addition of the air Tatsumaki Senpukyaku and the invincibility of the Tatsumaki Senpukyaku at his disposal, Ryu is the arguably the best *Street Fighter II Turbo* character. Use the LK hurricane kick when fighting in close quarters (since it has invincibility) to stop many of your opponent's moves. This is also the only version of Ryu that can two-in-one a Tatsumaki Senpukyaku in the air and make it connect. Ryu's Shoryuken also knocks down opponents in this version, so when you combo it your opponent will be floored. This tactic enables you to prepare Hadoken traps or other waiting/zoning games.

COMBOS

STREET FIGHTER II

Cross-up HK, ↓ + LK x 4

 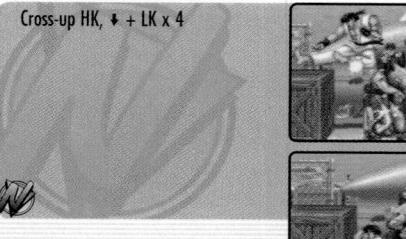  

Jump in HP, HP, Hadoken

STREET FIGHTER II CHAMPION EDITION

Jump in HK, ↓ + MP, HK Tatsumaki Senpukyaku

Cross-up HK, ↓+ MK, Shoryuken

STREET FIGHTER II TURBO

Jump in HP, ↑ + HK, HK Tatsumaki Senpukyaku

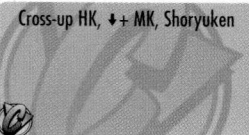   

Crossup FK, ↓ + MP, ↓ + MK, HP Hadoken

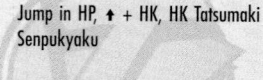   
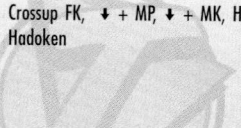   

GOOD MATCH-UP

VS E. HONDA

When fighting E. Honda, you should be in the drivers seat. E. Honda's Headbutt is almost useless against a good Ryu player. Throwing Hadoken's will stop most of the Headbutt's from connecting. Your opponent will likely resort to jumping or performing the sumo splash. Just keep your distance from Honda and you should fair well in the fight. You can actually use a crouching HK against all of E. Honda's jumping attacks, including the Sumo Splash. Don't get too close to E. Honda while he is on the ground. His excellent throw range and wakeup moves are high priority. If he gets too close to you, use an air Tatsumaki Senpukyaku to get away and start the process over again.

SUPER STREET FIGHTER II

Super Street Fighter II Ryu gained a new move and a new property for an older move. He now has the Shakunetsu (red) Hadoken, which was a glitch in earlier versions of the game and would only appear randomly. Due to the high popularity of this so-called glitched "Red Hadoken," it was added to his arsenal. The Shakunetsu Hadoken leaves an opponent in a burned state a little longer than the normal Hadoken. At close range, this move knocks down your opponent. This is crucial when attacking with crouching MK and chaining it into a Shakunetsu Hadoken. His new and improved Tatsumaki Senpukyaku now has a rainbow pattern that it follows. It starts close to the ground and makes an arc as it goes across the screen. You can also use it at the end of a jump (to maximize safety) and hit your opponent.

SUPER STREET FIGHTER II TURBO

One of the best things that Ryu received in his *Super Turbo* form is a super-fast overhead move. This move →
+ MP can hit ducking opponents and combo into almost anything. He also has a → + HP move that is excellent for a Frame Advantage when blocked. You can follow this move up with a throw, mix it up with an overhead attack, or use a crouching MK into Shinku Hadoken. Another new move is the jumping MP. This MP enables you to jump into the air and hit an opponent up to three times. Upon landing, you can use Shinku Hadoken and hit your adversay two additional times for a 5-hit juggle combo. This move also has a lot of priority in the air, so the chances of landing it are high.

COMBOS

SUPER STREET FIGHTER II

↓+LK, ↓+HP, Shakunetsu Hadoken

Crossup HK, ↓+MP, ↓ + HP, Shakunetsu Hadoken

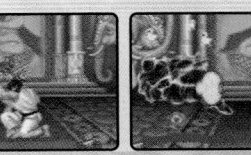

SUPER STREET FIGHTER II TURBO

On crouching opponent, → + MP, ↓ + MK, Shinku Hadoken

↓ + LK x 3, Shinku Hadoken

BAD MATCH-UP

VS VEGA

Vega has lots of strengths, so read onward to learn some key strategies. One advantage he has over Ryu is his speed. Your opponent can react to a Hadoken, jump over it, and hit you with a 2-hit combo fairly easily. Only throw Hadoken's from afar, or fake them up close to psych Vega into jumping straight into a Shoryuken. Another key advantage for Vega is his range. The claw on his hand gains him some extra reach to complicate things. Fortunately, all of Vega's normals can he stopped with a crouching HK. The only one that can't be countered in this manner is his crouching MK. Ryu's crouching LK will put an end to this attack. If your opponent starts utilizing Vega's Flying Barcelona Attack, use Ryu's LP Shoryuken. If you use an HP Shoryuken, your opponent can easily land before you and cause big damage. Lastly, don't get near Vega on wake up because he has more range in his throw than Ryu.

COSTUMES

LP

MP

HP

START

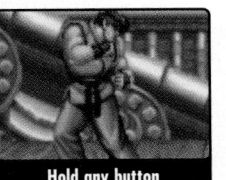
Hold any button

LK

MK

HK

NORMAL MOVES

STANDING

His standing moves haven't changed at all. He still has HK which is great for anti-air attacks if you don't have time to do a Shoryuken. His punches have range and can trade with projectile throwers a lot of the time.

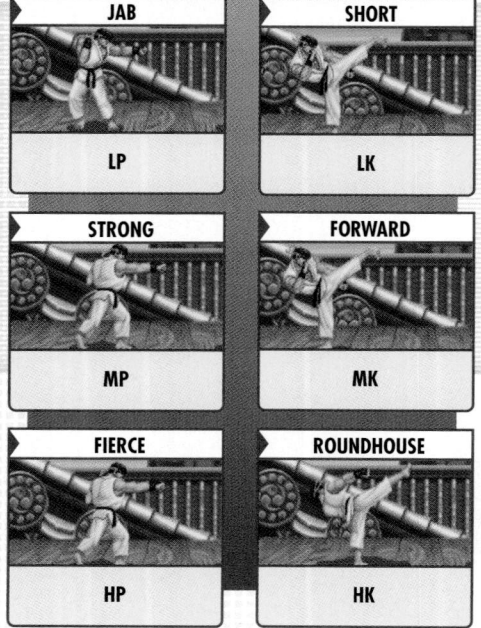

JAB	SHORT
LP	LK

STRONG	FORWARD
MP	MK

FIERCE	ROUNDHOUSE
HP	HK

STANDING CLOSE

A few changes here include the fact that Ryu's close-range MK can be followed up with any special move, and his HK Axe Kick hits twice instead of randomly.

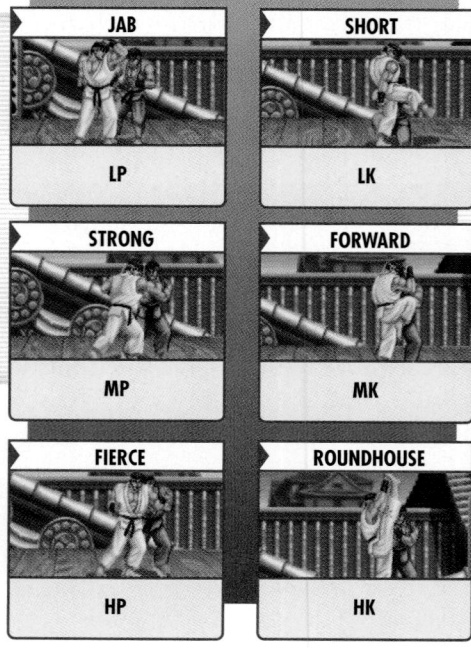

JAB	SHORT
LP	LK

STRONG	FORWARD
MP	MK

FIERCE	ROUNDHOUSE
HP	HK

CROUCHING

Ryu's crouching attacks are great for chaining together for big damage. Almost all of them can be used in conjunction with a two-in-one. His crouching MK has a lot of range, so use that a lot to follow it up with a Hadoken.

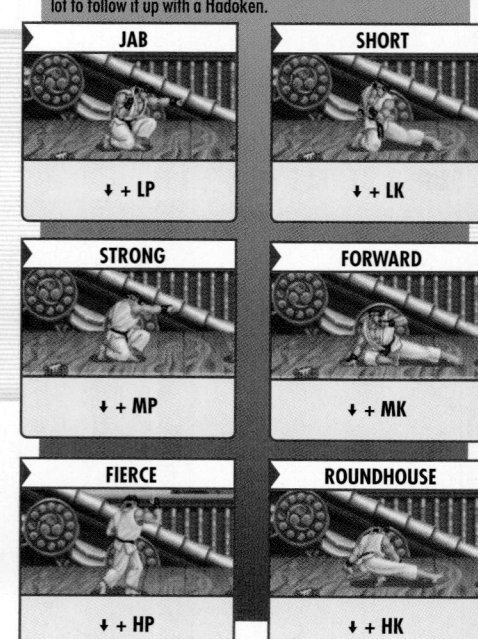

JAB	SHORT
↓ + LP	↓ + LK

STRONG	FORWARD
↓ + MP	↓ + MK

FIERCE	ROUNDHOUSE
↓ + HP	↓ + HK

THROWS

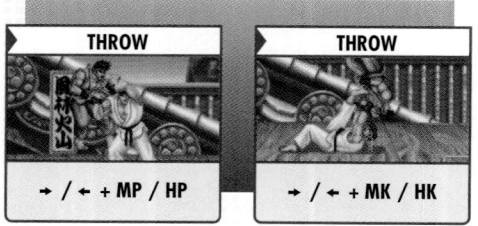

THROW	THROW
→ / ← + MP / HP	→ / ← + MK / HK

SPECIAL NORMALS

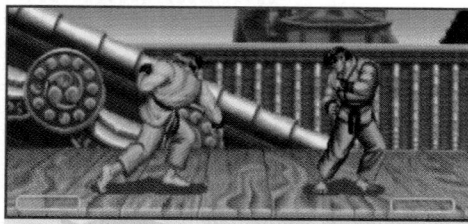

In close, → + MP

This move is a overhead attack, which means that if an opponent is ducking it will hit him or her while they are blocking. This is a great move to keep your opponent guessing. You can also use this move to start off a combo.

In close, → + HP

This move is an advancing move. Because of its incredible speed, it's possible to get next to your opponent very quickly. This is also effective when your opponent is blocking. It puts him or her in a pressure situation, since they must determine if an overhead attack or a low a Shinku Hadoken is on its way.

JUMPING

Ryu's primary goal when jumping is to land that all-important combo. Every single one of his jump-in moves can start a massive combo and almost dizzy the opponent.

Ryu's only change here is his ↘ / ↑ / ↗ + MP. This move can be repeated for a total of three hits, and it can be linked into a combo after a Shinku Hadoken. It also has great air priority.

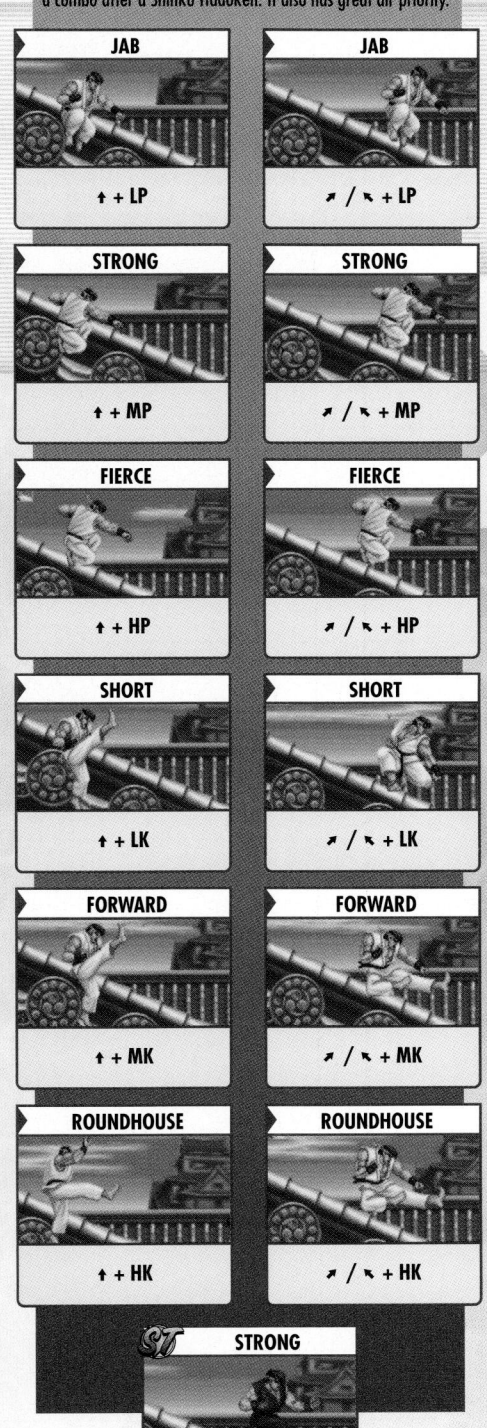

JAB	JAB
↑ + LP	↗ / ↘ + LP
STRONG	**STRONG**
↑ + MP	↗ / ↘ + MP
FIERCE	**FIERCE**
↑ + HP	↗ / ↘ + HP
SHORT	**SHORT**
↑ + LK	↗ / ↘ + LK
FORWARD	**FORWARD**
↑ + MK	↗ / ↘ + MK
ROUNDHOUSE	**ROUNDHOUSE**
↑ + HK	↗ / ↘ + HK

STRONG
↗ / ↘ + MP

SPECIAL MOVES

↓ ↘ → + Any P — Hadoken

This Hadoken is faster than its predecessor and it has a lot less recovery time than before. This makes the Hadoken a really good projectile. Not much else has changed with this move.

↓ ↙ ← + K — Tatsumaki Senpukyaku

Ryu's Tatsumaki Senpukyaku lost the invincibility from *Street Fighter II Turbo*, but it gained a rainbow effect that changes its trajectory. You can also use this move at the last moment while approaching the ground to minimize exposure. Either way, it almost always knocks down its target. Using the LK Tatsumaki in the air (before landing) is a great way to charge the Super Meter in *Super Street Fighter II Turbo*.

→ ↓ ↘ + P — Shoryuken

Ryu's Shoryuken uppercut is only one hit now with each punch button. It also knocks down your opponent every time regardless of the range.

← ↙ ↓ ↘ → + P — Shakunetsu Hadoken

The infamous Shakunetsu Hadoken. It can dizzy an opponent from great distances and knock him or her down at close-range.

SUPER COMBO

↓ ↘ → ↓ ↘ → + P — Shinku Hadoken

This Shinku Hadoken is the only super projectile in the game. It combines Ryu's power and unleashes five Hadokens in one. This is a great super on so many levels. If you're having a projectile fight and Ryu's Super Meter is charged, use the Shinku Hadoken to go through your opponent's projectile. This results in the loss of only one of the five Hadokens, while the other four hit your opponent. This Shinku Hadoken is also very effective at getting out of lockdown traps that have you stuck in the block stance. Since the Shinku Hadoken carries invincibility with it, it can also be used on wake up.

Zangief

STANDING

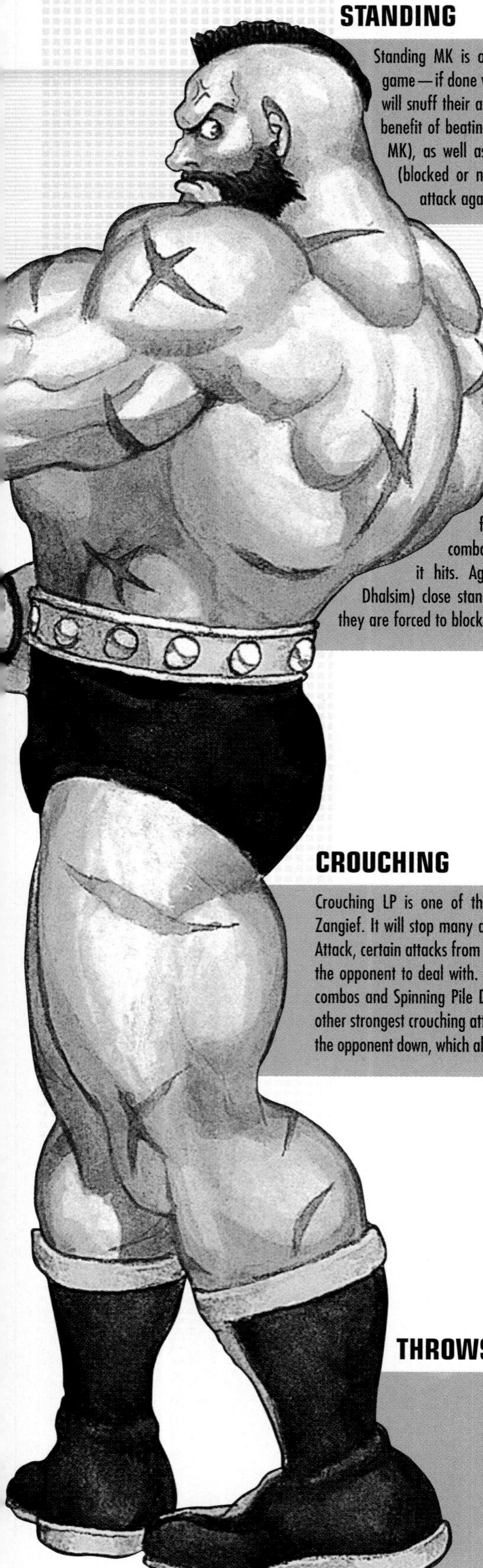

Standing MK is one of the best harassment moves in the game—if done versus Ken/Ryu as they throw a Hadoken, it will snuff their attempt. Standing LK from far away has the benefit of beating certain attacks (such as Guile's crouching MK), as well as setting up Spinning Pile Driver attempts (blocked or not). Standing HK is also a decent anti-air attack against certain jump in attacks.

JAB	STRONG	FIERCE
LP	MP	HP

SHORT	FORWARD	ROUNDHOUSE
LK	MK	HK

STANDING CLOSE

Use an early standing MK as the opponent is getting up and input the command for the Spinning Pile Driver, or you can combo a Spinning Pile Driver into a standing LK if it hits. Against some characters (especially versus Dhalsim) close standing MP becomes very important because they are forced to block it even when they are crouching.

JAB	STRONG	FIERCE
LP	MP	HP

SHORT	FORWARD	ROUNDHOUSE
LK	MK	HK

CROUCHING

Crouching LP is one of the many secret moves to playing a good Zangief. It will stop many attacks (Honda's Headbutt, Blanka's Rolling Attack, certain attacks from Dhalsim, etc.), as well as put up a shield for the opponent to deal with. Beyond all of that—it also sets up many combos and Spinning Pile Driver attempts. Crouching HK will be your other strongest crouching attack. Not only is it relatively fast—it knocks the opponent down, which allows for more Spinning Pile Driver attempts.

JAB	STRONG	FIERCE
↓ + LP	↓ + MP	↓ + HP

SHORT	FORWARD	ROUNDHOUSE
↓ + LK	↓ + MK	↓ + HK

THROWS

PILEDRIVER	FACE CLAW	SHOULDER THROW	ABDOMINAL CLAW
CLOSE, → + MP	AT CORRECT DISTANCE, → + MP	CLOSE, ↘ + MP	AT CORRECT DISTANCE, ↘ + MP / HP

JUMPING

There are going to be times when you are getting zoned out by projectiles, and you have to jump. Jumping HP is a good move to start with because it has a lot of range, and it avoids a lot of projectiles.

JAB	STRONG
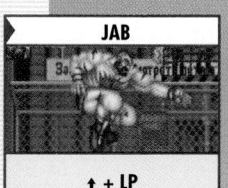	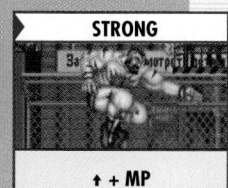
↑ + LP	↑ + MP

FIERCE	FIERCE
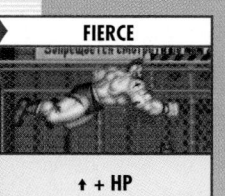	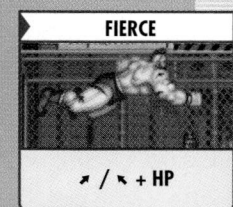
↑ + HP	↗ / ↖ + HP

SHORT	SHORT

↑ + LK	↗ / ↖ + LK

FORWARD	FORWARD

↑ + MK	↗ / ↖ + MK

ROUNDHOUSE	ROUNDHOUSE
	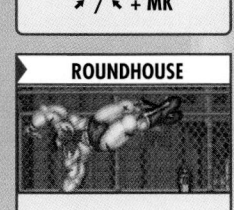
↑ + HK	↗ / ↖ + HK

SPECIAL MOVES

3 punch buttons — **Spinning Lariat**

When fighting versus anyone with a projectile, the Spinning Lariat is going to be what you will use half the match—either to avoid the projectile, or try to get in close while protecting yourself

In *Street Fighter II Champion Edition*, Zangief can move forward and backward during this move.

In *Street Fighter II Turbo*, 3 kick buttons initiates the same move, but he cannot be swept out of it.

360-degree controller motion + P — **Spinning Pile Driver**

Spinning Pile Driver is what makes or breaks Zangief players. Your goal is to not only land this move, but also to have your opponent fear it. Hopefully, this will put them into a mindset to commit mistakes, while trying to avoid it.

The Spinning Pile Driver not only does a lot of damage, but also has a lot of range. You will want to learn the ranges of your opponents attacks, so you can use the Spinning Pile Driver to counter their special moves.

SPECIAL NORMALS

↑ + MP / HP (on way up) — **Headbutt**

This is one of the strangest moves in the game. If this move is done in the early part of the round (first 5 seconds) it will stun on hit. This is huge early in a match because getting your opponent dizzy and then hitting them with a Spinning Pile Driver takes away almost 50% of their life bar.

↗ / ↖ + ↓ + HP — **Body Press**

When you are on top of the opponent, the Body Press (jump, ↓ + HP) is a really good move because it can cross the opponent up and it forces them to block standing.

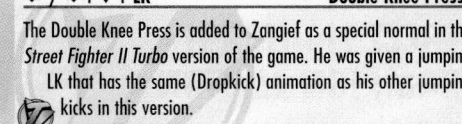

↗ / ↖ + ↓ + LK — **Double Knee Press**

The Double Knee Press is added to Zangief as a special normal in the *Street Fighter II Turbo* version of the game. He was given a jumping LK that has the same (Dropkick) animation as his other jumping kicks in this version.

ZANGIEF

SUPLEX	HEAD BITE	OVERHEAD TOSS	GERMAN SUPLEX	POWER BOMB
		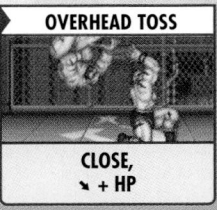		
CLOSE, → + HP	AT CORRECT DISTANCE, → + HP	CLOSE, ↖ + HP	→ + MK	→ + HK

COSTUMES

STREET FIGHTER II

COSTUME

STREET FIGHTER II

ALTERNATE COSTUME

CHAMPIONSHIP

COSTUME

TURBO

COSTUME

STREET FIGHTER II

Zangief is able to take damage, and you should always keep this in mind. Never be afraid to trade damage for information—if you jump in twice in a row, and the opponent does the same thing, chances are they will the third time and that is when you switch things up and go for a mix-up that will let you connect with a Spinning Pile Driver. You may have to be patient and sit on the other side of the screen for half the round, just so you can realize where the gap is in your opponents attacks and go in for the kill when the opportunity presents itself. Master the Spinning Pile Driver from both sides and you will soon see your opponents fear. Zangief in this mode is unique because after performing a successful Spinning Pile Driver, he doesn't bounce very far back from his opponent—close enough to keep applying pressure as soon as his opponent stands up.

STREET FIGHTER II CHAMPION EDITION

Gaining the ability to move around with the Spinning Lariat helps out a lot, since it gives him positioning advantages while also allowing him to avoid projectiles. After a successful Spinning Pile Driver, Zangief will bounces back very far from the opponent limiting his ability to go for another one as they wake up in this version. Although this takes away some of his options, he is still an opponent to be feared.

STREET FIGHTER II TURBO

Arguably the best version of Zangief ever! The Kick Lariat opens up a whole new world for Zangief. This move can put him right next to the opponent while being invincible to crouching attacks, allowing him to use a Spinning Pile Driver when he recovers from the Spinning Lariat. Not only that, but the 3 kick Spinning Lariat recovers much faster than the punch version, allowing for positional mixups when trying to get close to the opponent.

COMBOS

STREET FIGHTER II

Cross-up ↓ + HP in air, ↓ + LP x3, ↓ + HK

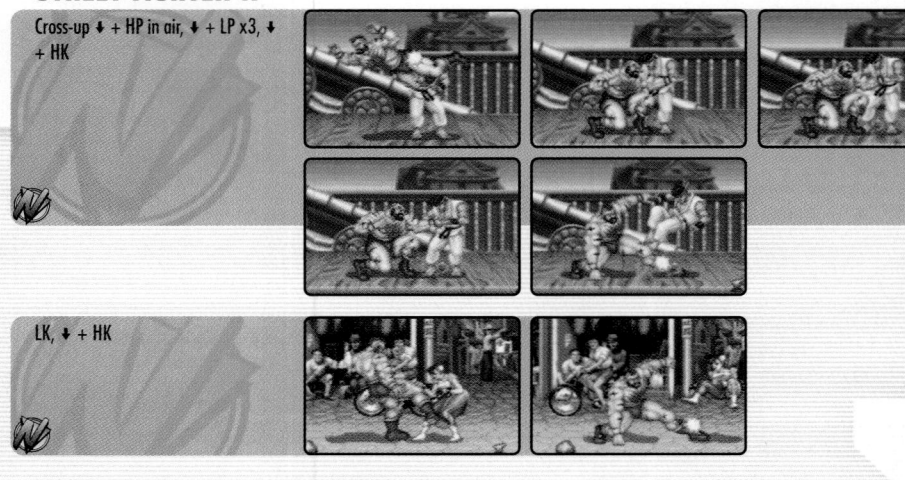

LK, ↓ + HK

STREET FIGHTER II CHAMPION EDITION

Cross Up ↓ + HP in air, MP, MK, ↓ + HK

Cross Up ↓ + HP in air, ↓ + MK, Spinning Lariat

STREET FIGHTER II TURBO

Cross Up ↓ + HP in air, ↓ + LP x 2, HP

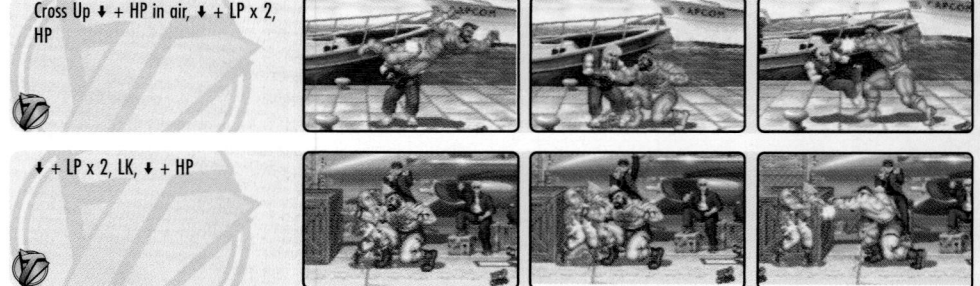

↓ + LP x 2, LK, ↓ + HP

GOOD MATCH UP

VS RYU

While Zangief does have a hard time versus many characters, his one winning matchup across the board seems to be versus Ryu. While your main goal against most characters is to try to get close and land a Spinning Pile Driver, you don't have to actually land one to win this matchup. What you do need is some patience and a good attack plan. While you are far away from each other, neither one of you can do much damage. Zangief can Spinning Lariat through Ryu's Hadokens and you can't attack him at all. So, the only time you will really hang out at this range is either when Ryu is running away trying to build up meter (*Super Turbo* Ryu), or you are taking a small breathing break trying to bait Ryu into coming closer to you. Around Mid Range (outside of Ryu's crouching MK) you will want to harass him your standing MK while trying to get inside his attacks. Look out for the occasional Hadoken and use your Spinning Lariat when you see it, or think it is coming. Even if you guess wrong you can either try to steer yourself backwards, or go for another one when you recover. Your main goal is to get in, so that you can get your standing LK to connect (blocked or not, you don't really care) to combo into the Spinning Pile Driver. Another good tactic is take a step back at this range and let Ryu throw a Hadoken, then do jumping HP to smack him in the head. A good mixup to use is a standing LK followed by a Spinning Pile Driver. For your next attack walk up and use a standing LK, and chain it into a crouching HK—this will combo if it is done correctly and the LK hits. The reason why this works so well is that a lot of people will block the standing LK then try to stop the Spinning Pile Driver attempt with a Shoryuken—if they mess up their attempt you will trip them and get another chance to land the Spinning Pile Driver. Another mind game layer is to do standing LK, pause (to see if they are going to use a Shoryuken, or block), and instead of using a crouching HK, do another standing LK and perform a Spinning Pile Driver. Note: you can actually combo standing LK, standing LK for a 2 hit combo.

SUPER STREET FIGHTER II

Starting with *Super Street Fighter II*, Zangief goes through some growing pains: losing the low invincibility with the 3 kick Spinning Lariat, gaining a throw whiff on the Spinning Pile Driver, having three different strengths of the Spinning Pile Driver (light punch does less damage than hard punch), and an air throw! However, his main strategy remains the same—try to get close and use the Spinning Pile Driver. The Double German Suplex/Flying Powerbomb gives him some fun options, when an opponent whiffs a normal attack right in front of him, you can attempt to grab them while they are in their recovery with it. It doesn't do that much damage, but the move is very fast.

SUPER STREET FIGHTER II TURBO

Realizing that *Super Street Fighter II Turbo* Zangief was never going to live up this his former *Street Fighter II Turbo* glory days, but they gave him a new move that nullifies projectiles while allowing him to move forward. An interesting move that doesn't necessarily replace the 3 kick Spinning Lariat from *Street Fighter II Turbo*, but it does bring a new dimension to Zangief allowing him to get closer and apply pressure to the opponent. His super combo is very scary, and can turn the tide quickly in a battle.

COMBOS

SUPER STREET FIGHTER II

Cross-up ↓ + HP in air, ↓ + LP x2, LK, HK

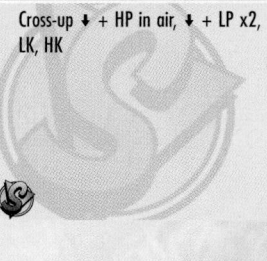

Cross-up ↓ + HP in air, MK, LP, ↓ + LP, ↓ + HK

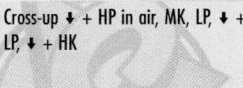

SUPER STREET FIGHTER II TURBO

Cross-up ↓ + HP in air, LP, ↓ + MK, Banishing Punch

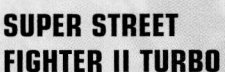

Cross-up ↓ + HP in air, ↓ + LP x4, LP, Banishing Punch

BAD MATCH UP

VS DHALSIM

You are going to spend a lot of time on the other side of the screen away from Dhalsim whether you like it or not. Between blocking Yoga Fire and his limbs, you will get pushed back nonstop. Just remember to be patient, and once you do get in, you are going to do a lot of damage, if not win the game. When your opponent uses a Yoga Fire, walk toward it and block it at the last possible second, so you don't get hit by it. Your goal is to get in and every little inch counts. You want to jump in with the Double Knee Press (down+MK) alternating between jumping and pressing button early, or late. You will often trade (usually losing out on damage), but sometimes trading is your best bet to get closer. When you do get pushed back, a crouching MP will hit some of his limbs depending on the attack. Don't be afraid to use a Spinning Lariat every now and then. Especially when a Yoga Fire is coming your way. Remember that you have the bigger throw range and a much better throw than he does. So, if Dhalsim tries to do any throw traps (slide into MP throw being the most common) use your Spinning Pile Driver. Also, since you have the bigger throw range almost every single time you can get a standing LK to hit him, and go for the Spinning Pile Driver. He has to Yoga Teleport to get out of this trap, but it is easier to talk about this escape than it is to perform it.

COSTUMES

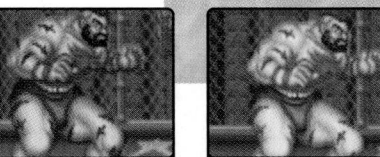

LP

MP

HP

START

Hold any button

LK

MK

HK

NORMAL MOVES

STANDING

His HK is great for anyone jumping in on you. Since it is a quick attack, it gets your opponent off of you.

JAB	SHORT
LP	LK

STRONG	FORWARD
MP	MK

FIERCE	ROUNDHOUSE
HP	HK

STANDING CLOSE

All his close normals are good for comboing into the Spinning Pile Driver.

JAB	SHORT
LP	LK

STRONG	FORWARD
MP	MK

FIERCE	ROUNDHOUSE
HP	HK

CROUCHING

Zangief's whole setup game is the tick-throw into the Spinning Pile Driver. Crouching LP is great for that.

JAB	SHORT
↓ + LP	↓ + LK

STRONG	FORWARD
↓ + MP	↓ + MK

FIERCE	ROUNDHOUSE
↓ + HP	↓ + HK

THROWS

Since the Spinning Pile Driver is his main throw, you don't want to use regular throws too much unless you are in a situation where you are trapped.

PILEDRIVER	ABDOMINAL CLAW
→ + MP	↘ + MP

FACE CLAW	SUPLEX
→ + HP	→ + MK

HEAD BITE	AIR THROW
→ + HK	IN AIR, → / ← / ↓ + MP / HP

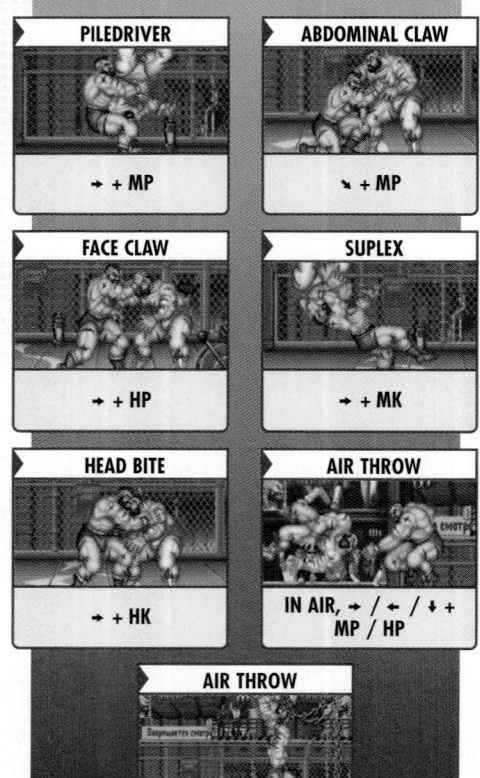

AIR THROW
IN AIR, → / ← ↓ + MK / HK

SPECIAL NORMALS

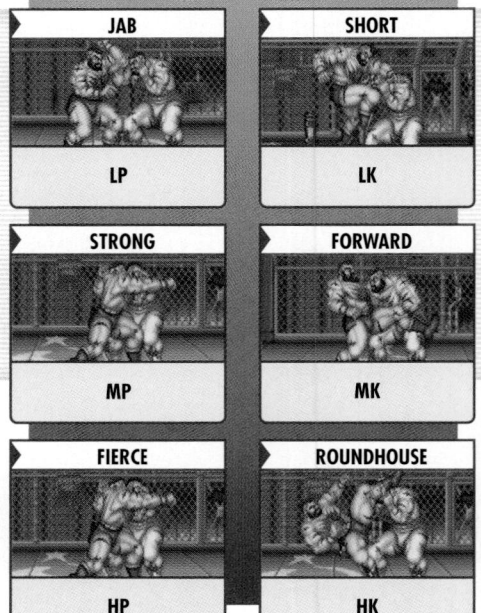

↗ / ↘, ↓ + LK / MK   **Double Knee Press**

The Double Knee Press is great for getting in on your opponent and having the option for the first move on the ground. Since it is so quick, you will be the first to act, and the mix-up game will be yours for the taking.

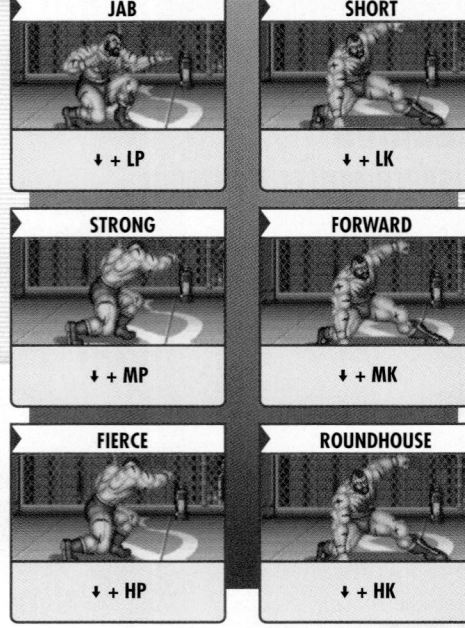

↑ + MP / HP (on way up)   **Headbutt**

This move lost its ability to dizzy in the opening seconds of a round, but has enormous potential when setting up the Spinning Pile Driver. Since it can only be done of a straight up jumping move, you must come down with the Headbutt, and immediately try for a Spinning Pile Driver. This move has great tick-throw potential.

↗ / ↖ ↓ ↓ + HP   **Body Press**

The Body Press can cross-up an opponent from any range, and often leads to big damage. If Zangief can get in close to an opponent, he has the upper hand. Use this move to confuse your opponent, and then go for a quick Spinning Pile Driver while they aren't looking!

JUMPING

Zangief spends a lot of time in the air since he has no projectile deterrent. A lot of his moves are high priority if you do them immediately when you leave the ground. Most of his air moves can also be used on the way down to setup a Spinning Pile Driver. His LK is extremely good for this purpose.

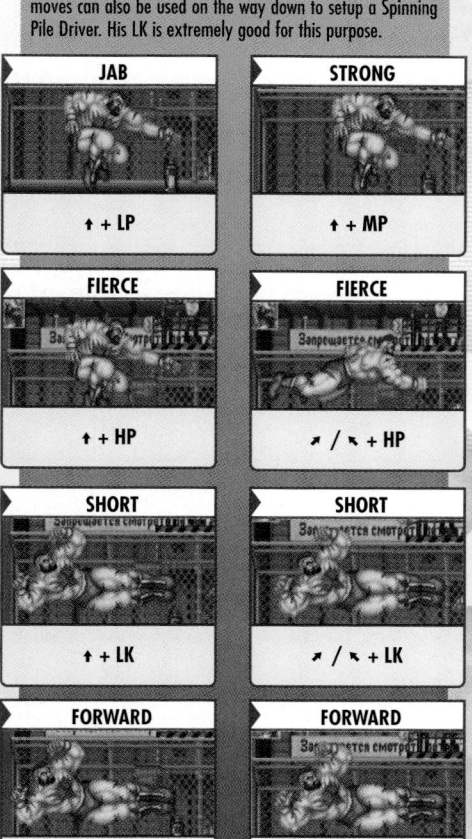

JAB	STRONG
↑ + LP	↑ + MP
FIERCE	FIERCE
↑ + HP	↗ / ↘ + HP
SHORT	SHORT
↑ + LK	↗ / ↘ + LK
FORWARD	FORWARD
↑ + MK	↗ / ↘ + MK
ROUNDHOUSE	ROUNDHOUSE
↑ + HK	↗ / ↘ + HK

SUPER COMBO

720 controller motion + P　　　**Final Atomic Buster**

It is harder to build up the Super Meter with Zangief than most characters. Even though you have to be next to your opponent while using this super combo, this move still strikes fear into opponents. Many of the setups are impossible to escape, such as jumping LK into the Final Atomic Buster, or standing LK into it. A really important aspect to master is blending the Banishing Punch motion into the Final Atomic Buster, so you can tack on a super combo after nullifying an opponent's projectile.

SPECIAL MOVES

3 punch buttons　　　**Spinning Lariat**

Zangief can still use this move as a great anti-air for people jumping in at him, and can also use it for passing through projectiles.

In close, 360-degree controller motion + K　　**Double German Suplex**

This attack dosen't have as much range as the Spinning Pile Driver, but it does have less start up (no throw whiff) making it a viable option when using tick-throw tactics against your opponent.

→ ↘ ↓ + P　　　**Banishing Punch**

While having the Spinning Lariat for years to deal with projectiles, this move gives Zangief another option to nullify projectiles, while advancing closer to the opponent.

360-degree controller motion + P　　**Spinning Pile Driver**

Due to gaining the throw whiff, you have to be a little more cautious with the Spinning Pile Driver. Before if you mis-timed the Spinning Pile Driver tick and peformed it while they were still in block stun, you would just get a a punch attack. In this version Zangief hugs some air and leaves himself wide open.

At correct distance, 360-degree controller motion + K Flying Powerbomb

This throws most people off, but you will only be able to get away with it once or twice before they start punishing you. Probably the best use for the move is to try to grab normal attacks that miss right in front of you.

ZANGIEF

55

Balrog

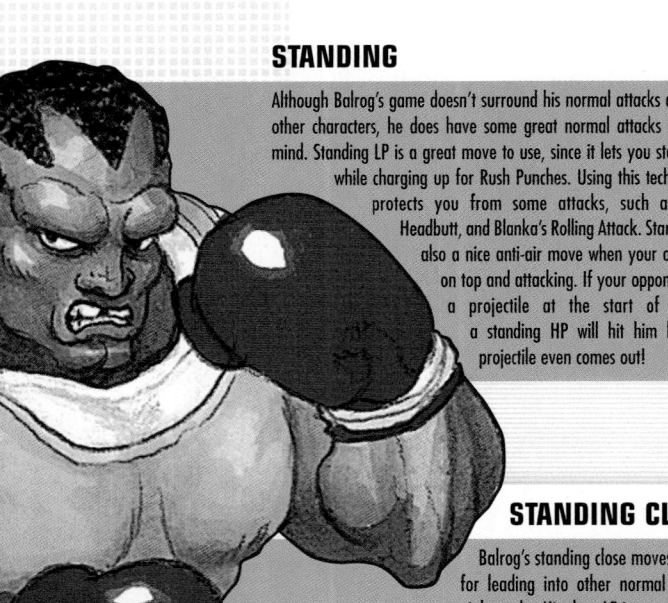

STANDING

Although Balrog's game doesn't surround his normal attacks as much as other characters, he does have some great normal attacks to keep in mind. Standing LP is a great move to use, since it lets you stay in place while charging up for Rush Punches. Using this technique also protects you from some attacks, such as Honda's Headbutt, and Blanka's Rolling Attack. Standing MP is also a nice anti-air move when your opponent is on top and attacking. If your opponent throws a projectile at the start of a round, a standing HP will hit him before the projectile even comes out!

JAB	STRONG	FIERCE

LP	MP	HP

SHORT	FORWARD	ROUNDHOUSE

LK	MK	HK

STANDING CLOSE

Balrog's standing close moves are great for leading into other normal moves or special attacks. His close LP is great for chaining together for big damage. Since he has no kick animations, everything that he does will come out in the form of a punch.

JAB	STRONG	FIERCE

LP	MP	HP

SHORT	FORWARD	ROUNDHOUSE

LK	MK	HK

CROUCHING

Crouching HP is an important anti-air attack (in addition to standing MP) in these versions of Balrog. Crouching HK is a decent sweep (although it looks like other attacks) and you can use it to poke your opponent.

JAB	STRONG	FIERCE
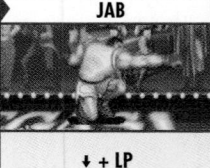		
↓ + LP	↓ + MP	↓ + HP

SHORT	FORWARD	ROUNDHOUSE

↓ + LK	↓ + MK	↓ + HK

JUMPING

Don't spend much time jumping with Balrog, but if you must (and you will have to every now and then) jumping HP and HK are usually the best options.

JAB	STRONG	FIERCE

↑ + LP / LK	↑ + MP / MK	↑ + HP / HK

THROWS

Balrog has one of the best throws in the game. Not only can you mash for more damage, but you also get to walk under an opponent while he is flipping in the air recovering from it! This sets up many mind games: walk under your opponent after the throw, use a crouching LP, then throw him again. You can also walk under your opponent and use a crouching HK to trip him. Or, take a step (so that it looks like you're going to walk under him) and perform a crouching HK so the attack hits your opponent from the other side. You can quickly turn the tide by throwing and doing one or two throw mixups.

An advanced throwing strategy is to throw with MP if you're going for a blocked move into a throw. If the opponent tries to jump out or counter in some fashion, the standing MP will often hit them.

THROW

→ / ← + MP / HP

SPECIAL MOVES

Hold 3 P or 3 K, release　　　　　　**Turn Punch**

This is one of the most powerful moves in the game, since you can hold down the buttons to charge the attack until you hear him say, "Final!" By releasing this attack, you will deplete 60% of the opponent's life bar. Mastering the Turn Punch is a very important part of playing as Balrog, because it enables the player to keep pressure on the opponent while also adding in pauses to Balrog's attack strings.

In *Street Fighter II Turbo*, Balrog is invincible against low attacks and projectiles if it is charged for less than two seconds—this makes Balrog quite a threat. Not only that, but you can store two separate charges, one with the three-punch buttons depressed and another one with the three-kick buttons. So, you can hold the three-punch buttons and release them to get "One"count Turn Punch, then release the three-kick buttons and get "Two" count Turn Punch right after the first one.

Another good thing to remember is that if you hold down all three kicks for the Turn Punch and you need to use a Dashing Uppercut, you can do so by inputting the command (charging back and moving toward) and releasing one of the kick buttons. Oftentimes, if the opponent knows you're charging up the Turn Punch, they will attempt to take advantage by jumping in, but you can surprise them with this technique.

Charge ←, → + P　　　　　　**Dash Straight**

The Dash Straight is the main attack, since your opponent can't duck under it. Even if they block, they still take block damage. It is also relatively easy to use this move in a combo off a crouching LP or a standing LP. These two options provide some quick combos that can serve up damage in short order.

Charge ←, → + K　　　　　　**Dash Uppercut**

Often used as an anti-air attack when an opponent is either jumping toward you from far away, or jumping away from you when they are up close. An opponent can duck under this attack, but this is another opportunity to create some mind games. If your opponent is blocking low and you perform a crouching LP, use another one to set up a Dash Uppercut (which will miss), but it will provide some time to throw them.

COSTUMES

STREET FIGHTER II
COSTUME

STREET FIGHTER II
ALTERNATE COSTUME

CHAMPIONSHIP
COSTUME

TURBO
COSTUME

STREET FIGHTER II CHAMPION EDITION

The main strategy here is to focus on trying to land Balrog's main dizzy combos (jump in HK, crouching LK, standing LK, LK Dash Uppercut, standing HP, or crouching LK, crouching LK, standing LK, LK Dash Uppercut, standing HP) while attempting to get close enough for a throw.

STREET FIGHTER II TURBO

This is where Balrog becomes interesting. Not only does he retain his powerful combos and his excellent throw, he also becomes invincible with the Turn Punch. Now he can go through the projectiles that so easily plagued him in *Champion Edition*. The best strategy here is to keep the Turn Punch charged at all times (flying through projectiles when needed), while throwing out a barrage of Dash Straights, Dash Uppercuts, standing HPs and an occasional throw.

COMBOS

STREET FIGHTER II CHAMPION EDITION

Jump in HK, ↓ + MK, LP Dash Straight

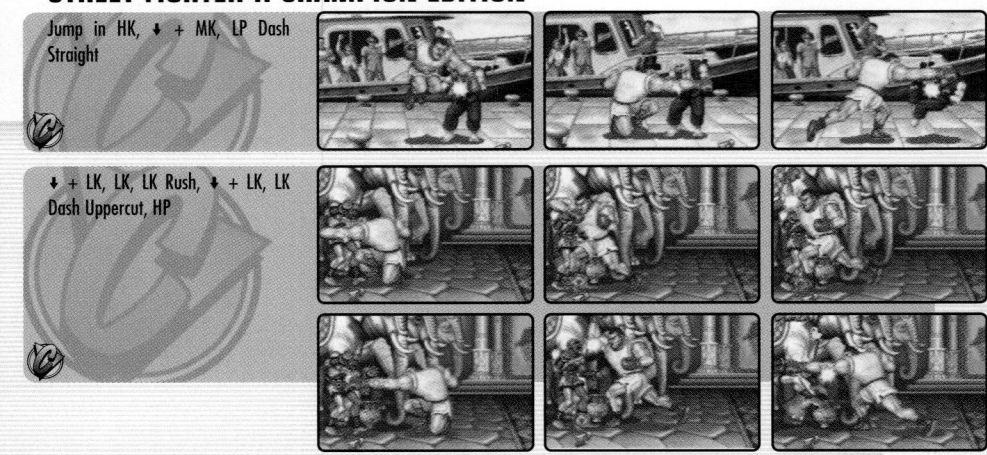

↓ + LK, LK, LK Rush, ↓ + LK, LK Dash Uppercut, HP

STREET FIGHTER II TURBO

↓ + LK, ↓ + LK, LK, LK Dash Uppercut, ↓ + HK

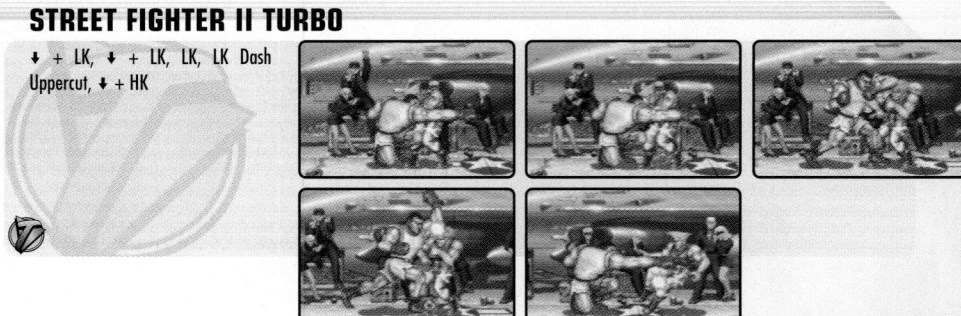

Jump in HP, ↓ + LP x 4, LP, LP Dash Straight

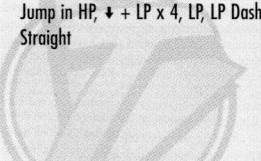

GOOD MATCH-UP

VS RYU

STREET FIGHTER II TURBO

The Turbo version of Balrog has the Turn Punch, which helps him get around projectiles. If Ryu links a lot of crouching HKs into Hadokens, unleash a Turn Punch through the projectile and punish him. Don't be afraid to throw out a standing HP if Ryu throws a Hadoken and keep the pressure on with the Dash punches. If an opponent starts using the Tatsumaki Senpukyaku to get out of trouble, smack him down with a crouching HP.

SUPER STREET FIGHTER II TURBO

This matchup changes slightly due to the Buffalo Headbutt, but the main strategies still apply: Stay on top of him, pressure him with standing HP, use the Dash Low, and use Turn Punches. After gaining the ability to use a super combo, look for any opening to land it. When Ryu throws a Hadoken, misses a Shoryuken, or a normal attack use the super combo to punish him. Even if the attack gets blocked, you should be safe and have a Frame Advantage that enables you to keep the pressure on. It is almost impossible for Ryu to perform a Cross-up on Balrog (except for an Air Tatsumaki Senpukyaku), so if he attempt one try to throw him and begin the High/Low mix-ups.

COMBOS

SUPER STREET FIGHTER II

Jump in HP, ↓ + LP, LP Buffalo Headbutt

Jump In HK, ↓ + LP x 3, LP Dash Straight

SUPER STREET FIGHTER II TURBO

Jump in MK, ↓ + MK, ↓ + MP, LP Dash Low

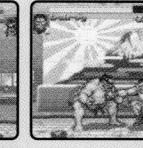 

↓ + LP x 4, Crazy Buffalo

 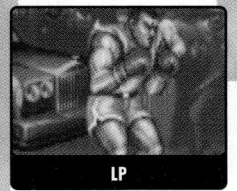 

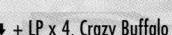

BAD MATCH-UP

VS STREET FIGHTER II SAGAT

While Balrog performs admirably against anyone with a projectile, things get more difficult against the original version of Sagat because his projectile traps are better than any other character. Use a standing HP to hit him when he tries a Ground Tiger Shot. The main goal in this match-up is to stay alive long enough to charge the super combo, which is when the whole dynamic of this match changes. At this point, Sagat can longer throw Tiger Shots randomly, since Balrog can use the super combo on him. This will occur when he throws high Tiger Shots (you can catch him almost full screen), but there isn't as much range on Ground Tiger Shots.

SUPER STREET FIGHTER II

While losing the ability to go through projectiles with the Turn Punch, Balrog gains a few new moves that keep him definitely in the game and make him a threat to any character. He has gained the Buffalo Headbutt which is invincible to projectiles, and a set of kick moves that act like sweeps to knock an opponent down.

SUPER STREET FIGHTER II TURBO

With the addition of the Dash Low Punch, Balrog can now knock down opponents when it connects. He also has the ability to float in the air with ↓ + HP, just like E. Honda. If he is about to land on a projectile, he will be able to avoid it last second. With these two new options, Balrog can be very aggressive, and he is a powerhouse to deal with.

COSTUMES

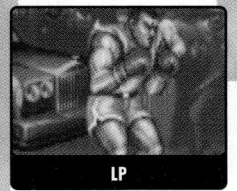 LP	 MP
 HP	 START
 Hold any button	 LK
 MK	 HK

NORMAL MOVES

STANDING

While gaining new animations for most of his normal attacks from *Champion Edition* and *Turbo*, their functionality is much the same. Use standing HP to hit opponents at a distance, use standing MP as an anti-air attack, and use standing LP to maintain a charge and for protection.

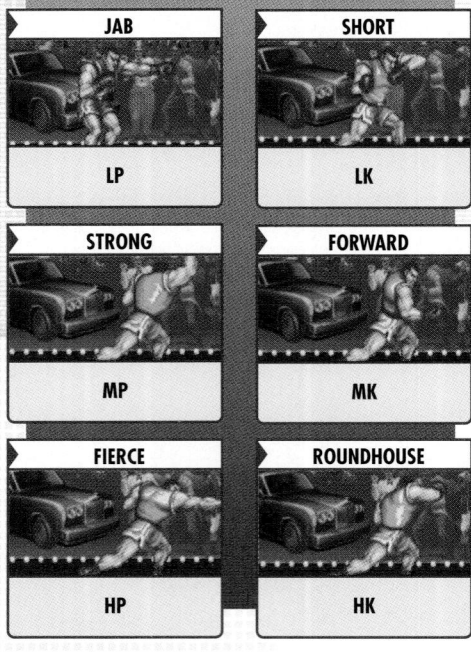

JAB	SHORT
LP	LK

STRONG	FORWARD
MP	MK

FIERCE	ROUNDHOUSE
HP	HK

STANDING CLOSE

When fighting in close, you won't use your standing normals very much. One thing to keep in mind, however, is that opponents can't duck under standing MK, which forces them to block.

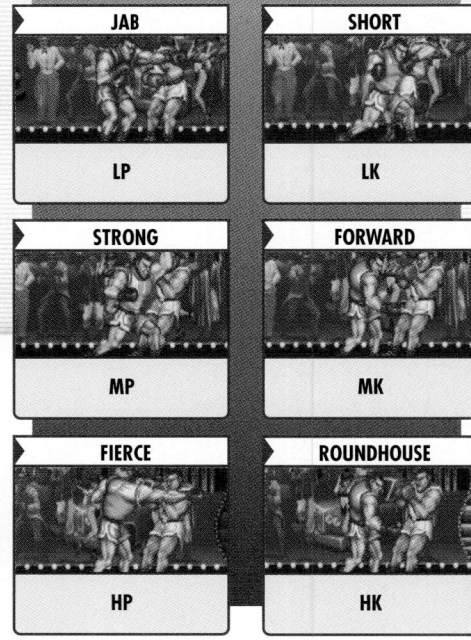

JAB	SHORT
LP	LK

STRONG	FORWARD
MP	MK

FIERCE	ROUNDHOUSE
HP	HK

CROUCHING

Balrog has great crouching normals and almost all of them have a use during a single match. Crouching LP/LK are standard pokes that enable you to keep the pressure on while maintaining a charge. Crouching MK must be blocked low and if it is performed early (when an opponent is getting up from a knockdown), it sets up very powerful mixups.

This move also counters many of the poke attacks that may have proven problematic previously, such as Guile's crouching MK. Crouching MP is a great shield to throw out non-stop because it counters many different special attacks (for example, M. Bison's Psycho Crusher/Scissors, Honda's Headbutt, etc.) and it can also be used to combo into a Dash Straight (or Dash Uppercut) if it hits an opponent on the ground. Crouching HP is a great anti-air attack, and Crouching HK is an excellent sweep.

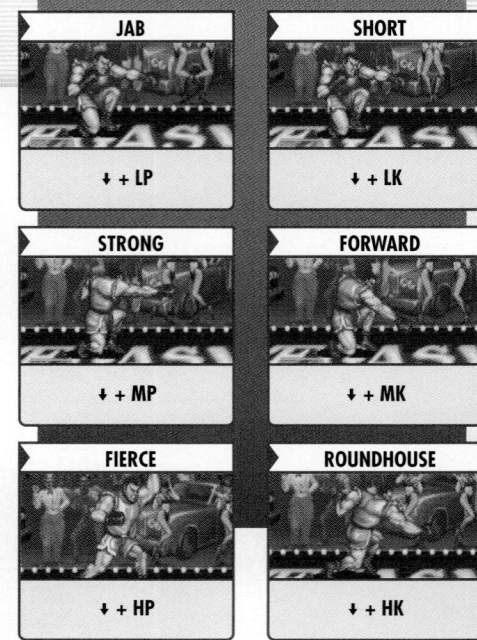

JAB	SHORT
↓ + LP	↓ + LK

STRONG	FORWARD
↓ + MP	↓ + MK

FIERCE	ROUNDHOUSE
↓ + HP	↓ + HK

SPECIAL MOVES

Hold 3P or 3K, release — **Turn Punch**

Although it can no longer go through projectiles, it is still effective at keeping pressure on an opponent while building up the Super Meter for Super Turbo Balrog. He still has his "Final" punch, while also maintaining the ability to store more than one of these devastating attacks.

Charge ←, → + K — **Dash Uppercut**

The Dash Uppercut is still just as good as it was in previous versions. It is useful for getting close to an opponent and throwing them. You can also "glitch" it into the super combo by inputting the command then, after it hits, press ←, → + any punch.

Charge ↓, ↑ + P — **Buffalo Headbutt**

Although he lost the ability to go through fireballs with the Turn Punch, Balrog gained a new move that makes him just as dangerous. The Buffalo Headbutt not only has amazing range, but it knocks down and very rarely trades damage with anything . This move is key in most match-ups in which an opponent has a projectile.

Charge ←, → + P — **Dash Straight**

In *Super Turbo*, Balrog's Dash Straight no longer hits crouching opponents, so you will likely use this move a lot. Since it is one of the faster special moves in the game, it's best to continually use this move over and over until your opponent proves that he or she can either block it or counter attack.

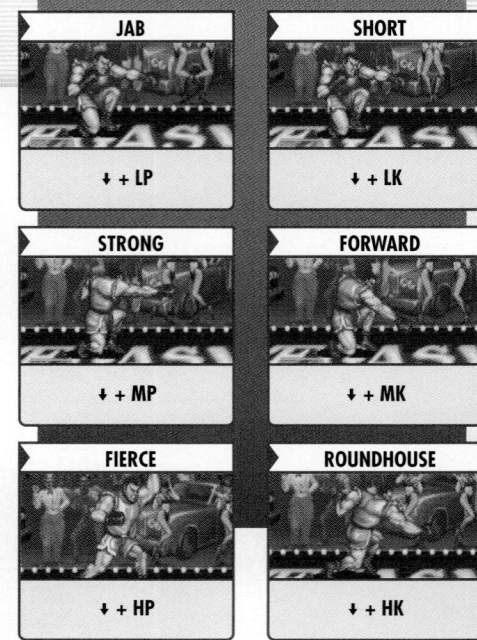

Charge ←, ↘ + P — **Dash Low**

This move resembles Balrog's normal Dash Uppercut, but it's much more powerful. Not only does it knock down your opponent (the original one doesn't), it ends in ↓/↘ which is very important. This is because the Buffalo Headbutt is performed by charging down, then pressing ↑ + Punch. The ↓/↘ motion qualifies as down, so you can charge for the Buffalo Headbutt during this move!

A really powerful tactic to use is a crouching MK, followed by a crouching MP into this move. Then, if your opponent thinks you're going to go for a throw, do a Buffalo Headbutt and hit his or her counter attack. If you are full screen away, against a character like Chun Li, use this version of the Dash Uppercut when she uses a projectile, Buffalo Headbutt to go through the projectile and hit her while she is still in her recovery animation.

JUMPING

Balrog gets some new animations in this version, which helps out his jumping game. Jumping MP is effective against projectiles because it hits farther out than it looks. Jumping MK is a great poke that hits at an odd angle, and usually forces an opponent to block. Lastly, jumping HP and HK are good to throw out early, or late, in Balrog's jump arc to counter attack various poke attacks.

THROWS

Balrog's wonderful throw from *Champion Edition* and *Turbo* make a comeback, and it is potentially better now that crouching MK leads to so much damage. The main strategies should revolve around walking under the throw, using a crouching MK, and either throwing the opponent again or using a crouching MP. If the crouching MK/crouching MP combo sequence gets blocked, perform a Dash Uppercut (it will miss), which will set you up for a throw.

JAB	JAB
↑ + LP	↗ + LP

STRONG	STRONG
↑ + MP	↗ / ↖ + MP

FIERCE	FIERCE
↑ + HP (→ / ←)	↗ / ↖ + HP

SHORT	SHORT
↑ + LK	↗ / ↖ + LK

FORWARD	FORWARD
↑ + MK	↗ / ↖ + MK

ROUNDHOUSE	ROUNDHOUSE
↑ + HK	↗ / ↖ + HK

THROW

→ / ← + MP / HP

SUPER COMBO

Charge ←, → ← → + P or K	Crazy Buffalo

Balrog has one of the best super combos in the game. Not only can he charge it up fast, but it also hits with lightning-fast speed and causes tremendous damage.

You can activate it with either Punch or Kick. With punch, the first move is a Dash Straight; with kick, the first move is a Dash Uppercut. No matter what you use, if you press kick during the super combo your attacks will change to Dash Uppercuts. This makes it very handy to juggle an opponent if you catch them in the air.

BALROG

M. Bison

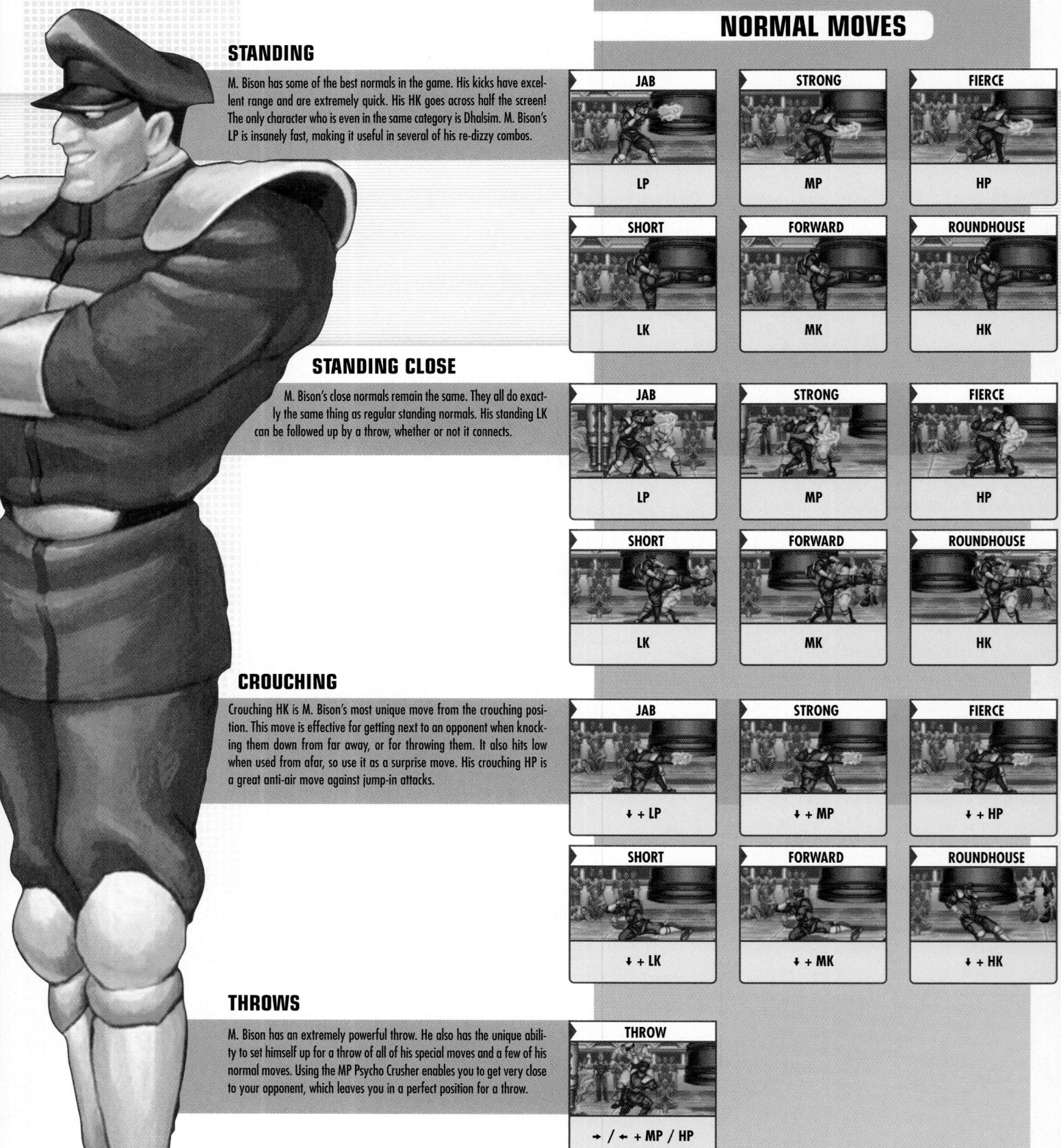

STANDING

M. Bison has some of the best normals in the game. His kicks have excellent range and are extremely quick. His HK goes across half the screen! The only character who is even in the same category is Dhalsim. M. Bison's LP is insanely fast, making it useful in several of his re-dizzy combos.

STANDING CLOSE

M. Bison's close normals remain the same. They all do exactly the same thing as regular standing normals. His standing LK can be followed up by a throw, whether or not it connects.

CROUCHING

Crouching HK is M. Bison's most unique move from the crouching position. This move is effective for getting next to an opponent when knocking them down from far away, or for throwing them. It also hits low when used from afar, so use it as a surprise move. His crouching HP is a great anti-air move against jump-in attacks.

THROWS

M. Bison has an extremely powerful throw. He also has the unique ability to set himself up for a throw of all of his special moves and a few of his normal moves. Using the MP Psycho Crusher enables you to get very close to your opponent, which leaves you in a perfect position for a throw.

NORMAL MOVES

JAB	STRONG	FIERCE
LP	MP	HP

SHORT	FORWARD	ROUNDHOUSE
LK	MK	HK

JAB	STRONG	FIERCE
LP	MP	HP

SHORT	FORWARD	ROUNDHOUSE
LK	MK	HK

JAB	STRONG	FIERCE
↓ + LP	↓ + MP	↓ + HP

SHORT	FORWARD	ROUNDHOUSE
↓ + LK	↓ + MK	↓ + HK

THROW
→ / ← + MP / HP

JUMPING

M. Bison's jumping normals look rather strange. All of his punch attacks place his body in a curved position as he jumps toward an opponent. His kicks are standard jump-ins, but his straight-up jump kicks have excellent priority.

JAB  ↑ + LP	**JAB** 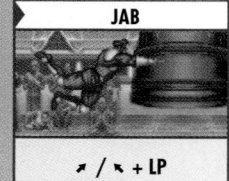 ↗ / ↖ + LP
STRONG 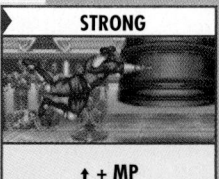 ↑ + MP	**FIERCE** 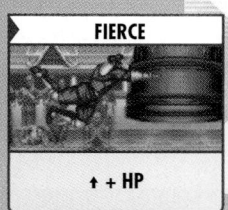 ↑ + HP
SHORT  ↑ + LK	**SHORT**  ↗ / ↖ + LK
FORWARD  ↑ + MK	**FORWARD**  ↗ / ↖ + MK
ROUNDHOUSE  ↑ + HK	**ROUNDHOUSE**  ↗ / ↖ + HK

SPECIAL MOVES

Charge ←, → + P   Psycho Crusher

The Psycho Crusher was extremely powerful in the arcade version of *Street Fighter II Champion Edition*. It hit six times on a block, causing heavy damage. In *Street Fighter II Anniversary Edition*, it only hits four times on a block, but it causes the same amount of damage. Use this move to end up next to an opponent with priority; this can lead to a combo or a throw.

Charge ←, → + K   Double Knee Press

M. Bison's Double Knee Press is a two-hit flying kick that hits high, then low. In *Street Fighter II Champion Edition* and *Street Fighter II Turbo*, the Double Knee Press doesn't knock down, but it leaves the opportunity to combo after it.

Charge ↓, ↑ + K   Head Press (P behind it)Somersault Skull Diver

This serves as a great counter against projectile-throwing characters. During this move, M. Bison speeds across the screen and instantly stomps on his opponent's head. After this occurs, you can go left or right and come down with a punch to start a combo! Note that the Headstomp and the punch are *not* a combo!

COSTUMES

STREET FIGHTER II
COSTUME

STREET FIGHTER II
ALTERNATE COSTUME

CHAMPIONSHIP
COSTUME

TURBO
COSTUME

STREET FIGHTER II CHAMPION EDITION

M. Bison is perhaps one of the best characters in *any version of Street Fighter II*. The block damage on his HP Psycho Crusher is really high, and his combos are powerful enough to dizzy… and re-dizzy! The charge time for his Double Knee Press is long, but he can still put together great pressure patterns like Double Knee Press, crouching MK, standing LK, LP Psycho Crusher, standing LK, standing LK, Double Knee Press, and so on. Don't be afraid to just use the HP Psycho Crusher back and forth across the screen, either.

STREET FIGHTER II TURBO

M. Bison was toned way down in this version of *Street Fighter II*, leaving him squarely at the bottom of the rankings. His HP Psycho Crusher hits about three times and there are even gaps in between it that enables a blocking opponent to use a Shoryuken! The charge time on his Double Knee Press is still long, but with no re-dizzy combos and seemingly reduced priority, it's tough to win with M. Bison. One trick is to knock down an opponent (with a throw, for example), then immediately use a crouching HK slide and charge up. Just before your opponent gets up, perform an LP Psycho Crusher. When timed correctly, this results in a weird cross-up attack that oftentimes hits an opponent who's attempting to block. When it hits, it knocks them down, so you can repeat the move again. When it gets blocked, perform a pressure string of crouching MK, crouching LP, crouching LP, and finish with a Double Knee Press.

COMBOS

STREET FIGHTER II CHAMPION EDITION

↓ + LP, LP, MK Double Knee Press, LP, HP Psycho Crusher

↓ + LP x 2, LP, MK Double Knee Press, ↓ + MP, MK

STREET FIGHTER II TURBO

Cross-up HK, ↓ + LP x ↗, LP, HP Psycho Crusher

Somersault Skull Diver, ↓ + HK

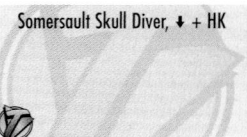   

GOOD MATCH-UP

VS VEGA

It's somewhat easy to stop Vega's Flying Barcelona Attack by jumping back and using an MP. If your opponent tries to use this move off his own back wall, use a HP Psycho Crusher to move the screen over. This prevents him from touching the wall, possibly making him land in M. Bison's Psycho Crusher. Random Double Knee Presses can go through most of Vega's ground pokes. If you guess wrong and he blocks, throw him. Make him block some standing MKs, and standing HKs for good measure. Bait his LK Flip Kick and, when he misses, use a standing HK or a Double Knee Press against it. Careful, Vega can beat M. Bison's Psycho Crusher attack and his Double Knee Press attack by jumping back and using HP. Also, if Vega gets a knockdown on M. Bison he can force you to rise into his cross-up Flying Barcelona Attack. This is difficult to block and M. Bison has no reversal attack to get out of it.

SUPER STREET FIGHTER II

M. Bison gets a few more normal moves, better priority, the Devil Reverse (similiar to the Head Press, but a punch), and a Double Knee Press that knocks down. He's generally much improved from *Street Fighter II Turbo*, but he still remains a shadow of his former self from *Street Fighter II Champion Edition*.

SUPER STREET FIGHTER II TURBO

M. Bison gains an improved Devil Reverse, an insanely high priority, a juggling jumping MP, and a good super combo. The jumping MP allows M. Bison to rule the air, even against Vega and Chun Li. The super combo passes through projectiles. When the super combo hits, tack on two extra jumping MPs. If the super combo gets blocked, go for a throw. A blocked Double Knee Press into throw is difficult to defend against. After knocking down an opponent, use a "meaty" crouching MK. For some reason, this move is difficult to reverse with a Shoryuken or any other reversal move. When a crouching MK hits, combo it into either a standing HK (if you don't have a charge) or a standing LK followed by a Double Knee Press. After a knock down, use a crouching HK slide to set up the crouching MK. Another option after a knock down is a cross-up combo. Jump in and cross-up right as the opponent gets up and use an MK or an HK while in the air. Additionally, M. Bison's standing MK and standing HK are excellent poking attacks. He can lock down lots of characters, especially Ken and Zangief, by just repeatedly giving them the MK, or HK boot.

Lastly, M. Bison is the only character without an instant reversal move. This means that he has no way to escape a corner once he gets into it. Therefore, it's extremely important when playing as M. Bison to be on the attack, lock down your opponent and don't get locked down in the process.

COMBOS

SUPER STREET FIGHTER II

Jump in HP, MP, HP Psycho Crusher

Jump in MK, LK, LK, HK Double Knee Press

SUPER STREET FIGHTER II TURBO

At a jumping opponent, jump + MP x 3 in the air, Knee Press Nightmare

Jump in HK, ↓ + LP x 2, LP, Knee Press Nightmare, Jump + MP x2

COSTUMES

LP

MP

HP

START

Hold any button

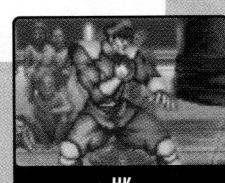

LK

MK

HK

BAD MATCH-UP

VS E. HONDA

When fighting in a corner and you block a single jump attack, you will likely lose the round. E. Honda's inescapable Ochio-Throw will force you to stand up into blocking a crouching LP into an Ochio-throw again and repeat. With no reversal move, M. Bison has no way out. At mid-screen, it's almost as bad. After an Ochio-Throw, expect to see E. Honda's Hundred Hands Slap if you attempt to jump away. Keep this in mind: never get into a position in which you must block a jump-in from Honda. You can try to chip away damage by doing LP Psycho Crushers at the top of the move's range. Honda can usually cause block damage with the Hundred Hand Slap, but it's very difficult to actually use his Headbutt against M. Bison's Psycho Crusher. You can also try the Head Press, but E. Honda can jump and LP, or use an MP to knock M. Bison out of the air. You can attempt an HP Psycho Crusher through E. Honda while at mid-screen (if he's close), but you may see a standing HK after passing him. Trying to use a standing MK or a standing HK against him is tricky, because he can use his Headbutt against those moves. Basically, just chip away damage whenever possible. Don't try to lock him down, or even get near him, because his Ochio-Throw can dominate the entire match.

NORMAL MOVES

STANDING

M. Bison received two changes to his standing line-up. His LK no longer extends outward; now it's a knee and it only goes short distances. His standing HP also changed, reverting to an uppercut motion.

STANDING CLOSE

There are two changes to mention here. When fighting up close, the LK unleashes a knee. This is a great move for tick-throw tactics.

CROUCHING

The only change here is M. Bison's crouching LP, which has lost all of its range. It only stretches about half the distance now.

JAB	SHORT	JAB	SHORT	JAB	SHORT
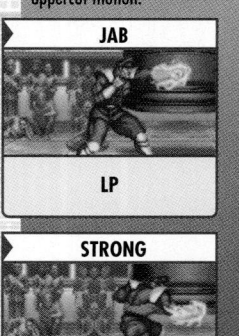	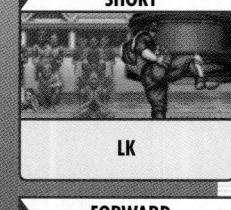	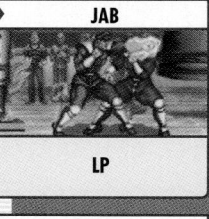			
LP	LK	LP	LK	↓ + LP	↓ + LK

STRONG	FORWARD	STRONG	FORWARD	STRONG	FORWARD
			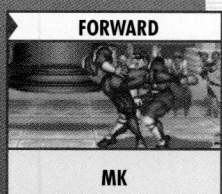		
MP	MK	MP	MK	↓ + MP	↓ + MK

FIERCE	ROUNDHOUSE	FIERCE	ROUNDHOUSE	FIERCE	ROUNDHOUSE
					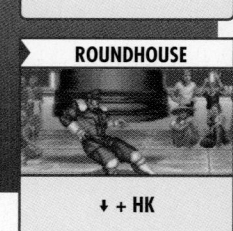
HP	HK	HP	HK	↓ + HP	↓ + HK

THROWS

M. Bison has no changes in the throw department. It's just his same old tricks.

THROW
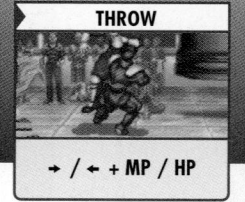
→ / ← + MP / HP

JUMPING

M. Bison received new jumping HP, MP, LK, and MK in *Super Street Fighter II* and *Super Street Fighter II Turbo*. He also received a new straight up LK. He is only one of two characters who can chain three MP hits in the air. You can also follow this up with a super combo.

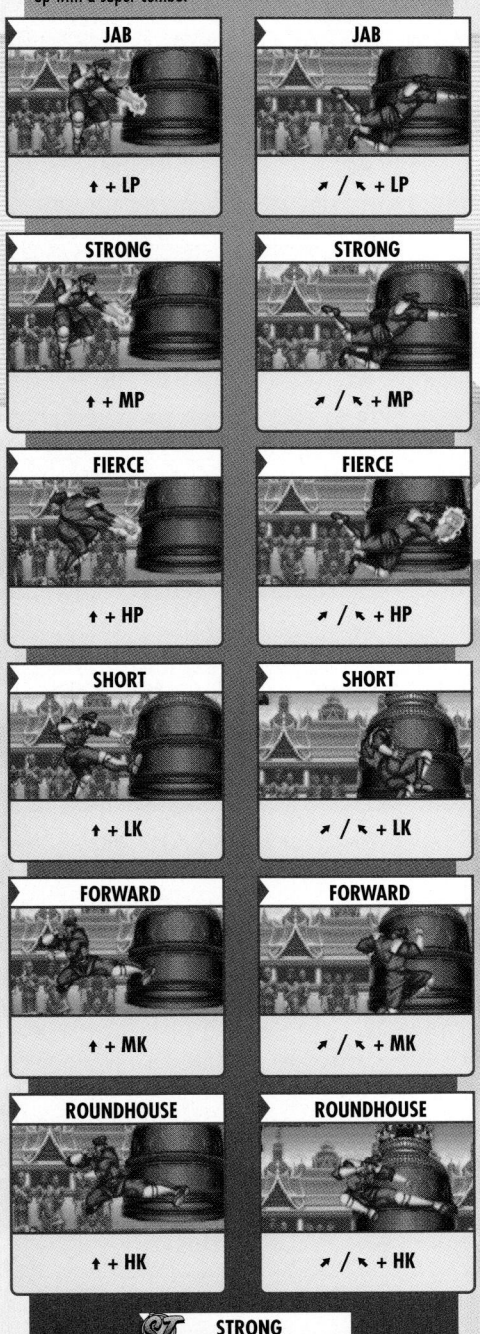

JAB	JAB
↑ + LP	↗ / ↖ + LP

STRONG	STRONG
↑ + MP	↗ / ↖ + MP

FIERCE	FIERCE
↑ + HP	↗ / ↖ + HP

SHORT	SHORT
↑ + LK	↗ / ↖ + LK

FORWARD	FORWARD
↑ + MK	↗ / ↖ + MK

ROUNDHOUSE	ROUNDHOUSE
↑ + HK	↗ / ↖ + HK

STRONG
↗ / ↖ + MP

SPECIAL MOVES

Charge ←, → + P   **Psycho Crusher**

This is a great move to throw out randomly against any opponent. Unless it gets detected by chance, your opponent will take up to three hits of block damage.

Charge ↓, ↑ + P   **Devil Reverse**
(changes in *Super Turbo*; must press P again)

In *Super Street Fighter II Turbo*, this move becomes somewhat of a fake Devil Reverse since it doesn't hit your opponent on top of the head. By pressing the second punch in the air, you control your landing spot. This is especially useful against characters with anti-air special moves. You must use both methods (the fake and the real attack) to keep your opponent guessing.

Charge ←, → + K   **Double Knee Press**

The only new thing about the Double Knee Press is the fact that it knocks down when it connects. There are no more insane combos like there are in the *Street Fighter II Champion Edition* version. Also, it's possible to use the HK Double Knee Press as a tick-throw setup.

Charge ↓, ↑ + K (P in air)   **Head Press**

This move hasn't changed at all, It still results in M. Bison stomping on your opponent's head. You can follow it up by moving left or right.

SUPER COMBO

Charge ←, → ← → + K   **Knee Press Nightmare**

The Knee Press Nightmare, perhaps M. Bison's greatest asset, is his only reversal move. Unlike the other characters who have special moves that can be used as reversals, this is only enabled when he has a full Super Meter. For characters using projectile traps against M. Bison, use this move to escape from a corner. You can also follow the super combo with a jumping MP for two additional hits.

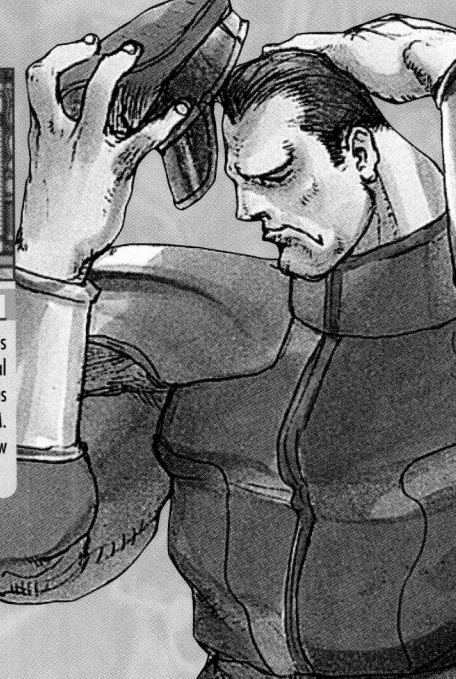

Sagat

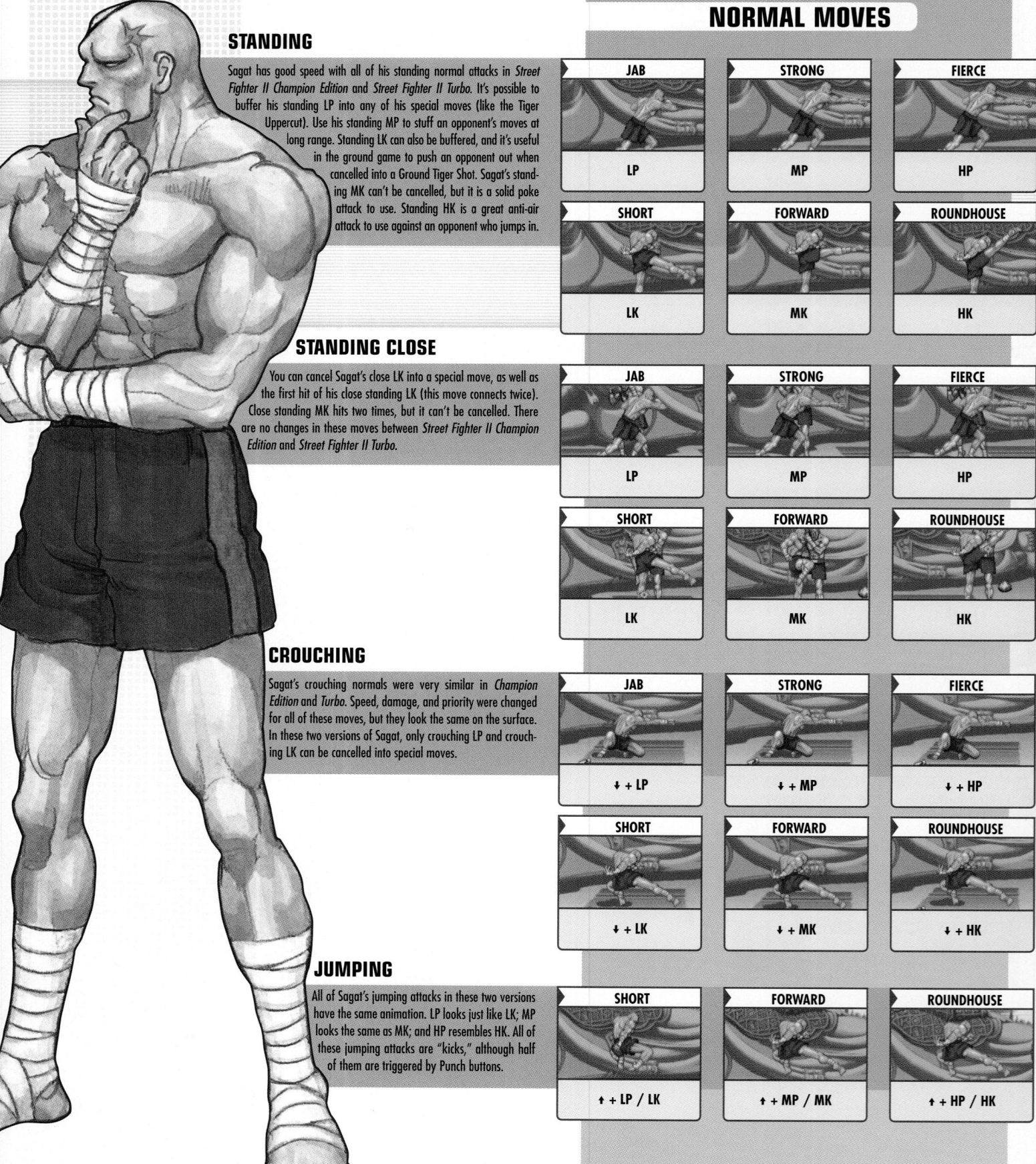

STANDING

Sagat has good speed with all of his standing normal attacks in *Street Fighter II Champion Edition* and *Street Fighter II Turbo*. It's possible to buffer his standing LP into any of his special moves (like the Tiger Uppercut). Use his standing MP to stuff an opponent's moves at long range. Standing LK can also be buffered, and it's useful in the ground game to push an opponent out when cancelled into a Ground Tiger Shot. Sagat's standing MK can't be cancelled, but it is a solid poke attack to use. Standing HK is a great anti-air attack to use against an opponent who jumps in.

STANDING CLOSE

You can cancel Sagat's close LK into a special move, as well as the first hit of his close standing LK (this move connects twice). Close standing MK hits two times, but it can't be cancelled. There are no changes in these moves between *Street Fighter II Champion Edition* and *Street Fighter II Turbo*.

CROUCHING

Sagat's crouching normals were very similar in *Champion Edition* and *Turbo*. Speed, damage, and priority were changed for all of these moves, but they look the same on the surface. In these two versions of Sagat, only crouching LP and crouching LK can be cancelled into special moves.

JUMPING

All of Sagat's jumping attacks in these two versions have the same animation. LP looks just like LK; MP looks the same as MK; and HP resembles HK. All of these jumping attacks are "kicks," although half of them are triggered by Punch buttons.

NORMAL MOVES

JAB	STRONG	FIERCE
LP	MP	HP

SHORT	FORWARD	ROUNDHOUSE
LK	MK	HK

JAB	STRONG	FIERCE
LP	MP	HP

SHORT	FORWARD	ROUNDHOUSE
LK	MK	HK

JAB	STRONG	FIERCE
↓ + LP	↓ + MP	↓ + HP

SHORT	FORWARD	ROUNDHOUSE
↓ + LK	↓ + MK	↓ + HK

SHORT	FORWARD	ROUNDHOUSE
↑ + LP / LK	↑ + MP / MK	↑ + HP / HK

THROWS

Sagat's throw has decent range and causes good damage, but it isn't intended to be used from an offensive standpoint. Due to Sagat's height, he can exploit the sacrifice throw. This involves taking a hit early on, so that you hold the advantage in the throw department.

THROW

→ / ← + MP , HP

SPECIAL MOVES

↓ ↘ → + P   **Tiger Shot**

The punch version of the Tiger Shot travels across the screen higher off the ground, making it difficult to jump over. Its speed can be modified by pressing LP, MP, or HP. For example, using LP throws a high, slow Tiger Shot. The Tiger Shot underwent several changes from *Champion Edition* Sagat to *Super Street Fighter II Turbo* Sagat. The version of Sagat in *Street Fighter II Champion Edition* has a very quick recovery, which was toned down in *Street Fighter II Turbo*.

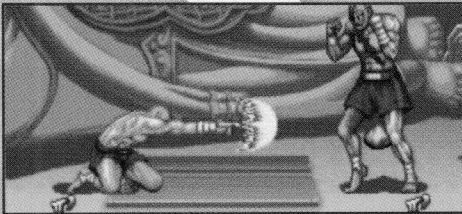

↓ ↘ → + K   **Ground Tiger Shot**

Sagat's Ground Tiger Shot is more useful than the standing version of the move. Although it travels low to the ground, it leaves Sagat free to counter attack when an opponent attempts to jump over it.

→ ↓ ↘ + P   **Tiger Uppercut**

The Tiger Uppercut is similar to the Shoryuken, because it can be used to blast an opponent who jumps in on you. This is useful in reversal situations in which your character has been knocked down and your opponent is jumping in. Don't miss with this move. If your opponent blocks it, or you completely whiff, Sagat becomes vulnerable to attack.

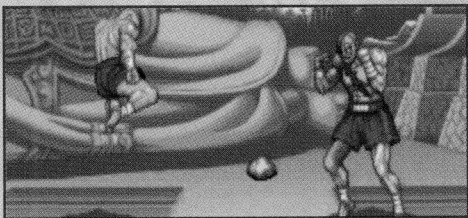

↙ ↓ ↘ → ↗ + K   **Tiger Knee**

Tiger Knee starts close to the ground and finishes high. The motion is tricky, so practice it repeatedly before attempting to use it. Use Sagat's Tiger Knee in combos and to quickly advance across the screen when your opponent gets knocked to the ground.

COSTUMES

STREET FIGHTER II
COSTUME

STREET FIGHTER II
ALTERNATE COSTUME

CHAMPIONSHIP
COSTUME

TURBO
COSTUME

COMBOS

STREET FIGHTER II CHAMPION EDITION

↓ + MP, ↓ LK, HK Tiger Shot

Jump in HK, LK, HK Tiger Knee

STREET FIGHTER II TURBO

Jump in HK, ↓ + LK, HP Tiger Uppercut

Crossup LK, ↓ + MP, HP Tiger Uppercut

STREET FIGHTER II CHAMPION EDITION

Sagat is one of the more powerful characters in *Street Fighter II Champion Edition*. He held a distinct advantage over many characters due to his ability to apply pressure from full-screen with his Tiger Shots. This is mainly due to the short recovery time associated with this move. Sagat's Tiger Uppercut is one of the more punishing anti-air moves; if an opponent chooses to jump at Sagat, use a Tiger Uppercut or a standing HK.

STREET FIGHTER II TURBO

Sagat's Tiger Shot was slowed down slightly in *Street Fighter II Turbo*. Also, his delay after throwing his projectiles was modified. This enabled other projectile characters (such as Guile, Ken, and Ryu) to better compete in a long-range battle. While not the dominating force he was in *Street Fighter II Champion Edition*, Sagat is still a formidable character.

GOOD MATCH-UP

VS. CHUN LI

One of Sagat's better match-ups is against Chun Li, who has one of the highest jumps in the game. When she jumps in at Sagat, you have many options, including his standing HK and, of course, his Tiger Uppercut. Throw Tiger Shots at Chun-Li to apply pressure, forcing her to jump. This puts Sagat at a tremendous advantage, since the recovery time for his Tiger Shots enable him to throw them one after the other with very little recourse. Even if Chun-Li jumps over a Tiger Shot, it leaves her open to a Tiger Uppercut.

BAD MATCH-UP

VS. DHALSIM

Dhalsim is perhaps Sagat's biggest challenger. In most fights, Sagat can throw fast, Ground Tiger Shots. Dhalsim's Drill Kicks and Drill Headthrusts make this tactic a lot less effective, since Dhalsim can use this attack over Ground Tiger Shots. If you throw one of Sagat's high Tiger Shots, your opponent can use a crouching HP or crouching HK to (slide) out of the way. Sagat's recovery for his Tiger Shots is one of the better ones in the game, but missing a high Tiger Shot makes him vulnerable to Dhalsim's attacks.

SUPER STREET FIGHTER II

Sagat gained the ability to two-in-one off the second hit of his standing LK, and his standing MK is used in the same manner in this version (both the first and second hit can be buffered into a special move). His standing HK can be buffered as well, but use it only in a combination. Sagat's Tiger Knee was modified in this version, too. Now it starts lower and travels farther. The controller motion was also changed slightly, with less of a 540-degree feel (← ↙ ↓ ↘ →) to more of a ↙ to ↗ feel.

SUPER STREET FIGHTER II TURBO

In this version, Sagat's Tiger Uppercut was changed from a single devastating blow to a multi-hit version with less priority. His Tiger Shots were watered down significantly, in both projectile speed and recovery time. However, he did gain a cross-up normal move, as well as the Tech Escape from throws that is included for all of the characters.

ADDITIONAL COMMENTS

The "Old" *Super Street Fighter II Turbo* version is regarded as one of the most powerful characters in the game. He possesses many of the characteristics of the *Super* version of the character, but combined with the game-engine of *Super Turbo*, he's a force to be reckoned with. Many tournament pros rarely underestimate their opponent if this character is chosen in tourney play. To choose "Old" Sagat, hold down the START button while choosing the *Super Street Fighter II* version of Sagat. Notice that the logo at the bottom of his feet is the *Super Street Fighter II Turbo* logo (blue), but you won't have a super combo bar.

COMBOS

SUPER STREET FIGHTER II

Jump in HP, HK, HP Tiger Uppercut

Jump in LK, LP, LK (one hit only), HK Tiger Knee (5 hits)

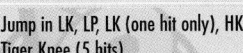

"OLD" SUPER STREET FIGHTER II TURBO

Cross-Up LK, crouching LP, LK (2 hits), HK Tiger Knee

SUPER STREET FIGHTER II TURBO

CORNER ONLY——Jump in HK, HP, HP Tiger Uppercut, HP Tiger Uppercut

Jump in HP, ↓ + MK, Tiger Genocide, HP Tiger Uppercut, HP Tiger Uppercut

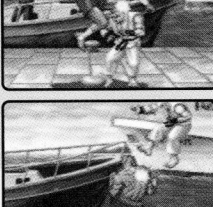

COSTUMES

LP	MP
HP	START
Hold any button	LK
MK	HK

NORMAL MOVES

STANDING

Several of Sagat's normal moves were modified in *Super Street Fighter II*, then again in *Super Street Fighter II Turbo*. In *Super Street Fighter II*, it's possible to cancel his Standing MP and HP. This is highly useful in the poking and keep-away game. Standing MK can also be buffered, making it difficult to get close to Sagat. Standing HP also dishes out a decent amount of damage, making it key for snuffing out projectiles at maximum distance. Note that many of the cancel properties of some of these moves were removed in *Super Street Fighter II Turbo*. Standing LK, MK, and MP were all changed in this version to prevent them from being buffered into a Tiger Shot. The frame rate for standing MP and HP were also reduced slightly. Sagat still has a potent standing HP, plus standing LK and MK are still good pokes.

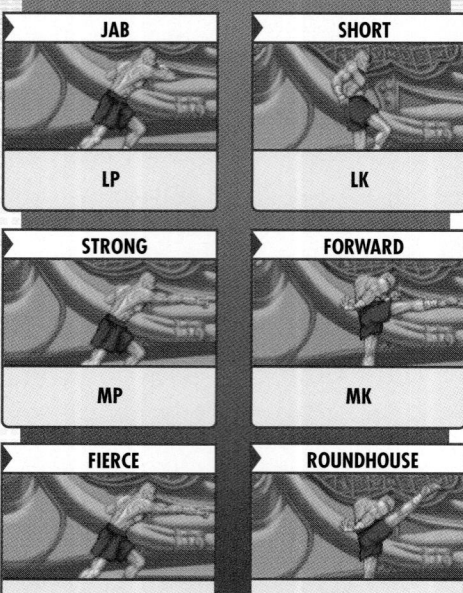

JAB	SHORT
LP	LK

STRONG	FORWARD
MP	MK

FIERCE	ROUNDHOUSE
HP	HK

STANDING CLOSE

You can cancel all of Sagat's close standing attacks into special moves. Either hit of the close standing LK or MK can be buffered into a Tiger Shot, too. Close standing HK can be cancelled as well, but only during powerful combos.

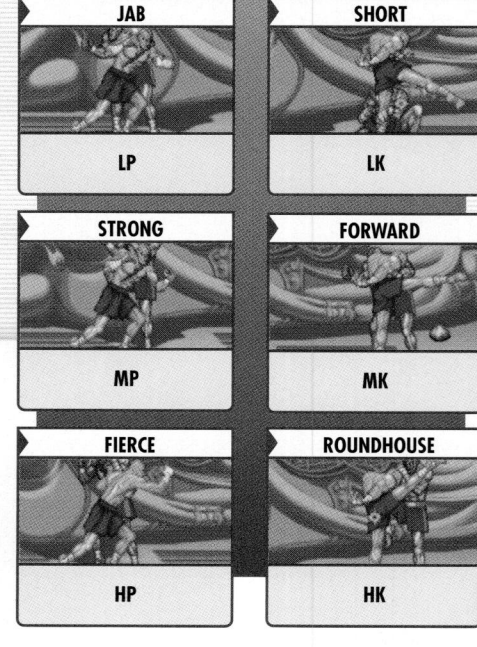

JAB	SHORT
LP	LK

STRONG	FORWARD
MP	MK

FIERCE	ROUNDHOUSE
HP	HK

CROUCHING

Several of Sagat's crouching attacks were modified in *Super Street Fighter II* and *Super Street Fighter II Turbo*. Crouching LK now looks different than MK and HK. LK and MK can now be cancelled, and similar changes were made to his crouching punching attacks. Crouching LP and MP could be cancelled, but neither crouching HP or HK could be buffered.

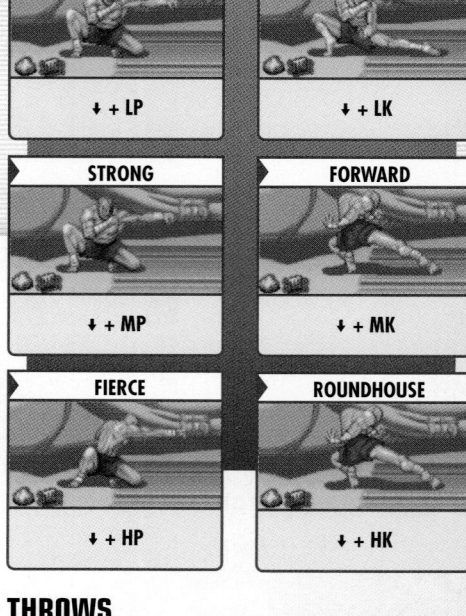

JAB	SHORT
↓ + LP	↓ + LK

STRONG	FORWARD
↓ + MP	↓ + MK

FIERCE	ROUNDHOUSE
↓ + HP	↓ + HK

THROWS

THROW
→ / ← + MP OR HP

72

JUMPING

Sagat gained some jumping punch animations for LP, MP, and HP in *Super Street Fighter II*, and they carried over to *Super Street Fighter II Turbo*. His punch attacks aren't very strong, but his jumping LK and jumping HK are great attacks. LK has very good priority and HK is a good starter for combos.

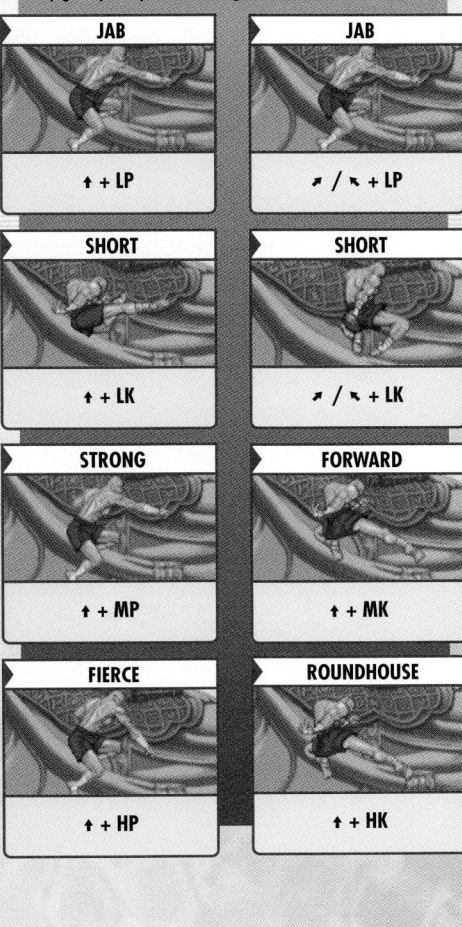

JAB	JAB
↑ + LP	↗ / ↖ + LP

SHORT	SHORT
↑ + LK	↗ / ↖ + LK

STRONG	FORWARD
↑ + MP	↑ + MK

FIERCE	ROUNDHOUSE
↑ + HP	↑ + HK

SPECIAL MOVES

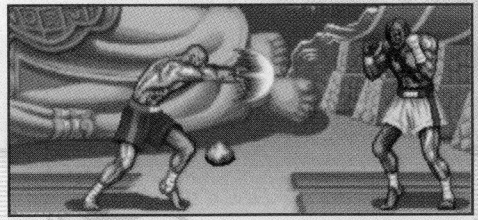

↓ ↘ → + P — **Tiger Shot**

In *Super Street Fighter II*, Sagat's Tiger Shots returned to their original glory from *Street Fighter II Champion Edition*. In *Super Street Fighter II Turbo*, however, they get less powerful. The recovery time for this version is quite poor, and the speed of the projectile is slowed down from the *Super Street Fighter II* version.

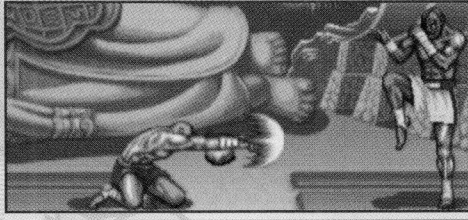

↓ ↘ → + K — **Ground Tiger Shot**

The Ground Tiger Shots are not as dominant as the high ones. Because a lot of characters have special moves that go over these, they are only useful in the "OLD" version of Sagat. Characters like M. Bison can use the Psycho Crusher torpedo to go over the Ground Tiger Shots and hit Sagat.

→ ↓ ↘ + P — **Tiger Uppercut**

In *Super Street Fighter II*, the Tiger Uppercut hits once. In *Super Street Fighter II Turbo*, though, it hits five times and spreads the damage into five separate parts. This is extremely ineffective as an anti-air attack, as only certain portions of the Tiger Uppercut hit the opponent.

↙ ↓ ↘ → + K — **Tiger Knee**

Now in *Super Street Fighter II*, the Tiger Knee can combo, plus it moves from a low to a high position when it hits. In *Super* and *Super Turbo*, it hits most ducking opponents instead of going over their heads.

SUPER COMBO

↓ ↘ → ↓ ↘ + P — **Tiger Genocide**

You can use Sagat's super combo up close to pass through projectiles and punish an opponent with a Tiger Knee animation that combos into a Tiger Uppercut. This Super Combo has decent invincibility at the start. It doesn't have much horizontal range, so only use it in close fighting situations. When this Super Combo gets blocked, Sagat becomes extremely vulnerable. This super can also be followed up by two hits in the corner.

Vega

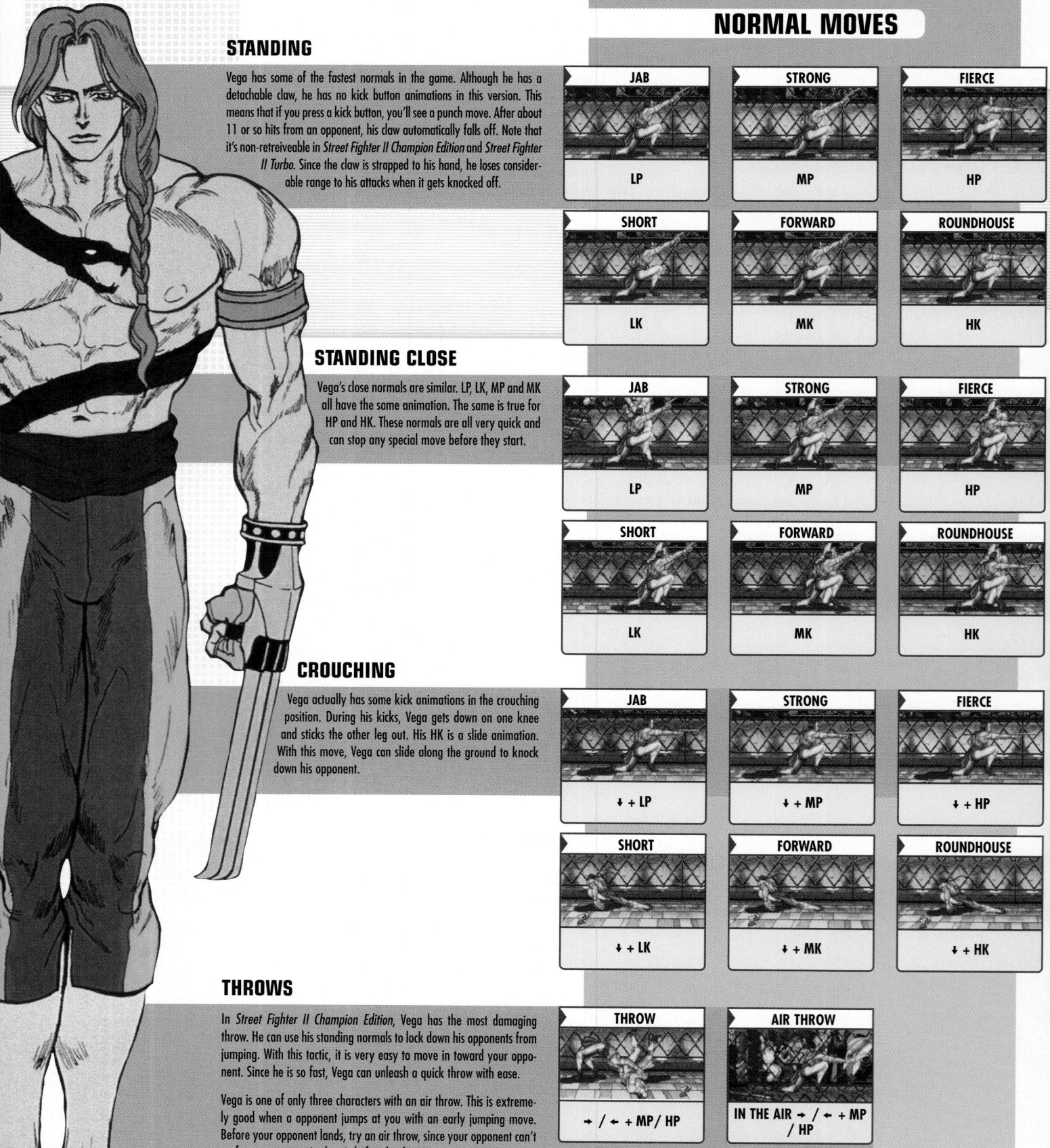

STANDING

Vega has some of the fastest normals in the game. Although he has a detachable claw, he has no kick button animations in this version. This means that if you press a kick button, you'll see a punch move. After about 11 or so hits from an opponent, his claw automatically falls off. Note that it's non-retrieveable in *Street Fighter II Champion Edition* and *Street Fighter II Turbo*. Since the claw is strapped to his hand, he loses considerable range to his attacks when it gets knocked off.

STANDING CLOSE

Vega's close normals are similar. LP, LK, MP and MK all have the same animation. The same is true for HP and HK. These normals are all very quick and can stop any special move before they start.

CROUCHING

Vega actually has some kick animations in the crouching position. During his kicks, Vega gets down on one knee and sticks the other leg out. His HK is a slide animation. With this move, Vega can slide along the ground to knock down his opponent.

THROWS

In *Street Fighter II Champion Edition*, Vega has the most damaging throw. He can use his standing normals to lock down his opponents from jumping. With this tactic, it is very easy to move in toward your opponent. Since he is so fast, Vega can unleash a quick throw with ease.

Vega is one of only three characters with an air throw. This is extremely good when a opponent jumps at you with an early jumping move. Before your opponent lands, try an air throw, since your opponent can't perform two moves in the air before landing.

NORMAL MOVES

JAB	STRONG	FIERCE
LP	MP	HP

SHORT	FORWARD	ROUNDHOUSE
LK	MK	HK

JAB	STRONG	FIERCE
LP	MP	HP

SHORT	FORWARD	ROUNDHOUSE
LK	MK	HK

JAB	STRONG	FIERCE
↓ + LP	↓ + MP	↓ + HP

SHORT	FORWARD	ROUNDHOUSE
↓ + LK	↓ + MK	↓ + HK

THROW	AIR THROW
→ / ← + MP / HP	IN THE AIR → / ← + MP / HP

JUMPING

Vega's air normals contain no punch moves. Since Vega is all about speed, use these attacks to easily jump over projectiles.

SHORT

↑ + LP / LK

SHORT

↗ / ↖ + LP / LK

FORWARD

↑ + MP / MK

FORWARD

↗ / ↖ + MP / MK

ROUNDHOUSE

↑ + HP / HK

ROUNDHOUSE

↗ / ↖ + HP / HK

SPECIAL MOVES

Charge ←, → + P　　　　　　　**Rolling Crystal Flash**

The Rolling Crystal Flash is a great move to use in a combo. It's also efficient at putting an opponent in a repeated block stun while chipping away at his or her health.

Charge ↓, ↑ + K, P　　　　　**Flying Barcelona Attack**

The Flying Barcelona attack is great at catching an opponent off-guard. If you press punch early on—not next to your opponent—Vega will attack with his claw instead of a throw.

SPECIAL NORMALS

Tap ← ←　　　　　　　　　　　**Backflip**

The backflip is a crazy move in which Vega jumps back and actually performs a backflip. It's important to note that he is completely invincible during this time. This move is great at getting out of projectile traps or when an opponent jumps in.

Press 3 Punch buttons　　　　　　　**Backflip**

In *Street Fighter II Turbo*, the input command for the Backflip is all three punch buttons pressed simultaneously.

Charge ↓, ↑ + K, → + P　　　　　　**Izuna Drop**

Press → + HP when Vega is next to an opponent after the Flying Barcelona attack to perform the Izuna Drop. This is the move to perform when using the Flying Barcelona attack. If you're playing on Vega's stage, you'll gain a special ability. He doesn't jump off the side wall, but instead jumps off the cage in the background. He doesn't take any damage while on the cage.

COSTUMES

STREET FIGHTER II

COSTUME

STREET FIGHTER II

ALTERNATE COSTUME

CHAMPIONSHIP

COSTUME

TURBO

COSTUME

COMBOS

STREET FIGHTER II CHAMPION EDITION

⬇ + MK, ⬇ + MK, ⬇ + MP

⬇ + LP, HP Rolling Crystal Flash, HP
(Redizzy)

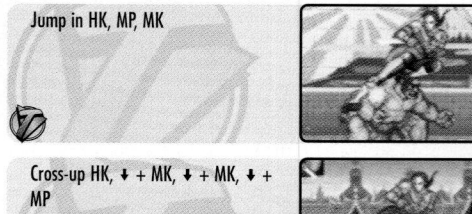

STREET FIGHTER II TURBO

Jump in HK, MP, MK

Cross-up HK, ⬇ + MK, ⬇ + MK, ⬇ +
MP

STREET FIGHTER II
CHAMPION EDITION

Vega's normal throw inflicts more damage than any character in *Street Fighter II Champion Edition*. His standing LP is really fast and it can be used repeatedly to lock down any of the bigger characters, or an enemy Vega. Also, his crouching HP and standing HK have high anti-air priority. His crouching HK slide is arguably the best in the game. Crouching MP is his staple attack for poking.

STREET FIGHTER II TURBO

Vega was toned down in this version. One noticeable change is that his throw causes less damage. His attacks seem to have slightly less priority and less range than in *Street Fighter II Champion Edition*, which makes this version of Vega a little less desirable.

GOOD MATCH-UP
VS. GUILE

The key to this match is sliding. As soon as Guile blocks a crouching HK slide, slide again and again to prevent him from using his Sonic Boom or Somersault Kick (the slide hits the start-up of his Sonic Boom and his Somersault Kick just misses). Guile can't hit Vega's slide with any of his ground normal moves in this situation either. However, Guile can jump straight up and come down with a HP, or jump in and perform a cross-up with LK. Reducing your opponent's set of moves to just one or two options (both jumping) means that you are already way ahead of the game. Use jump HK, standing HK, or a Flip Kick to counter his jumping attacks. Don't be afraid to use off-the-wall special moves against Guile, especially after a knockdown.

SUPER STREET FIGHTER II

Vega has a fuller set of normal moves with better priority in this version. His standing HP is now long range. His crouching MP is an excellent poke, and his crouching HK slide is still as good as ever.

SUPER STREET FIGHTER II TURBO

Vega gets his Flip Kick, the Sky High Claw, and a mildly useful super combo in this version. Note that the super combo (like Zangief's and T. Hawk's) cannot whiff; it will only come out if it connects. The Sky High Claw is fairly useful when cornered and an opponent jumps in to kick a normal Flying Barcelona Attack. If you use the Sky High Claw when Vega touches the wall, he'll start his high-priority attack and hit his opponent.

COMBOS

SUPER STREET FIGHTER II

In corner only—Vertical Jump HP, ↓ + MP, HP Sky High Claw

Wall Jump, in Air HK, ↓ + LP, MP Rolling Crystal Flash, ↓ + MP

SUPER STREET FIGHTER II TURBO

↓ + MK, Flip Kick two hits, Flip Kick

Jump in HP, HP, ↓ + MP

BAD MATCH-UP

VS. E. HONDA

If you use the Flying Barcelona attack behind E. Honda, he can jump and use LP or MP to stop you before you hit the wall. If you use it off of the wall behind you, he can LP Headbutt at the last moment to cause damage. He can also LP Headbutt to hit Vega's regular jump-in, or anything else you do from close quarters. So, it's very important to stay ahead in this match. By staying ahead, you can "out turtle" your opponent. Charge up Vega's Flip Kick to prevent E. Honda from jumping in. If he walks up, poke him away with a crouching MP. If you get behind, the Flying Barcelona attack (the one behind E. Honda) is a great option. Lure him into doing other moves to safely reach the back wall without getting hit by his jumping LP or MP. If you succeed, you'll cause E. Honda to lose the charge-up for his Headbutt (since you're on the other side), and you can attack him with the Sky High Claw and—hopefully—land the Izuna Drop. After doing so, go to the wall behind you again to prevent E. Honda from getting a charge for his Headbutt and repeat the sequence.

COSTUMES

LP

MP

HP

START

Hold any button

LK

MK

HK

VEGA

NORMAL MOVES

STANDING

There are a lot of changes to Vega in this version. He has kicks now, as well as normal moves, and his standing punches all do something different. His standing MP has great distance and it's extremely fast. Use it for a great poke attack. His standing LK, a short-range knee attack, is lightning-fast.

STANDING CLOSE

Vega received many updates to his normal moves in this version. The standing close LK is extremely fast, and it is an excellent attack to use with tick-throw techniques.

CROUCHING

The only change here is that Vega's HP no longer goes straight when crouching. Instead, it goes up at an angle, so it can be used as an anit-air attack.

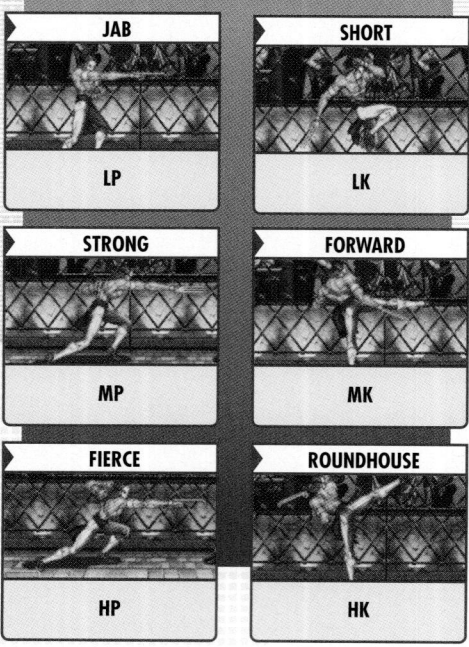

JAB	SHORT
LP	LK
STRONG	FORWARD
MP	MK
FIERCE	ROUNDHOUSE
HP	HK

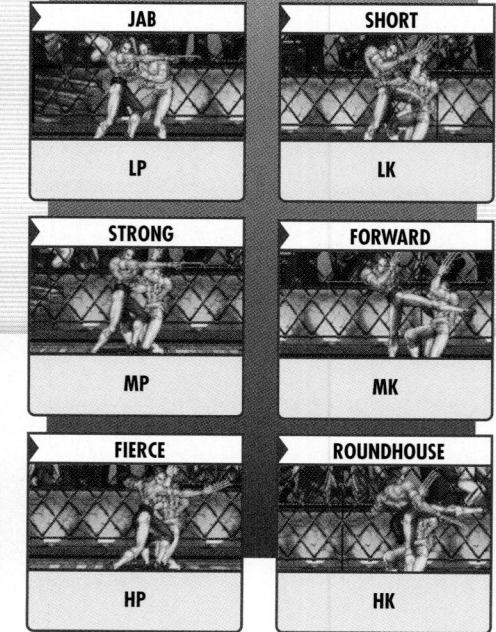

JAB	SHORT
LP	LK
STRONG	FORWARD
MP	MK
FIERCE	ROUNDHOUSE
HP	HK

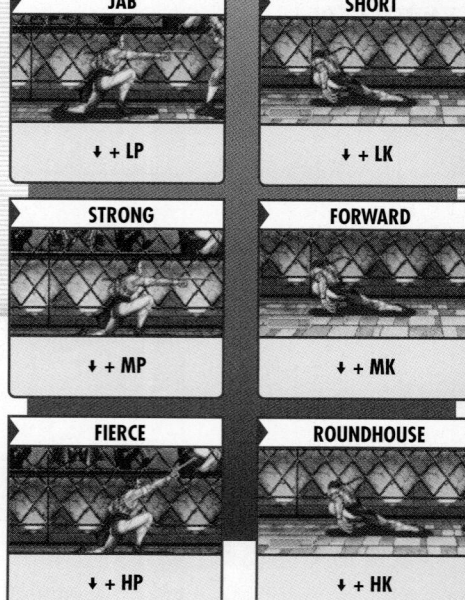

JAB	SHORT
↓ + LP	↓ + LK
STRONG	FORWARD
↓ + MP	↓ + MK
FIERCE	ROUNDHOUSE
↓ + HP	↓ + HK

THROWS

His air throw remains the same. Since it has priority over regular air moves, use it frequently to knock an opponent out of the air.

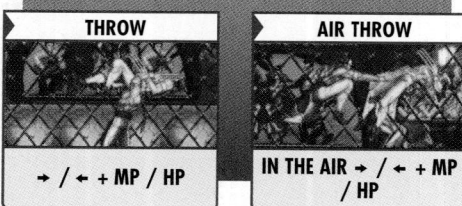

THROW	AIR THROW
→ / ← + MP / HP	IN THE AIR → / ← + MP / HP

SPECIAL NORMALS

3P — Backflip

Vega's Backflip is a great way for him not to get crossed-up on wake up. He is invincible during this move. This move also doesn't hit your opponent at any time, and should only be used to evade.

3K — Backflip

Vega's other Backflip is the quicker of the two. He only does half a flip and is immediately back in action ready to attack. This move also doesn't hit your opponent at all, and is completely invincible to moves or attacks.

JUMPING

Vega finally gets a set of jumping punch moves in the air in *Super Street Fighter II* and *Super Street Fighter II Turbo*. Jumping in with HP is a good way to start a combo.

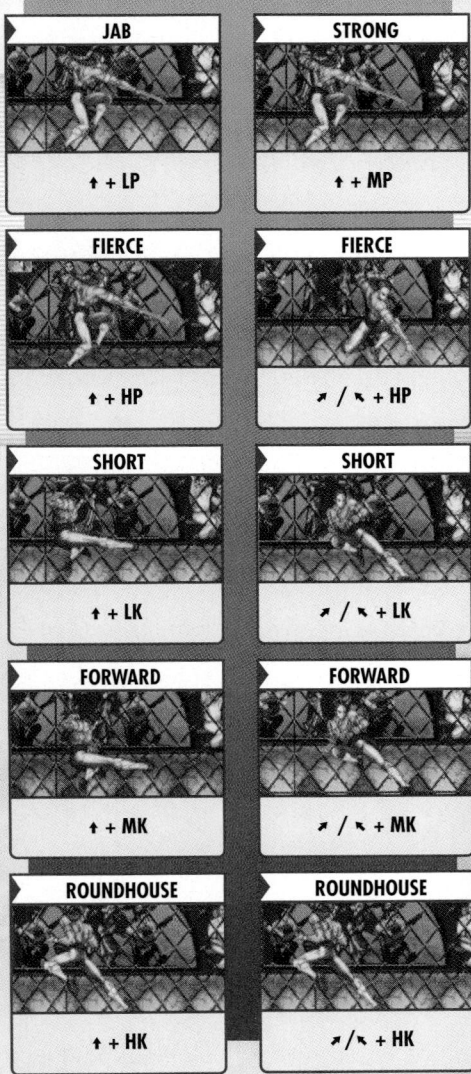

JAB	STRONG
↑ + LP	↑ + MP
FIERCE	**FIERCE**
↑ + HP	↗ / ↖ + HP
SHORT	**SHORT**
↑ + LK	↗ / ↖ + LK
FORWARD	**FORWARD**
↑ + MK	↗ / ↖ + MK
ROUNDHOUSE	**ROUNDHOUSE**
↑ + HK	↗ / ↖ + HK

SPECIAL MOVES

Charge ←, → + P   Rolling Crystal Flash

The Rolling Crystal Flash got slower in *Super Street Fighter II* and *Super Street Fighter II Turbo*, and it no longer strings all the hits together as one combo. It might glitch every now and then and combo, but most of the time it fails.

Charge ↓, ↑ + P   Sky High Claw

This is a fairly risky move to perform, but it looks really cool when it works. Vega jumps off the wall and darts toward his opponent really fast. If it connects, your opponent will have no time to retaliate.

Charge ←, → + K   Flip Kick

This is Vega's new anti-air move and his only reversal move. Like the Backflip, it now moves forward and hits an opponent twice in the air. You can follow it up for another hit by performing it again after the first hit for a total of three hits!

Charge ↓, ↑ + K, P   Flying Barcelona Attack

This move got a little more priority in *Super Street Fighter II Turbo*, but it is still susceptible to anti-air attacks.

Charge ↓, ↑ + K, → + P   Izuna Drop

This move got faster with the version change, and it inflicts incredible damage for an air throw. Use it to cross-up an opponent (knock them down first), then perform the Izuna Drop immediately after it.

SUPER COMBO

Charge ↙ ↘ ↙ ↗ + K, → + P   Rolling Izuna Drop
(when near opponent)

This super combo is a great move, even when your opponent isn't in the air. It will still do a air throw if you're close enough. The great thing about this move is that your opponent won't know he's getting hit by it unless it connects. So, basically, keep using the Flying Barcelona attack and when your opponent sits there and does nothing, nail him with a Rolling Izuna Drop.

VEGA

Cammy

STANDING

Cammy's fast walking speed is complemented nicely by the speed of her standing pokes. Some of them, like her standing MK and HP, have great priority. By dancing back and forth a few character widths in front of your opponent and throwing out these moves, you can hit opponents as they try to do their own pokes and special moves. This tactic may force your opponent into situations that are easy to predict and counter, such as poorly timed jumps or projectiles.

STANDING CLOSE

Many of Cammy's normal moves change significantly when she moves closer to an opponent, creating several new modes of attack, especially as an opponent is getting up. Her close standing LK becomes a great tick-throw tool, enabling you to throw an opponent when the block stun ends. Close standing HP is bufferable into all of her special moves, links to her crouching MK, and links into her crouching HK normals when done early enough as an opponent is rising from the ground. Close standing HK can be used to counter cross-up attacks, and some jump-in attacks.

CROUCHING

In general, MK and MP are the crouching moves of choice. The MK's long range makes it a great hit-and-run poke, especially against projectile characters (such as Ken). Crouching MP has a great deal of priority, making it useful for hitting an opponent's own crouching pokes. As a bonus, it links to itself, leading to easy, powerful combos when used as a wake-up attack. Both of these moves can be buffered into specials.

THROWS

Normal throws are not a big part of Cammy's game, simply because she spends so much time at the range of her crouching MK and standing HP. However, once she scores a knockdown, a few well-placed tick-throws in a match can make an opponent overly cautious and leave them open to other tactics.

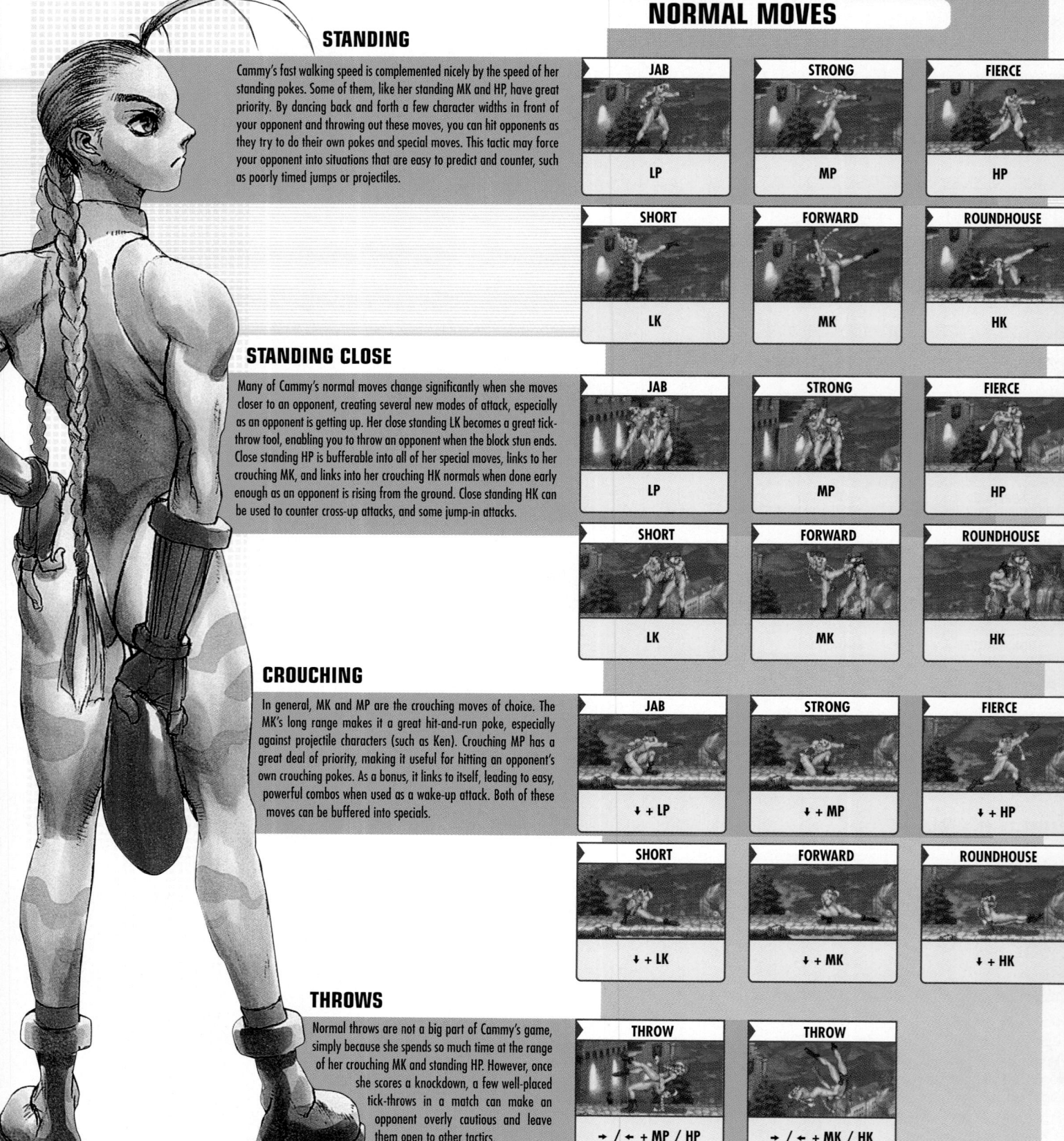

NORMAL MOVES

JAB — LP	STRONG — MP	FIERCE — HP
SHORT — LK	FORWARD — MK	ROUNDHOUSE — HK

JAB — LP	STRONG — MP	FIERCE — HP
SHORT — LK	FORWARD — MK	ROUNDHOUSE — HK

JAB — ↓ + LP	STRONG — ↓ + MP	FIERCE — ↓ + HP
SHORT — ↓ + LK	FORWARD — ↓ + MK	ROUNDHOUSE — ↓ + HK

THROW — → / ← + MP / HP	THROW — → / ← + MK / HK

JUMPING

Cammy has several good options in the air. By using her high-priority, fast ground pokes, you can bait an opponent into mistakes. One of her most powerful weapons is the jumping MP. This move has high priority, allowing you to jump in with impunity on some characters, beating or trading with most common anti-air moves (including Ryu and Ken's Shoryuken special attacks). Her jumping LK is an excellent cross-up move, and it leads to some deadly combos against some of the wider characters (like Dhalsim and Guile). Her jumping HK has deceptive reach, making it useful for punishing errant projectiles.

JAB	**STRONG**
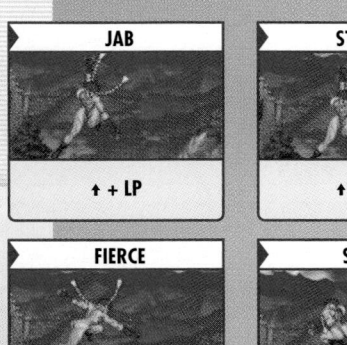	
↑ + LP	↑ + MP
FIERCE	**SHORT**

↑ + HP	↑ + LK
FORWARD	**ROUNDHOUSE**
↑ + MK	↑ + HK

AIR THROWS

AIR THROW	**AIR THROW**
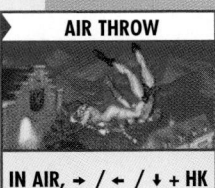	
IN AIR, → / ← / ↓ + HK	IN AIR, → / ← / ↓ + MP/HP

SPECIAL MOVES

← ↙ ↓ ↘ → + P **Spin Knuckle**

Cammy takes a short hop into the air and comes down with her fist extended, with an animation similar to her standing HP. The strength of the button used determines how far she travels. The Spinning Knuckle has several frames of invulnerability at its start, which lets you pass harmlessly through projectiles and some standing attacks. However, the hit properties are such that opponents can actually throw her between the point that she lands on the ground, and the point that it actually starts hitting! As such, this move is a little unreliable to use in actual combat. This move also serves well as a wake-up attack if you can time it so that her fist is extended as the opponent is getting off the ground. Cammy's Spinning Knuckle in *Super Street Fighter II Turbo* looks and acts exactly as it does in *Super Street Fighter II* with one exception: The invulnerability has been restricted to only the LP one. This makes the MP and HP versions somewhat useless. It can still be used as a wake-up attack, however, this move is best used sparingly.

↓ ↘ → + K **Cannon Drill**

Cammy straightens her legs and slides along the ground during this move. It doesn't hit low, although it appears to do so. The strength of the button determines how far along the ground Cammy slides, with LK being the shortest and HK being the farthest. Additionally, the HK version hits twice when performed next to an opponent. Like her normals, Cammy's Cannon Drill is an excellent poking tool, as long as it is spaced properly. It can be used to punished whiffed moves that have long recovery periods, such as sweeps or Shoryuken-type attacks. By mixing up her normal pokes (such as crouching MK, standing MK and MP), you can get an opponent to commit to a ground game. Upon doing so, punish his or her own pokes with Cannon Drill attacks. Make sure you distance the Cannon Drill properly, though. Using it too close leaves Cammy in recovery long enough for an opponent to cause damage! Try to connect with the very tip of Cammy's legs as the move is ending and she is sliding on the ground.

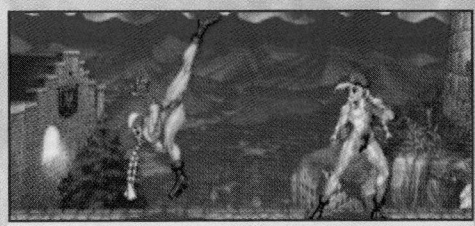

→ ↓ ↘ + K **Cannon Spike**

This is Cammy's all purpose anti-air move. She launches herself at an angle into the air, leg first. If this move gets blocked, she bounces away from the opponent; otherwise, she flies into the air and comes straight back down. This move has a fair amount of invulnerability at the start, although it will occasionally trade with some jump-in attacks. Unlike a Shoryuken, the Cannon Spike isn't a great move to use against an opponent's limbs during a poking game. If it misses, it leaves Cammy next to her opponent and vulnerable. As such, it is best saved for anti-air attacks and use in combos.

←, ↙, ↓, ↘, →, ↗ + P **Hooligan Combo**

Cammy tucks her legs into her body and rolls into a tight ball, flying toward her opponent. If no buttons are pressed, she will land and slide along the ground, which will knock down your opponent if it connects. Taunt your opponent with a few normal moves (such as crouching MK and standing HP) to lure your opponent into a poking game, then suddenly pull out a Hooligan.

During Hooligan Combo, K **Hooligan Throw**

When Cammy is still on the upward trajectory of the roll, she performs a neck breaker throw that will put her on the opposite side of her opponent. If she is on the downward trajectory, she'll perform a rolling throw, slamming her opponent into the ground with her legs.

During Hooligan Combo, K **Hooligan Cancel**

By pressing one of the kick buttons before she begins the downward part of the Hooligan roll, Cammy will cancel out of the roll and land lightly on her feet with a brief recovery period.

COSTUMES

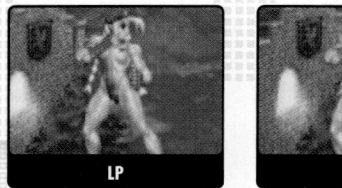
LP

MP

HP

START

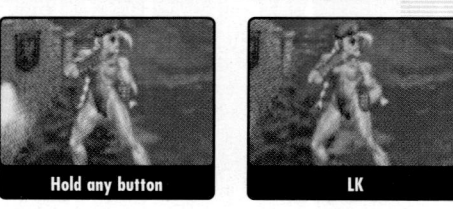
Hold any button

LK

MK

HK

SUPER STREET FIGHTER II

Cammy's only move in this version that is better than the *Super Street Fighter II Turbo* version is her Spinning Knuckle. The HP one goes through projectiles much better than the *Super Street Fighter II Turbo* version. Those who rely heavily on projectiles should be wary of this fact.

SUPER STREET FIGHTER II TURBO

Cammy received a few upgrades in the transition from *Super Street Fighter II* to *Super Street Fighter II Turbo*. She gained two special moves: the Hooligan Combination and her super combo, the Spin Drive Smasher. Her Spinning Knuckle was also changed slightly. These changes, however, significantly added to her game, making her more versatile and giving her more options in combat. Be careful when using Cammy's ground punch throw from *Super Street Fighter II Turbo* against another *Super Street Fighter II Turbo* character. *Super Turbo* characters have the ability to soften throws, and Cammy has a lot of recovery time after her ground punch throw. Against characters like Zangief, this can lead to easy Spinning Piledriver setups, which is a poor tradeoff for the damage of a softened throw!

COMBOS

SUPER STREET FIGHTER II

Cross-up HP, HP, ↓ + MK, HK Cannon Drill

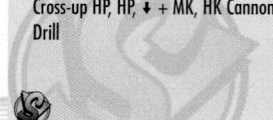

Jump-in HK, HP, HK Cannon Spike

SUPER STREET FIGHTER II TURBO

Cross-up jumping LK, crouching MP, close standing HP, HK Cannon Drill

Jump-in HK, ↓ + MP, ↓ + MK, Spin Drive Smasher

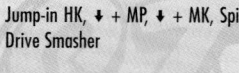

SUPER COMBO

↓ ↘ → ↓ ↘ → + K	Spin Drive Smasher

Cammy performs a multi-hit Cannon Drill, followed by a multi-hit Cannon Spike. Unlike a normal Cannon Spike, she won't bounce away if the Spin Drive Smasher gets blocked. This move has enough invulnerability to move through projectiles, normals, most special moves, and some super combos. However, it leaves her very vulnerable if it gets blocked due to the lack of a bounce back. Once you have the super meter to use it, this move becomes difficult to counter well-spaced Cannon Drills, since you can activate the Spin Drive Smasher as soon as Cammy recovers from the Cannon Drill! By performing the motion for the super combo as the drill is recovering, you can wait to see if your opponent throws out any moves. If they do, press a kick button to activate the super combo.

GOOD MATCH-UP

VS DHALSIM

The priority on Cammy's jumping MP almost single-handedly wins this fight. This jumping attack will beat or trade with all of Dhalsim's limbs and slides, enabling you to attack relentlessly. Cammy's slim character sprite, and somewhat high jump, makes it easy to jump straight up and down over projectiles. She can come down with MP to beat any limbs Dhalsim may throw out as she falls. The wide horizontal arc of Cammy's Cannon Spike enables you to keep Dhalsim from jumping away with air attacks. By keeping on the pressure, you can harass Dhalsim with the Hooligan Throw, which is easy to connect after a close standing HP.

BAD MATCH-UP

VS M. BISON

The difficulty in this match is in the superiority of M. Bison's pokes. His standing MK and HK have more range and they cause more damage than Cammy's pokes. Additionally, he can use his jumping MP to beat out Cammy's Hooligan Combo (*Super Street Fighter II Turbo* only), which leaves her with Cannon Drills and Cannon Spikes, both of which are risky to use. Cammy is also a good target for cross-ups and M. Bison's jumping MK is one of the best in the game. It's difficult to beat M. Bison's pokes with Cammy's, so don't try it. If you elect to go this route, your opponent will be forced to use his Psycho Crusher or Knee Press. Try to anticipate these moves and use a Cannon Spike to counter them, although this is proves difficult because of the range difference. If you can bait an HP Psycho Crusher from M. Bison, jump backward and punish it with a jump-in combo. You have some options if you knock him down. Either use a wake-up close LK into a regular throw, or a Hooligan Combo (*Super Street Fighter II Turbo* only), or try to land a cross-up jumping LK. This is risky, though, as it is difficult to time the cross-up.

Dee Jay

STANDING

Dee Jay's standing normal moves make for a good arsenal of both defensive and offensive attacks. Standing MP is great against jump-ins, especially characters with great jumping ability, like Chun-Li. Standing HP can be used in the same manner(priority is not as good), but it should be used when an opponent jumps from farther away. Standing LK is a great poke that has decent range. Both MK and HK are also good pokes, but because of their slow recovery time do not abuse them.

JAB	STRONG	FIERCE

LP	MP	HP

SHORT	FORWARD	ROUNDHOUSE

LK	MK	HK

STANDING CLOSE

Several of Dee Jay's close normals are useful in combos, because many of them link easily together. For example, you can link two standing MP attacks from close range, or a standing MP into a standing HP. One of his better close normals is MK, which can be used in combos or as a reversal attack.

JAB	STRONG	FIERCE

LP	MP	HP

SHORT	FORWARD	ROUNDHOUSE

LK	MK	HK

CROUCHING

Dee Jay's crouching normal attacks are extremely versatile and very important to his game. His crouching MP has excellent priority against many attacks (for example, Dhalsim's limbs) and it can be linked into combos. Crouching HP can be used as an anti-air attack, and it has great priority against other normal attacks. It inflicts solid damage on its own, but when worked into combos, it unleashes some serious damage.

JAB	STRONG	FIERCE

↓ + LP	↓ + MP	↓ + HP

SHORT	FORWARD	ROUNDHOUSE

↓ + LK	↓ + MK	↓ + HK

THROWS

Dee Jay has a very good punch throw (→/← + MP) with great range. Mixing up throws with cross-up attempts is a very strong tactic to employ. If you can stay on top of your opponent and keep him guessing how to block, it's much easier to get in a throw. The punch throw has good recovery, enabling you to advance toward an opponent. His kick throw is not as strong, though. In a throw situation, it's best to use the punch version.

THROW	THROW
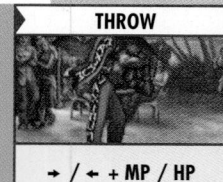	
→ / ← + MP / HP	→ / ← + MK / HK

JUMPING

While in the air, Dee Jay has several options depending on his opponent. Air-to-air his jumping LP is effective if it is used before an opponent can use his. This move stays out for a very long time, and it has a very high priority. It's great to jump in when you have an opponent in the corner and they are being forced to jump out (Bison trying to use a jump MP, for example). Dee Jay's jumping LK attacks (regular and special) differ significantly. The regular version isn't the greatest, however, the special normal (↓ + LK) has good priority in the air and it can be used to start combos. Jumping HP is an excellent combo starter, and it will snuff several anti-air specials (Chun's Whirlwind Kick, for example). The timing is difficult, tough; press HP earlier than normal. Jumping MK is one of the best cross-ups in the game and a great way to start combos. Jumping HK has great range for jumping over projectiles and hitting an opponent's hands during recovery. You can also start combos with it and use it as a cross-up in some situations.

SPECIAL NORMAL

| In air, ↓ + LK | Knee Shot |

Dee Jay has an alternate jumping LK, which has very strange properties in how it hits. In addition, you can cross-up your opponent with this move.

SPECIAL MOVES

| Charge ←, → + P | Max Out |

DeeJay's Max Out is a fast projectile once it gets going, however, it's initial release time is a little long. In addition, the Max Out has considerable lag after release. The projectile is long, which makes jumping over it difficult, especially when an opponent is trying to jump straight up. It's useful at negating other projectiles, though. Use it in combos and to apply pressure at full-screen.

| Charge ←, → + K | Double Dread Kick |

The Double Dread Kick is a special move that hits one or two times, depending on which button you use. MK and HK both hit two times, so use them in combos only. Trying to hit with the second hit of the MK version is an interesting strategy, because you can advance toward an opponent and if the first hit misses, the second move comes out very fast. Use the LK version in close quarters, since it goes over crouching attacks.

| Charge ↓, ↑ + P, P rapidly | Hyper Fist |

The Hyper Fist is a move that can really swing the fight in your favor once mastered. Although the *Super Street Fighter II* version was invincible on start-up, this feature was removed in *Super Street Fighter II Turbo*. However, timing the buttons in the right pattern can yield many hits. It's best used after hitting with a cross-up attack followed by a crouching normal.

| Charge ↓, ↑ + K | Maximum Jacknife |

The Maximum Jacknife acts as a good anti-air attack. The LK version has high priority and is great against an opponent who is jumping in. The LK version hits once, the MK connects twice, while the HK hits three times. When used as a reversal, use the LK version. This move is great in combos, since you can juggle with two hits of a super combo after hitting with the HK version.

JAB
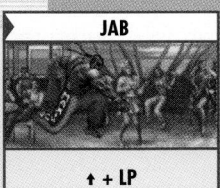
| ↑ + LP |

JAB
| ↗ / ↖ + LP |

STRONG

| ↑ + MP |

STRONG
| ↗ / ↖ + MP |

FIERCE

| ↑ + HP |

FIERCE
| ↗ / ↖ + HP |

SHORT

| ↑ + LK |

SHORT
| ↗ / ↖ + LK |

FORWARD

| ↑ + MK |

FORWARD
| ↗ / ↖ + MK |

ROUNDHOUSE

| ↑ + HK |

ROUNDHOUSE
| ↗ / ↖ + HK |

DEE JAY

COSTUMES

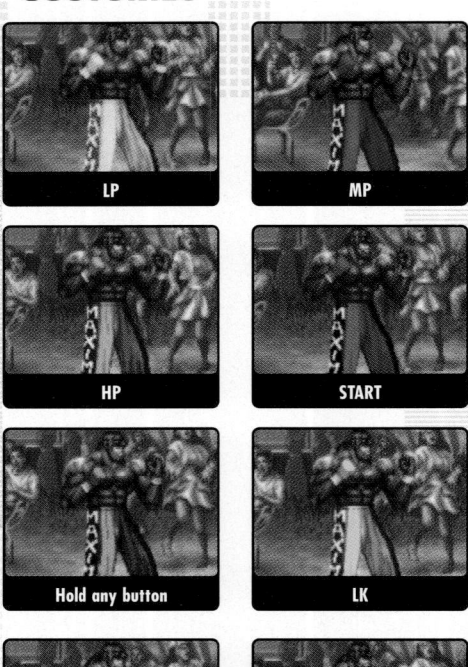

LP	MP
HP	START
Hold any button	LK
MK	HK

COMBOS

SUPER STREET FIGHTER II

Cross-Up MK, ↓ + LP x3, Standing MP, HK Double Dread Kick

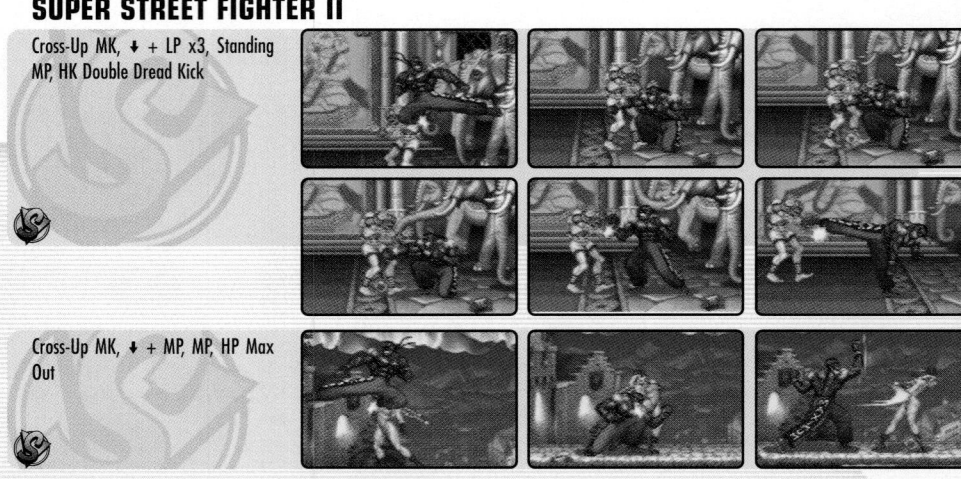

Cross-Up MK, ↓ + MP, MP, HP Max Out

SUPER STREET FIGHTER II TURBO

Cross-up MK, Crouching LP, Crouching HP, Hyper Fist

Cross-up MK, Crouching MP, Crouching LK, HK Maximum Jackknife, Dread Carnival

SUPER STREET FIGHTER II

Dee Jay was an unknown commodity when he was first introduced. It quickly became apparent that he is better suited for close-quarters combat than full-screen. His Hyper Fist could pass through projectiles, and it was also useful as an anti-air special attack. Several combos help his game, as well as decent overall speed, but he is not a dominating force. He is most effective fighting at close range, mixing up throws and using his powerful combos.

SUPER STREET FIGHTER II TURBO

Super Street Fighter II Turbo Dee Jay is a very strong character in some aspects, but weak in others. He is at his best while on top of an opponent after knocking them down. His gameplan centers around mixing up his powerful combos with throws and tick-throws, tempered with his ability to keep an opponent pinned in the corner. Avoid playing in the traditional "Guile" mindset (sit and throw projectiles until an opponent jumps, then Somersault Kick); if not, you'll get eaten alive because of his weakness against projectiles. Instead, get a mid-screen knockdown and mix up some of the deadly cross-ups into Hyper Fists for dizzy potential, or use Maximum Jacknife kicks for position. Pin your opponent in the corner and use Dee Jay's high priority normal attacks and his arsenal of special moves (such as HP Max Out and LK Dread Kick). The addition of a super combo does add another dimension to his arsenal. It provides a legitimate reversal move and a method to punish close projectiles.

SUPER COMBO

charge ← → ← → + K	Dread Carnival

At close range, this super combo passes through projectiles and smacks your opponent four times. During the execution of the move, charge down for two seconds. Then, when the Dread Carnival finishes executing, unleash a Maximum Jacknife to juggle for two more hits. This super combo is great to twitch out in close range when playing footsies, especially if an opponent flinches with a slower normal attack.

GOOD MATCH-UP

VS FEI-LONG

When fighting against Fei-Long, the priorty of Dee Jay's normal attacks, plus the ability to pressure from a distance with Fast Max Outs, creates an advantage. You don't need to jump toward Fei-Long; instead, let Fei-Long come to you. The one thing to look out for is Fei-Long's standing HP/Forward Hop kick trap, because it will force you to block high and lose the charge for a Maximum Jacknife. However, if you are blocking low while Fei-Long uses his standing HP, then you should have time to execute an Maximum Jacknife to escape the trap.

BAD MATCH-UP

VS RYU

Dee Jay has a decent projectile in his Max Out, however, he has much more delay on it compared to other projectiles (Guile's Sonic Boom, for example). This keeps him at a disadvantage against Ryu's faster Hadoken. A paitent player can pepper you with the Hadoken, forcing you to jump. Ryu can often recover quickly enough from his Hadoken to use his Shoryuken on any of Dee Jay's jump attacks. To succeed in this fight, try to knock Ryu down as soon as possible and stay on top of him. Throws work well, as does baiting a Shoryuken. The odds are good that the person playing as Ryu will try a Shoryuken on wake-up. If your opponent doesn't use a Shoryuken, try a fast sweep with crouching MK to knock him back down. Stay on top of Ryu and don't let your opponent dictate the pace of the fight with projectiles.

Fei Long

STANDING

Fei-Long is built for attacking and offense, and his normal moves reflect this. His pokes have high priority and many of them link together, allowing him to land devastating combos with ease. Additionally, all of Fei-Long's standing normal attacks (with the exception of standing HK) can be buffered into his Rekka Ken rushing punches. Standing HP is Fei-Long's standing poke of choice. This attack may discourage players who like to throw projectiles constantly.

STANDING CLOSE

Fei-Long's close standing normals complement his game very well, because so many of them link together. All of them (except HK) can be buffered into his Rekka Ken punches. MP, HP, and MK are probably the most viable close-range options. Close standing MP easily links to his close standing HP or his crouching HK sweep, leading to a knock down or additional damage. Close standing HP is one of Fei-Long's best options, especially when an opponent is rising. Although it normally has a long recovery, it can be performed early, allowing you to link more normals after it!

CROUCHING

Fei-Long's crouching attacks complement his attack game with decent range, good priority, and the ability to buffer into his Rekka Ken punches. Crouching HP is one of Fei-Long's greatest assests. Although it doesn't combo into his Rekka Ken punches, it has a great deal of priority, range, and a high dizzy potential. If this move is used as a wake-up attack against an opponent, you can link it to another crouching HP, which has a high chance of dizzying your opponent. With the exception of HP and HK, all of Fei-Long's crouching normals can be buffered into his Rekka Ken punches. This enables him to keep pressure on opponents and it provides several different looks via links.

THROWS

His punch throw tosses an opponent into the air in the direction you choose. The kick throw is similar, although he throws them by the neck instead.

After a knockdown, Fei-Long can move next to an opponent and unleash a standing or crouching attack while his opponent is rising, forcing them to block. From there, you can walk forward and perform a throw as your opponent recovers from the blocked attack or use the overhead special normal (→ / ← + MK), or even a Rising Dragon Kick. With his huge damage potential, opponents must be wary when getting off the ground.

NORMAL MOVES

JAB	STRONG	FIERCE

LP	MP	HP

SHORT	FORWARD	ROUNDHOUSE

LK	MK	HK

JAB	STRONG	FIERCE

LP	MP	HP

SHORT	FORWARD	ROUNDHOUSE

LK	MK	HK

JAB	STRONG	FIERCE
		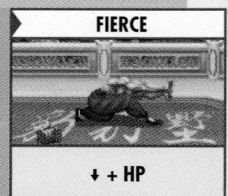
↓ + LP	↓ + MP	↓ + HP

SHORT	FORWARD	ROUNDHOUSE

↓ + LK	↓ + MK	↓ + HK

THROW	THROW	AIR THROW
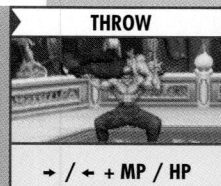		
→ / ← + MP / HP	→ / ← + MK / HK	IN AIR →/←/↓ + MK / HK

JUMPING

With great ground mobility (due to the Rekka Ken punches), it's not necessary to take to the air often. When he does, however, he has a formidable array of options. His jumping HK is an excellent jump-in, useful for both cross-ups and starting combos. His jumping LP stays out for a long time, allowing him to throw it out early and jump in against an opponent. The only jumping normal move to visibly receive a change (for reasons that become evident) is HK. This move is now a straight legged kick, rather than the odd twisting kick from before. This move also lacks the cross-up properties of the old jumping HK.

JAB	JAB
	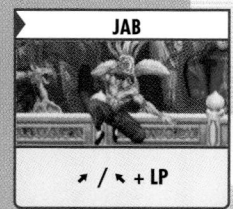
↑ + LP	↗ / ↖ + LP

STRONG	STRONG

↑ + MP	↗ / ↖ + MP

FIERCE	FIERCE
	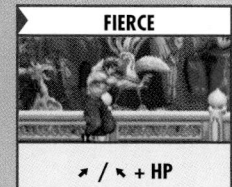
↑ + HP	↗ / ↖ + HP

SHORT	SHORT

↑ + LK	↗ / ↖ + LK

FORWARD	FORWARD

↑ + MK	↗ / ↖ + MK

ROUNDHOUSE	ROUNDHOUSE

↑ + HK	↗ / ↖ + HK

ROUNDHOUSE

↗ / ↖ + HK

SPECIAL NORMALS

→ / ← + MK   **Forward Hop**

Fei-Long has two special normals. The first one is a quick overhead hopping kick. Without this move, opponents could simply block low with no fear of attacks that can hit high. By occasionally including this move during close-range combat, you can land a few extra hits in the poking game and swing matches back in your favor. When an opponent retaliates after this move, counter with a Rising Dragon Kick.

← / → + MK   **Forward Hop**

Although this move hasn't changed from a visible standpoint, Fei-Long now hops forward slightly when → is held. Otherwise, he simply hops in place as in *Super Street Fighter II*.

→ + HK   **Roundhouse Hop**

The other special normal (→ + HK) isn't quite as useful, but it still has its place. This forward-moving kick hits twice at close range, leaving Fei-Long close to his opponent. It can cover a great deal of distance, but comes out a little slow. Unfortunatley, the move can be punished before it actually hits if it is performed too far away.

COSTUMES

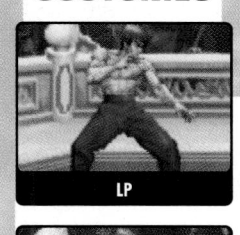	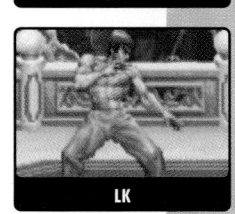
LP	**MP**

HP	**START**

Hold any button	**LK**

MK	**HK**

SPECIAL MOVES

↓ ↘ → + P (repeat up to 3 times)   **Rekka Ken**

Fei-Long slides along the ground, extending his fist. The punch used determines the distance he travels (HP goes the farthest). Three Rekka Ken attacks can be performed in succession, creating an easy 3-hit combo. When one connects, use the same strength button to finish the combo; if not, it may miss.

The Rekka Ken is Fei-Long's bread and butter. Because so many of his normal moves can be buffered into the Rekka Ken, you will almost always throw these out in some way. They also serve well as pokes, allowing you to pressure blocking opponents not only with his normals, but with the chip damage from blocking the Rekkas and the threat of them actually connecting.

The Rekkas should be considered an extension of his poking game. By using Fei-Long's high-priority normal pokes, and dragging an opponent into a ground-based poking game, you can switch to using his Rekka Kens for punishing whiffed (or dodged) normal moves with recovery time. Also, his Rekka Kens are relatively safe when blocked, as long as he hits his opponent at the end of the sliding motion. This takes practice, but it is well worth the effort.

← ↓ ↙ + K   **Rising Dragon Kick**

This is Fei-Long's anti-air flaming kick. He spins into the air, one leg on fire, whirling the other one around him. The stronger the kick button used, the further into the air he goes. The HK version hits twice.

This move serves a variety of purposes. It is normally used as an anti-air attack, discouraging opponents from jumping. It also works well in combos, since it causes very good damage and it's more reliable than the Rekka Ken punches. It can be used to hit pokes from opponents at close range, especially following Fei-Long's overhead kick special normal.

Be very careful with the HK version of this move. Although it can hit twice, if the opponent is too far away, the second hit will whiff and the opponent will not get knocked down.

← ↙ ↓ ↘ → ↗ + K   **Dragon Arc Kick**

The Dragon Arc Kick is a fantastic move that helps Fei-Long's offense. Performing this move causes Fei-Long to launch into the air toward an opponent, using the animation similar to his jumping HK from *Super Street Fighter II*. This move can hit up to three times. The kick button used determines the distance he travels across the screen.

By performing a normal attack that causes a lot of block stun (close standing HP, for example), Fei-Long can buffer it into the Dragon Arc Kick, leaving only a small window of opportunity for an opponent to attempt to hit him out of it. This is especially difficult for certain charge characters, or those without good reversal moves. Since Fei-Long recovers instantly upon landing, perform the normal move when he lands and buffer it into the Dragon Arc Kick!

This move is extremely versatile, allowing Fei to hop over projectiles and land big damage combos and juggles. While the motion is slightly peculiar, it's definitely a move you'll want to learn.

SUPER STREET FIGHTER II

Super Street Fighter II brought us the martial arts master Fei-Long. He brought a unique style to the game, utilizing high-priority ground moves in the form of his Rekka Ken punches, and a decent anti-air attack with his Rising Dragon Kick. Playing as Fei-Long means sacrificing any kind of long-range strategy in return for huge damage potential. His Rekka Ken punches link together, making them excellent for punishing a missed poke attack or moves that have a lot of recovery. You may experience difficulty fighting characters who have good defense (such as E. Honda) and those who are skilled at keeping opponents away (such as Sagat and Dhalsim). However, even against these opponents, he can slowly work his way in close where his skills rise.

SUPER STREET FIGHTER II TURBO

Fei-Long's Dragon Arc Kick is a powerful new tool, plus he retains most of his high-damage combos from *Super Street Fighter II*. The Dragon Arc Kick enables him to work into close range against opponents, which means he's no longer at a disadvantage against long-range characters like Sagat and Dhalsim. However, because his game is so ground-based, he still has difficulty cracking open a tough defense. Fei-Long's game is still based around his Rekka Ken punches. By repeatedly poking with these punches, you can slowly force opponents back into the corner. By using different strength versions of the Rekka Ken, it's possible to bait out a poke from an opponent that will miss, thus allowing you to rush in for a powerful combo or knockdown. Fei-Long is most dangerous against an opponent who gets knocked down, because his high-priority normal moves serve as great wake-up attacks. When opponents begin to fear the damage potential of Fei-Long's combos, it leaves them open to his throws.

SUPER COMBO

↓ ↘ → ↓ ↘ → +P   **Rekka Shin Ken**

Fei-Long performs five consecutive Rekka Ken punches in this combo. Although this move leaves him very vulnerable if it whiffs, he is completely safe if an opponent blocks it and it is invulnerable for most of the duration of the move! This provides a fantastic anti-projectile technique, as well as creating options after a blocked Rekka Ken series or a Dragon Arc Kick.

COMBOS

SUPER STREET FIGHTER II

Jump in HP, ↓ + LP, HP, HP Rekka Ken x 3

→ + HK, ↓ + HP

SUPER STREET FIGHTER II "OLD"

Close standing MP, crouching MP, Rekka Ken X3

↓ + HP, ↓ + LK, HP Rekka Ken x3

SUPER STREET FIGHTER II TURBO

Cross-up MK, MP, Rising Dragon Kick

Dragon Arc Kick, LP, ↓ + LP, Rekka Shin Ken, Dragon Arc Kick

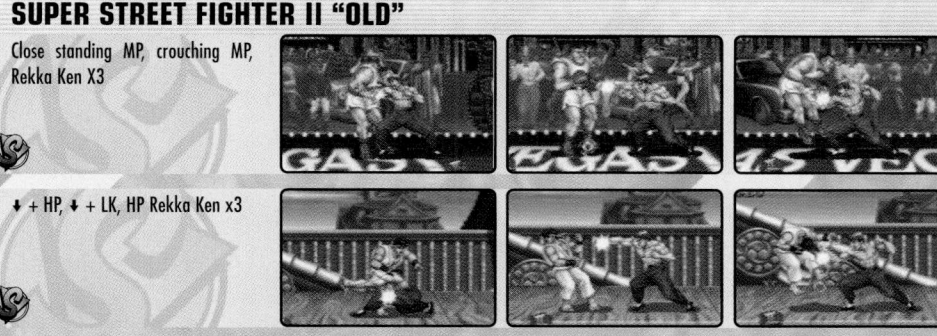
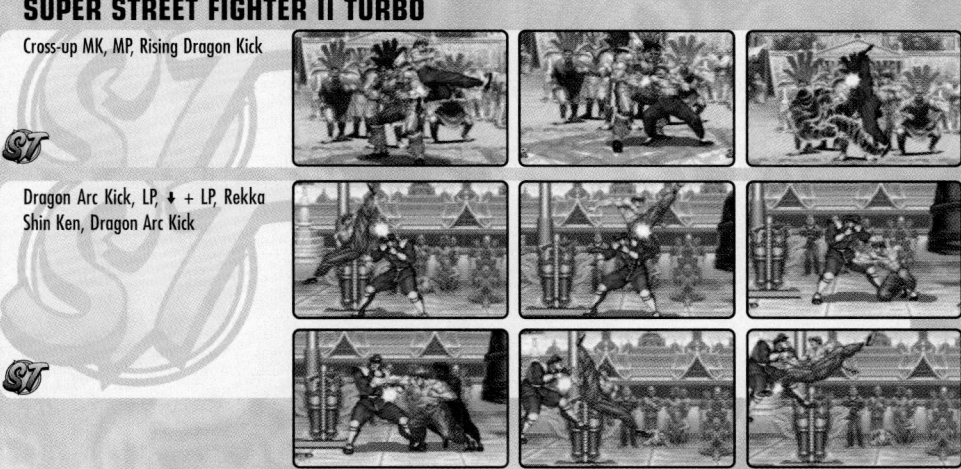

GOOD MATCH-UP

VS ZANGIEF

While it seems that Fei-Long's need to get close to opponents would hurt him against Zangief, his normal moves save the day. In particular, his standing HK and crouching HP. The standing HK will beat any jump-in that Zangief attempts, including his Body Splash. This prevents Zangief from setting up his Spinning Pile Driver, leaving him with his crouching HK and standing MK moves. Both of these moves can be harried by a crouching HP. Additionally, a whiffed crouching HK from Zangief can be punished by HP Rekka Kens.

BAD MATCH-UP

VS E. HONDA

This match heavily favors the Sumo wrestler due to Fei-Long's lack of viable offensive options. E. Honda's LP Headbutt can beat any of Fei-Long's jump-ins, including the Dragon Arc Kick (*Super Street Fighter II Turbo* only). This leaves only ground strings and Rekka Kens to rely on. E. Honda's defense is powerful against any character without a projectile. Try to bait HP Headbutts from E. Honda to make him jump backward to counter it. Crouching HP can also beat many of E. Honda's pokes, but it runs a serious risk of being hit by a Headbutt.

T. Hawk

STANDING

T. Hawk's normal moves are primarily poking moves that enable him to get in close to set up throw attempts with his Storm Hammer. Standing HK is good for punishing missed moves from far away, while the standing MP is useful for stopping or trading with projectile attempts.

STANDING CLOSE

Most of T. Hawk's close normals are useful for setting up throw attempts with his Storm Hammer and combos. Close LP, LK, and MK are excellent moves to force an opponent to block in order to throw them. Close MP and MK are the primary moves to combo into Thunderstrike to knock them down. Close MP is also a good anti-air against players who try cross-ups.

CROUCHING

T. Hawk's crouching normals compliment his standing normals as poking tools to frustrate an opponent and get closer. His crouching MP is probably his highest priority ground normal, trading with or beating a large number of attacks. Crouching MK is also good for trading with moves that crouching MP can't beat.

THROWS

Because T. Hawk has a more powerful special move for a throw, you may shy away from using his normal throws. His best throw is the HK version, because it's impossible to tech regardless of the version being played. In addition, it sets up perfectly for either a well-timed jump-in or ground poking game. If you decide to use a ground poking game, use his Storm Hammer or attempt a combo.

NORMAL MOVES

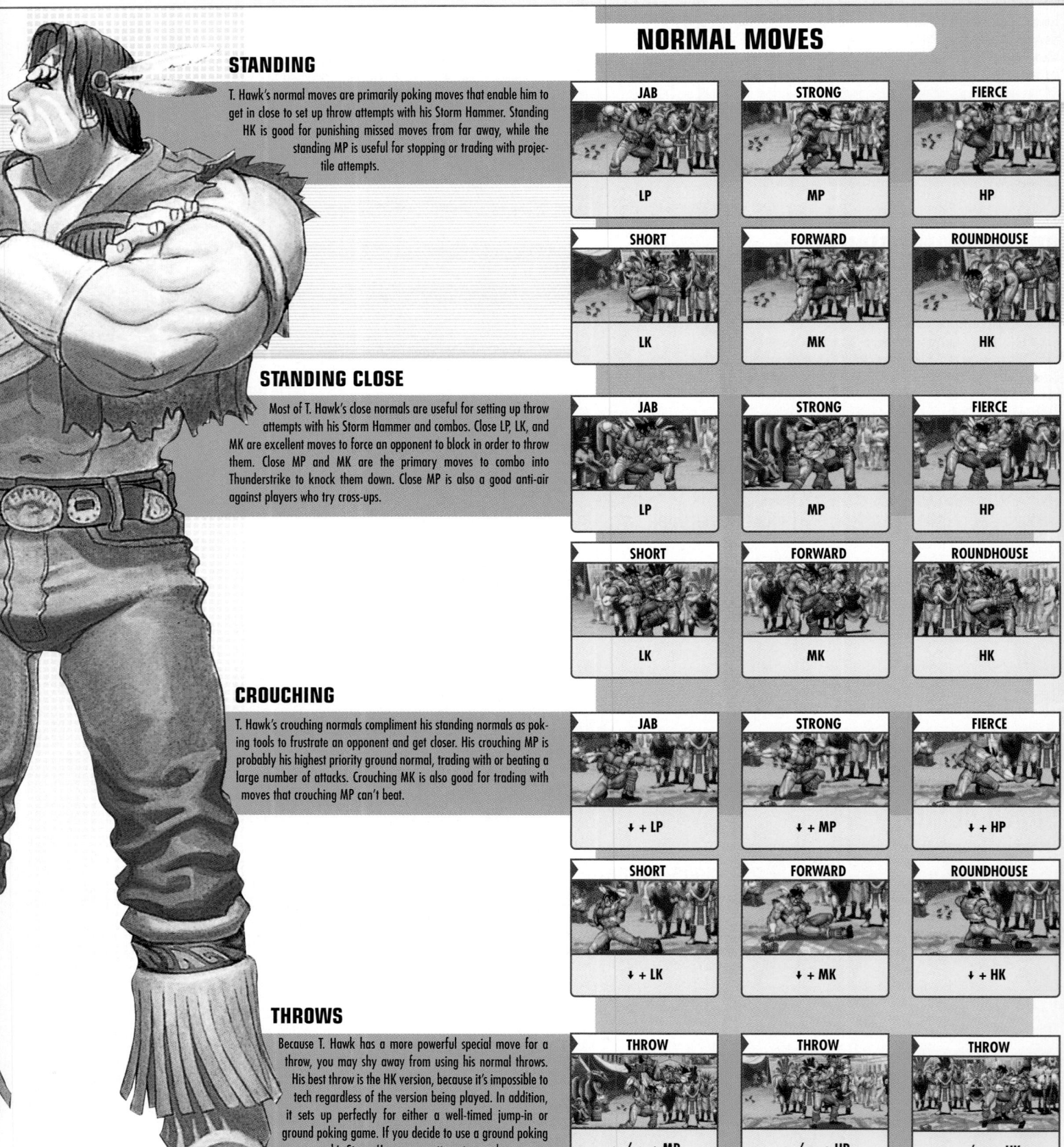

STANDING		
JAB — LP	STRONG — MP	FIERCE — HP
SHORT — LK	FORWARD — MK	ROUNDHOUSE — HK

STANDING CLOSE		
JAB — LP	STRONG — MP	FIERCE — HP
SHORT — LK	FORWARD — MK	ROUNDHOUSE — HK

CROUCHING		
JAB — ↓ + LP	STRONG — ↓ + MP	FIERCE — ↓ + HP
SHORT — ↓ + LK	FORWARD — ↓ + MK	ROUNDHOUSE — ↓ + HK

THROWS		
THROW — → / ← + MP	THROW — → / ← + HP	THROW — → / ← + HK

JUMPING

T. Hawk's best air move is his jumping LP. It stays out a long time, has great priority to trade or stop various air counters, and the move sets up his Storm Hammer perfectly. The only problem with his jump LP is that some characters have a perfect counter for it (i.e. the crouching MK of Cammy, M. Bison, and Blanka). In this case, jumping HP can be used to stop these attacks. T. Hawk's jumping MK is his primary cross-up attack. If you're playing the *Super Street Fighter II* version of T. Hawk, however, his Heavy Body Press will also cross-up.

JAB	JAB

↑ + LP	↖ / ↗ + LP

STRONG	STRONG

↑ + MP	↖ / ↗ + MP

FIERCE	FIERCE

↑ + HP	↖ / ↗ + HP

SHORT	SHORT

↑ + LK	↖ / ↗ + LK

FORWARD	FORWARD
↑ + MK	↖ / ↗ + MK

ROUNDHOUSE	ROUNDHOUSE
	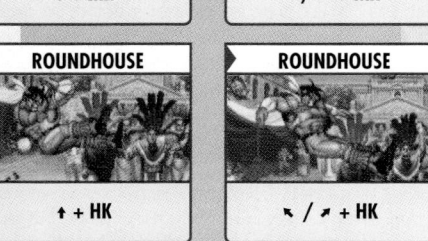
↑ + HK	↖ / ↗ + HK

SPECIAL NORMAL

In air, ↓ + HP   **Heavy Body Press**

T. Hawk's Body Press is the second best cross-up in the game, only trailing behind Zangief. This move is great for starting combos off with big damage, or putting your opponent in block stun, and forcing them to escape the Storm Hammer (Which is extremely hard to do). If the Body Press hits a crouching opponent, the window of opportunity is expanded, allowing you more time to connect a bigger combo.

SPECIAL MOVES

360 + P   **Storm Hammer**

T. Hawk's Storm Hammer is the most powerful non-super combo move in the game. Use it to punish whiffed moves and tick-throw after blocked normals (like his jumping LP, standing or crouching LP, or close MK). The range for this throw is not as good as Zangief's Spinning Piledriver, but there is no whiff animation, which makes this move a bit safer if you are too far away.

In air, all 3 Punch buttons   **The Hawk**

The Hawk can be a great suprise move. When used properly, it can punish projectiles (or other slow attacks) that have a longer delay. You can also use it after a Storm Hammer, and you can land right next to your opponent and set up another Storm Hammer attempt as they wake up.

→ ↓ ↘ + P   **Thunderstrike**

The Thunderstrike is T. Hawk's best anti-air move. It has decent priority and can be used as a wake-up reversal. It is even an option at close range to go through projectiles to hit an opponent. Avoid using the MP and HP versions of this move, except in combos. The reason being is that only the second hit of the move will knock down.

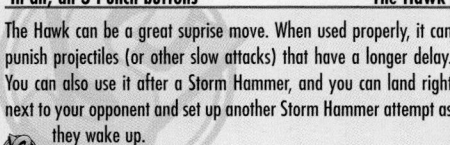

COSTUMES

LP

MP

HP

START

Hold any button

LK

MK

HK

SUPER STREET FIGHTER II

T. Hawk's primary strategy revolves around getting close to land his Storm Hammer. From further away, you can use his standing HK, standing MP, crouching MP, and MK to beat or trade with moves to make your opponent hesitate about sticking anything out. If an opponent is keeping you out with projectiles, use The Hawk move against slower ones, and jump straight over the quicker ones to advance close enough to use standing HK or standing MP. If your opponent doesn't have a good anti-air move, get in close and unleash T. Hawk's jumping LP to set up some throw attempts. The Thunderstrike is a good attack up close to knock down an opponent. After a knockdown, T. Hawk gains the advantage. Use cross-up MK or the Heavy Body Press, crouching LPs, crouching MP, and close standing MK against an opponent who is waking up to force them to block. Then you can go for tick throws with T. Hawk's Storm Hammer.

SUPER STREET FIGHTER II TURBO

T. Hawk's biggest addition to his arsenal is his super combo. Depleting about half of an opponent's life bar, this is the most powerful move in the entire game. His Heavy Body Press is now much more difficult to use as a cross-up, and it is impossible to use against some smaller characters. Also, his standing HK no longer hits crouching opponents.

COMBOS

SUPER STREET FIGHTER II

Cross-up MK, MP, HP Uphawk

In air, Cross-up ↓ + HP, ↓ + LP, MK, LP Uphawk

SUPER STREET FIGHTER II TURBO

Cross up MK, ↓ + MK, ↓ + LP, HP Uphawk

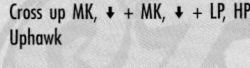   

Cross-up MK, ↓ + LP x 2, standing LP, LP Uphawk

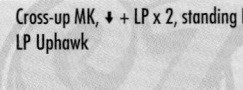   

SUPER COMBO

720 + P	Double Typhoon

With the Super Meter filled, use this move in place of any Storm Hammer for added damage. Like all super combos, your character is invincible at the beginning of the move and it's possible to tick-throw to make some nearly unescapable setups. It will grab a lot of reversal moves, including Tiger Uppercuts and Shoryukens!

GOOD MATCH-UP

VS CHUN-LI

Although T. Hawk doesn't have an advantage in this fight, it is much less of an uphill battle than a lot of other possible matches. With the exception of a properly timed Whirlwind Kick, Chun-Li will experience difficulty against T Hawk's jumping LP. Take advantage of this by performing the Storm Hammer. Ground to ground, Chun-Li's normals are faster and have more priority than T. Hawk's, so you may be limited to standing and crouching MP to attempt to trade or beat her moves. Be patient against her poking game and wait for an opportunity to tick-throw her. If you can get her in the corner with a knockdown, unleash repeated tick-throw attempts to make it difficult for her to escape.

BAD MATCH-UP

VS HONDA

Against a defensive-minded E. Honda player, T. Hawk will have a hard time causing much damage. T. Hawk cannot jump in or poke very well for fear that E. Honda's Headbutt will cause a lot of damage. Your best bet is to move close to E. Honda and bait a Headbutt from him that you can jump over and punish. If E. Honda isn't charged, go for the attack. Without his charge, he cannot defend against T. Hawk's jumping LP as well. Be careful with tick-throw attempts against the *Super Street Fighter II Turbo* version of E. Honda, though, because he has his own special move throw that can be used to reversal out of a tick-throw attempt. Try to space any tick attempts so that you are too far away for him to throw you, but you are still in range with T. Hawk's Storm Hammer. If you get the advantage in this fight, step back and take a more defensive approach. T. Hawk's crouching LP can stop offensive Headbutt attempts. If E. Honda tries a Sumo Splash , block it as he comes down and use the Storm Hammer when he lands. If he attempts to advance toward you, simply attack because he won't have his charge for his Headbutt.

Akuma

Akuma is the boss of all bosses and his power scares the most hardcore players. Because Akuma is a secret character and all of his moves have an unfair advantage, he is considered one of the best boss characters created for a fighting game. His Zanku Hadoken and Shakunetsu Hadoken moves are extremely powerful. Akuma can deplete almost 90% of your character's health bar with a single hit.

To select Akuma in battle, choose the Super T mode from the menu and let the cursor rest on Ryu for four seconds. Then move to T. Hawk for two seconds, then on to Guile for two seconds, then move it to Cammy for two seconds. Lastly, move the cursor back to Ryu for two more seconds. After doing so, press the START button and all three Punch buttons at the same time to make Ryu's picture turn completely black. This means you have successfully picked Akuma!

NORMAL MOVES

STANDING

Due to Akuma's great speed and the fact that he has the same normals as Ryu and Ken, his normals are twice as good!

JAB	STRONG	FIERCE
LP	MP	HP

SHORT	FORWARD	ROUNDHOUSE
LK	MK	HK

STANDING CLOSE

Akuma is very similar to Ryu when it comes to close normal moves. His close MK can be followed up with a special move, and his HK hits twice.

JAB	STRONG	FIERCE
LP	MP	HP

SHORT	FORWARD	ROUNDHOUSE
LK	MK	HK

CROUCHING

Akuma has the same basic crouching moves as Ryu. His crouching MK is good for two-in-ones. Crouching HK is great at knocking an opponent off his feet, plus the move is extremely fast.

JAB	STRONG	FIERCE
↓ + LP	↓ + MP	↓ + HP

SHORT	FORWARD	ROUNDHOUSE
↓ + LK	↓ + MK	↓ + HK

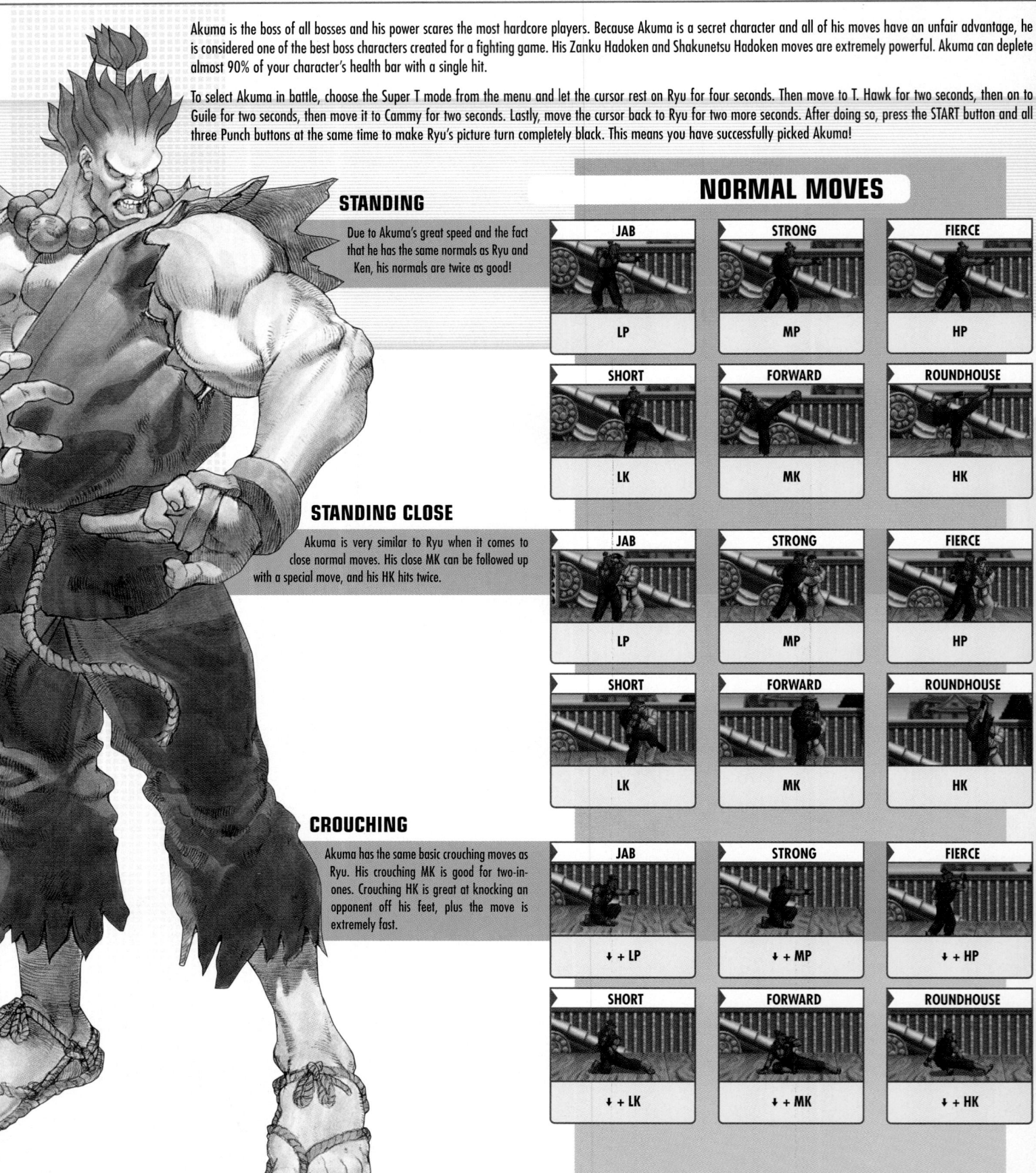

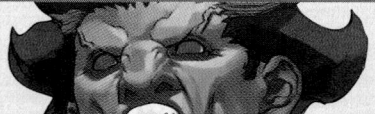

JUMPING

His air moves are somewhat standard. He doesn't really need anything, since he has the best air move in the game.

JAB	JAB
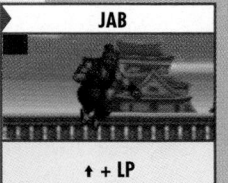	
↑ + LP	↗ / ↖ + LP
STRONG	STRONG
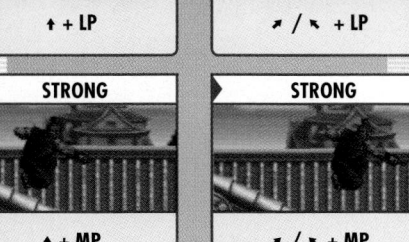	
↑ + MP	↗ / ↖ + MP
FIERCE	FIERCE

↑ + HP	↗ / ↖ + HP
SHORT	SHORT
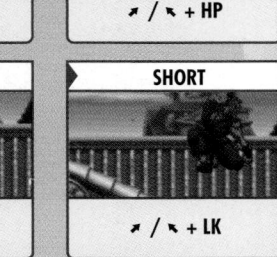	
↑ + LK	↗ / ↖ + LK
FORWARD	FORWARD

↑ + MK	↗ / ↖ + MK
ROUNDHOUSE	ROUNDHOUSE

↑ + HK	↗ / ↖ + HK

THROWS

Because Akuma has blinding speed, his throw game is ridiculous! He can lock down an opponent with his Zanku Hadoken or the Shakunetsu Hadoken, then swoop in for a quick throw.

THROW	THROW

→ / ← + MP / HP	→ / ← + MK / HK

SPECIAL MOVES

↓ ↘ → + Any P **Go Hadoken**

His Go Hadoken is unbelievably fast. This Hadoken comes out of nowhere and can take down its target in no time at all.

↓ ↙ ← + K **Tatsumaki Senpukyaku**

Akuma's Tatsumaki Senpukyaku is incredibly fast and it has juggle potential. You can link up to three hits in the air, with any combinations of Shoryukens or Tatsumaki Senpukyakus.

→ ↓ ↘ + P **Go Shoryuken**

Akuma's Go Shoryuken uppercut hits three times (like Ken's), but it does so with any Punch button. It also hits three times as an anti-air move.

← ↙ ↓ ↘ → + P **Shakunetsu Hadoken**

The infamous Shakunetsu Hadoken can knock down an opponent at any distance, plus it hits three times. This is one of two moves that Akuma has that makes him far superior to any character in the game. Since it has almost zero recovery time, this move can keep opponents permanently locked down.

In air, ↓ ↘ → + P **Zanku Hadoken**

This move is perhaps the most feared by opponents. This move puts any opponent into a blocking animation for at least three or four seconds, and it can trigger massive 8-hit combos.

COMBOS

SUPER STREET FIGHTER II TURBO

Jump in HK, ↓ + MK, HP Shakunetsu Hadoken

Cross-up HK, ↓ + MK, HK Tatsumaki Senpukyaku, LP Shoryuken

In air LP Zanku Hadoken, standing HP, Shakunetsu Hadoken

In air LP Zanku Hadoken, jump in HP, jump up HP Zanku Hadoken, ↓ + MP, standing MP, HK Tatsumaki Senpukyaku, MP Shoryuken

GLOSSARY OF TERMS

Before you dive into this comprehensive strategy guide, take a few minutes to read through this glossary of gaming terms. These terms are mentioned throughout the guide, so your familiarity with them is paramount.

360 MOTION

Spin the controller or joystick in a circle. Basically, only six consecutive points on the joystick (or controller) must be hit.

720 MOTION

Spin the controller or joystick in a circle twice. Basically, only 12 consecutive points on the joystick (or controller) must be hit.

ABSOLUTE GUARD

After blocking the first hit of a combo, the rest of the hits are blocked automatically. *Street Fighter III: 3rd Strike* is the first *Street Fighter* game to remove absolute guard.

AMBIGUOUS CROSS UP

A jumping attack that may or may not cross up. It should be executed in such a way as to confuse an opponent's ability to block on reaction.

ANTI AIR

A move used to attack a jumping opponent from the ground.

BAIT

To lure an opponent into attacking.

BLOCK

To successfully guard against an attack. Blocking can be done from a high or low position.

BLOCK STUN

The time in which a character is frozen on-screen after a move connects. The stronger the move, the longer the block stun. Opponents cannot be thrown during a block stun.

BUFFERING

To conceal the joystick and button presses of a move during the execution of another move. This makes cancels and certain combos easier to perform. It is also useful for "Psychic" moves that automatically come out only if the first move hits.

CANCEL

To interrupt an attack to begin a new attack before the first attack finishes. Only certain moves can be canceled. Generally, normal attacks can be canceled into special moves and super arts. Special moves can be canceled into super arts. This is crucial for multi-hit combos. It also has advanced applications.

CHAIN

A series of moves that connect or cancel into each other to form a combo.

CHARGE

Press in a direction (almost always ↓ or ←) for two seconds.

CHARGE PARTITIONING

A way to break up the charge times of a charge special move into pieces. This enables a character to be active while charging for a special move.

CHIP DAMAGE

Damage inflicted to opponents with a special attack or super art while they are blocking.

COMBO

A combination of attacks, special attacks, and super arts strung together to hit opponents in sequence before they leave hit stun.

CROSS UP

A method used to get on the other side of opponents. Any jumping attack that starts in front of an opponent then hits from behind is called a cross up. Opponents must block a cross up in the other direction, basically the direction in which they face.

COUNTER MASH

A defensive mash. Press the buttons repeatedly to reduce the number of hits on certain throws.

DAMAGE REDUCTION

Attacks inflict less damage than normal when they are part of a combo. The more hits in the combo, the less damage (a reduced amount of its standard damage) each additional move causes. Canceling and super canceling also decreases the damage of all the attacks that follow. Damage reduction resets after the combo is completed.

DIZZY

Synonymous with stun. When the stun bar gets maxed out, the character becomes paralyzed and cannot do anything until he gets hit or the dizzy state ends. Mash the buttons to reduce the amount of dizzy time.

DOUBLE TAPPING

Quickly pressing the same button twice in a row.

DRUMMING

Quickly pressing all three punch or kick buttons in succession.

EX

A faster, more powerful version of a special attack that usually causes more hits than the normal version. EX moves consume the Super Meter.

FOOT GAMES (FOOTSIES)

Fighting on the ground from a distance with low kick attacks. A big part of foot games is to bait opponents to attack while your character is out of range, then counter attack during their recovery from the whiffed move.

FRAME ADVANTAGE

The recovery of an attack is quick enough where your character can move or attack again before your opponent leaves hit/block stun.

GROUND CROSS UP

To cross up an opponent on the ground. In general, this is accomplished by dashing over an opponent's body as he or she quick recovers.

GUESSING GAME

Any situation that arises in which there is no way to know what an opponent will do, so you must make an educated guess.

HIGH ATTACK

An attack that must be blocked high but cannot be parried low.

HIT STUN

The time when opponents are paralyzed from being struck by an attack. They cannot move, block, or attack until the hit stun wears off. Opponents cannot be thrown during hit stun unless they have been turned around. Hit Stun is only present on an attack that does not knock down.

HIT VERIFICATION

Canceling or linking into the next move of a combo only after seeing that the first attack connects. You must verify that the next attack will combo before you do it.

JUGGLE

A combo that knocks an opponent into the air.

JUGGLE STATE

A state in which an opponent is susceptible to a hit by more juggles.

KARA CANCEL

A Japanese term that means "empty cancel." It is used to describe a situation in which you cancel out a normal attack into a special move before even seeing the normal attack come out. Usually used to gain extra range on special attacks, such as throws.

KNOCKDOWN

Opponents are hit or thrown to the ground. Opponents cannot be hit during a knockdown, with the exception of a few OTG situations.

LIFE BAR

The long bar at the top of the screen. Any hits taken decreases the life bar. When the life bar is depleted, that fighter loses the round.

LOW ATTACK

An attack that must be blocked low, but cannot be parried high.

MATCH RESET

When neither player has a positional advantage over the other.

MASH

To press the buttons repeatedly. This tactic is often used to gain extra hits for certain moves.

MEATY ATTACK

An attack that starts while an opponent is on the ground. The move stays out long enough to where the opponent gets up into the move while it is still hitting. This enables the attack to hit at a later time than it normally would. It is good for linking after the attack, thus making it difficult for opponents to execute a wakeup reversal.

METER

The long bar at the bottom of the screen that indicates the number of super arts that are available. The longer the meter, the more super arts and EX moves you can do. You can build the meter by whiffing moves, connecting with moves (hit or blocked), or by being hit.

MID ATTACK (MID-LEVEL ATTACK)

An attack that can be blocked high or low, and usually also parried high or low.

MIND GAMES

Anything from playing tricks on opponents, to forcing them into unfavorable situations in which they must guess. The opponent playing mind games is generally the one controlling the momentum of the match.

MIX UP

Any pattern or series of moves intended to confuse opponents and create an opening.

MOVE

(Used as a noun) Synonymous with attack. For example, a "special move" (a special attack).

NEGATIVE EDGE

Releasing a pressed button. It's possible to execute special attacks with the negative edge release of a button. For example, to execute a Hadouken with a negative edge button release, press punch, then ↓, ↘, → + release Punch. Negative edges are used to simplify complex input commands and make it easier to time a button press for a linked special attack or super art.

NEUTRAL POSITION

When the controller or joystick is in the center. Basically, when the joystick (or controller) isn't being pressed.

ON REACTION

Refers to the ability to react to something in time to either block/parry/execute a super art, etc.

OPTION PARRY

A type of option select. You cover your character with a parry before committing to a move.

OPTION SELECT
Inputting a command that covers your character for multiple situations. Usually used in situations in which guessing is involved.

OTG (OFF THE GROUND)
A combo that hits opponents even though they have already fallen to the ground.

OVERHEAD
An attack that hits high. It cannot be blocked or parried low.

PARRY
A technique that nullifies an opponent's attack and provides a short period of time to counter the attack. There are two types of parries: high and low. Proper parrying involves a lot of guesswork.

PERSONAL ACTION
HP +HK. Each character performs a personal action that gives him or her some sort of power-up. Also known as "taunting."

POKE
Usually a low attack, it is used to hit opponents from a distance.

PROJECTILE
An attack that travels independently from a character's body.

PSYCHIC
Any attack can be considered psychic if an opponent guesses at the right time and lands a hit. Only moves that can't be verified are usually considered psychic. Although highly risky, a psychic attack can really change the momentum of a match.

PUNISHMENT SITUATION
A situation in which an opponent is in the middle of a long recovery from an attack and is completely open, leaving himself open for a combo.

QUICK RECOVERY
Tap ↓ after a knockdown as soon as your character hits the ground. The character will roll backward and recover to his or her feet quicker than normal. This is good for retreating away from opponents after a knockdown. However, many characters are at risk to being crossed up on the ground during their quick recovery.

RECOVERY
All attacks take a certain amount of time after their hit phase to finish before a character can move, block, or attack again. This is known as "recovery." Recovery is also used to describe when a character gets back to his or her feet.

RED PARRY
A variation of a parry that can only be done when a character is in block stun. The absence of absolute guard in *Street Fighter III: 3rd Strike* enables characters to leave block stun during a combo and red parry the next attack.

RESET
A situation in which you finish a combo with a move that knocks opponents back to their feet. You can usually start a new combo before the opponent hits the ground, thus resetting the combo. Resets are also used to create ambiguous cross up situations.

REVERSAL
To perform a special move or super art at the first opportunity after being knocked down, or after coming out of block stun.

SHOTO
Short for Shotokan. Used to describe the character types of Ryu, Ken, and Akuma.

STOCK
A term used to describe a sufficient amount of meter for a super art.

STUN
Synonymous with dizzy. When the stun bar gets maxed out, the character is paralyzed and cannot do anything until hit, or the stun state ends. Mash the buttons to reduce the amount of time stunned.

STUN BAR
The smaller bar under the life bar. Each hit taken increases the stun bar. When the stun bar gets maxed out, the character becomes stunned and cannot do anything for a brief time. The stun bar gradually decreases on its own.

SUPER ART
Sometimes known simply as "super." Every character has at least three super arts. These moves, which require complex joystick and button inputs, are usually a character's most powerful attack. You must have a full super meter to use them.

SUPER JUMP CANCEL (SJC)
To cancel an attack into a super jump. To do so, press the button for the normal attack, then quickly tap ↓ ↑. Only a certain few normal attacks, special moves, and super arts can be super jump canceled.

TARGET CHAIN
A series of chainable moves that is a pre-set combo.

TECH
To escape a throw attempt.

TICK
A quick move used to set up a throw or any other tricky maneuver. The "ticked" move is usually blocked.

TRIP GUARD
When characters jump they can block the moment they land, provided they did not attack while in the air. This is called trip guard. Any parry that occurs while either player is in the air resets trip guard.

TURNED AROUND STATE
Certain attacks hit opponents and turn their bodies around so that their backs face your fighter. This is the only time in which you can throw an opponent in hit stun.

UNBLOCKABLE
Two attacks with overlapping hit boxes cause a situation in which you cannot block both attacks at the same time, thereby causing an unblockable situation. Unblockables are guaranteed hits unless parried, or an invulnerable move is used to escape it.

UNIVERSAL OVERHEAD (UOH)
An overhead attack that is universally available to all characters. In general, press MP + MK. Each character's UOH is shown at the start of his or her strategy section.

WAKEUP
The time in which opponents get off the ground.

WAKEUP SUPER
An opponent performs a reversal super the moment he or she gets off the ground.

WHIFF
When a move does not connect with an opponent. Sometimes whiffing an attack is useful for building the super meter or setting up another attack. Whiffed moves also tend to be vulnerable to counter attack on their recovery.

ZONE (ZONING)
(Used as a verb). To control space and keep your character at a distance so that you can dictate the flow of the match.

CONVENTIONS

QCF
Quarter circle forward (↓ ↘ →)

QCB
Quarter circle back (↓ ↙ ←)

HCF
Half circle forward (← ↙ ↓ ↘ →)

HCB
Half circle back (→ ↘ ↓ ↙ ←)

JAB
Least damaging punch button - LP

STRONG
Medium damage punch button - MP

FIERCE
Most damaging punch button - HP

SHORT
Least damaging kick button - LK

FORWARD
Medium damage kick button - MK

ROUNDHOUSE
Most damaging kick button - HK

+
Used to show an action occurs at the same time. For example, ← + MP means to tap back on the controller and press MP at the same time.

→
Used to show a sequence of events, most often for combo explanations. For example, X → Y either means X is canceled into Y, or that Y happens immediately after X finishes if X is not a cancelable move.

Basic Universal Tactics

COMMAND INPUTS

ALL COMMANDS IN THIS GUIDE ARE PRESENTED WITH THE ASSUMPTION THAT THE FIGHTER IS FACING TO THE PLAYER'S RIGHT, THE DIRECTION THE 1P FIGHTER FACES WHEN A ROUND BEGINS.

FORWARD DASH

→ →

Tapping forward twice makes your character perform a forward dash. Dashes are effective for quickly closing distances. Each character's dash has different speeds and properties, including start-up, overall travel time, and recovery period at the end of the dash.

BACKWARD DASH

← ←

Quickly tapping back twice makes your character do a retreating dash. If you need to create space between your fighter and the opponent, start back dashing. Some characters have back dashes that are designed to be effective up close. Ryu's back dash covers an extremely short distance. Use this to your advantage, as he can back dash out of an opponent's throw range. After the throw whiffs, punish the opponent with a combo. Each character has a different back dash; learn each one's strengths and weaknesses.

JUMP

↖ / ↑ / ↗

Pressing Up makes a character jump. You can jump toward (press ↗) an opponent or backward (press ↖). The jump is a very daring choice in *Street Fighter*. Although it's commonly the first thing lots of people choose to do in an attempt to be on the offensive, most characters have multiple anti-air options they can use to deal damage for jumping. Even with the parry, jumping is never safe. An opponent can vary which anti-air options they use and do other tricks to throw off your parry timing during a jump and score free damage. It's very important to experiment and determine when to jump to minimize the risk involved in jumping.

JUMPING/CROUCHING SHORTHAND

FOR MOVES INVOLVING A JUMP, IF ONLY ↑ IS LISTED, THEN THE SAME ATTACK EMERGES FROM ↖ AND ↗ AS ↑.

THE SAME HOLDS TRUE OF CROUCHING. IF ONLY ↓ IS LISTED, THEN ENTERING ↙ OR ↘ SHOULD PERFORM THE SAME MOVE.

EXCEPTIONS TO THE ABOVE ARE NOTED IN EACH CHARACTER'S LIST OF MOVES.

SUPER JUMP

↓ ↑

A jump that covers more distance, both vertical and horizontal. Super jumps are easier to use in cross ups and when jumping over projectiles.

BLOCKING

← vs. standing or jumping attacks

↙ vs. low attacks

The basic defense against an opponent's attacks. Blocking makes fighters immune to normal attacks. While blocking an attack, fighters go into a state called "block stun." During this condition, the character is helpless so he/she can only block or red parry. The stronger the attack, the longer block stun lasts.

Blocking has two major weaknesses. First, special attacks still inflict some damage if blocked (damage is reduced by more than 90%). Second, throws cannot be blocked. Knowing when to block is key to taking less damage in tight situations. Learn to watch for overheads and throw attempts while blocking low to reduce the overall damage taken when opponents are close.

PARRY

→ vs. high attacks, or while in the air

↓ vs. low attacks

Parrying is a new technique introduced in *Street Fighter III*. It is an offensive maneuver that nullifies an attack and provides a brief period of time to counter opponents before they recover from their move. Many mid-level attacks can be parried either high or low. The controller must come from the neutral position before inputting the parry command. You cannot mash in a direction, trying to parry all the time. The controller must return to neutral and stay there for a fraction of a second before you can attempt another parry.

You take no damage from parrying an attack. You get frame advantage to hit opponents while they are caught in the recovery of their move. The weaker the attack, the more frame advantage you have before they start to recover. The parry input must be done a split second before their move is going to hit your fighter.

Parrying is a high risk, high gain maneuver. There are low and high attacks on the ground, and you can only attempt a parry in one direction at a time. If you guess correctly and parry an opponent's attack, you have the opportunity to land a big combo. However, if you guess wrong, your character will take damage from their attack, which could lead to a big combo. Parrying is a tactic that can change the momentum of a match in a big way. Use it strategically; sometimes the risk is worth the reward. Sometimes, however, it's better just to block. Consider the consequences before attempting a parry.

You can also parry while in the air. Any parry that occurs when either fighter is in the air resets the trip guard. An attempted parry in the air that does nothing because your opponent did not attack does *not* affect trip guard.

Street Fighter 3rd Strike also introduces red parries. A red parry is a parry that comes from a block stun. Red parries are possible because *Street Fighter 3rd Strike* does not have absolute guard. In most other SF games, when you block a combo, even if you release the joystick after the first hit, the rest of the combo hits are blocked automatically. However, in *Street Fighter 3rd Strike*, if you release the joystick your character will start to get hit. The absence of absolute guard creates the option to stop blocking in the middle of a combo. The only options at this point are to either get hit by the next combo hit, or interrupt the opponent's combo with a red parry. While blocking, wait for a space between the hits of the attack string, then return the stick to neutral, then input a parry in the proper direction before the next hit. When timed correctly, your character will stop blocking and flash red as you parry the next hit that you normally would have blocked. Red parrying is useful for parrying multi-hit moves, or for attack sequences in which you are fairly confident you know what will come next.

THROW

LP + LK

Pressing LP + LK next to an opponent makes your character execute a throw, inflicting a decent amount of damage and stun damage. Throws cannot be blocked, making them ideal to use against blocking opponents. Normal throws are very fast, coming out in three frames, so they can sometimes seem unbeatable at certain ranges.

There are a variety of ways to counter throws. "Teching" the throw is one option. Another simple way to offset a throw is to jump straight up just as an opponent tries to throw, which should enable you to avoid it completely. Throws also cannot offset any normal attack with a three-frame start up. If a normal attack and a throw come out at the exact same time, a normal attack always wins.

Also remember that most throws don't have great range, meaning you can back out of throw range to make it impossible to land. Throws will also never defeat meaty attacks on wake up, or most moves with invincibility. Regardless, throws are a major part of mix up games in *Street Fighter III*. When close to an opponent, mix in a throw when you think the opponent will block. Then use attacks when you think your adversary will attempt to tech a throw attempt. Add them to your close-range gameplan and force your opponent to guess.

TECH THROWS

LP + LK immediately upon being thrown

When an opponent attempts to throw your fighter, press LP + LK when they activate the throw to counter it. The result is that both players bounce away from each other and take no damage.

QUICK RECOVERY

↓ upon touching the ground after a knockdown

Quick recovery makes characters immediately roll backward and stand up after they have been knocked down. This is helpful for keeping opponents from maneuvering into a potentially dangerous position. Your fighter is completely invulnerable during a quick recovery. The only weakness in this situation is that many characters can dash through an opponent's body during a quick recovery. This enables opponents to dash behind your character and attack on wake up, which can be very difficult to block. However, only certain characters can do this against a very specific set of characters.

UNIVERSAL OVERHEAD (UOH)

MP + MK

This is an overhead attack available to each character. These attacks come out quickly and are helpful in setting up guessing games. However, they can leave your fighter susceptible to damage if done too close to an opponent. By performing one on wake-up (or from farther away so it hits on a later frame than normal), you kill the recovery and get a significant amount of frame advantage. This allows for linked super arts or other attacks. This is great for wake up mix-up games, since this gives your character a potential to cause damage with an overhead. However, attempting a UOH early enough to get frame advantage makes the overhead more noticeable and easier to block.

PERSONAL ACTIONS

HP + HK

Personal actions are basically character-specific taunts. There are other benefits to performing them, outside of looking cool and boosting your super meter.

PERSONAL ACTIONS BREAKDOWN

AKUMA

Akuma's attack power and stun damage increase.

ALEX

Alex's attack power increases. Pressing and holding HP + HK keeps Alex in his taunt stance, which builds his attack power to a specific limit. Performing the taunt repeatedly builds attack power, maxing out after the fourth taunt.

CHUN-LI

The bonuses Chun-Li receives depend upon the type of taunt she performs. Chun-Li has four variations to her taunt:

> When she yawns, Chun-Li's stun gauge recovery rate increases. This can be stacks up to three times.
>
> When she cracks her neck, Chun-Li's attack power increases for all attacks *except* for throws.
>
> When she pats her shoulder, Chun-Li gets a defense increase.
>
> When she arches forward, Chun-Li gets an attack and defense power increase.

DUDLEY

Dudley gets an attack power increase while tossing a rose into the air that zeroes in his opponent. Dudley will end up holding a rose if additional taunt attempts are tried before the first rose disappears from the screen. In this case, Dudley still gets an attack increase but no super meter increase.

ELENA

Elena gets a stun damage increase. The stun damage increase stacks up to a total of four times.

GILL

Gill gets an attack power increase.

HUGO

Hugo gets an attack power bonus for all attacks *except* for throws. While holding HP + HK, he performs a taunt that increases throw damage. Any time a taunt is performed, Hugo gets an additional defense bonus, which stacks up to times.

IBUKI

Ibuki leaps toward her opponent and, when it connects, she leapfrogs over her opponent and gets an attack increase. Ibuki does not receive the bonus if the taunt does not hit.

KEN

Ken receives an attack power increase for all of his attacks *except* for throws. Ken's taunt also hits twice, although the hits do not combo.

MAKOTO

Makoto's taunt has three segments. Taunting once is the first segment and holding HP+ HK after the first taunt leads to additional taunts (if the buttons are held down long enough). The first taunt hits once for minor damage and gives Makoto an attack power and stun gauge recovery increase. The second gives Makoto another attack power and stun gauge recovery increase. The third taunt gives Makoto another stun gauge recovery increase.

NECRO

Necro receives an attack power increase for all of his attacks *except* for throws. Hold it down to make Necro continue to flail his tongue.

ORO

Oro's stun gauge is lowered slightly. Hold down the buttons to gradually lower his stun gauge.

Q

Q gets a defense bonus for the rest of the round. This bonus stacks up to three times.

REMY

Increases Remy's stun damage. Stacks up to four times.

RYU

Increases Ryu's stun gauge recovery rate. Stacks up to three times.

SEAN

Sean throws a basketball that zeroes in on his opponent. When it hits, Sean gets a stun damage increase, which stacks up to three times. The basketball must hit each time for Sean to receive the stun damage increase.

TWELVE

Twelve disappears a limited period of time during his personal action. When hit Twelve reappears, blocks an attack, throws his opponent, or performs a super art. Taunting while invisible also makes Twelve reappear.

URIEN

Urien gets an attack power increase. Strangely enough, if the taunt hits an opponent, Urien does *not* receive the attack power bonus.

YANG

Yang gets an attack power increase, but his throws only receive one point of increased damage. Yang's taunt also hits opponents.

YUN

Yun's spinning hat can hit on every rotation. He gets a full attack increase for all of his special attacks, and a minor increase for throws, normal, and special attacks. Hold HP + HK to make Yun continue to spin his hat, which gradually increases his overall attack power. Taunting eight separate times has the same effect.

UNIVERSAL CHARACTER ABILITIES

This section covers the universal character abilities.

SPECIAL ATTACKS

Special attacks range from projectiles to multi-hit punch attacks that are great for combos. Learn each character's special attack commands to perform them smoothly and swiftly.

EX SPECIAL ATTACKS

These attacks are alternate, upgraded versions of a character's special attacks. To perform an EX attack, press two punch or kick buttons (depending on the special attack) instead of one. Performing an EX move depletes a certain amount of super meter, but it is worth the cost. Many EX special attacks are vastly superior to the original. They are so much better, in fact, that it's possible to base some characters (like Ryu) entire game around EX special attacks.

SUPER ARTS

All characters have three super arts and you can choose one before each round. Super arts have varying super meter sizes and stock amounts. Super art selection changes the way any particular character is played, so choose the super art that best fits your style of play.

STUN GAUGE

There is a second bar under a fighter's life bar. Each time a fighter gets hit, the bar fills slightly. When it fills up, the character falls over and gets up in a "dizzy state." During this time, the fighter is completely vulnerable to attacks. When your character is dizzy, wiggle the controller while mashing buttons to escape from dizzy state. Learn to keep an eye on your character's stun gauge and defend yourself if it's high. Experiment and determine which combos and attacks cause the most stun damage so that you can dizzy opponents when the opportunity arises.

COMBO SYSTEM

Combos are a combination of a character's attacks, special attacks, and super arts strung together to form an inescapable string of attacks. Some combos are flexible, safe ways to cause damage in situations where an attack is not always guaranteed. Others combos are good for when an opponent is completely open to attack, possibly inflicting enough damage in one shot to end the round. Learning each character's most important combos—and when they are most useful—is an important part of being successful in *Street Fighter III*.

When a character gets hit by an attack that does not knock down, he or she goes into a short period of recovery known as hit stun. During this time, a character cannot move, attack, or defend until this window of recovery ends. It's possible to attack opponents before they leave this recovery and the end result is a combo.

Because the period of time for hit stun is usually short, you can't simply follow attacks one after the other to form a combo. A variety of methods exist in creating combos, each of which have different uses. It's important to learn all of these methods to deal the maximum amount of damage while still being safe from attack.

COMBO TYPES

CHAIN COMBOS

Chains are combos that use normal attacks that are "canceled" into each other. The reason why chain combos work is because you're canceling the recovery of the first normal attack into a second normal attack, just before opponents leave hit stun. The cancelled attack should never fully animate; the next attack in the chain should come out almost immediately after the first attack hits. Most chains consist of repeated jabs or shorts strung together, like crouching short → crouching short with Ken or Ryu. However, a specific type of chain, called a target combo, usually consists of a variety of normal attacks.

TARGET COMBOS

Target combos are character specific; no two characters have the same target combo. Target combos work in the same manner as chain combos, so they are often referred to as target chains, or simply chain combos.

Example: Select Ken and stand next to an opponent. Perform a close standing MP, then execute a HP just as it hits. When timed correctly, Ken should immediately go straight into a standing fierce after the MP hits without going into a recovery animation.

Target combos are specific and only work with a small set of normal attacks. Some characters only have one or two chains—others don't have any!

LINK COMBOS

Links are the opposite of chain combos. You are not canceling the recovery of an attack, instead, the starting attack hits the opponent and recovers *before* the opponent leaves hit stun. This enables you to "link" another attack after it. In essence, the recovery from executing the attack is shorter than recovering from being hit by it.

For a link to work, the first hit must have a significant amount of frame advantage after it, and the second attack must come out fast enough to hit an opponent while he or she is still in hit stun. The window of time to link an attack after another is short. So, since you must wait for the first attack to recover before following up, the timing for links is vastly different.

Although difficult to execute, links are useful for one big reason: verification. Because the starting attack must recover completely before you can link an attack after it, the recovery of that normal attack can be observed. This enables you to decide on whether or not to finish the combo. In *Street Fighter III*, this is known as "verification," which is important when it comes to landing specific super arts.

Example: Ken has a significant amount of frame advantage after his crouching strong hits. Although he doesn't have any normal attacks fast enough to take advantage of this, Shippuu-jinrai-kyaku comes out fast enough to link into it. Ken's crouching strong recovery can be observed before committing to linking into his super art. If the low strong hits, go straight into Shippuu-jinrai-kyaku. If the low strong is blocked, there's no need to do the super art, which leaves Ken wide open when blocked.

The ability to verify attacks before launching another attack keeps your combos safe, plus it prevents you from giving opponents any easy openings. The same idea applies to some chains as well, as chains with multiple hits and cancelable endings can be used to verify attacks before canceling into a special attack or super art.

JUGGLES

Many attacks knock opponents into the air. When this occurs, it's possible to hit an opponent again as he or she falls from these attacks. This is what is known as a "juggle."

Example: Select Ryu and perform an EX Joudan Sokuto Geri. After this attack hits—and just after the opponent bounces off the wall—perform a Shoryuken (HP) to juggle your adversary.

The number of attacks that put opponents into a "juggle state" (and sometimes what is available to continue the juggle) are limited. Juggles often lead to a large amount of damage. This makes them important for combos, because they can be started in a variety of positions—not just during a ground-based combo.

CANCEL

After specific normal attacks hit, it's possible to cut off the recovery and go straight into a special attack or super art. This is called a "cancel." This is one of the most basic and classic combo types in every *Street Fighter* game. For a cancel to work, you must complete the motion for the special attack just as your chosen normal attack hits. When done correctly, the normal attack does not finish its recovery, but instead cuts off and goes into the special attack or super art.

Example: Select Ryu and perform a low MK and, just as it hits, input the command for Hadouken (HP). When done correctly, the crouching forward should cancel directly into the Hadouken, resulting in a two-hit combo.

Not all normal attacks are cancelable; some are only cancelable into super arts. It's important to know what normals can cancel into a special attack and which special attacks are best suited for canceling.

SUPER CANCEL

Some special attacks can be canceled into a super art after they hit. This is great for additional damage in combos. It works just like a normal cancel: Perform a super cancelable special attack, then input a super art as the special attack hits.

Example: Select Makoto and Seichuu-godan-zuki. Position her next to the opponent and perform an Oroshi (LP). As the overhead chop connects, quickly input the super art. The motion must finish for the super as the Orochi connects. When done correctly, the overhead chop should cancel directly into the super art.

Although some super cancels can add damage to a combo, some super cancels might cause less damage than if you were to cancel directly into a super. Super cancels have an interesting property that can help with execution. It's possible to use the motion from a previous special attack within the super attack motion.

Example: Select Ryu and Shinkuu-hadouken. Perform Hadouken (HP), then as the Hadouken hits, input ↓ ↘ → + HP. When timed correctly, the Hadouken should cancel directly into a Shinkuu Hadouken. This only works if the special attack you're canceling from and the super art you're canceling into have similar input motions. For instances in which the motions are not similar, do the full super art command when the special attack hits. Still, this shortcut method can be helpful for making a variety of combos easier.

BUILDING EFFECTIVE COMBOS

Now that you know what's possible, combine all of these elements and build combos that are effective for gameplay. Some combos should be built on the basis of flexibility, whether it's verifiable, safe if blocked, or it can't be parried both high and low. Other combos are purely for maximum damage output. It may not be safe, but if you get an opening it's worth trying. Note that the combo that can cause the most damage probably doesn't fit into both the flexible and most powerful categories. It's important to build multiple combos that are good for every situation.

Experiment and have fun!

Advanced Universal Tactics

KARA CANCELING

Street Fighter games are lenient on coordinating joystick motions and button presses in order to execute special moves. For example, the command for a Hadouken is ↓ ↘ → + (any punch button). However, you do not have to press punch and → at the same exact moment. Pressing punch early (at ↘ instead of →), it is still possible to execute a Hadouken. At first, the game registers ↘ + punch, which starts the animation of a crouching punch. By quickly rolling the controller to → and finishing the Hadouken's input, the game engine cancels out the low punch in its early frames. This happens so fast that you may not see the punch come out in front of the Hadouken. This feature makes executing complex special moves easier.

However, this feature can be used in another way. If you cancel out a normal attack that moves your character forward in its very first frames, then the special move that cancels out the normal attack will start from your character's new position. Use this cancelling property to move your character forward in order to gain extra range on special attacks.

ADVANCED APPLICATION 1: KARA THROWING

You can cancel out any normal attack with a throw because a throw is considered a special attack. Find a move that moves your character forward in its first few frames, then quickly press LP + LK to cancel that move and execute a throw.

Here is a list of each character's best kara throw moves:

AKUMA: → + MP	DUDLEY: → + LK	IBUKI: MK	ORO: MK	RYU: → + MP	URIEN: NONE
ALEX: → + HP	ELENA: → + MK	MAKOTO: LK	Q: ← + MP	SEAN: → + HP	YANG: HK
CHUN LI: MK	HUGO: MK	NECRO: MP	REMY: MP, HK	TWELVE: MP	YUN: LK

There is one disadvantage to kara throwing. The start up time for the throw is slightly greater than normal throw. If you are in range for a normal throw attempt, there is no reason to kara throw. Only use kara throws when you are outside of normal throw range.

ADVANCED APPLICATION 2: KARA UNIVERSAL OVERHEAD

Universal Overhead (UOH) attacks are also considered special moves, so they also make use of kara canceling. Do a normal attack that moves your character forward, then cancel it out in its first few frames by pressing MP + MK.

Many characters kara cancel with either MP or MK. In order to execute a kara UOH in this case, you must negative edge the button pressed for the kara canceled move. For example, Chun Li's kara cancel is with MK. To execute a kara UOH with Chun Li, you must press MK, then negative edge MP + MK.

Any characters that require a directional input to execute their kara-canceled move must release the controller before pressing MP + MK. For example, for Ryu to kara UOH, he must press → + MP, then reset to neutral, then input (negative edge) MP + MK. A UOH can only be executed when the controller is in the neutral position.

THROW TECH DEFENSE

There are two ways to defend, or 'tech', against being thrown. The first way is if both characters attempt to throw at the same time. In order for this to happen, both characters must be standing and within their respective throw ranges. If this happens, both tech the throw and neither player lands a throw.

The other way to tech a throw is to press LP + LK within the first few frames of being thrown by an opponent. This option does not require you to stand up, which makes your character vulnerable to low attacks. Also, you can input the throw tech attempt later than the other method, thus giving you more time to react to any throw attempts. By using this method, you never need to stand up to tech a throw again. You can continue to block low, which is generally safe, and tech after being thrown.

ADVANCED APPLICATION 3: KARA SPECIAL MOVES

Kara canceling can also be used to add range to certain special moves. The controller motions to achieve this vary according to each attack. Generally, you input as much of the special command as possible, input the normal attack on the *second to last* controller motion, then kara cancel it with the final controller input + button press.

If you anticipate incorrectly, and your opponent doesn't try to throw, your character's low jab will come out when you press LP + LK from ↙. Low jab is generally a fast move, so it's a good choice from close proximity. Positioning from ↙ is usually the safest way to tech throws while simultaneously defending against low attacks.

However, this method has one drawback. If you anticipate a throw correctly, and press LP + LK from ↙ *at the same time* that an opponent tries to throw, expect to be thrown. This is because low jab does not execute quickly enough to beat the throw. (Chun Li is the only exception to this, because her low jab comes out fast enough to beat throws.) In order to tech throws safely from ↙, you must wait until after being grabbed, then quickly press LP + LK.

CROSS UP

A way to hit your opponent from behind.

JUMPING CROSS UP

A jumping attack that hits opponents from behind. Your fighter jumps over their head and hits from behind, then lands behind them. Crossing up is a great way to confuse an opponent's blocking.

GROUND CROSS UP

A way to cross up on the ground. This is generally done by dashing over fallen opponents as they quick recover. Many characters have dashes that are considered airborne for a brief period. Use this property to go over opponents while they are rolling during their quick recovery.

CHARGE PARTITIONING

Charge Partitioning is the ability to split up the charge times for some special moves. As long as you aren't fully charged, it's possible to charge a fraction of the total charge time, then move around or do a move quickly, before you resume charging. Splitting up the charge into several pieces achieves some interesting results. This technique allows many charge-based characters to move around and remain active while also charging for their special moves. This helps out a great deal, because without this technique, most characters are forced to sit back and charge ↓ or ← or ↙ while waiting for the charge to complete. With charge partitioning, these fighters can actively fight and still manage to build up a charge.

ADVANCED TECHNIQUE 1:
BUFFERING

Buffering is the idea of carrying over the controller inputs and button presses of one move in the execution of another move. This is extremely important for basic combos that involve canceling. For instance, in order to do ↓ + MK → super art with Ken, you must cancel the ↓ + MK before a certain point in the move's animation. As soon as you input ↓ + MK, immediately begin the doubled QCF motion while the ↓ + MK is hitting, then press P on the second →.

Buffering is also extremely helpful with the timing of links and late cancels. For instance, Ken can link a Shippu-Jinrai-Kyaku after a ↓ + MP if it hits. You can do the ↓ + MP, and start to buffer the QCF (x2) during the execution of the punch. Time the second QCF motion to coincide with the moment Ken fully recovers from ↓ + MP. If the move hits, press kick to link the super art. If the punch doesn't hit, don't press kick. The idea is to do the super art motion during the move to prepare for the possible hit and link. This makes doing links and late cancels much easier.

Buffering can also be used for "psychic" moves. For instance, Ken sticks out ↓ + MK from a distance where it normally would whiff. Buffer the QCF (x2) super art motion during the execution of ↓ + MK. As long as the move is out of range and whiffs, the super art will not come out if you complete QCF (x2) + K before ↓ + MK recovers. If you time it correctly, the super art comes only if the move being done hits an opponent. This allows you to set up a 'psychic' situation where the super art comes out automatically only on a hit. Position your fighter outside of the move's maximum range; do the move and buffer the super art motion. If the opponent does anything to run into the move, such as dashing or poking with a low attack, the attack automatically cancels into the super art. This is a good and generally safe way to cancel into super arts via low attacks that are too fast to cancel on reaction to a hit.

ADVANCED TECHNIQUE 2:
NEGATIVE EDGE

It is possible to execute special attacks with the negative edge release of a button. For example, to execute a Hadouken with a negative edge button release, press punch, then ↓ ↘ → + (release punch). Negative edges are used to simplify complex input commands and make it easier to time a button press for a linked special attack or super art. Negative edges go hand and hand with the button drumming technique to make timing a link much easier. Also, certain kara cancels can only be done with a negative edge button release.

ADVANCED TECHNIQUE 3:
DRUMMING

Drumming the buttons means pressing all three punch (or kick) buttons in succession. This is very handy when trying to get the timing correct for a linked super art. Instead of trying to press one button at the precise, required moment, you can drum all three buttons to give yourself more time to hit the button press at the proper moment. Drumming all three buttons gives you three chances to hit the button at the right time. You can take this a step further and negative edge all of the button presses in series after drumming the buttons. For example, if the move you are trying to time correctly is with punch, you press in sequence: LP, MP, HP, then release LP, MP, HP. This technique provides six chances to score a button press at the proper time. You can start early and end late, in effect covering all possible times so that you will get the super art to come out every time. This technique is useful for hard-to-time links, such as Ken's Inazuma Kakato Wari linked into Shippu-jinrai-kyaku.

ADVANCED TECHNIQUE 4:
DOUBLE TAPPING

Double tapping is a very simple technique. It is done for the same reason as drumming the buttons—to make sure you hit the button at the right time. Every time you press a button, press it with one finger, then immediately use a second finger to press it again really quickly. This gives you two chances to hit the button at the proper time to input whatever move you are trying to do.

ADVANCED APPLICATION:
SUPER JUMP CANCEL.

Certain characters can cancel a normal attack into a super jump, and before they leave the ground, cancel the first frames of the super jump into a super art. This allows attacks that normally cannot be super canceled to link into super arts. Also, because no special cancel or super cancel is used, there are no damage reduction effects from canceling involved in the combo to follow.

ADVANCED TECHNIQUES

ADVANCED EXECUTION TECHNIQUES

There are many controller input and button pressing techniques that you can use to improve your game play and help you to execute some of the advanced techniques easier.

FRAME ADVANTAGE

Every attack comes out in a certain number of frames. When the attack connects, it also has a certain number of frames of recovery before you can move/block/attack again. If you can move before opponents can, then the move has what is called frame advantage. If your opponent can move/block/attack before you can, then the move has what is called frame disadvantage. There are two different types of frame advantage: hit advantage and blocked advantage.

Hit advantage is how much frame advantage you have when a move hits opponents. If a move has a large hit advantage, then you recover from your move and are able to attack again while they are still paralyzed from the attack you just did. They are said to be in hit stun. This is how links are possible. You recover in time to hit opponents with another move before they can block again. The hit advantage is longer for the same move if an opponent is crouching when hit.

There is also hit disadvantage. Some moves allow you to hit opponents where they recover from the hit while you are still in the recovery phase of your attack. In these situations, if the disadvantage is long enough, opponents can attack you before you finish your move, even though you hit them.

Blocked advantage is similar to hit advantage. You recover from your attack while the opponent is still in block stun. You have the advantage to move or attack again while the opponent is immobilized.

Blocked disadvantage is when you attack and an opponent blocks your move, and the recovery of your move is slow enough where the opponent recovers before you do. If the blocked disadvantage of your move is long enough, your opponent can hit you before you fully recover from your attack.

HIT CONFIRMATION (HIT VERIFICATION)

Hit confirmation is a way to eliminate guesswork in your attacks. You only follow up an attack with a special move or super art if the first attack connects with a hit. For some attacks, this is impossible because the window to cancel the move is too brief. However, other moves can be cancelled late into their recovery, making it possible to confirm by sight that the move actually hit, then cancel into a super art. This is even easier with links because you generally have more time to watch the move and look for a hit before doing the super art.

Verifying a hit is important because your super meter is limited. You don't want to waste a super art by canceling an attack that is blocked. Also, many super arts are vulnerable if they are blocked, so it's too risky to guess. Whenever possible, always try to verify that your move has hit before you proceed to your next attack in the desired combo. The most common ways to hit confirm an attack before doing a super art are with chainable moves, late cancels, links, cancelable target chains, and meaty attacks.

It's also possible to confirm that your attack will hit based on the action of opponents. If you see an opponent stick out a move that's slow to recover, you can hit quick enough to know that it will hit before the opponent can block. In this situation, it's safe to immediately cancel into a super art, even off of moves that normally can't be verified. Another situation that often comes up is a throw whiff. If you see a character attempt a throw that whiffs, you have enough time to punish it. After the initial hit, cancel into a super art immediately.

GUESSING GAMES, MIND GAMES

Many situations come up where there is no way to know what is going to happen. You must guess to get it right. Many of these situations have two possible choices, so they are known as 50/50 situations. Examples of these are blocking (high or low), parrying (high or low), throwing (throw or no throw), wakeup move (hit, whiff). Parrying is the most notorious 50/50 situation in *Street Fighter III: 3rd Strike*. However, there is more involved in parrying than just high or low. Throws and hesitation moves combat parrying, as well, so it's better to refer to it as a rock, paper, scissors mind game.

It is generally in your favor to get opponents into these guessing game situations and force them to make a choice. They can't always guess correctly, so pressure them in this manner, especially when there are more than two options. The best 50/50 situations are the ones where you force opponents to choose between block-

ing left or right (or up or down). Examples of this are ambiguous cross ups. If they guess wrong, you land a big combo. If they guess right, they block, but you are still safe. So, it's ideal to try to create as many of these safe 50/50 situations as you possibly can. Consider it free damage 50% of the time.

Wakeup situations are 50/50 guessing games that come up all the time. The player who scores the knockdown has many options, including attack high / attack low / throw / do nothing / etc. The waking up opponent's options include block low / block high / parry low / parry high / wakeup move / etc. Although some overhead attacks are slow enough to react to, most other attacks are not. Therefore, the waking up opponent usually must guess what opponents will do, then decide what is the best option. The opponent pressuring the waking up opponent has the advantage in this situation because of the ability to attack first.

FOOT GAMES (FOOTSIES)

Foot games, or footsies, are a big part of many characters' offense. Footsies involve low kick attacks between two players on the ground. It is a step up from merely poking. You are essentially trying to invite an attack, then punish it. This is usually done by staying just outside of the maximum poke range of an opponent. Walk back and forth, making it look like you are vulnerable and in range for an attack, trying to draw out an attack. If the attack whiffs, quickly hit them during the recovery of their move. Some characters can base their entire strategy on just foot games. Those characters usually have a super art that can combo easily from their longest low poke. Make it hard for opponents to get near you, and hover outside of their range. Get opponents to flinch, thinking you are about to use an attack that is vulnerable, but you should actualliy do a poke that recovers quickly. Foot games are very effective against impatient opponents, and they do not need to be complex to garner large rewards.

HOW TO READ CHARACTER MOVE DATA

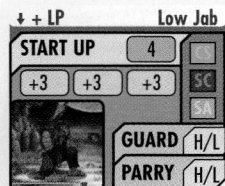

START UP
The number of frames from the beginning of the attack animation until the attack actually hits. The lower the number, the faster the attack.

BLOCKED ADVANTAGE, HIT STANDING ADVANTAGE, HIT CROUCHING ADVANTAGE
The frame advantage or disadvantage for the different outcomes of an attack. If a D is listed, then the attack knocks down.

GUARD H/L
The ability to block an attack High (with ←), Low (with ↙) or either.

PARRY H/L
The ability to parry an attack High (with →), Low (with ↓) or either.

CHAIN INTO SELF (CS)
SPECIAL CANCELABLE (SC)
SUPER ART CANCELABLE (SA)
White text indicates that it is possible to chain a move into itself, cancel into a special attack or cancel into a super art.

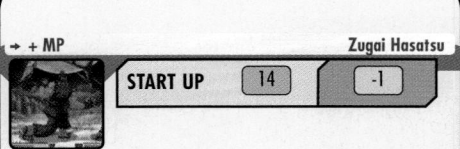

START UP
The number of frames from the beginning of the attack animation until the attack actually hits. The lower the number, the faster the attack.

BLOCKED ADVANTAGE
The frame advantage or disadvantage if the attack is blocked. If a D is listed, then the attack knocks down.

 THROW FRAME DATA
ALL THROWS USING LP + LK HAVE A TWO FRAME START UP, EXCEPT IBUKI'S AND ORO'S AIR THROWS, WHICH HAVE A SIX FRAME START UP.

 COSTUMES
THE COSTUME SELECTION INFORMATION GIVEN ASSUMES THE DEFAULT CONTROLLER SETTINGS ARE BEING USED.

COMBO DAMAGE
THE DAMAGE DATA FOR COMBOS WAS ACQUIRED AGAINST A STANDING RYU, UNLESS THE COMBO SPECIFIES OTHERWISE. SINCE CHARACTERS TAKE DAMAGE AT DIFFERENT RATES, THE VALUES PRESENTED IN THIS GUIDE SHOULD BE USED FOR COMPARISON PURPOSES ONLY.

START UP
The number of frames from the beginning of the attack animation until the attack actually hits. The four numbers represent Light attack, Medium attack, Hard attack and EX attack (where applicable).

BLOCKED ADVANTAGE
The frame advantage or disadvantage if the attack is blocked. If a D is listed, then the attack knocks down.

Akuma

NORMAL MOVES

STANDING

Outside of ↓ + LK range, MK is Akuma's best poke. His foot extends out and goes over most low attacks, yet it has a wide enough hitbox to hit most characters as they attempt an attack. Use this to beat other characters' pokes.

HK covers a wide hit area. Use it from long range to catch large characters at the beginning of jumps, or use it as a universal anti-air. Effective at almost any time, stick this out to confuse parry attempts.

LP		Jab
START UP		4
+4	+4	+4
GUARD		H/L
PARRY		H/L

LK		Short
START UP		4
+2	+2	+2
GUARD		H/L
PARRY		H/L

MP		Strong
START UP		5
+4	+5	+5
GUARD		H/L
PARRY		H

MK		Forward
START UP		5
-7	-6	-5
GUARD		H/L
PARRY		H

HP		Fierce
START UP		8
-6	-4	-2
GUARD		H/L
PARRY		H

HK		Roundhouse
START UP		9
-7	-5	-3
GUARD		H/L
PARRY		H

STANDING CLOSE

Close MP is a good poke. Akuma has frame advantage off of it, so it's good for tick throw setups and other mix-ups. For example, after a blocked MP, hesitate, then walk up and repeat, or use ↓ + LK twice. The trick is to make it look like a throw attempt, which should lead to an opening. MP links to Messatsu-Goushouryu, and is the only verifiable high attack into it.

In close MK hits high, so mix it in versus would-be low parriers. It easily links into Messatsu-Gouhadou.

LP		Close Jab
START UP		3
+3	+3	+3
GUARD		H/L
PARRY		H/L

LK		Close Short
START UP		4
+2	+2	+2
GUARD		H/L
PARRY		H/L

MP		Close Strong
START UP		5
+1	+2	+3
GUARD		H/L
PARRY		H/L

MK		Close Forward
START UP		4
+2	+4	+6
GUARD		H/L
PARRY		H

HP		Close Fierce
START UP		4
-4	-2	0
GUARD		H/L
PARRY		H

HK		Close Roundhouse
START UP		9
-6	-4	-2
GUARD		H/L
PARRY		H

COSTUMES

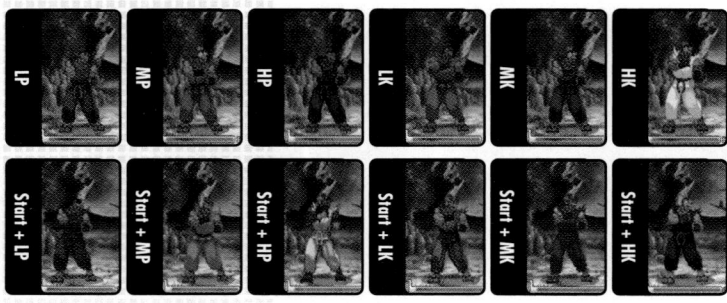

THROWS

LP + LK	Seoi Nage

← + LP + LK	Tomoe Nage

SPECIAL NORMALS

→ + MP		Zugai Hasatsu
START UP	14	-1

↗ + MK		Tenma Kuujin Kyaku
START UP	9	—

CROUCHING

↓ + LK has many uses. It's a quick poke, ideal for tick throw setups and mind games. After a blocked ↓ + LK, there are a few options: throw, hesitate and ↓ + LK twice to follow up, dash back and punish an incorrect reaction, etc. It chains into itself, so combo ↓ + LK (x2) into any standard super art.

Akuma's best poke for mid-range distance fighting is ↓ + MK. Combo it into Messatsu-Gouhadou from long range to punish whiffs or to apply pressure. While good from a distance, up close it can be countered by a few super arts because of its blocked frame disadvantage.

Good for punishing whiffed normals when you don't have a super meter, ↓ + HK comes out fast and knocks down. However, it has a terrible recovery, and is vulnerable to combos if blocked close, and some super arts from further away. Don't use it unless you know it will connect.

↓ + LP		Low Jab
START UP		4
+3	+3	+3
GUARD		H/L
PARRY		H/L

↓ + LK		Low Short
START UP		5
+1	+1	+1
GUARD		L
PARRY		L

↓ + MP		Low Strong
START UP		5
+3	+4	+5
GUARD		H/L
PARRY		H/L

↓ + MK		Low Forward
START UP		6
-3	-2	-1
GUARD		L
PARRY		L

↓ + HP		Low Fierce
START UP		5
-8	-6	-4
GUARD		H/L
PARRY		H/L

↓ + HK		Low Roundhouse
START UP		7
-15	D	D
GUARD		L
PARRY		L

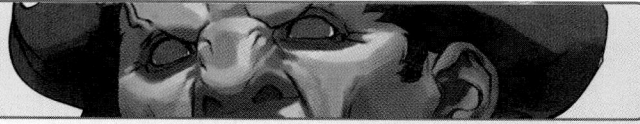

JUMPING

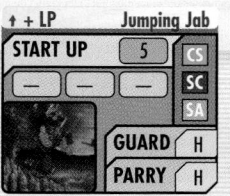

↑ + LP — Jumping Jab

START UP		5	CS
—	—	—	SC
			SA
	GUARD		H
	PARRY		H

↑ + MP — Jumping Strong

START UP		5	CS
—	—	—	SC
			SA
	GUARD		H
	PARRY		H

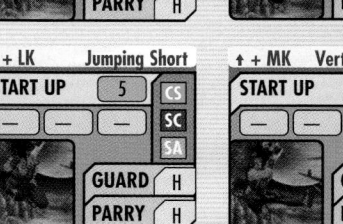

↑ + HP — Vertical Fierce

START UP		6	CS
—	—	—	SC
			SA
	GUARD		H
	PARRY		H

↖ / ↗ + HP — Jumping Fierce

START UP		6	CS
—	—	—	SC
			SA
	GUARD		H
	PARRY		H

↑ + LK — Jumping Short

START UP		5	CS
—	—	—	SC
			SA
	GUARD		H
	PARRY		H

↑ + MK — Vertical Forward

START UP		5	CS
—	—	—	SC
			SA
	GUARD		H
	PARRY		H

↖ / ↗ + MK — Jumping Forward

START UP		5	CS
—	—	—	SC
			SA
	GUARD		H
	PARRY		H

↑ + HK — Vertical Roundhouse

START UP		6	CS
—	—	—	SC
			SA
	GUARD		H
	PARRY		H

↖ / ↗ + HK — Jumping Roundhouse

START UP		6	CS
—	—	—	SC
			SA
	GUARD		H
	PARRY		H

SPECIAL MOVES

↓ ↘ → + P — Gohadouken

8	8	8	—
-11	-11	-11	—

In air, ↓ ↘ → + P — Zanku Hadouken

12	12	12	—
—	—	—	—

→ ↓ ↘ ↙ ← + P — Shakunetsu Hadouken

14	19	24	—
-23	-18	-15	—

→ ↓ ↘ + P — Gou Shouryuken

3	2	1	—
-24	-30	-34	—

Shakunetsu Hadoken travels slowly and hits multiple times. The button used affects the speed at which it travels and the number of hits. With a heavy start up and recovery, the uses for this attack are limited. Score a knock down and throw a meaty Shakunetsu Hadoken from semi close range. Your opponent has no choice but to try to parry. If the parry is successful, super cancel into Shungokusatsu, which grabs out of the parry stance.

An all purpose defensive attack, Gou Shoutryken has a small window of invulnerability at start up, meaning in wake up or anti-air situations it has the ability to consistently beat an opponent's attack. It hits multiple times, making it especially irritating to parry in anti-air situations. It's also an important combo option, specifically because it juggles off LK or MK Tatsumaki Zankuukyaku for heavy damage.

↓ ↙ ← + K (also in air) — Tatsumaki Zankuukyaku

5	5	5	—
—	—	—	—

Use this move in combos that inflict heavy damage. LK and MK versions put opponents into a juggle state, leaving them open to Gou Shouryuken or a super art to tack on damage at the end of it. Unfortunately, this move is extremely unsafe if blocked, meaning there are few (if any) consistent and/or safe ways to land this move. Good in punishment situations or off of successful option select parries. The aerial version of this move can be used to cross someone up.

→ ↓ ↘ / ← ↓ ↙ + PP / KK — Ashura Senkuu

→ ↓ ↘ makes Akuma teleport forward, while ← ↓ ↙ makes Akuma travel backwards. PPP makes Akuma travel further than KKK. Use Ashura Senkuu to avoid hairy situations where Akuma might get cornered, or to avoid block damage from a projectile super art. Although Akuma will pass through a character and most attacks, he is vulnerable to certain super arts.

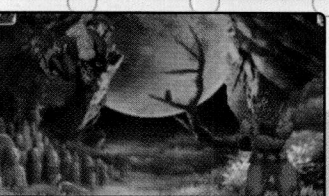

→ ↓ ↘ + K — Hyakki Shuu

—	—	—	—
—	—	—	—

The button used determines how far Akuma travels. During the jump, there are several options:

During Hyakki Shuu, no input — Hyakki Gouzan

40	40	40	—
-11	-D	-D	—

Hyakki Gouzen can be tricky to block in a few limited situations if opponents are worried about getting hit by Hyakki Goushou. If this move is blocked, expect trouble.

During Hyakki Shuu, Pq — Hyakki Goushou

6	6	6	—
—	—	—	—

A leaping overhead punch with heavy recovery. Mix up with Hyakki Gouzan to increase effectiveness.

During Hyakki Shuu, K — Hyakki Goujin

3	3	3	—
—	—	—	—

Strangely, Hyakki Goujin is not an overhead. When blocked, Akuma ends up with a slight frame advantage. Use it to get close and start mix-up patterns.

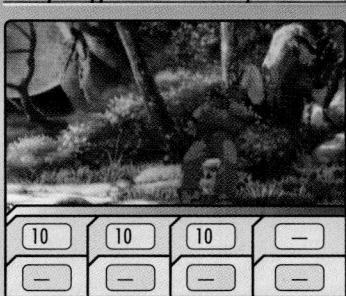

During Hyakki Shuu, LP + LK when directly on top of opponent — Hyakki Gousai

10	10	10	—
—	—	—	—

A nice throw added to the mix of other attacks off of Hyakku Shuu.

SUPER ARTS

SUPER ART I

Messatsu-Gouhadou
↓ ↘ → ↓ ↘ → + P

| 4 | -13 |

Tenma-Gouzanku
In air, ↓ ↘ → ↓ ↘ → + P

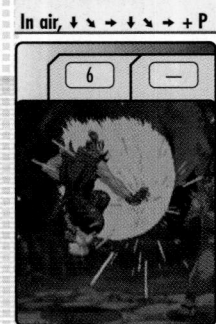

| 6 | — |

Messatsu-Gouhadou has many uses and does nice damage when comboed without a super cancel. Combo into Messatsu-Gouhadou from ↓ + MK to prevent an offensive rush. Use it to punish whiffed moves, or up close, verify a combo into it through doubled up ↓ + LKs, or link behind a MK. This provides both a low and high avenue to land Messatsu-Gouhadou to discourage attempted parries.

Use Gou Shouryuken → Messatsu-Gouhadou to stop all jump ins. Even if parried, Akuma recovers well before an opponent is done parrying, leaving the option to attack again (to mess up the parry timing) or teleport away to safety. Finally, counter a jump in with ↗ and MK. If Akuma lands first, reset with Messatsu-Gouhadou.

Tenma-Gouzanku isn't as useful as the ground variation because you can't verify it, but it does have uses. If you expect an anti-air counter to a jump in, unload Tenman-Gouzanku, which defeats anti-air moves that don't have a long invulnerability window. It can also be effective for chip damage kills when an opponent only has a few pixels of health left. If parried, dash up and hit low for an almost sure hit.

SUPER ART II

↓ ↘ → ↓ ↘ → + P   **Messatsu-Goushouryu**

| 1 | -25 |

Messatsu-Goushouryu inflicts impressive damage when comboed with a super cancel. Verify it with ↓ + LK (x2), or MK link. The downside to this super is its limited range. Akuma has a wide range of offensive options where he is constantly moving. If you must concentrate on getting close to deal big damage, Akuma loses some other offensive pressue tactics. Messatsu-Goushouryu does not allow Akuma to punish ground pokes, which is an option with Messatsu-Gouhadou.

SUPER ART III

Messatsu-Gourasen
In air, ↓ ↘ → ↓ ↘ → + K

| 3 | -35 |

Messatsu-Gourasen
In air, ↓ ↘ → ↓ ↘ → + K

| 8 | — |

Messatsu-Gourasen is Akuma's anti-air super. You can also perform it in the air against airborne opponents. Unfortunately, it inflicts less damage than his other super arts. It also doesn't have much use other than as anti-air. It's possible to combo into it on the ground, but the only way to verify it is off of doubled up ↓ +LK, which means he will be prone to down parries. If you have an opening to land ↓ + MK → Tatsumaki Zankuukyaku, you can juggle with the super art, but the damage isn't that good. It's better to finish that combo off with Gou Shouryuken (HP) and save the meter for an anti-air opportunity.

SUPER ART MAX

Shungokusatsu
LP LP → LK HP

| 1 | — |

Shungokusatsu is available in all super arts. It requires two full stocks of super meter. Opponents must anticipate the super art before you actually do it in order to escape. Use this to your advantage to play mind games; for example, wait for a jump escape attempt from the assumed Shungokusatsu, then attack with an air Tatsumaki Zankuukyaku.

Shungokusatsu is invincible at start up, so you can use it to pass through projectiles or any attacks from an opponent. You can also use Shungokusatsu to punish jump in attempts. As someone jumps in, crouch and input LP (x2). At the last moment possible, finish the Shungokusatsu input to pass through any attack and catch the jumper upon landing. An alternate way is to press ↘ instead of → after the second LP. With this method, Akuma remains crouching, leaving you more time to input the Shungokusatsu command and catch the opponent's jump in at the last possible moment. You can also use this invincibility to pass through ground moves. If you connect a ↓ + MK → Tatsumaki Zankuukyaku (LK); instead of finishing them off with a Shouryuken (HP), hit with HP → Tatsumaki Zankuukyaku (LK) to knock them back over. Tatsumaki Zankuukyaku (LK) whiffs, but Akuma lands right next to the opponent. If they attack, Akuma passes through it with a Shungokusatsu.

SUPER ART MAX

Kongouko-kuretsuzan
↓ ↓ ↓ + PPP

| 16 | -25 |

Kongouko-kuretsuzan is also available from all three super arts. Its first hit is unparriable, making it ideal for chip damage kills. It's also a safe wake up move against jump in cross up attempts. Another way to land this super art is in a reset situation. After a ↓ + MK → Tatsumaki Zankuukyaku (LK) combo, walk up LP to reset, then immediately Kongouko-kuretsuzan. In an air reset situation, the opponent's only option is to parry, but Kongouko-kuretsuzan's first hit is unparriable. Be cautious about using this super art in other situations because Akuma is quite vulnerable to a counter attack if it is blocked.

An interesting note about this super art: if Akuma taunts once, it does 100% damage to another crouching Akuma or a Twelve that is transforming back from an X.C.O.P.Y.

Recommended Super Art: Messatsu-Gouhadou

Akuma does not have access to EX moves, and all his super arts have two stocks with access to both super arts MAX abilities. Therefore, the only thing to consider is super art usage. In that regard, Messatsu-Gouhadou is the clear winner. Akuma mounts an offense from multiple distances, so it is best to have a super art that accommodates this style.

COMBOS YOU NEED TO KNOW

6 HITS

TOTAL DAMAGE: 37

↓ + LK, ↓ + LP → forward Tatsumaki Zankuukyaku, Juggle with a strong Gou Shoryuuken.

One of the few verifiable ways to land damage without a super art. Unfortunately, the combo has many range limitations and doesn't work versus most crouching opponents. The juggle after the Tatsumaki Zankuukyaku is also inconsistant mid-screen. Use with caution.

5 HITS

TOTAL DAMAGE: 53

HP → Tatsumaki Zankuukyaku (LK), juggle with a semi late Gou Shoryuuken (HP)

Simple, high damage, non super art option. Good for punishment situations. Knocks down.

6 HITS

TOTAL DAMAGE: 50

↓ + MK from max distance → Tatsumaki Zankuukyaku (LK), juggle with a late close LP→ Gou Shouryuken (HP)

Similar to the above combo, hits from further away.

5 HITS

TOTAL DAMAGE: 41

HP →Tatsumaki Zankuukyaku (LK), juggle with a late close LP → Tatsumaki Zankuukyaku (HK)

Less damaging non-super art combo than the above. Good for punishment situations and pushing opponents into the corner. Knocks down.

4 HITS

TOTAL DAMAGE: 37

Hyakki Shuu →Hyakki Goujin, land and immediately link a Gou Shouryuken (HP)

Easy damage off of a connected dive kick. Verifiable. Knocks down.

6 HITS

TOTAL DAMAGE: 59

Hyakki Shuu → Hyakki Goujin, land, link a close MK → Tatsumaki Zankuukyaku (MK), juggle with a Gou Shouryuken (MP)

Heavy damage off of a successful dive kick hit. Knocks down.

13 HITS

TOTAL DAMAGE: 51

↓ + LK, ↓ + LK → Messatsu-Gourasen

Verifiable way to land Messatsu-Gourasen. Whiffs vs. crouching characters however. Use carefully. Knocks down.

7 HITS

TOTAL DAMAGE: 64

Close MK linked into Messatsu-Gouhadou

Verifiable way to land a super off of a mid-level hit. Knocks down.

9 HITS

TOTAL DAMAGE: 57

↓ + LK, ↓ + LK → Messatsu-Goushouryu

Verifiable way to land a super art. Flexible. Still fairly close and you have a slight frame advantage to work with to start another attack. Knocks down.

8 HITS

TOTAL DAMAGE: 64

Close MP linked into Messatsu-Goushouryu

Verifiable way to land Messatsu-Goushouryu with a mid level hit.

13 HITS

TOTAL DAMAGE: 74

Jump in HP, land, close HP → Tatsumaki Zankuukyaku (LK), Gou Shouryuken (HP) on the second hit → Messatsu-Gouhadou, juggle with an early Gou Shouryuken (MP)

High damage jump in using super meter. Good in situations where the damage is guaranteed, whether opponents are dizzied or you parry a slow anti-air. It's possible to super cancel the Gou Shouryuken (MP) into another Messatsu-Gouhadou, then juggle again with another Gou Shouryuken. However, the damage difference is minimal and usually not worth the super meter usage.

16 HITS

TOTAL DAMAGE: 88

Jump in HK from a distance, land, HK → Shungokusatsu

Not exactly useful, but the only way to combo a Shungokusatsu. Massive damage. Knock down.

STRATEGY

Straight

Akuma has multiple offensive abilities to keep pressure on defensive opponents. Akuma can control the air and keep an opponent grounded through the use of properly timed Zankuu Hadokens. Use them as a safe way to jump in on opponents. Jump towards the opponent, then execute a Zankuu Hadoken near the end of Akuma's jump to land safely, leaving opponents blocking the projectiles. Do not use a Zankuu Hadoken too early in Akuma's jump arc or else opponents can dash under him and land a combo.

Once you get opponents in block stun from the Zankuu Hadokens, you gain the advantage, allowing you to walk up and attack first. Akuma's command overhead is a good move in this situation because it is fast and most players' instincts are to block low after a jump in. After the overhead, you're in a good position to MK over any poke they might try, or jump straight up and Zankuu Hadoken. Mix it up with kara throws, ↓ + LK (x2), and close MK to create super art opportunities, and keep opponents guessing.

Hyakki Shuu is a good way to keep on the offensive pressure. If opponents block the kick variation, keep pressuring them when you land. It's possible to cancel the ground moves into another Hyakki Shuu to continue the offensive assault. A trick you can use to get in close to execute the kick variation a split second before you hit the ground. No move will come out and you will land right in front of them. It is very quick and gives you the opportunity to land a quick throw or Shungokusatsu. Although the Hyakki Shuu can be blocked low, it is sometimes difficult to distinguish it from a normal jump, so take advantage of that fact and try ↓ + LK x2 after this Hyakki Shuu trick.

Zone opponents and keep them out of the air with Zankuu Hadokens and on the ground with ↓ + MK pokes. Punish any whiffed ground pokes with ↓ + MK → Messatsu-Gouhadou. If Akuma is getting pressured, use an Ashura Senkuu.

There are many anti-air options available if Akuma is being attacked. Gou Shouryuken (HP) → Messatsu-Gouhadou is the safest, although it burns super meter. Close LP → Tatsumaki Zankuukyaku (HK) is a good maneuver to throw off air parry attempts. Akuma always has the option to dash under opponents when they jump. If they commit to an attack, ↓ + MK combo them. Another fairly safe anti-air is close HP, and cancel into Ashura Senkuu if they parry to run away from danger. An air Tatsumaki Zankuukyaku is good for an air to air situation. It's hard to punish if parried, and creates combo opportunities. For style points, hit with an anti-air Shungokusatsu when they jump in.

When Akuma has a guaranteed combo opportunity, go for the biggest non-super, meter-burning combo available. Akuma does good damage off of normal juggle combos. It's better to save super meter for situations where only a super art can be comboed, such as ↓ + LK (x2) or a max range ↓ + MK.

WAKEUP GAME

With Messatsu-Gouhadou and Messatsu-Goushouryu, Akuma has both high and low options to verify combo into a super art, which is important to thwart parry attempts. Zugai Hasatsu is fast and useful if you're looking for stun damage. Messatsu-Gouhadou and Messatsu-Goushouryu can both be comboed off of a meaty UOH on wakeup. Akuma can also combo Tatsumaki Zankuukyaku (MK) after a meaty UOH to set up a juggle. Mix in kara throw setups to get people to react to a possible throw.

Akuma, as well as the other shotos, have many quick fake out maneuvers available to trick opponents on wake up. For example, whiff a LP over their head right before they get up, then immediately throw. This makes it look like you're going for something other than a throw, which often gets opponents to block, then eat the throw. Next time on wake up, whiff the LP, then go low into ↓ + LK (x2) → super art. You can do the same sequence with whiffed ↓ + LK into throw, then next time do a high move that is verifiable into a super art. Another good tactic is to option parry into a throw as they are getting up. Do this right in their face; many players expect Akuma to throw from his maximum kara throw range. Surprise them with an in-your-face throw. Finally, to totally fake out opponents, dash back on wake up to bait a throw attempt or wake up move, then ↓ + MK combo for big damage and another knockdown to repeat the process.

When Akuma is the one knocked down, he has the traditional wake up options, such as a psychic Gou Shouryuken, parrying, or blocking. It is also fairly safe to teleport to the other side of the screen. Beware of certain super arts that can hit Akuma during the Ashura Senkuu. A wake up Tatsumaki Zankuukyaku (MK / HK) beats most normal pokes on wake up. If they tick or do any hesitation move, a good counter is a quick ↓ + LP, ↓ + LK combination. If they block, they get pushed away to a safer distance. If it hits, finish the combo with Messatsu-Gouhadou.

ADVANCED SHUNGOKUSATSU APPLICATIONS

Shungokusatsu is the only move in the game that is super cancelable from any ground move. This permits many interesting setups. The first thing that should be noted is that Shungokusatsu can be comboed off of far HK. Normally grab super arts cannot be comboed into, but HK puts opponents in a turned around state in which it's possible for the throw to hit. A tricky way to pull this off is to stay at almost a dash distance away and make it seem like you are going for dash in Shungokusatsu. If they were thinking about jumping away, HK hits while they are still on the ground, allowing you to combo into Shungokusatsu.

The fact that you can cancel ANY move leads to more than just combo opportunities to land Shungokusatsu. A classic set up is to do a ↓ + HK from very close range, anticipating it to be blocked. ↓ + HKs from Shotos have terrible recovery and can almost always be punished. Knowing this, bait a counter, then cancel the recovery of ↓ + HK into a Shungokusatsu, and pass right through the attempted poke. This works because it's possible to cancel any move at any point into Shungokusatsu.

Another move that can take advantage of late canceling is Tenma Kuujin Kyaku. Cancel the last recovery frames of the dive kick the moment Akuma hits the ground to dive kick on opponents without fear. If they parry the kick and try to hit Akuma upon landing, cancel into Shungokusatsu and pass through their attack.

Taking this idea of canceling moves a bit further, Akuma can kara cancel the very first frames of his Zugai Hasatsu (or ↓ + HK) to increase the range of Shungokusatsu. With the additional range on the Shungokusatsu, Akuma has many more possibilities to land it since he doesn't need to be at point blank range. The command input for this is LP LP (→ + MP) LK HP.

You can also mix up the classic shoto tick throw setups into Shungokusatsu setups. For example:

↓ + LK, whiffed LP, kara Shungokusatsu

LK, kara Shungokusatsu

MP, kara Shungokusatsu

Akuma also has many setups where he positions himself just outside of throw range, then performs a kara Shungokusatsu to make up the extra space. If opponents throw out an attack, or blocked an attack, they will get hit.

Here are a few examples to set this up:

1. After a blocked Tenma Kuujin Kyaku, dash back, kara Shungokusatsu

2. Whiff a Tenma Kuujin Kyaku in front of an opponent, kara Shungokusatsu

3. Whiff Hyakki Goujin from full screen, land, kara Shungokusatsu. You must do the kick as late as possible so it doesn't actually come out. Most players expect the kick and stay blocking while Akuma attacks with a Shungokusatsu.

Another simple yet effective setup is to dash from further than full dash distance, then kara Shungokusatsu to make up the extra range. This is a good setup to bait an attack and slip past it. Other long range setups include Hyakki Goujin and have the opponent block it. Once you land, dash and use a Shungokusatsu. The trick to dash Shungokusatsu is to hide the two LP during the dash, then finish the input after the dash has completed. This setup works often because most players expect some sort of an attack after the jump in.

SETUPS

Ranges setups for UOH → super art

Against small and medium sized characters:

(↓ + LK, ↓ + MP), UOH → Messatsu-Gouhadou

Against medium sized characters:

(↓ + LK, dash back), UOH → Messatsu-Gouhadou

Against wide characters:

(↓ + LK (x3)), UOH → Messatsu-Gouhadou

Against Hugo:

(close MP, ↓ + MP), UOH → Messatsu-Gouhadou

Against Oro:

No setup is required. UOH → Messatsu-Gouhadou or Messatsu-Goushouryu works at close distance on crouching Oro.

RESETS:

Reset 1: After connecting a Tatsumaki Zankuukyaku (LK), close LP to reset, then Messatsu-Gouhadou (both ground and air variations work). If they parry, Akuma recovers in time to continue attacking while they are in the air.

Reset 2: After connecting a Tatsumaki Zankuukyaku (LK), close LP to reset, then immediately cancel into Kongouko-kuretsuzan. This is a guaranteed hit situation because the first hit of Kongouko-kuretsuzan is unparriable.

Reset 3: In an air-to-air situation, connect jump → + MK so that Akuma lands before the opponent. As soon as you hit the ground, use Messatsu-Gouhadou.

PARRY SETUPS AND TACTICS

If you're fishing for damage, and ↓ + LK (x 2) is blocked, an effective pattern is to ether walk up a step and kara throw, walk up ↓ + LK x 2 again, or let the controller go back to neutral, tap ↓, then hit ↓ + MK soon after. If your opponent hits a button to try to stop what they think is a throw, and it's a low attack (which it often is in that situation), you parry the attack, ↓ + MK hits, then you can cancel ↓ + MK into a super art or special attack on reaction to the parry. If they don't press anything, ↓ + MK comes out to push them away. The key is not to cancel into a super art if you don't visually see the parry happen.

FAVORABLE MATCH UP: HUGO

Hugo is big and slow. Keep him away with Zankuu Hadokens and pressure him. It's possible to throw Hugo with Hyakki Gosai from midscreen during the upward arc of his jump. It's hard for Hugo to react to this and he tends to get thrown often. Even if Hugo gets close, simply teleport away to safety. Hugo is too slow to keep up with Akuma's ability to run away.

UNFAVORABLE MATCH UP: MAKOTO

Makoto needs to get in close to do damage, and Akuma is generally good at keeping people the right distance away. The reason this match does not go Akuma's way is because Makoto only needs to hit Akuma once. If Akuma messes up and allows Makoto to dash under an Zankuu Hadoken or successfully parry an attack, it's all over. If Makoto grabs Akuma with her Karakusa, it's a guaranteed stun, which can lead to an easy 100% combo.

Akuma must keep Makoto away as best he can in order to win this match. Whenever Makoto is close to Akuma, the only safe offensive maneuver is to throw. Sticking out any poke could lead to a parry into a 100% damage combo.

AKUMA

Alex

NORMAL MOVES

STANDING

MP is a good anti-air move and it can be comboed into EX Air Knee Smash. It is also a good poke to whiff across screen to build meter and hide charges in. Alex's HP isn't the fastest overhead, but it gets the job done. Useful in Alex's wakeup game, although it has a tendency to trade with other wakeup moves.

MK is a great ground poke with extremely long range, which goes over most low attacks and still hits crouching characters. Use this to hit other character's low pokes. HK has a slow startup time and terrible recovery, but is strong and has good priority. Use with caution.

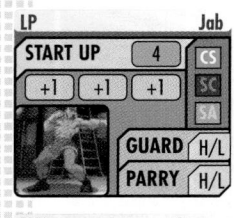

LP — Jab

START UP	4			CS
+1	+1	+1		SC
				SA
GUARD	H/L			
PARRY	H/L			

LK — Short

START UP	5			CS
0	0	0		SC
				SA
GUARD	H/L			
PARRY	H/L			

MP — Strong

START UP	4			CS
-1	0	+1		SC
				SA
GUARD	H/L			
PARRY	H			

MK — Forward

START UP	5			CS
0	+1	+2		SC
				SA
GUARD	H/L			
PARRY	H			

HP — Fierce

START UP	14			CS
-1	+1	+3		SC
				SA
GUARD	H			
PARRY	H			

HK — Roundhouse

START UP	16			CS
-13	0	+2		SC
				SA
GUARD	H/L			
PARRY	H			

STANDING CLOSE

Close MK is a good mid level attack to use in combos. It can be done meaty to make it easier to verify a cancel. It is possible to cancel off of a hit confirmation into Boomerang Raid from this move, although it must be done quickly.

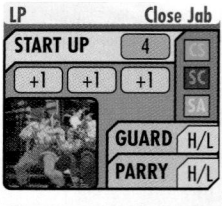
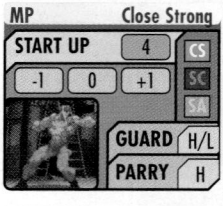

LP — Close Jab

START UP	4			CS
+1	+1	+1		SC
				SA
GUARD	H/L			
PARRY	H/L			

LK — Close Short

START UP	5			CS
0	0	0		SC
				SA
GUARD	H/L			
PARRY	H/L			

MP — Close Strong

START UP	4			CS
-1	0	+1		SC
				SA
GUARD	H/L			
PARRY	H			

MK — Close Forward

START UP	11			CS
-1	0	+1		SC
				SA
GUARD	H/L			
PARRY	H/L			

HP — Close Fierce

START UP	14			CS
-1	+1	+3		SC
				SA
GUARD	H			
PARRY	H			

HK — Close Roundhouse

START UP	16			CS
-13	0	+2		SC
				SA
GUARD	H/L			
PARRY	H			

COSTUMES

 LP
 MP
 HP
 LK
 MK
 HK
 LP + MK + HP

 Start + LP
 Start + MP
 Start + HP
Start + LK
Start + MK
Start + HK

SPECIAL NORMALS

→ + MP — Chop

START UP	7	-2

Good for hitting jumping opponents early in their jump. This move is also decent against ground opponents.

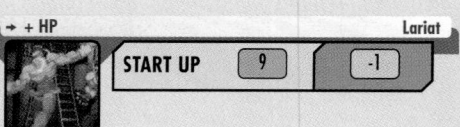

→ + HP — Lariat

START UP	9	-1

Great for catching opponents early in their jump from mid range and further. Can also be used as a traditional anti-air. In the corner, it knocks down and sets up throws. Do not use this attack against an opponent on the ground. It whiffs versus most characters.

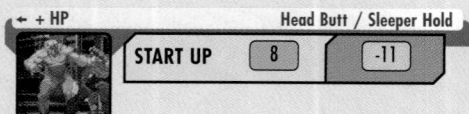

← + HP — Head Butt / Sleeper Hold

START UP	8	-11

Command grab. Head butt from the front, Sleeper from the back, which can be mashed for additional damage. After Sleeper Hold, Alex can link Boomerang Raid. Vulnerable if it doesn't hit.

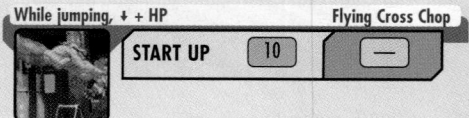

While jumping, ↓ + HP — Flying Cross Chop

START UP	10	—

Very slow and easy to see coming. Too risky. If it hits air-to-air, it can set up a juggle, but it is hard to time this attack and connect with it.

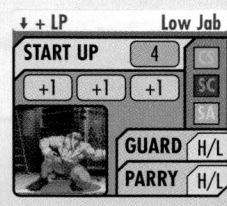

SPECIAL MOVES

CROUCHING

↓ + MP is Alex's best low poke, with good priority and decent range. The only drawback is that it can be parried high or low.

↓+ HP is a 2 hit tackle move. Great when used as anti-air. If it hits early for only one hit, juggle with an Air Knee Smash. It can also be used to confuse and cross up grounded opponents. Use it right next to them to hop to the other side and hit them on wakeup.

↓ + LP		Low Jab	
START UP		4	CS
+1	+1	+1	SC
			SA
	GUARD	H/L	
	PARRY	H/L	

↓ + LK		Low Short	
START UP		5	CS
+2	+2	+2	SC
			SA
	GUARD	L	
	PARRY	L	

↓ + MP		Low Strong	
START UP		7	CS
0	+1	+2	SC
			SA
	GUARD	H/L	
	PARRY	H/L	

↓ + MK		Low Forward	
START UP		8	CS
-1	0	+1	SC
			SA
	GUARD	L	
	PARRY	L	

↓ + HP		Low Fierce	
START UP		13	CS
-9	D	D	SC
			SA
	GUARD	H/L	
	PARRY	H/L	

↓ + HK		Low Roundhouse	
START UP		11	CS
-15	D	D	SC
			SA
	GUARD	L	
	PARRY	L	

JUMPING

Jumping HP is Alex's best combo starter. Jumping LP is also a solid option; however, it does not stay out for the entire length of his jump like LK.

Jumping LK stays out for the entire length of Alex's jump. Use it to tick into Power Bombs.

↑ + LP		Jumping Jab	
START UP		4	CS
			SC
			SA
	GUARD	H	
	PARRY	H	

↑ + LK		Jumping Short	
START UP		4	CS
			SC
			SA
	GUARD	H	
	PARRY	H	

↑ + MP		Jumping Strong	
START UP		5	CS
			SC
			SA
	GUARD	H	
	PARRY	H	

↑ + MK		Jumping Forward	
START UP		9	CS
			SC
			SA
	GUARD	H	
	PARRY	H	

↑ + HP		Jumping Fierce	
START UP		8	CS
			SC
			SA
	GUARD	H	
	PARRY	H	

↑ + HK		Jumping Roundhouse	
START UP		8	CS
			SC
			SA
	GUARD	H	
	PARRY	H	

THROWS

LP + LK		Body Slam	
START UP		3	

↓ ↘ → + P	Flash Chop

12	16	20	10
-2	-1	-1	-1

MP and HP put opponents in a turned around state that is susceptible to throws. Jab and EX versions (EX adds one hit and knocks down) are good for combos and pressure after a canceled MK. HP version comes out slow, but works best in a guaranteed hit situation to set up grabs and combos.

→ ↘ ↓ ↙ ← + P	Power Bomb / Back Drop

7	8	9	—
—	—	—	—

Command grab. The stronger the punch button used, the more damage done, but the slower the move comes out and the greater recovery it has; it also bounces Alex further away from the opponent. If done from behind, Alex performs Back Drop.

→ ↘ ↓ ↙ ← + K	Spiral D.D.T.

21	24	27	—
—	—	—	—

Command grab that hits standing opponents, but not crouching opponents. Button pressed determines how far Alex jumps. Can be tricky sometimes and has limited uses.

↑ ↓ ↘ + K	Air Knee Smash

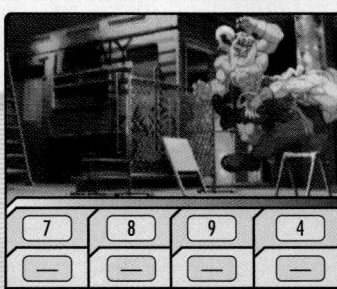

7	8	9	4
—	—	—	—

EX version hits opponents on the ground. Normal version has very limited use. Juggles after an anti-air low HP that only hits once. Cancel MP into EX Air Knee Smash for a solid anti-air option. EX version is also a high priority wake up move.

Charge ← → + K	Slash Elbow

16	19	21	10
-2	-8	-8	-6

Button used affects the distance traveled. Jab version is virtually unpunishable. Use it often to pressure and get in on opponents. EX version comes out extremely fast, adds one hit and knocks down. Good for surprise attacks and hitting moves in their recovery. Can cancel into Boomerang Raid off of a hit. Be careful, some characters can punish a blocked EX Slash Elbow.

Charge ↓ ↑ + K	Air Stampede

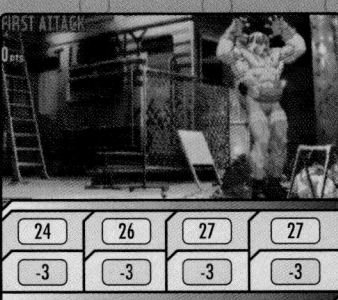

24	26	27	27
-3	-3	-3	-3

Overhead attack that knocks down. EX version has homing property. Button used determines how far Alex jumps. Good for mid screen mix ups, it crosses up, and is decent as a wakeup move.

ALEX

SUPER ARTS

SUPER ART I

360 motion + P	Hyper Bomb

Alex has a small window of invulnerability at start up of Hyper Bomb and he can grab characters through any of their normal moves. The only way to connect with Hyper Bomb with 100% certainty is to grab an opponent during a move. Grabbing opponents from behind leads to an

3	—

alternate version that inflicts more damage. Ideal after parries or if you anticipate an opponent's attack. Hyper Bomb is too slow to grab characters in any other situation. Opponents on the ground can always jump away from Hyper Bomb after it is activated, as long as they didn't commit to a move beforehand. Hyper Bomb only has one stock of meter, so it is not recommended for EX usage.

SUPER ART II

↓ ↘ → ↓ ↘ → + P	Boomerang Raid

The damage is not that high, but Boomerang Raid gives Alex some much needed combo possibilities. Alex can easily verify Boomerang Raid from up close from ↓ + LP (x2), or after traveling across the screen with a Slash Elbow, then canceling if it hits. Alex can also cancel close MK into

3	—

Boomerang Raid on reaction. The timing is tough, but it gives Alex a much needed mid attack to verify a super art.

The best feature of Boomerang Raid is its two stocks of super meter. Alex's EX Slash Elbow is a big part of his offense, and having plenty of meter means it's available often. If you plan to use EX moves, Boomerang Raid is the super art of choice.

SUPER ART III

↓ ↘ → ↓ ↘ → + P	Stun Gun Head Butt

If Alex connects with Stun Gun Head Butt, it's a guaranteed stun, leaving enough time to do any combo behind it. The button used determines the distance Stun Gun travels. It is invulnerable on the way up, but highly vulnerable on the way down. In fact, every character can jab Alex out

27	—

of Stun Gun Head Butt. It is unlikely that this super art will land against a grounded opponent. It can be used in a limited fashion as anti-air, although it is not very good in that role either. With only one stock of super meter, it limits the use of EX moves.

An interesting note about this super art: under very specific circumstances, it can be used in combos against juggled mid air opponents, but it's not applicable in a real match.

Recommended Super Art: Boomerang Raid

Boomerang Raid may not have the highest damage potential, but it is Alex's most consistent super art. Hyper Bomb and Stun Gun have too many flaws that make them unreliable.

TARGET COMBOS

↓ + LK → ↓ + MK	6
Strangely enough, Alex's only safe combo starting off a low attack.	-1

↓ + LK → ↓ + HK	6
Does not combo, so it has little value.	-15

COMBOS YOU NEED TO KNOW

3 HITS

TOTAL DAMAGE: 41

Close MK → EX Flash Chop

Basic Alex combo. Does good damage and it's safe. Knocks down.

7 HITS

TOTAL DAMAGE: 56

↓ + LP (x2) → Boomerang Raid

Flexible, verifiable way to land Boomerang Raid. Knocks down.

2 HITS

TOTAL DAMAGE: 49

Flash Chop (HP) linked into Power Bomb (HP)

High damage. Good for punishment situations. Knocks down.

4 HITS

TOTAL DAMAGE: 58

Flash Chop (HP) linked to close MK → EX Flash Chop

Another high damage variation off of fierce Flash Chop. Punishment situations only. Knocks down.

7 HITS

TOTAL DAMAGE: 66

Flash Chop (HP) linked to MK → Boomerang Raid

Heavy damage. Good for punishment situations when you have a super art available. Knocks down.

2 HITS

TOTAL DAMAGE: 40

Close MP → EX Air Knee Smash

Great anti-air combo. Knocks down.

3 HITS (CORNER ONLY)

TOTAL DAMAGE: 54

Anti-air Flying Cross Chop, land then juggle with close MP → EX Air Knee Smash

A hard to set up anti-air combo in a corner. Inflicts impressive damage if it lands. Knocks down.

6 HITS

TOTAL DAMAGE: 80

Flash Chop (HP) → Hyper Bomb

Only way to combo a Hyper Bomb. Massive damage. Knocks down.

7 HITS

TOTAL DAMAGE: 86

Flash Chop (HP) → Stun Gun Head Butt (LP), dizzies opponent; follow up with Flash Chop (HP) link to Power Bomb (HP)

Good way to combo Stun Gun Head Butt in punishment situations. Knocks down.

STRATEGY

Flying Knee

Alex has the tools to do well from all ranges (grappler mind games from close range, decent pokes and rushing attacks to fight from a distance), although he fights best in close. He has a basic, and effective mix up with Power Bomb/HP/↓ + HK.

Alex's Slash Elbow is the perfect move to rush in on opponents. The LP version is virtually unpunishable, so use it to pressure constantly. EX Slash Elbow is great from longer ranges when you have trouble getting in close, and you can use it to punish whiffed attacks. Charge during a Slash Elbow to have the option of an Air Stampede or another Slash Elbow as a follow up.

Alex has trouble getting close to characters with good low pokes. He also has the ability to make it hard for opponents to get close to him. Alex's MK goes over most low pokes and has great range. Use ↓ + MP to keep people away. Against players that poke constantly, wait for the recovery of the move, then dash in for a kara throw. Alex's dash is pretty quick, enhancing his kara throw ability. After a knock down, start a mix up pattern.

↓ + HP is good as an all purpose anti-air. It hits twice, so you can mix up the timing of it to confuse parry attempts. If it hits for only the second hit, juggle with Air Knee Smash. Another solid anti-air option is MP → EX Air Knee Smash. This is difficult to parry, and works well with an option parry beforehand.

Against airborne opponents, jumping MK and HK are both good options due to their range. When Alex is jumping on an opponent, HP is great to start combos off of, provided it connects. Otherwise, jump in with an early LP or LK. These moves hit from high up, and act as a nice tick throw setup. You can mix it up by landing and doing close MK → Flash Chop to mix it up and punish any attempt to tech or counter throw.

WAKEUP GAME

Many of Alex's knockdowns cause an opponent to bounce away. Always dash forward and stay on top of opponents afterward. A Power Bomb on wake up is a good tactic. It knocks down and allows Alex to continue to pressure on wake up. This also makes it seem like blocking is not safe; many players might choose to jump to escape Power Bomb attempts. However, as Alex likes to say, "You can't escape!" Mix it up with close MK → EX Flash Chop to punish opponents for not blocking when they try to jump. Change it up from time to time with HP and ↓ + HK, and you have enough to keep opponents guessing at all times.

Another viable option to do on wakeup, or after any successful jump in, is to jump straight up and use LP on the way down. Use it as a tick and Power Bomb when Alex lands. Against taller characters, jump straight up and do HP early enough so that, on the way down, they are out of hit/block stun and open for a Power Bomb.

After a mid-screen knockdown or a successful Air Stampede, you can set up a tricky wake up situation. Stay as close as possible and hold ↓. As soon as the opponent gets up off the ground, use close MK and immediately cancel into a Air Stampede (HK), which crosses up. Opponents end up in block stun while this happens, so they can't get out of the way and must block or parry. If Air Stampede hits, it knocks down, and you are in position to charge again and repeat the trick. Mix this up by canceling into an Air Stampede (MK) instead of HK. This version does not cross up, so opponents must actively choose which way to block. As long as you keep hitting them, they will keep getting knocked down. Continue dropping boots until they figure out how to block this trick. If they've figured it out and are going to block the next time, cancel the MK into a Spiral D.D.T.

When Alex gets knocked down, he has a good answer to opponent's wake up tactics: EX Air Stampede. It generally goes through and punishes all ground pokes and is fairly fast. It is not completely safe if blocked, but it is hard to react to it in time, so generally do not fear doing a wake up Air Stampede.

ADVANCED TACTIC: CHARGE PARTITIONING

Take advantage of charge partitioning to invent new setups to land Alex's Smash Elbow and Air Stampede in situations where it normally couldn't happen. The idea of Charge Partitioning is simple, just divide the charge time of a move into pieces. Charge for a little bit, do something, then finish the charge and execute the move. Here are some examples of how you can incorporate charge partitioning into Alex's game:

Do a Smash Elbow and begin charging. Dash backwards after it hits and finish charging during the dash. When the dash finishes, immediately execute an EX Smash Elbow. Opponents often try to poke or dash after Alex as he dashes back. Surprise them with a quick EX Smash Elbow.

Tap down for a split second before jumping, then jump forward with a MK to strike an opponent fairly high during the jump. During the jump, charge so that when you land, it's possible to immediately cross up with an Air Stampede. This works because most opponents try to hit or throw Alex when he lands. This setup works great with Alex's jump LP and LK, as well.

From across the screen, start charging back and do two MP for timing purposes, then dash forward and use Smash Elbow with either LP or MP. Keep charging so you can dash back and use an EX Smash Elbow.

It's also possible to charge for an Air Stampede while walking back and forth. This is extremely useful against zoning characters, such as Ken and Chun-Li. These characters tend to walk back and forth just outside of Alex's longest poke reach. Shadow them and make it seem like you're playing into their poke/counter poke game. If they take a step forward, you take a step back. If they step back, you step forward. With each step, tap down for just a second. If you time it right, after three taps you should have a full charge to surprise them with an Air Stampede. Cross up and score a knock down, which is a perfect way to get close against defensive players. Most players never expect an Air Stampede in this situation because Alex is walking back and forth. Usually a charge character stays crouching before a charge move.

One more setup that can catch people is a close MK, then start charging ↓. Do a UOH and finish the charge. As soon as the UOH whiffs in front of the opponent, cross up with an Air Stampede. Upon seeing the UOH, most players react with a high block, which usually leads to a whiffed UOH. Most opponents reaction to the whiff is an attack, but by then Alex should be on his way in the air, ready to drop his boots on their head.

SETUPS

Ranged set ups for UOH → super art

Against small and medium sized characters:

(→ + MP), UOH → Boomerang Raid

Against medium sized characters:

(↓ + LP), UOH → Boomerang Raid

Against Oro:

No setup is required. UOH → SA2 works at close distance on crouching Oro.

PARRY SET UPS AND TACTICS

Alex's MP → EX Air Knee Smash is a great anti-air that does good damage. To make it even better, option parry forward right before doing the MP. If a jumping opponent sticks out an attack, you will parry and counter. If they did not attack, you continue on with the anti-air as originally planned. This covers Alex against moves that HP won't beat.

Alex's kara throw is → + HP → throw. When executing a kara throw, first tap → a split second before pressing HP. This option parry covers Alex in case the opponent tries any mid level attacks. Alex will parry first, then continue on and throw.

GROUND CROSS UPS

Alex can cross up Necro, Twelve, Hugo in any corner.

FAVORABLE MATCH UP: SEAN

Alex can control the tempo of the match against Sean. On the ground he can consistently out-range Sean and beat out his low pokes with MK, and he can rush in easily with Smash Elbow. Use jumping HP to jump in at Sean with little fear. Alex's jump is fairly fast and low to the ground. Sean generally doesn't have enough time to counter Alex with HK. His only anti-air quick enough to beat Alex's jump in is an EX Dragon Smash. If Sean must burn meter for anti-airs, he loses any ability to do big damage to Alex on the ground.

When Alex has Sean cornered on wake up, Sean is in a similar predicament, needing to burn meter in order to get clear of Alex. Alex should be able to control Sean on the ground. Sean will have difficulty jumping in due to Alex's option parry into MP → EX Air Knee Smash.

UNFAVORABLE MATCH UP: IBUKI

Alex must play defensively against Ibuki, and that doesn't suit his style at all. Ibuki is a momentum character, and once she gets going, it's hard to stop her. Expect her attacks against Alex to come from all over: jumping, crossing up, and dashing through Alex. This makes it hard for Alex to keep a charge. Ibuki's LP hits Alex when he is crouching, so Alex has a hard time finding an opening against Ibuki. Alex's pokes aren't fast enough to interrupt her attack patterns. From mid-range Ibuki can keep Alex pressured with Bonshougeri because it hits him while he's crouching.

Even if Alex is fortunate enough to score a knockdown, there isn't much he can do because of Ibuki's EX Kazakiri, which beats every thing Alex can do to her on wakeup. Alex also has the misfortune of not being able to counter Ibuki's Koubekudaki command overhead with anything other than a super. And, if Alex is using Boomerang Raid, he can only manage to land two hits in this situation, so it's not even worth trying. In the worst case scenario where Alex doesn't have enough meter for a super art, Ibuki is free to pressure with this move all day.

For Alex to win this match up, he may have to resort to parrying. When Ibuki is pressuring with repeated LPs, try to react to the first jab and parry the second one. If she doesn't jab, chances are she will go low with ↓ + HK. A down parry should still work in that situation. Alex is too slow to get out of the way of Ibuki's jumping assault, so try to parry all her jump-ins and counter.

Chun-Li

NORMAL MOVES

STANDING

HP is Chun-Li's main, all-purpous poke with ridiculous range and damage. It's a fantastic whiff punisher and safe if blocked.

HK is a good offensive poke that goes over a variety of low attacks. It has good recovery and links into a Houyouku-Sen if it hits against a crouching opponent.

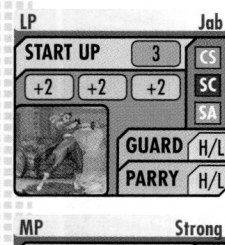

LP — Jab
START UP: 3
+2 +2 +2
CS / SC / SA
GUARD: H/L
PARRY: H/L

LK — Short
START UP: 3
+1 +1 +1
C / SC / SA
GUARD: H/L
PARRY: H/L

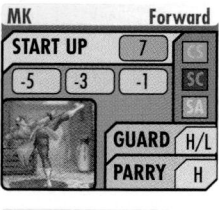

MP — Strong
START UP: 6
-2 -1 0
SC / SA
GUARD: H/L
PARRY: H

MK — Forward
START UP: 7
-5 -3 -1
CS / SC / SA
GUARD: H/L
PARRY: H

HP — Fierce
START UP: 8
-2 0 +2
SC
GUARD: H/L
PARRY: H

HK — Roundhouse
START UP: 12
0 +2 +4
CS / SC / SA
GUARD: H/L
PARRY: H

STANDING CLOSE

In close, HK hits hard and cancels into a super jump, which is useful in a number of ways. If an opponent parries the attack and tries to throw Chun-Li, she can safely cancel close HK into a super jump to avoid the throw completely. Super jump cancelable normals also have the ability to cancel into super arts in a strange manner: by canceling into a super jump, then inputting a super art command before leaving the ground. This must be done quickly in one big motion for it to work. Because Chun-Li can super jump cancel close HK so late into its recovery, there is just enough time to verify the attack, then super jump cancel into a super art if it does hit, giving Chun-Li another safe way to land a super art.

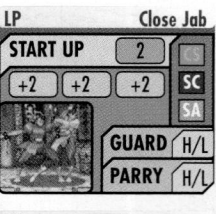

LP — Close Jab
START UP: 2
+2 +2 +2
CS / SC / SA
GUARD: H/L
PARRY: H/L

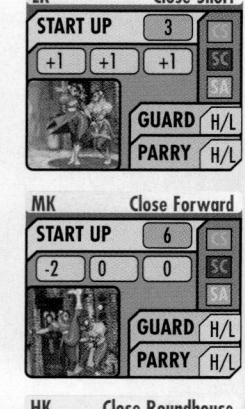

LK — Close Short
START UP: 3
+1 +1 +1
SC / SA
GUARD: H/L
PARRY: H/L

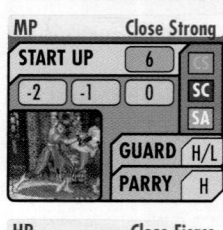

MP — Close Strong
START UP: 6
-2 -1 0
SC / SA
GUARD: H/L
PARRY: H

MK — Close Forward
START UP: 6
-2 0 0
SC / SA
GUARD: H/L
PARRY: H/L

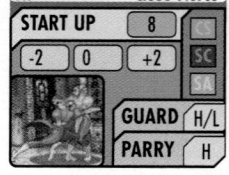

HP — Close Fierce
START UP: 8
-2 0 +2
SC
GUARD: H/L
PARRY: H

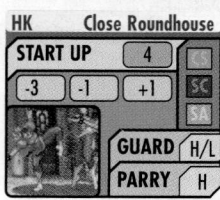

HK — Close Roundhouse
START UP: 4
-3 -1 +1
CS / SC / SA
GUARD: H/L
PARRY: H

SPECIAL NORMALS

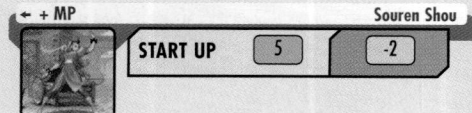

← + MP — Souren Shou
START UP: 5 | -2

A two-hit slap that's cancelable off both hits. Whiffs against crouching characters, and decent in punishment situations where the hit is guaranteed and you want to land a super art behind it.

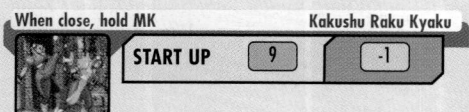

When close, hold MK — Kakushu Raku Kyaku
START UP: 9 | -1

Multi-hit heel kick with limited uses.

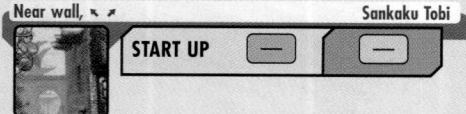

Near wall, ↖↗ — Sankaku Tobi
START UP: —

Use Sankaku Tobi to get Chun-Li out of corners. When an opponent is cornered, do a Yousou Kyaku, then as Chun-Li recovers from the stomp mid-air, bounce off the wall. On the way down, Chun-Li can parry any anti-air attempt, and if the opponent tries to meet her with a low attack, hit HK on the way down, or do nothing and just block as Chun-Li lands.

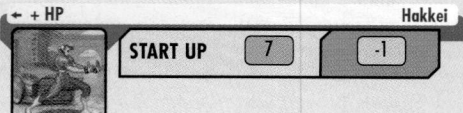

← + HP — Hakkei
START UP: 7 | -1

A cancelable palm thrust with almost unfair priority. Notorious for being able to beat a large assortment of pokes. During foot games, use this move to beat anticipated poke attempts. It's also a good way to land a super art in punishment situations.

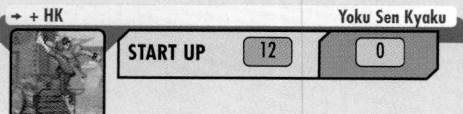

→ + HK — Yoku Sen Kyaku
START UP: 12 | 0

The moving version of HK with essentially the same properties. Possible to link a Houyouku-Sen afterward if it hits against crouching characters.

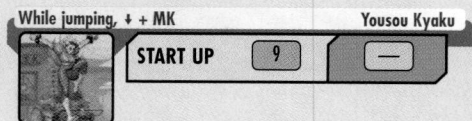

While jumping, ↓ + MK — Yousou Kyaku
START UP: 9

Hit or blocked, Yousou Kyaku allows Chun-Li to recover completely after bouncing off of an opponent's head, meaning she can execute another jump attack or parry on the way down. Somewhat limited, but has some use in aerial combos.

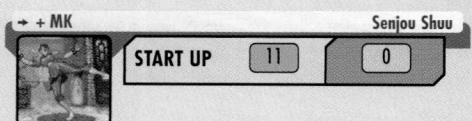

→ + MK — Senjou Shuu
START UP: 11 | 0

Lunging kick that moves Chun-Li forward. Useful during foot games as it rarely whiffs. When blocked, set up option select parries or minor guessing games, such as walk up kara throw or Hakkei after recovering. Used sparingly, it makes a decent addition to her ground game.

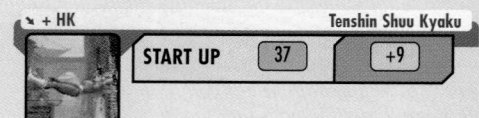

↘ + HK — Tenshin Shuu Kyaku
START UP: 37 | +9

Slight frame advantage afterward, but it's possible to link a Houyouku-Sen after it hits. Extremely slow, very easy to parry on reaction.

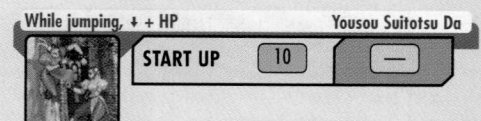

While jumping, ↓ + HP — Yousou Suitotsu Da
START UP: 10

Yousou Suitotsu Da sends opponents flying toward the ground if it hits while they are airborne. Has one use inside an awkward anti-air combo. Do an early anti-air Yousou Kyaku, juggle with a semi late Yousou Suitotsu Da before landing, then just as Chun-Li touches down, juggle with an immediate ↓ + LP. Sets up a ground cross up opportunity.

CROUCHING

One of the fastest normal moves in the game, ↓ + LP is good defensively for stopping throw attempts and other mix up patterns.

↓ + MK is the main opening for landing a super art. It possesses passable range, and recovers quickly (for a medium strength attack), making it difficult to punish. It serves as a good whiff punisher, although Chun-Li must be close to do so. It also cancels into special attacks and super arts after it hits much later than most normal attacks; late enough that it's possible to verify the move before starting the super art.

↓ + HK has a wide hit box and can be used to beat a variety of normals from a distance. Decent anti-air in limited situations.

↓ + LP	Low Jab	
START UP		2	CS
+3	+3	+3	SC
			SA
GUARD		H/L	
PARRY		H/L	

↓ + LK	Low Short	
START UP		4	CS
+3	+3	+3	SC
			SA
GUARD		L	
PARRY		L	

↓ + MP	Low Strong	
START UP		8	
-4	-3	-2	SC
			SA
GUARD		L	
PARRY		L	

↓ + MK	Low Forward	
START UP		6	
-2	-1	0	SC
			SA
GUARD		L	
PARRY		L	

↓ + HP	Low Fierce	
START UP		8	
-1	+1	+3	SC
			SA
GUARD		H/L	
PARRY		H/L	

↓ + HK	Low Roundhouse	
START UP		7	CS
-7	D	D	SC
			SA
GUARD		H/L	
PARRY		H/L	

JUMPING

↑ + LP	Vertical Jab	
START UP		4	CS
—	—	—	SC
			SA
GUARD		H	
PARRY		H	

↖ / ↗ + LP	Jumping Jab	
START UP		2	CS
—	—	—	SC
			SA
GUARD		H	
PARRY		H	

↑ + MP	Vertical Strong	
START UP		7	CS
—	—	—	SC
			SA
GUARD		H	
PARRY		H	

↖ / ↗ + MP	Jumping Strong	
START UP		4	
—	—	—	SC
			SA
GUARD		H	
PARRY		H	

↑ + HP	Vertical Fierce	
START UP		10	
—	—	—	SC
			SA
GUARD		H	
PARRY		H	

↖ / ↗ + HP	Jumping Fierce	
START UP		9	SC
—	—	—	
			SA
GUARD		H	
PARRY		H	

↑ + LK	Vertical Short	
START UP		5	
—	—	—	SC
			SA
GUARD		H	
PARRY		H	

↖ / ↗ + LK	Jumping Short	
START UP		5	
—	—	—	SC
			SA
GUARD		H	
PARRY		H	

↑ + MK	Vertical Forward	
START UP		6	
—	—	—	SC
			SA
GUARD		H	
PARRY		H	

↖ / ↗ + MK	Jumping Forward	
START UP		6	
—	—	—	SC
			SA
GUARD		H	
PARRY		H	

↑ + HK	Vertical Roundhouse	
START UP		8	
—	—	—	SC
			SA
GUARD		H	
PARRY		H	

↖ / ↗ + HK	Jumping Roundhouse	
START UP		10	
—	—	—	SC
			SA
GUARD		H	
PARRY		H	

THROWS

LP + LK	Koshuu Tou

In air, LP + LK	Ryuusei Raku

SPECIAL MOVES

← ↙ ↓ ↘ → + P	Kikouken

14	13	11	16
-17	-10	-4	-7

Button strength determines how far the projectile travels and how fast it recovers. HP version has limited uses in simple combos like Hakkei → Kikouken (HP). However, it is not safe versus fast super arts if it hits or misses. EX version recovers slowly, but travels at a slow speed with no range / damage deduction. Use as a shield for Chun-Li to dash behind it to get in close on opponents. Still, it remains a risky move to do in general, and isn't important to Chun-Li's ground game.

Tap K rapidly	Hyakuretsu Kyaku

6	6	5	3
+3	+1	-1	-3

Perform it meaty on wake up to inflict block damage if an opponent is pixels away from death. EX version does more damage and knocks down. It is possible to link Houyouku-Sen after the LK version if the opponent is standing, but the damage the super art does is greatly diminished.

→ ↘ ↓ ↙ ← + K	Hazan Shuu

22	24	29	31
-2	-2	-1	-2

A slow command overhead that can be canceled into behind normals. The EX version comes out slower, but knocks down and cannot be quick recovered. It's risky due to being somewhat easy to parry on reaction.

Charge ↓ ↑ + K	Spinning Bird Kick

12	14	17	12
-2	-2	-2	-8

Possesses some limited use in combos: ↓ + HP → Spinning Bird Kick (MK) is Chun-Li's most damaging non super art combo. However, this move whiffs against crouching characters, making it completely unsafe. Save it for punishment situations. The EX version does more damage, knocks down, and hits crouching oponents. It also functions as a wake up because it has some invincibility and has limited use in basic combos, although still not safe if blocked. Use with caution.

COSTUMES

LP · MP · HP · LK · MK · HK

Start + LP · Start + MP · Start + HP · Start + LK · Start + MK · Start + HK

LP + MK + HP

CHUN-LI

SUPER ARTS

SUPER ART I

↓ ↘ → ↓ ↘ → + P **Kikou-Shou**

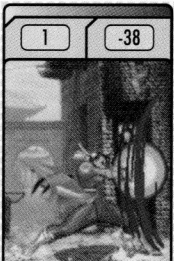

| 1 | -38 |

Kikou-Shou is one of the fastest super arts in the game. With a single frame start up, it is one of the only super arts that can hit the recovery of Dudley's Dart Shot, and is the only super art that can hit Ken after a blocked MP → HP target combo. Kikou-Shou links after all her important moves: Hakkei, HP, ↓ + HP, far HK, and towards + MK. She can also hit confirm it off of late cancels from: ↓ + MK, MP, and super jump canceled close HK. Almost any hit from Chun-Li can lead to a super. Kikou-Shou is also a solid anti air option. At 20 hits, it is unlikely that every hit will be parried.

Although it combos so easily, Kikou-Shou does less damage the further away it hits. This is not good because most of Chun-Li's game revolves around keeping people at a distance with her high priority pokes. Also, with only one meter of super stocked, Chun-Li will be struggling to do damage after she uses her super.

SUPER ART II

↓ ↘ → ↓ ↘ → + K **Houyouku-Sen**

| 3 | -23 |

Houyouku-Sen paired with ↓ + MK is the sole reason why Chun-Li is a dominant force in *Street Fighter III: 3rd Strike*. Houyouku-Sen is fast, powerful, has two stocks of super meter, and combos nearly as easily as Kikou-Shou. It's possible to verify Houyouku-Sen from late cancels of ↓ + MK, MP, and Hakkei, as well as super jump canceling it from close HK. It links easily from HK and Tenshin Shuukyakku. Almost any hit can lead to a super art, and even at maximum poke range, Houyouku-Sen hits for full damage. Most opponents are reluctant to attack Chun-Li from close range. Use this to your advantage to inflict damage off of kara throws.

Houyouku-Sen is invincible versus certain moves at start up and travels a significantly long distance on its first hit. Use it to pass through projectiles and hit opponents while they are stuck in recovery. It allows Chun-Li to punish whiffs from half a screen away, and punish many moves when blocked.

The last hit of Houyouku-Sen is super jump cancelable, allowing Chun-Li to jump in the air and juggle for two additional hits, then use these hits to gain position over a grounded opponent, or reset them and go for an ambiguous ground cross up situation mid screen.

SUPER ART III

↓ ↘ → ↓ ↘ → + K **Tensei-Ranka**

| 3 | -30 |

Tensei-Ranka gives Chun-Li a good anti-air move. It has three stocks of super meter, so it can be used often. However, anti-air is essentially its only use. There's no potential for high damage combos on the ground with Tensei-Ranka. Chun-Li's EX special attacks are lacking, so there is little reason to select this super art and its three stocks of super meter.

Recommended Super Art: Houyouku-Sen

Houyouku-Sen is so good that there is really no reason to consider her other super arts. Her ability to control the fight on the ground is unmatched by her other two super arts. While Chun-Li lacks a solid anti-air with Houyouku-Sen, the way it dominates it on the ground more than justifies selecting it. With two levels of super meter, one ↓ + MK hit can potentially lead to a double super combination, almost ensuring victory that round.

TARGET COMBOS

↖ / ↗ HP → HP

	9
	—

Passable in air-to-air situations and for juggles after Houyouku-Sen. Use it to build super meter by jumping backward and whiffing the HPs.

COMBOS YOU NEED TO KNOW

6 HITS

TOTAL DAMAGE: 42

↓ + HP → EX Spinning Bird Kick

Good for punishment situations. Knocks down.

20 HITS

TOTAL DAMAGE: 67

↓ + MK → Houyouku-Sen, super jump cancel the last hit and juggle with HP → HP

Does a ridiculous amount of damage and leads to the high/low set up of your choice after the air chain in the corner.

20 HITS

TOTAL DAMAGE: 66

Close HK, super jump cancel → Houyouku-Sen, super jump cancel the last hit and juggle with HP → HP

Does a ridiculous amount of damage and leads to the high/low set up of your choice after the air chain in the corner.

20 HITS

TOTAL DAMAGE: 72

CROUCHING OPPONENTS ONLY

HK linked into Houyouku-Sen, super jump cancel the last hit and juggle with HP → HP

Verifiable. HK goes over an assortment of low attacks, making this a good way to land a super art if it hits. Does massive damage and leads to the high/low set up of your choice after the air chain in the corner.

21 HITS

TOTAL DAMAGE: 58

Close HK, super jump cancel → Kikou-Shou

Verifiable and inflicts decent damage. Knocks down.

21 HITS

TOTAL DAMAGE: 57

↓ + MK → Kikou-Shou

3 HITS

TOTAL DAMAGE: 24

Anti-air Yousou Kyaku, juggle with a semi-late Yousou Suitotsu Da before landing; immediately upon touching the ground, juggle with ↓ + LP.

Setting up an opponent to get hit by this combo is tricky. After the ↓ + LP juggle, dash to the other side of the opponent just before the flip recovery for a confusing side switch trick. It's possible to dictate which side Chun-Li ends on by dashing forward at different times: earlier to get behind, and later to stay on front.

STRATEGY

Kakutsuken

Chun-Li's strategy is to control the ground. With Houyouku-Sen, she is the dominant zoning fighter. She outranges and outpokes almost every other character. Anytime she has a single stock of super meter, she becomes a scary opponent. Any hit can combo into a super art, leading to an opponent's life bar being halved. Concentrate on landing ⬇ + MK. ⬇ + MK ➜ Houyouku-Sen is the only combo Chun-Li needs. Everything else is style points (which aren't tallied by the game). HK goes over all low pokes and links into super arts. Close HK provides an up-close mid attack that verifies into a super art. Hakkei and MP beat out almost every other ground move, and cancel into super art on reaction. All of these moves' ability to combo into Houyouku-Sen make Chun-Li's ground game nearly unbeatable.

⬇ + MK is especially important; it's fast, has a great reach, and is practically unpunishable. It's possible to cancel ⬇ + MK into Houyouku-Sen at any point in the move, even into the very last recovery frames. This luxury of time and ability to verify deeply into the move makes Chun-Li absolutely deadly. Keep opponents at bay by zoning with ⬇ + MK. If anyone gets close, they are instnatly at risk of ⬇ + MK ➜ super art. Position Chun-Li just outside of her opponent's longest low poke range. Do whatever it takes to bait an attack, then quickly ⬇ + MK ➜ super art the recovering limb. This strategy is so frustrating to play against, it often causes other players to go on the defensive, or resort to unsafe tactics to beat Chun-Li. Against slower characters, stay well out of range and buffer super art motions while using Hakkei or ⬇ + HP.

If an opponent starts playing defensively, start kara throwing repeatedly. Chun-Li's kara throw range is outside the reach of most fast pokes. At her maximum kara throw range, she is safe from most forms of verifiable counter attack. Opponents are forced to guess whether a throw is coming. In order to tech a throw, opponents must either stand up and throw, or option select and commit to ⬇ + LP. Performing either of these in anticipation of a throw leaves them open to ⬇ + MK, and Houyouku-Sen.

When Chun-Li is less of a threat when she doesn't have any super meter stocked. She has no high damaging combos or means to punish whiffs in a big way. Play a similar game plan by staying out of range, zoning with ⬇ + MK and Hakkei, and punishing whiffs from long range with HP until she builds up a super meter stock. Another option is to keep away and build meter before attacking. Whiffing Hakkei builds meter quickly, and stops dashes and rush down pokes at the same time. If an opponent gets close, use jump HP ➜ HP. Jumping back and forth and using this chain is a good way to control space if Chun-Li's super meter is empty.

Backing into corners can be turned to your advantage when trying to play keep away. Super jump toward the wall and use Sankaku Tobi to get clear of pursuing opponents, or use Yousou Kyaku if the opportunity presents itself. If the Yousou Kyaku is blocked, Chun-Li bounces off and continues in her original direction. Once Yousou Kyaku connects (by blocking, hitting, or being parried), Chun-Li's jump state is reset, allowing another move, attempt to hit, or air parry any counter attack. With at least one full meter available, there is no need to run away anymore. Stay on the ground and start up with ⬇ + MKs. As soon as one connects, cancel into Houyouku-Sen. Then concentrate on building up meter again.

Chun-Li lacks a solid, all-purpose anti-air move, but she has ways to deal with incoming attackers. Chun-Li walks quickly, allowing her to walk under most cross up attempts. Use ⬇ + MK or close HK to punish them

upon landing. If you feel confident that they will not attack in the air, hit them out of the air with stand jab. As they flip over and land, dash under them for a sneaky cross up. If you possess quick reflexes, jump and meet opponents in the air with either HP ➜ HP, or air throw. Another great air option for players with quick reflexes is to super jump toward opponents and use Yousou Kyaku. If it hits, juggle with Yousou Suitotsu Da, land, and juggle with ⬇ + LP for a reset. From there, dash under for a ground cross up.

WAKEUP GAME

Chun-Li is deadly staying at her maximum kara throw range or moving close to a waking opponent,. From close up, throwing is always an option. Most players expect Chun-Li to throw from far away, so an in-your-face throw is always a surprise. A tick throw with ⬇ + LK is a good option. ⬇ + LK has frame advantage, so Chun-Li is able to attack again before they can hit her. The two best options off of a ⬇ + LK tick are ⬇ + MK, and close HK. ⬇ + MK can't be parried high. If it hits, cancel into Houyouku-Sen. Close HK can't be parried low. Super jump cancel on reaction and cancel into Houyouku-Sen. If either option is blocked, Chun-Li is still in a good, close range to walk up and kara throw, or get into position for a UOH ➜ super art. At this distance, opponents may try to attack. This is a good time to go for a HK over their poke. If it hits, link into super art.

When getting off the ground, Chun-Li has a great wakeup move. EX Spinning Bird Kick goes through all low attacks, and can be used from up close, or from a short distance away. It also has the property of sucking in opponents. Don't rely on it solely; certain high attacks beat it and it's vulnerable if blocked. ⬇ + LP is great in wake up situations. It is the fastest normal move and cleanly defeats any move or throw attempt. If parried, immediately cancel into EX Spinning Bird Kick. Close HK is another good move in close situations. It comes out reasonably fast and has high priority. Use it to beat throws and low parry attempts (of the anticipated ⬇ + LP). If it hits, super jump cancel, then cancel into Houyouku-Sen. If the oppponent parries, super jump cancel into the air to escape any throw attempt.

SETUPS

Double Houyouku-Sen Tricks: The last hit of Houyouku-Sen is super jump cancelable. There are many ways to set up opponents for an ambiguous cross up, or high/low situation that's difficult to react to properly. This is the perfect position to land a second Houyouku-Sen. Landing one Houyouku-Sen can generally lead to a second super art about half of the time.

Setup 1: (Against everyone in the corner). After the super jump cancel, HP ➜ HP early in the jump so only the first HP hits, leading opponent to flip back and recover. While the screen stays concentrated on the recovering character, Chun-Li lands off-screen. Immediately UOH upon landing. It should be a perfectly timed meaty UOH that links another Houyouku-Sen. It is hard to react to because Chun-Li is off-screen while starting the UOH.

Setup 2: (Against most characters mid screen). After the super jump cancel, jump LK to cause the opponent to flip back and recover. Chun-Li lands off screen. Walk forward while the opponent falls back to the ground. Walk under the moment the opponent lands, setting up a ground cross up situation. Hesitating just a little bit allows you to uncross up. This is a difficult situation for opponents because they can't see where Chun-Li is until they land. HK as they land to provide enough time to verify super jump cancel, then cancel into another Houyouku-Sen. To make this even trickier, use ⬇ + MK. Chun-Li's crouching animation is low to the ground. The falling player won't be able to see which side Chun-Li is on until they are hit.

Setup 3: (Against most characters mid screen). After the super jump cancel, jump MP to cause the opponent to flip back and recover. Immediately UOH when Chun-Li lands. It should be perfectly meaty to link into another Houyouku-Sen.

Setup 4: (Against small characters mid screen). After the super jump cancel, Yousou Suitotsu Da to knock opponents down on the ground. Quickly dash up and UOH over their bodies as they are getting up for a ground cross up opportunity. Close HK immediately, super jump cancel, then cancel into super art if that hits. To increase confusion, change up the timing of the dash or UOH or how much you walk forward or backwards.

Setup 5: (Against Chun-Li mid screen). After the super jump cancel, Yousou Kyaku, jump LK, land and dash under the falling Chun-Li, close HK, super jump cancel, then cancel into Houyouku-Sen on a hit.

Setup 6: (Against Chun-Li in the corner). After the super jump cancel, Yousou Kyaku, jump LK, land, and immediately UOH. Link Houyouku-Sen or a low poke.

RANGES SETUPS FOR UOH ➜ SUPER ART

Against small, medium, and wide characters:

(⬇ + LK, ⬇ + HK), UOH ➜ Houyouku-Sen

Against medium sized characters:

(⬇ + LK, close HK), UOH ➜ Houyouku-Sen

(⬇ + LK, close HK, ⬇ + MK), UOH ➜ Houyouku-Sen

Against Oro:

No setup is required. UOH ➜ works at close distance on crouching Oro.

RESETS

Reset 1: In an air-to-air situation, hit the other airborne opponent with Yousou Kyaku, then immediately Yousou Suitotsu Da to juggle. Land and juggle with ⬇ + LP to reset. Dash under to cross up just as the opponent lands.

PARRY SET UPS AND TACTICS

Chun-Li doesn't have a perfect anti-air move, so mixing in option select parries helps deal with jump-ins. As jumping opponents get near, tap ➜, then LP a split second later. Timed properly, and the opponent attacked, Chun-Li parried, then hit with LP. LP recovers quickly, so Chun-Li is not in very much danger.

GROUND CROSS UPS

Chun-Li can cross up Twelve, Alex, Dudley, Necro, Hugo, and Urien in any corner.

FAVORABLE MATCH UP: KEN

Chun-Li is the only character that can shut down Ken. Chun-Li's pokes are quicker and deadlier than Ken's. A patient Chun-Li can counter attack any of Ken's whiffed low forwards with ⬇ + MK ➜ Houyouku-Sen. Stay just outside of Ken's maximum range. Chun-Li must keep Ken away. If Ken can't get close, Chun-Li has little to fear. If Ken tries to jump in, walk under him and ⬇ + MK or HK. Always maintain distance until you score a knockdown.

If Ken corners you, learn his poke ranges like they were your own. There is a certain distance where Ken's low forward no longer hits Chun-Li, but roundhouse will. At that distance, it is reasonably safe for Chun-Li to stand up for a split second to catch the HK if he uses it. If Chun-Li blocks Ken's HK high, punish him with a super art during his recovery. Chun-Li must block it high, because she recovers from block stun quicker when standing. A low block recovers from stun one frame too late.

UNFAVORABLE MATCH UP: YUN

There isn't much Chun-Li can do to ward off an aggressive Yun player. Chun-Li must be patient and deal with the attacks as they come. Chun-Li's dominance comes from her ability to control the ground. If Yun is constantly jumping and Dive Kicking, he's not open to ⬇ + MK ➜ Houyouku-Sen. If Yun starts running away and building meter for Genei Jin, try to back Yun into a corner before he can activate it.

A good strategy is to try to always stay on the same plane as Yun. If he jumps, so should you. Don't let him get higher, where Chun-Li can't fight him off. Vertical roundhouse is good to keep Yun away. If you are on the ground and he Dive Kicks, option parry a with close HK to cover a short whiffed Dive Kick attempt. If you score a knock down, then you're ready to take control. Yun really has no way to get Chun-Li away from him in a wake up situation. Use this to your advantage to throw him repeatedly, then fake him out and try to land ⬇ + MK ➜ super art. One knockdown could be all Chun-Li needs to win. Getting that one knock down is the hard part.

CHUN-LI

Dudley

NORMAL MOVES

STANDING

HP is a decent poke at close range, still inflicting good damage with moderate range. MK is a great mid level attack. Completely safe if blocked, and it barely pushes Dudley away so he is still standing right next to opponents, ready to attack again. Links into Rocket Upper and Corkscrew Blow easily.

HK possesses a fairly large frame advantage after it and can be used to verify and link Rolling Thunder. It's possible to whiff this move just outside of poke range in the midst of inputting an EX Machine Gun Blow. If opponents attack, HK hits and cancels into the EX Machine Gun Blow, scoring damage and a knock down.

LP		Jab	
START UP		3	CS
+3	+3	+3	SC
			SA
GUARD			H/L
PARRY			H

MP		Strong	
START UP		3	CS
+1	+2	+3	SC
			SA
GUARD			H/L
PARRY			H

HP		Fierce	
START UP		7	CS
-1	+1	+3	SC
			SA
GUARD			H/L
PARRY			H

LK		Short	
START UP		5	CS
+2	+2	+2	SC
			SA
GUARD			H/L
PARRY			H/L

MK		Forward	
START UP		5	CS
0	+2	+2	SC
			SA
GUARD			H/L
PARRY			H

HK		Roundhouse	
START UP		5	CS
+4	+6	+8	SC
			SA
GUARD			H/L
PARRY			H

CROUCHING

Doubling up ↓ + LK is a great opening for all of Dudley's supers. Fast, hits low, and it's flexible. ↓ + HK is a two-handed sweep with mediocre range. It's a juggle setup, and can lead to a ton of damage. This move is completely safe if blocked. Great for reset patterns.

↓ + LP		Low Jab	
START UP		3	CS
+1	+1	+1	SC
			SA
GUARD			H/L
PARRY			H/L

↓ + MP		Low Strong	
START UP		4	CS
+2	+3	+4	SC
			SA
GUARD			H/L
PARRY			H/L

↓ + HP		Low Fierce	
START UP		7	CS
0	+2	+2	SC
			SA
GUARD			H/L
PARRY			H/L

↓ + LK		Low Short	
START UP		4	CS
0	0	0	SC
			SA
GUARD			L
PARRY			L

↓ + MK		Low Forward	
START UP		9	CS
-12	D	D	SC
			SA
GUARD			L
PARRY			L

↓ + HK		Low Roundhouse	
START UP		15	CS
+1	D	D	SC
			SA
GUARD			H/L
PARRY			H/L

COSTUMES

 LP
 MP
 HP
 LK
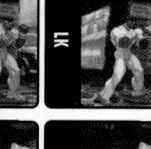 MK
 HK
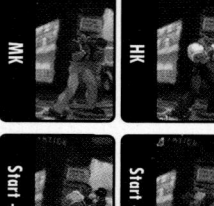 Start + LP / Start + MP
 Start + HP
 Start + LK / Start + MK / Start + HK
 LP + MK + HP

SPECIAL NORMALS

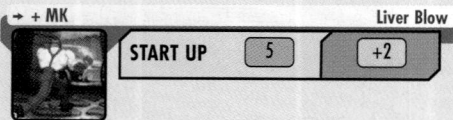

→ + LP		Slipping Jab	
START UP	4		+1

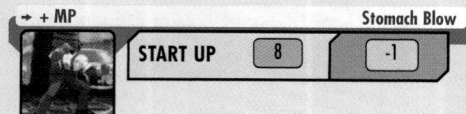

→ + MK		Liver Blow	
START UP	5		+2

Very fast and a decent amount of frame advantage after it. Liver Blow can be linked into a Rocket Upper or Corkscrew Blow. It also keeps Dudley close when blocked, allowing him to set up guessing games afterward. Cancelable and has some use in juggle combos.

→ + MP		Stomach Blow	
START UP	8		-1

Gut punch that moves Dudley forward. Okay poke at close range.

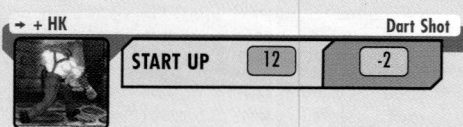

→ + HK		Dart Shot	
START UP	12		-2

Very fast overhead. Can be chained into MK for extra damage. Also links into a Rocket Upper or Corkscrew Blow against crouching opponents.

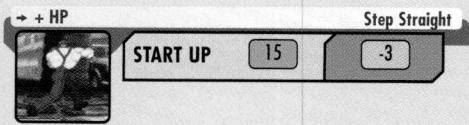

→ + HP		Step Straight	
START UP	15		-3

A moving version of Dudley's HP. Super art cancelable and a good poke with terrific range. Hard to avoid during foot games and safe from the right ranges.

JUMPING

Dudley can hit with HK extremely early in his jumping arc and still have enough time to link a super art when he lands due to its enormous hit stun. Excellent jump-in.

↑ + LP Jumping Jab	↑ + MP Jumping Strong	↑ + HP Jumping Fierce	↑ + LK Jumping Short	↑ + MK Jumping Forward	↑ + HK Jumping Roundhouse
START UP 3	START UP 4	START UP 7	START UP 3	START UP 4	START UP 11
GUARD —	GUARD H	GUARD H	GUARD H	GUARD H	GUARD H
PARRY H	PARRY H	PARRY H	PARRY H	PARRY H	PARRY H

THROWS

LP + LK Liver Crusher	→ + LP + LK Dynamite Throw

SPECIAL MOVES

→ ↘ ↓ ↙ ← + P Cross Counter	← ↙ ↓ ↘ → + P Machine Gun Blow	→ ↓ ↘ + P Jet Upper	→ ↘ ↓ ↙ ← + K Short Swing Blow

2 / 2 / 2 / 4	8 / 15 / 17 / 16	4 / 4 / 3 / 3	17 / 20 / 23 / 17
— / — / — / —	-3 / -9 / -15 / -15	-23 / -30 / -38 / -37	0 / 0 / 0 / -3

Cross Counter is just that, a counter attack. If Dudley is hit during this move, he counters with a rushing punch. The damage of the counter attack depends on the damage of the attack used against him, meaning the more damage it was set to do, the more damage they take. Note that Dudley still takes damage from the attack, so it's possible for Dudley to do the counter, then get knocked out afterward. The move is limited, so stick to using defensively in desperate situations where you're having trouble beating an opponent's offense. The EX version hits more times and does more damage.

Rapid fire punch combo with great range. Passable for punishing whiffed attacks, it can also be used in combination with HK to beat and punish some normal attacks on start up. It's a huge threat during foot games against some characters as Dudley can punish some normal attacks on startup, especially with an EX Machine Gun Blow. The EX version is a juggle setup, and can be used in combos to score big damage.

Good as a reversal or in some combos, plus it inflicts impressive stun damage. The EX version is faster and does more damage.

Fantastic for avoiding and punishing throw attempts in wake up situations. If it's done just as an opponent tries to throw, the throw whiffs, which should be punished with the gut punch. The punch at the end can be super canceled for extra damage. The EX version of this move does a 3 hit combo at the end, which knocks down.

← ↙ ↓ ↘ → + K Ducking	During Ducking, P Ducking Strait	During Ducking, K Ducking Upper

— / — / — / —	20 / 19 / 21 / —	19 / 18 / 20 / —
— / — / — / —	-7 / -7 / -7 / —	-12 / -12 / -12 / —

Very good for keeping close after failed attacks. Cancel into Ducking from HK to set up high/low/throw mix up games. Use the LK version to punish whiffed normals during foot games, ending with a Corkscrew Blow. Ducking can be used to pass through most projectiles.

Whiffs against most crouching characters, but use it against large characters to their punish whiffed attacks.

Mainly used to keep opponents from attacking or throwing Dudley out of Ducking during its recovery. Ducking Upper has some use in juggle combos, like after a mid screen ↓ + HK. Use the MK version to punish whiffed attacks during foot games.

SUPER ARTS

SUPER ART I

↓ ↘ → ↓ ↘ → + P	Rocket Uppercut

Rocket Uppercut works well as anti-air and does reasonable damage in combos. This super art can be verified and comboed into from some of Dudley's most effective attacks in wake up situations, like ↓ + LK (x 2), Liver Blow, and Dudley's amazing overhead, Dart Shot. Rocket Uppercut has 2 super meters to work with which is rather important to Dudley as EX Machine Blow can lead to impressive damage and a knock down during foot games. Although this super art by itself is only good at close ranges, having bar for EX Machine Gun Blows makes Dudley a threat at a greater distance.

1	-31

Recommended Super Art:
Rocket Upper or Corkscrew Blow

Both supers provide enough stock for EX moves, keeping EX Machine Gun Blow available to help Dudley's poke game. Both supers also combo off of Dudley's most important attacks. Although Corkscrew Blow has a few more uses, Rocket Uppercut does more damage consistently than Corkscrew Blow.

COMBOS YOU NEED TO KNOW

3 HITS

TOTAL DAMAGE: 39

HK →Jet Upper (HP)

3 HITS

TOTAL DAMAGE: 36

↓ + HK, juggle with an immediate Ducking Upper (MK)

4 HITS

TOTAL DAMAGE: 48

↓ + HK → walk up a bit and juggle with a late Liver Blow →Jet Upper (HP)

11 HITS

TOTAL DAMAGE: 59

HK → EX Machine Gun Blow, walk up a step and juggle with a late Liver Blow →Jet Upper (HP)

13 HITS

TOTAL DAMAGE: 59

↓ + LK, ↓ +LK → Rocket Upper

7 HITS

TOTAL DAMAGE: 45

↓ + LK, ↓ + LK → Corkscrew Blow

6 HITS

TOTAL DAMAGE: 56

CROUCHING OPPONENTS ONLY

Dart Shot linked to Corkscrew Blow

12 HITS

TOTAL DAMAGE: 68

CROUCHING OPPONENTS ONLY

Dart shot linked into a Rocket Upper

7 HITS

TOTAL DAMAGE: 71

↓ + HK, walk up and juggle with a late Liver Blow → Jet Upper (HP) → Cork Screw Blow

9 HITS

TOTAL DAMAGE: 67

HK linked into Rolling Thunder

10 HITS

TOTAL DAMAGE: 65

↓ + LK, ↓ + LK → Rolling Thunder

22 HITS

TOTAL DAMAGE: 71

HK → EX Machine Gun Blow, walk up a step and juggle with a late Liver Blow →Jet Upper (HP) → Rocket Upper

6 HITS

TOTAL DAMAGE: 57

WORKS ONLY AGAINST CHUN-LI, Q, ORO, ALEX, IBUKI, MAKOTO, ELENA, NECRO

↓ + HK, juggle with another ↓ + HK just before they hit the ground, repeat 3 more times, then jump forward and juggle with a jumping HP

SUPER ART II

↓ ↘ → ↓ ↘ → + P (tap P rapidly)	Rolling Thunder

Dudley's most damaging super art. It has great range and can be comboed into from ↓ + LK (x 2), or verified and linked after a maximum range HK. However, the damage is not as good as it could be for a super art with a meter this size. Dudely gets a single super meter stock, meaning no EX moves. Rolling Thunder does not combo off of Dudley's Dart Shot, which is a huge disadvantage considering how good Dudley's wake up game is when he can link off of that move.

2	-9

TARGET COMBOS

LP → MP → MK	3
The first and last hits miss crouching characters. The last hit is super cancelable but the damage is hardly worth the effort.	+1

→ + LP → MP	4
The second hit is cancelable, however it whiffs versus most crouching characters. There isn't much Dudley can cancel into, except a super art, that will hit from that range.	0

↓ + LK → MK	4
Quick chain starting off of a low attack. Doesn't do much damage, but it's safe and keeps Dudley close after it hits. One of Dudley's few safe low options.	-2

MK → HK → HP	5
Starts off of a mid level attack, hits crouching characters, and does passable damage.	0

LK → MK → MP → HP	5
Dudley's second most damaging chain. Whiffs versus crouching opponents. Would be a better choice for punishment situations if HK Jet Upper (HP) didn't do significantly more damage, stun damage, and knocked down.	0

SUPER ART III

↓ ↘ → ↓ ↘ → + P	Corkscrew Blow

Dudley's least damaging, but most flexible super art. The super meter is small, but you get three stocks which great for EX usage. This super art comes out quickly and has plenty of priority. Use it to punish a variety of blocked normals that are usually safe from close ranges.

Corkscrew Blow also combos behind Dudley's most important close range attacks, like ↓ + LK (x2), Liver Blow, and Dart Shot. Corkscrew Blow can also be used in combination with Ducking, which goes through projectiles, to punish an opponent's projectile recovery. Punish whiffed normals with Ducking (LK) → Corkscrew Blow, although you must be fast.

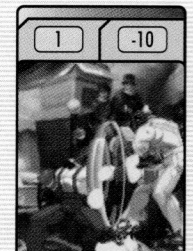

1	-10

→ + MK → MK → HP	5
Dudley's most damaging chain. Starts off of a mid level attack and does good damage. Fairly safe as well.	-4

↓ + LK → ↓ + MP→ ↓ + HP	4
More damaging chain opening with ↓ + LK. The last hit tends to whiff against crouching characters. Still, it's possible to verify if whether the opponent is standing or not when going for this chain. Use with caution.	-2

MP → MK → HP	3
Has bad range and misses crouching characters. Not Dudley's best option.	-4

→ + HK → MK	12
Decent damage and worth doing if you don't have a super art to link off of it.	-2

STRATEGY

Jumping Elbow

Dudley is a great character if you like to attack. His jump gives him great ability to attack effectively. Dudley keeps close to the ground, so attacks are available early in his jump when compared to other characters. Add to this the fact that he has two incredible jumping attacks with great hit stun: jumping HP and HK. Dudley can hit with jumping HK from the apex of his jump, then still have time to land and link a super art, which makes jumping in easy. Opponents must react quickly to Dudley's jump, and since he can use HK at any point in his jump and still connect a super art when he lands, it is difficult to parry this jump-in.

Once Dudley jumps in, he is usually positioned right next to the opposing fighter. From there he has a variety of mix up options that stem from Dart Shot mind games. The block stun from his jumping attacks is long, so it is just like he is in a wakeup situation. However, if a jumping attack lands, go ahead and tack on a combo for big damage. If a jumping HK hits, immediately Rocket Upper upon landing. If jumping HP connects, juggle with a big EX Machine Gun Blow combo.

After a blocked jump in, the best move to go for is Dart Shot. It comes out quickly, and generally hits in this situation because most players habitually block low after a jump in. However, Dudley's fast overhead breaks all the rules. Blocking low is never safe against Dudley. You are forced to guess when caught in this situation. If Dudley gets close and he has meter, a super art is guaranteed half of the time if he keeps mixing it up between high (Dart Shot) and low (↓ + LK (x2)). This is why Dudley must attack and get in close. He barely has a ranged game. He is all about getting in an opponent's face and dealing damage.

Dudley has many other options that score some damage and create openings when he is close after a jump-in. Immediately jumping straight up upon landing works very well. Hit foes with jumping HK early on the way up, then land and do either the high/low mix-up, or throw. Alternately, jump in with HP, but hesitate before throwing an opponent after landing. For the next time, jump in with HP, then immediately Swing Blow (LK) after landing. If the opponent tries to anticipate a throw and whiffs, cancel into a super art on reaction to a hit. If they block, you remain safe.

Another option when jumping in is to do nothing, and land and hit low with ↓ + LK, ↓ + MP, ↓ + HP ground chain. It starts low, and hits more often than it should because players tend to block high after a Dudley empty jump. Throwing behind an empty jump in is a good option as well. This is a good setup for the next empty jump in, which should be an immediate Short Swing Blow canceled into a super art, to hit throw attempts. Parrying is also another option for Dudley when jumping in. His jump is so low that he is usually nearing the end of his jump by the time opponents react to it and start an anti air. The timing to parry the anti air should be around the same time near the end of Dudley's jump.

For the rare occasions where you aren't being aggressive and are in a ground game (anytime you don't have any super meter), HP and HK are good pokes. Against some characters (such as Hugo), sit back and buffer EX Machine Gun Blows into his HP as Dudley whiffs them from across the screen. If the tips of any pokes are hit, the Machine Gun Blow automatically comes out and leads to a juggle opportunity.

MP is another good poke on the ground in situations where an opponent gets close. Buffer Duckings into whiffed MPs; if any MPs hit, a Ducking executes automatically and moves Dudley close enough to his opponent to cancel into a super art. This tactic is especially useful after teched throws. Characters with fast dashes might dash in after a teched throw to continue to pressure. Stick out MP to stop these dashes and create an opportunity to land a super art.

Dudley has a few good anti air choices. HP by itself is good if he is far enough away from opponents. It cancels into a Jet Upper to juggle for extra damage and defeat parry attempts. An EX Jet Upper also works well as anti-air. An interesting anti-air maneuver is to do a Ducking (HK) under opponents to cross them up on the ground, then either Corkscrew Blow or Rocket Upper from behind, which is fairly easy to do. Input the command for Ducking, then do another QCF + punch in the same direction and the super art automatically comes out, but in the other direction, towards the opponent. Dudley pulls this off quickly and it is hard to react to. Great for confusing opponents that like to jump in and parry often.

WAKEUP GAME

Dudley has the most intimidating wakeup game out of the entire cast of characters. What makes him so scary is his → + HK overhead attack. It comes out too quick to react to. Dudley can link super arts 1 or 3 after a hit for easy verified damage. He can also go low into his super arts via ↓ + LK x2. Both of these attacks are nearly instantaneous, so your opponent has to guess which way to block on wake up. This can lead to Dudley landing a super nearly 50% of the time on wake up. Knockdowns are incredibly important to Dudley. Against characters that can get hit by low roundhouse x6, they also have the misfortune of being able to lose a ton of life without Dudley even having to use any super meter. There is no right answer for what they should do in this situation. Dudley simply owns you on wakeup.

Even if Dudley's moves are blocked, he is still in range to remain a threat. After doubling up ↓ + LK, Dudley remains in perfect range to attempt a Dart Shot and link into super art if it hits. A UOH linked in to super art should be able to reach as well. After a blocked Dart Shot, Dudley is within range to either walk up and throw, or walk up and ↓ + LK (x2) and verify a super art after a hit. Dudley always has quick and easy ways to land a super art from up close and is a legitimate threat when he is close on the ground.

After Dudley knocks down an opponent, especially in the corner, throw his rose to hit opponents on wakeup. The rose keeps them pinned down if they try to jump. It even beats some wakeup moves. If time allows for it, always taunt and throw the rose on wakeup. It forces opponents to stay on the ground and guess between high or low.

The main thing Dudley must worry about when he is pressuring opponents on wakeup is random super arts and high priority moves. Throwing the rose virtually eliminates this threat. Opponents may be able to do a super art through the rose and hit Dudley, assuming he does a move, that is. Since they can't jump away, their only options are block, parry, or wakeup super art. If Dudley blocks after throwing the rose, he creates a stalemate. Neither character gets a hit, but Dudley wins because he remains close, exactly where he wants to be.

When Dudley is the one getting up off the ground, he has a few decent options to keep pressuring opponents off of him. An EX Jet Upper works great, although it's risky. All of his super arts work great as wakeup options if you don't mind taking a big risk. Parrying is always an option, although blocking is much safer. Doing a Short Swing Blow on wake up is a good idea. It get Dudley away from throws and ↓ + LK ticks.

SETUPS

Ranges setups for UOH → super art

Against small, medium and wide sized characters:

(↓ + LP (x2)), UOH → Rocket Uppercut, Rolling Thunder, Corkscrew Blow

(↓ + MP), UOH →Rocket Uppercut, Rolling Thunder, Corkscrew Blow

RESETS

Reset 1: Against characters that Dudley can connect ↓ + HK (x6) in the corner, he can reset them back on their feet at the last hit to set up a mix-up that can lead to more damage. Connect with five ↓ + HK, then jump towards them and use HP to reset them. When they land, expect opponents to block low, which is the safest thing to do in this situation. Right when Dudley lands, use Dart Shot, and link into Rocket Uppercut or Corkscrew Blow. The next time you are able to connect with ↓ + HK five times, reset with jumping HP again, and as opponents recover, they will probably block high in anticipation of the incoming overhead attack. Hit them with ↓ + HK and juggle them for 5 more hits. You could even juggle with a super art on the way down.

Reset 2: After hitting with an air to air HP, and Dudley lands first, immediately do a Ducking (HK) to catch up with your falling opponent, and immediately cancel into Corkscrew Blow for the reset juggle.

PARRY SETUPS AND TACTICS

Dudley is often going to attack a waking up opponent with Dart Shot. It comes out fast, so even changing its timing even slightly can throw off an opponent's attempts to parry it. Some players may try to hit Dudley before he gets this move off. Since the command involves a forward tap of the controller, press it forward a split second before pressing HK. This way Dudley option parries any mid level attacks that might be thrown his way before going into Dart Shot.

GROUND CROSS UPS

Dudley can cross up Twelve, Hugo, Necro, in any corner.
Dudley can cross up Yun, Yang, and Chun Li mid screen.

FAVORABLE MATCH UP: TWELVE

Twelve is very annoying to fight against from the start. He flies around and is hard to hit. He jumps much higher than Dudley and beats him out in the air easily. However, if Dudley is able to score a knockdown, it's all over for Twelve. Twelve has no answer for Dudley's wakeup game. Nothing short of a random X.N.D.L. is going to get him out of a corner. If Twelve has no meter, he's done. All Dudley needs to do is throw the rose to keep him grounded, then keep mixing it up between high and low attacks.

UNFAVORABLE MATCH UP: RYU

Jumping is Dudley's main way to get close to setup his wicked guessing and mind games. However, Ryu can keep Dudley from getting in by zoning with his HK. It can hit Dudley at any time during his jump, even at the very beginning. That move covers plenty of space, and it is hard for Dudley to get over it. It also beats Dudley's HP and ↓ + HK when done at the right time. Also, Dudley must always be on the lookout for the random EX Hadouken.

For Dudley to win this match, he must score a knockdown so he can get close to start his mind games. Jumping isn't the best avenue to achieve this. Look for Ryu to whiff a HK, then do a Ducking (HK) to get close before he fully recovers and knock him down. From there, Dudley must get in Ryu's face and keep landing super arts and knocking him down. Don't get discouraged. Be patient, and wait for Ryu to leave himself an open for an attack.

Elena

NORMAL MOVES

STANDING

LK is good for setting up tick throw and guessing games in general. This move has a decent amount of frame advantage after it. HK comes out high, moves Elena forward and goes over low attacks. This move is a great offensive normal at close range.

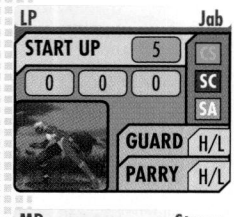

LP			Jab
START UP	5		CS
0	0	0	SC
			SA
GUARD			H/L
PARRY			H/L

LK			Short
START UP	3		CS
+4	+4	+4	SC
			SA
GUARD			H/L
PARRY			H/L

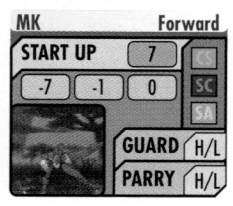

MP			Strong
START UP	6		CS
-2	-1	0	SC
			SA
GUARD			H/L
PARRY			H

MK			Forward
START UP	7		CS
-7	-1	0	SC
			SA
GUARD			H/L
PARRY			H/L

HP			Fierce
START UP	13		CS
-4	-2	0	SC
			SA
GUARD			H/L
PARRY			H

HK			Roundhouse
START UP	10		CS
-2	-1	0	SC
			SA
GUARD			H/L
PARRY			H

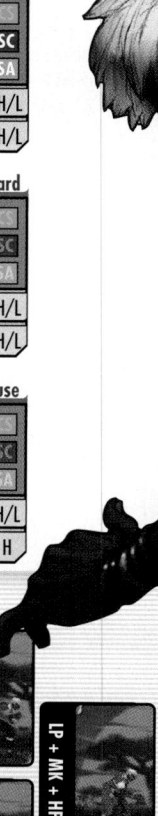

COSTUMES

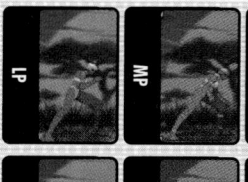  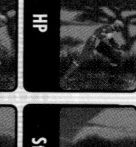    

LP — MP — HP — LK — MK — HK — LP + MK + HP

Start + LP — Start + MP — Start + HP — Start + LK — Start + MK — Start + HK

SPECIAL NORMALS

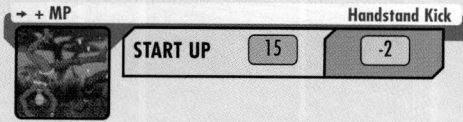

→ + MP — Handstand Kick

START UP	15	-2

Fast overhead with amazing range. Can be done from very far away.

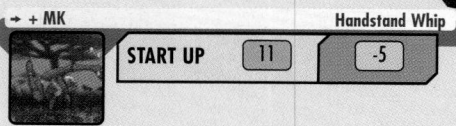

→ + MK — Handstand Whip

START UP	11	-5

Very fast overhead that moves Elena forward. Good range. However, it has a rather large frame disadvantage after it when blocked, making it rather unsafe. Kill this recovery issue and add frame advantage to the move by doing it early against a fallen opponent waking up, so that it hits meaty. Although difficult, not only does it make the move safe, but you can even link a Spinning Beat or a Brave Dance after it.

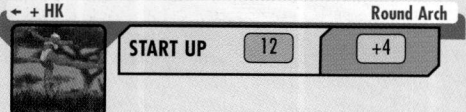

← + HK — Round Arch

START UP	12	+4

A leaping kick that moves Elena backward. Unbelievable priority. Because Elena is considered airborne while doing this move, it is invulnerable to throws and low attacks on start up. Can even beat a Gigas Breaker when timed correctly. To add to its usefulness, it has a nice frame advantage after it, making it completely safe if blocked. It's even possible to link a Brave Dance after this move if done meaty on a character waking up!

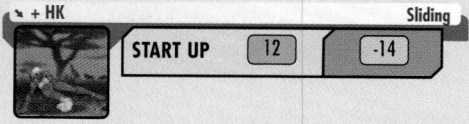

↘ + HK — Sliding

START UP	12	-14

Good range. Good during foot games as it's hard to make it whiff. Catches many players standing up trying to walk backward. Vulnerable if blocked from close range.

CROUCHING

↓ + MP is a mid level crouching kick and is Elena's main opener for combos. It has the strange property allowing her to cancel it into super arts much later into its recovery than most normal attacks. Just enough time to verify a hit before canceling into a super art, although it's difficult to execute.

↓ + MK is fast with good range. It works as a decent offensive poke.

↓ + LP		Low Jab	
START UP	4		CS
-1	-1	-1	SC
			SA
	GUARD	H/L	
	PARRY	H/L	

↓ + LK		Low Short	
START UP	4		CS
-2	-2	-2	SC
			SA
	GUARD	L	
	PARRY	L	

↓ + MP		Low Strong	
START UP	6		CS
-3	-2	-1	SC
			SA
	GUARD	H/L	
	PARRY	H/L	

↓ + MK		Low Forward	
START UP	8		CS
-3	-2	-1	SC
			SA
	GUARD	L	
	PARRY	L	

↓ + HP		Low Fierce	
START UP	7		CS
-7	-5	-3	SC
			SA
	GUARD	H/L	
	PARRY	H	

↓ + HK		Low Roundhouse	
START UP	11		CS
-9	0	0	SC
			SA
	GUARD	L	
	PARRY	L	

JUMPING

Jumping MK is a decent cross up and and can be used in combination with a super jump for ambiguous cross ups. Jumping forward or backward with HP adds a frame to its startup, but otherwise remains identical.

↑ + LP		Jumping Jab	
START UP	4		CS
—	—	—	SC
			SA
	GUARD	H	
	PARRY	H	

↑ + LK		Jumping Short	
START UP	5		CS
—	—	—	SC
			SA
	GUARD	H	
	PARRY	H	

↑ + MP		Jumping Strong	
START UP	6		CS
—	—	—	SC
			SA
	GUARD	H	
	PARRY	H	

↑ + MK		Jumping Forward	
START UP	7		CS
—	—	—	SC
			SA
	GUARD	H	
	PARRY	H	

↑ + HP		Jumping Fierce	
START UP	6		CS
—	—	—	SC
			SA
	GUARD	H	
	PARRY	H	

↑ + HK		Jumping Roundhouse	
START UP	9		CS
—	—	—	SC
			SA
	GUARD	H	
	PARRY	H	

THROWS

LP + LK	Leg Lift Throw

SPECIAL MOVES

→ ↘ ↓ ↙ ← + P		Mallet Smash	

21	24	27	21
0	+1	+4	+4

Rotating overhead kick. Has a very slight frame advantage after it. Fairly slow and vulnerable to parries if abused. MP version can be linked after with a Spinning Beat or Brave Dance, while HP version can links into a Spinning Beat, Brave Dance, or a LK →Scratch Wheel (HK). The EX version comes out faster and has a slightly longer frame advantage at the end of it. It's possible to link a Spinning Beat, Brave Dance, or a LK →Scratch Wheel (HK) after it.

→ ↓ ↘ + K		Scratch Wheel	

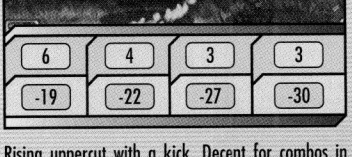

6	4	3	3
-19	-22	-27	-30

Rising uppercut with a kick. Decent for combos in punishment situations and as a reversal. EX version hits more times and has more priority.

← ↓ ↙ + K		Lynx Tail	

11	14	16	10
-17	-15	-15	-15

Multi-hit low kick attack with good range but terrible recovery. Linking an LK or EX version from ↓ + MP are both possibilities. The EX version hits more times. However, the last hit completely whiffs vs. most crouching characters. There's no reason to use this move over an EX Spin Scythe.

← ↓ ↘ → + K		Rhino Horn	

14	18	23	11
-3	-4	-6	-2

Button strength determines how far the Rhino Horn travels. It has frame disadvantage, although the block stun is deceptively long, usually making it safe if blocked. Whiffs versus most crouching characters. Can be rather annoying for large characters, like Hugo and Q, that cannot duck under it. EX version is faster, does more damage, and puts characters into a hardly noticeable juggle set up. Can be used in combos starting with an EX Spin Scythe for massive damage and juggle opportunities.

↓ ↙ ← + K		Spin Scythe	

15	16	17	10
-2	-6	-8	-15

Input ↓ ↙ ← + K again after the second hit for a 2 hit follow up.

Very slow and standard inputs do not combo. Can be used to set up the following guessing game: do QCB + HK, after the second hit, don't do the follow up, instead opt for a walk up throw. The next time you get a chance, do QCB + HK, when opponents anticipate the throw after the second hit, do the two hit follow up. The EX version of this move comes out faster, is comboable, and puts opponents into a juggle set up if you don't do the 2 hit follow up, which is extremely useful for high damage combos. The EX version's follow up doesn't put opponents into a juggle set up, and does about the same amount of damage. Heavy recovery too. It's best to avoid using it.

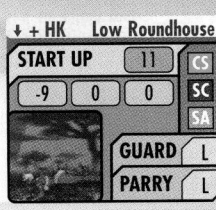

SUPER ARTS

SUPER ART I

↓ ↘ → ↓ ↘ → + K   **Spinning Beat**

| 1 | -12 |

Ilena does three repeated Scratch Wheels for a decent amount of damage. This super art has a high juggle potential in the corner. Use it to finish an EX juggle. It combos on the ground easily, and you can hit confirm it with a late ↓ + MP cancel, but only from close range. Spinning Beat cannot be used to punish whiffs or stop dashes from mid range. It can work as a decent anti-air. With 3 stocks, and a small super meter, Elena will be able to use Spinning Beat and her great EX moves often. Because Elena can only combo directly into Spinning Beat from such close range, this super could also be used solely to stock meter for EX moves to fight from longer ranges.

SUPER ART II

↓ ↘ → ↓ ↘ → + K   **Brave Dance**

| 1 | -30 |

In the corner, tack on an extra hit after the super with a Scratch Wheel (MK). It has a longer super meter than Spinning Beat, but it also does much more damage. It stocks two super meters, so Elena has the option to use EX moves and still have her super art available. Brave Dance combos nicely off of ↓ + LK and ↓ + MP. You can late cancel ↓ + MP to verify a combo into Brave Dance from almost the entire length of the move, and if you cancel it early, it combos from the very tip of her foot. This gives opponents a reason to fear her in close. Used in tandem with her long kara throw, Elena is sure to find openings to land a clean ↓ + MP → super art. Brave Dance has a quick start up, use it to punish any blocked moves with heavy recovery.

One thing to look out for, Elena flies forward with a slight upward incline as this super art starts up. It has a tendency to randomly go over Chun-Li and miss her completely, even if comboed into, because of how low her couching animation is.

SUPER ART III

↓ ↘ → ↓ ↘ → + P   **Healing**

| — | — |

Elena recovers up to 1/3 of her health with this super art. As she is healing, she is completely vulnerable. You can stop the super before fully healed by pressing PPP. The safest set up to use healing is after a throw. Elena throws opponents away far enough to where she can fully heal without getting hit. One throw can change the outlook of the round. Unfortunately, Healing only stocks one super bar, so if Elena plans to heal herself, she cannot use any of her EX moves. Without EX moves or a super art that does damage, Elena's combo possibilities are rather limited. Elena must rely on her fast pokes, overhead attacks, and kara throws to do most of her damage. Elena's normal moves are good, but she must hit opponents many more times than if she was landing Spinning Beat or Brave Dance often. Sometimes you may only get 1 or 2 openings for big damage in a round. Healing Elena will not be able to capitalize on these opportunities.

Recommended Super Art: Brave Dance

Brave Dance gives Elena the necessary range to verify into super arts that makes her ground game much more solid. ↓ + MP → Brave Dance allows Elena to keep people from rushing in on her, and apply pressure from her exceptionally long kara throw range. The constant threat of ↓ + MP → Brave Dance allows you to constantly kara throw, and it is the constant barrage of throws that leads to openings for ↓ + MP → Brave Dance.

COMBOS YOU NEED TO KNOW

4 HITS

TOTAL DAMAGE: 35

↓ + MP → Roundhouse Scratch Wheel

Okay for punishment situations when you don't have super meter for anything else. Knocks down.

7 HITS

TOTAL DAMAGE: 47

↓ + MP → EX Spin Scythe, when you recover, jump towards opponent and juggle with a semi early MP → HP air chain

High damage combo that leaves Elena with a positional advantage that could lead to more damage. Good for punishment situations. After the air chain Elena is free to dictate which side she will be on when opponents land, by either dashing under and behind before they land from the air chain, or walking forward to stay in front. Ambiguous and hard to react to.

7 HITS

TOTAL DAMAGE: 58

CORNER ONLY

↓ + MP → EX Spin Scythe, when you recover, immediately juggle with a Scratch Wheel (LK), when you recover, juggle again with a Scratch Wheel (HK)

High damage corner variation of the typical EX Spin Scythe juggle. Good for punishment situations.

10 HITS

TOTAL DAMAGE: 64

↓ + MP-> EX Spin Scythe, when you recover, immediately juggle with EX Rhino Horn, juggle again with a late Scratch Wheel (HK)

High damage combo that's good for punishment situations. Knocks down.

8 HITS

TOTAL DAMAGE: 54

Meaty Handstand Whip linked into Spinning Beat

Verifiable. Okay way to land a super art from an overhead. Difficult, and Handstand Whip must be done early against an opponent waking up.

11 HITS

TOTAL DAMAGE: 70

Meaty Handstand Whip linked into Brave Dance

Verifiable. Okay way to land a super art off an overhead. Difficult, Handstand Whip must be done early against an opponent waking up.

8 HITS

TOTAL DAMAGE: 51

↓ + MP → Spinning Beat

Verifiable way to land a Spinning beat. Knocks down.

11 HITS

TOTAL DAMAGE: 65

↓ + MP → Brave Dance.

Verifiable way to land a Brave Dance. In the corner, juggle with a Scratch Wheel (MK) after recovering from the super art versus most characters for extra damage. Generally not worth the effort, but does knocks down.

TARGET COMBOS

JUMPING (x2) LP → JUMPING MK

4
—

Fast 2 hit air chain. Good versus players who often anti-air parry. Although Elena has a variety of multi hit jump attacks and chains, this is by far the most flexible as it can be done much later in the jump than others.

JUMPING (x2) MP → JUMPING HP

6
—

Slower, more damaging 2 hit air chain. Steep upward angle, good for meeting another player in the air with a jump attack in anti-air situations. Not only does it do good damage and hit twice, giving opponents more to parry, but if it hits jumping opponents, Elena lands before they do, allowing her to dash under and behind them just before they land for an ambiguous side switch trick. Create further confusion into this trick by sometimes not dashing at all, staying in front of opponents just before they land, effectively making them guess which side Elena ends up on. In ether situation, mix up with the combo of your choice, UOH linked into Brave Dance or Spinning Beat, or a throw if you think they will guess correctly and block.

HP → HK

13
+1

Slow, damaging 2 hit chain. Slow start up and bad range, must be directly next to opponents to guarantee both hits connect. It has a small frame advantage after it, meaning it's completely safe. Elena's only safe non super combo. Still, not extremely useful.

MK → ↓ + HP

7
-11

2 hit chain ending with a launching kick. Knocks opponents fairly high into the air, allowing Elena to get into prime attack range just before they get up, whether they quick recover or not. However, the last hit of this chain has a huge frame disadvantage after it, meaning it's heavily open to attack if blocked.

STRATEGY

Knee Attack

Elena has some of the game's best pokes, which keep opponents frustrated at long range. ↓ + HK and Sliding are great for sneaking under high attacks, and her two command overhead attacks will keep them guessing. Use ↓ + MP as her main poke at a distance and to punish whiffs, beat out other attacks, and prevent characters from rushing in on the ground.

Elena does most of her damage off of Brave Dance and kara throws. The more you throw, the more likely they will make a mistake that leads to an opening for ↓ + MP → super art. Elena never has to get too close if she doesn't want to. Stay at her maximum kara throw range and frustrate opponents with repeated throws. Get them to attempt a tech, then react with a ↓ + MP → super art.

Elena has many great jumping attacks. Most come out fast and hit from far away. Elena jumps high and can usually outreach and outrange opponents. Many of Elena's jumping attacks and air chains allow her to land before opponents. Use this as a chance to dash under them before they land to quickly cross them up.

Elena has many anti-air options when she is on the ground. Scratch Wheel is her most basic anti-air. If you can react quick enough to an opponent's jump, meet them in the air and use any of Elena's multi-hitting air moves. Elena also has a fast dash, and she is fairly low to the ground as she does it. Use this to avoid cross ups and jumping attacks from close range by dashing under opponents and counter-attacking as they land.

Elena's Round Arch is one of the best special normals in the game. Use this move often to go over low attacks and beat throw attempts. Whenever you are not sure what to do, go ahead and use Round Arch. Most likely it will do you some good.

WAKEUP GAME

Elena has many options on waking opponents because her kara throw range is so great. At that maximum range, many characters' quickest low pokes whiff. Elena is free to kara throw at will. ↓ + MP also connects into super arts from this range. Throwing repeatedly is effective, but mix it up and hesitate, trying to make opponents react to a possible kara throw. Punish their reaction with ↓ + MP → Brave Dance. When you don't have enough meter for a super art, use Round Arch often to go over all low pokes and to stop throws.

At very close range, ↓ + LK is Elena's best tick. Follow it up with either a kara throw, ↓ + MP → super art, or Round Arch. Both ↓ + LK and ↓ + MP can be parried low, so Elena has some other wake up options to discourage parry attempts. She can do either Round Arch or Handstand Whip meaty and link Brave Dance after it. Throwing immediately on wake up works often because many players will not expect a throw from such close range.

When Elena is the one getting off the ground, if you decide not to block, Scratch Wheel is good for getting people off of her, particularly the EX version. A safer option is to block on wake up, and look for an opening to land ↓ + LK / ↓ + MP → super art. Round Arch at any time really helps Elena get out of trouble. She can't be thrown or hit by most low attacks, so it is really safe.

SETUPS

Ranges setups for UOH → super

Against most characters:
↓ + LK (x2), UOH → Spinning Beat / Brave Dance

Against Oro:
No setup is required. UOH → Spinning Beat / Brave Dance works at close distance on crouching Oro.

CORNER TRICKS

After a throw in the corner, Elena can set up an ambiguous cross up situation that is difficult to block correctly. After the throw, jump and press HK before hitting the ground. Time Elena's jump to land exactly at the moment the opponent gets up off the ground. Elena lands directly on top, and her jump HK extends her over both sides of the character. It is hard to tell whether Elena is going to cross up or not, leading to a guessing game for opponents. This is even trickier against opponents that Elena can only cross up in her own corner (against shots, for instance). Always be aware of which characters you can cross up and where you can do so.

RESETS

Reset 1: If Elena has enough super meter, she can turn an EX juggle combo into a setup for a perfectly distanced UOH linked into Brave Dance for massive damage. If you are able to combo into an EX Spin Scythe mid screen, juggle with an EX Rhino Horn, then hit with LK to reset the combo and have them flip recover. Walk up a tiny step, then UOH. It must be timed perfectly to link into Brave Dance if it hits. This does not work on characters that aren't juggled by all of the hits of the EX Rhino Horn.

Reset 2: If Elena lands a mid air HK, she usually lands before opponents. You can hit them before they land with Spinning Beat. To get the most hits, save this trick for the corner.

PARRY SETUPS AND TACTICS

Elena's kara throw is very good and a big part of her game. Take advantage of an option parry to cover Elena from mid level attacks when kara throwing. Elena's kara throw is → + MK → throw. Instead of pressing → at the same time as MK, press → a split second earlier than is necessary. Continue to hold → while finishing the input for the kara throw. With this method, you parry any potential mid level attacks before throwing.

GROUND CROSS UPS

Elena can cross up Dudley, Alex, Hugo, Necro, Twelve, and Urien in any corner.

Elena can cross up Oro, Elena, and Chun Li only in her own corner.

FAVORABLE MATCH UP: RYU

Elena only has one real concern when fighting Ryu, EX Hadoukens. If Elena can avoid random EX Hadoukens, there is not much else Ryu can hit Elena with if she is played correctly. Ryu has a hard time landing his bread and butter ↓ + MK → EX Hadouken combo on Elena because of Round Arch. This move goes over every single one of Ryu's ground attacks. Ryu must resort to throwing EX Hadoukens from a much greater distance because when he gets in close, he is always at risk of eating a Round Arch counter. Ryu will not be able to kara throw either, because Round Arch cannot be thrown. Use Round Arch like it is her only move.

Once you get Ryu trained not to stick out ↓ + MK or kara throw, he must play much more defensively. Get in close and mix up kara throws and ↓ + MP. Keep up the pressure and try to land ↓ + MP → Brave Dance.

UNFAVORABLE MATCH UP: CHUN-LI

When Chun Li has super meter, Elena is constantly at risk. Most of Elena's best pokes lose cleanly to Chun Li's Hakkei and ↓ + HP. Chun-Li has greater range, and can keep Elena away. Even if Elena gets close, she is always at risk for Chun-Li's ↓ + MK → Houyokusen.

For Elena to have a chance, take advantage of the first round when Chun-Li doesn't have enough meter for Houyokusen. Chun-Li is much less of a threat without meter. Stay out of range of her HP, and ↓ + HK, using Sliding to get under them and punish her. Whenever Chun-Li is close, Round Arch over her ↓ + MK. Elena can similarly do repeated ↓ + MPs and cancel into super arts upon a hit when Chun-Li tries to use her ↓ + MK. This match is winnable, but expect a tough battle.

Hugo

NORMAL MOVES
STANDING

MP looks like a patty cake slap and moves Hugo forward slightly. Goes over some low attacks, catches anticipated jumps. It has good range and good recovery; it's a fantastic poke, so abuse it!

LK is fast enough to beat some low attacks from the right range. Hard to punish if whiffed. Used to tick into Moonsault Press; it's also cancelable.

Press ← or → to move forward or backward during HK. Can be used to go over a variety of low attacks. This move has awful recovery, so use it with caution.

LP		Jab
START UP	4	CS
-1	-1	-1	SC
			SA
GUARD		H/L
PARRY		H/L

LK		Short
START UP	5	CS
+1	+1	+1	SC
			SA
GUARD		H/L
PARRY		H/L

MP		Strong
START UP	10	CS
-5	0	+1	SC
			SA
GUARD		H/L
PARRY		H

MK		Forward
START UP	9	CS
-4	+1	+3	SC
			SA
GUARD		H/L
PARRY		H

HP		Fierce
START UP	16	CS
-3	-1	+1	SC
			SA
GUARD		H
PARRY		H

HK		Roundhouse
START UP	21	CS
-13	+3	+3	SC
			SA
GUARD		H
PARRY		H

COSTUMES

LP | MP | HP | LK | MK | HK | LP + MK + HP

Start + LP | Start + MP | Start + HP | Start + LK | Start + MK | Start + HK

SPECIAL NORMALS

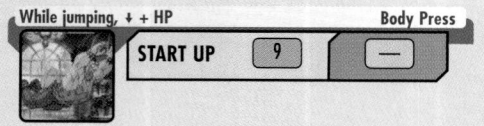

While jumping, ↓ + HP		Body Press
START UP	9	—

Great cross up, but tough to get into a position to use it. After it's blocked, use the fairly large amount of frame advantage to execute Moonsault Press or Ultra Throw ticks.

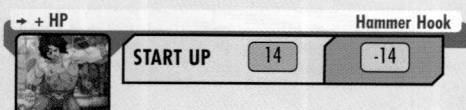

→ + HP		Hammer Hook
START UP	14	-14

SPECIAL MOVES

CROUCHING

↓ + MP is an overall good poke. It beats some attacks from the right ranges, plus it's fast and safe.

↓ + MK has great range and is a great whiff punisher. Use with some caution as it can be punished by some fast supers if blocked too close.

↓ + LP		Low Jab	
START UP	4		CS
-1	-1	-1	SC
			SA
	GUARD	H/L	
	PARRY	H/L	

↓ + LK		Low Short	
START UP	3		CS
+2	+2	+2	SC
			SA
	GUARD	L	
	PARRY	L	

↓ + MP		Low Strong	
START UP	4		CS
-2	-1	0	SC
			SA
	GUARD	H/L	
	PARRY	H/L	

↓ + MK		Low Forward	
START UP	8		CS
-5	D	D	SC
			SA
	GUARD	L	
	PARRY	L	

↓ + HP		Low Fierce	
START UP	4		CS
-29	D	D	SC
			SA
	GUARD	H/L	
	PARRY	H/L	

↓ + HK		Low Roundhouse	
START UP	11		CS
-43	D	D	SC
			SA
	GUARD	H/L	
	PARRY	H/L	

JUMPING

Jumping HK is a drop kick with amazing priority. It beats a variety of anti-air normals while covering large amounts of space. Jumping forward or backward MP has a start up of seven frames. Jumping forward or backward HP has a startup of thirteen frames.

↑ + LP		Jumping Jab	
START UP	3		CS
—	—	—	SC
			SA
	GUARD	H	
	PARRY	H	

↑ + LK		Jumping Short	
START UP	3		CS
—	—	—	SC
			SA
	GUARD	H	
	PARRY	H	

↑ + MP		Jumping Strong	
START UP	7		CS
—	—	—	SC
			SA
	GUARD	H	
	PARRY	H	

↑ + MK		Jumping Forward	
START UP	5		CS
—	—	—	SC
			SA
	GUARD	H	
	PARRY	H	

↑ + HP		Jumping Fierce	
START UP	13		CS
—	—	—	SC
			SA
	GUARD	H	
	PARRY	H	

↑ + HK		Jumping Roundhouse	
START UP	11		CS
—	—	—	SC
			SA
	GUARD	H	
	PARRY	H	

THROWS

LP + LK   Neck Hanging Three

←/→ + LP + LK   Body Slam

↓ ↙ ← + P — Giant Palm Bomber

17	19	22	22
+11	+16	+19	+10

Slow start up, but has an absolutely ridiculous amount of frame advantage afterwards. Great for combos and pressure patterns up close. Use the frame advantage in wake up situations to secure an attack and mix up with ↓ + MK, Moonsault Press, or HP. The EX version hits three times and sets opponents up for a juggle.

360 Motion + P — Moonsault Press

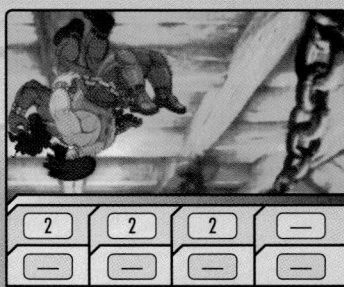

2	2	2	—
—	—	—	—

Hugo's main weapon. Moonsault Press is a fast command throw with great range that deals a ton of damage. Very scary at close ranges. So scary in fact, that opponents will do whatever they can to avoid it completely, making them play in an unsafe and awkward manner. Expect opponents to react to this move in a variety of ways in an attempt to counter it (jumping is the most effective way). Learn to anticipate attempts to jump away from this move and counter with an anti-air of some sort.

↓ ↘ → + K — Monster Lariat

11	15	24	7
-8	-10	-11	-22

A fast move with good range, but whiffs against crouching opponents, diminishing its value. Use it to catch back dashes or anticipated jump attempts. The EX version comes out faster and does more damage.

→ ↓ ↘ + K — Shootdown Backbreaker

5	17	13	—
—	—	—	—

A flying air grab mainly for use against anticipated jumps used to avoid Moonsault Press. Has absolutely no priority, losing to jumping attacks rather easily. It must be done early, just as an opponent is leaving the ground. Fairly heavy recovery when Hugo lands. A risky attack to use in general, utilize with caution.

360 Motion + K — Meat Squasher

17	19	22	22
—	—	—	—

Running command grab with heavy start up. Very slow and easy to counter. It does immediately drag opponents to the closest corner, a big plus for Hugo. The start up looks like the opening animation for a whiffed throw, which doesn't really help anything because the last thing you want is an opponent trying an attack.

→ ↘ ↓ ↙ ← + K — Ultra Throw

7	7	7	—
—	—	—	—

Command throw that bounces opponents off of a wall for a juggle opportunity. Can lead to big damage in combination with Megaton Press or EX Giant Palm Bomber when near a corner. Ultra Throw Shootdown Backbreaker is an okay combo to quickly corner opponents, however it does much less damage than a Moonsault Press (HP).

HUGO

SUPER ARTS

SUPER ART I

720 Motion + K	Gigas Breaker

With its one frame start up, Gigas Breaker is one of the quickest super arts in the game. Any opponent on the ground when Hugo starts Gigas Breaker will be caught. Opponents must anticipate Gigas Breaker before Hugo does it and jump before the super freeze in order to escape. Gigas  Breaker has invulnerability at start up, so it grabs opponents through their moves. Gigas Breaker only has one meter for its super art, so EX moves are not recommended.

1	—

SUPER ART II

↓ ↘ → ↓ ↘ → + K	Megaton Press

Hugo jumps and catches airborne opponents and slams them to the ground. The button pressed determines the angle at which Hugo jumps. Extremely good damage for an anti-air. Unfortunately, almost any air attack can knock Hugo out Megaton Press. Megaton Press stocks 2 super meters, and is usable as the last hit of a juggle combo.

LP 3 / MP 5 / HP 7
—

SUPER ART III

↓ ↘ → ↓ ↘ → + P	Hammer Frenzy

Hugo runs towards opponents and hits them with a bombardment of powerful moves, one of which is an overhead. Hugo can combo into Hammer Frenzy from ↓ + LP (x2). This is the only super art that makes Hugo's cross up a real threat. Use it in wake up situations to go through any pokes. If Hugo guesses wrong and the opponent blocks, try to trick them with a delayed release. By holding the punch button, Hugo continues running for a short time. Release the punch and Hugo starts his attack string. Holding the button for too long results in Hugo stopping, and never starting the attack. Hugo is vulnerable while running, and at the end of the super art. With a window of invulnerability at the beginning of the move, it's possible to pass through projectiles and pokes. Hammer Frenzy stocks 2 supers.

4	-29

Recommended Super Art: Hammer Frenzy

Hammer Frenzy gives Hugo his only real combo possibilities that don't involve command throws. It makes his jump-ins a threat, and gives him his only solid way to verify big damage. There's no need to guess with Shootdown Backbreaker when you think someone might jump away because of the threat of a Moonsault Press. ↓ + LP (x2) instead and cancel into Hammer Frenzy to punish their attempted escape.

COMBOS YOU NEED TO KNOW

7 HITS
TOTAL DAMAGE: 65

↓ + LP, ↓ + LP → Hammer Frenzy

Verifiable way to land a Hammer Frenzy. You must be directly next to an opponent for this to work or Hammer Frenzy might not combo. Knocks down.

3 HITS
TOTAL DAMAGE: 46

Giant Palm Bomber (HP); when Hugo recovers, link into Giant Palm Bomber (LP); when Hugo recovers, link into ↓ + MK

Decent damage and safe if you verify off of the first two Giant Palm Bombers. Knocks down.

2 HITS
TOTAL DAMAGE: 34

Ultra Throw, immediately juggle afterwards with Shootdown Backbreaker (HK)

Easy and reliable mid screen combo off of Ultra Throw. Knocks down.

4 HITS
TOTAL DAMAGE: 54
CORNER ONLY

Ultra Throw, juggle with a semi-late EX Giant Palm Bomber for 2 hits; when Hugo recovers, immediately juggle again with a Shootdown Backbreaker (HK)

Damaging option off of Ultra Throw in the corner. The EX Giant Palm Bomber MUST miss 1 of its 3 hits, or you cannot juggle after it with the Shootdown Backbreaker. Knocks down.

3 HITS
TOTAL DAMAGE: 59

Ultra Throw, immediately juggle afterwards with a Megaton Press

Easy way to land a Megaton Press mid screen. Ok damage. Knocks down.

4 HITS
TOTAL DAMAGE: 66
CORNER ONLY

Ultra Throw, juggle with a late fierce Giant Palm Bomber → Megaton Press

High damage option off of his Ultra throw in the corner. Knocks down

9 HITS
TOTAL DAMAGE: 27
CORNER ONLY

Neutral throw while opponent is cornered, after the 8th hit (when Hugo lets go), juggle with an immediate EX Monster Lariat

Juggle option off of his neutral throw in the corner. Does only 3 less damage then neutral throw → Megaton Press, which isn't remotely worth the bar usage. Knocks down.

STRATEGY

Knee Attack

Hugo requires patience. He inflicts an impressive amount of damage with only a few command grabs, but getting close enough to land them is no easy task. Hugo is slow and a big target for many characters. His size becomes an advantage when it comes to his poking game. MP and ↓ + MK outreach almost every character's longest pokes. MP hits many characters when they are crouching. That, combined with its range, works to stop many character's ground games.

Getting close enough to grab opponents is tough, but Hugo has some moves that help out. Use random Meat Squashers (LK) to catch opponents off guard while running towards them. If you can land a Meat Squasher, Hugo will slam your opponent against the wall and put them exactly where you want them; the corner. Any time you can land one of these Hugo takes control of the match. So if you are having difficulty fighting from mid screen, make it your goal to land a Meat Squasher. If you can get close enough to land a LK, Hugo can cancel into this attack and possibly catch them while they block low. This is extremely effective if you have been making use of his Palm Bombers and canceling into those off of stand short.

Palm Bombers really help Hugo out if he wants to get close. A blocked Palm Bomber carries significant frame advantage, so Hugo can dash up after one and start being a threat from up close, his ideal range. LK and low short are two excellent long reaching pokes Hugo can use to cancel into a Palm Bomber and then dash up. Instead of dashing, Hugo can use his opponent's long block stun period as a chance to cross them up with his Body Press. If you connect with a Body Press, do ↓ + LP (x2) → Hammer Frenzy. If they block, Hugo is up close where he wants to be. Hesistate just a second and Moonsault Press. If you think they might jump, Hugo's standing fierce overhead is really good in this situation. It has the dual effect of hitting crouching characters and stopping jump attempts. When you are this close, always consider an Ultra Throw, Shootdown Backbreaker as an option. While it does less damage than a Moonsault Press, it will move Hugo's opponent closer to the corner, exactly where Hugo wants them.

Hugo's ground game will prevent many opponents from poking at him, so they might try to jump in at Hugo. Use Shootdown Backbreaker as an anti-air to catch opponents quickly before they attack. It's quick and does good damage, although it can be beat if the jumping opponent attacks early. Hugo can attack opponents from the air from long range with jumping HP and HK attacks. These attacks are not necessarily good for getting in close, but are merely a way to keep pressure on jumping opponents. If either attack is parried from the ground, Hugo can hit from so far away that many opponents have difficulty hitting him when he lands.

WAKEUP GAME

Hugo's wake up game is limited because whenever he knocks down opponents, and they quick recover, he is too slow to keep in close. On the other hand, if Hugo manages to trap anyone in the corner, he is a terrifying opponent. Use Shootdown Backbreaker on anyone that tries to jump over Hugo, effectively keeping them trapped in the corner. Hover over opponents and keep trying Moonsault Press. If you are too obvious in Moonsault Press attempts, and opponents start to jump, be prepared to pay the price. Hugo has a large recovery on his throw whiffs, so he is vulnerable to being hit. Hesitation moves can be very tricky and lead to some chances to land throws. For instance, walk backwards a step as opponents are getting up, trying to make it look like you are being cautious, then Moonsault Press at its maximum range. A combo off of an Ultra Throw is also a great way to deal damage in the corner.

If opponents want to pressure Hugo on wakeup, they must get in close. When Hugo is the one getting up, he is scary. Hugo wants opponents near, which leaves him in range for his most powerful moves. A Moonsault Press on wakeup is always an option. If Hugo expects that an opponent is anticipating this, block on wake up and look for the opponent to jump. If they do so, quickly use a Shootdown Backbreaker. Hugo's opponents must be careful when they are close. Any tick throw setup or hesitation move could be an opening for a Moonsault Press. Moonsault Press has a quick start up, so unless Hugo's opponent ticks with a move that has significant frame advantage, Hugo can usually Moonsault Press before their next move out.

ADVANCED TACTIC: WALK UP GIGAS BREAKER

The command for a Gigas Breaker is a 720 motion of the controller, followed by punch. While it is possible to do a 720 on the ground without making Hugo jump, it is extremely difficult, and almost impossible to do with any consistency.

Think of the motion for a Gigas not as a 720, but as two 360 degree rotations. A 360 degree motion is six consecutive points on the controller. The game's engine provides plenty of leeway when doing complex controller motions. It's possible to do the first 360 (six consecutive points) motion, then wait a full second before doing the second 360 motion to complete the Gigas Breaker command. Take advantage of this delay to buffer the first 360 motion into a move so Hugo does not jump off the ground, then walk up 2 steps, and do the second 360 motion to surprise opponents with a Gigas Breaker. For example, walk towards an opponent and whiff a LK. Do the first 360 motion during the LK, then continue to walk towards the opponent and do a quick 360 motion + punch to execute a Gigas Breaker. Another tricky way to buffer the first 360 motion is during a dash. Dash just outside of Gigas Breaker range, then walk forward and 360 + punch.

RESETS

Reset 1: After a neutral grab in the corner, juggle once with ↓ + MP to cause opponents to flip recover and land back on the ground. Dash in and Moonsault Press, run and Meat Squasher, or just sit back and bait opponents into doing something in which Hugo can counter.

PARRY SET UPS AND TACTICS

Hugo has a tremendous amount of frame advantage off any Palm Bomber. Use this to set up opponents; after a blocked Palm Bomber Hugo is pushed away, so only low pokes can hit him. Stutter step back and forth to bait opponents into attacking, then down parry and Mounsault Press.

Against jumping opponents, Hugo's Shootdown Backbreaker is good, but susceptible to being beat by certain attacks. Use an option parry in this situation to cover Hugo before you using an anti-air. Before executing a Shootdown Backbreaker, return the controller to neutral for a split second. This way, when you input → for the Shootdown Backbreaker command, you will automatically parry a potential jumping attack, then counter with Shootdown Backbreaker upon completion of the command. If the attacker does nothing, they are still caught by Shootdown Backbreaker. So if you tend to walk around or crouch often with Hugo, get into the habit of returning the controller to neutral just before you Shootdown Backbreaker.

FAVORABLE MATCH UP: SEAN

Hugo doesn't have any one thing in particular that makes his match against Sean go in his favor. It has more to do with the fact that Sean doesn't really have any good way to attack Hugo. If Hugo just stands outside of Sean's longest poke range and uses plenty of MP and ↓ + MKs, there isn't much Sean can do. Don't just stick out moves, make sure they hit, or else Sean can sometimes hit back. Keep him away and you should do fine. If you manage to get in on Sean, that's great. Mix up Moonsault Presses and his overhead. If you don't manage to get close, don't worry. Hugo should have no problem winning this match with his superior range alone.

UNFAVORABLE MATCH UP: AKUMA

Akuma is mobile and can keep Hugo pinned down with a barrage of quick attacks and air fireballs. Hugo is susceptible to getting hit by Hyakki Gousai early in Akuma's jump arc, even when Hugo is crouching. It is hard for Hugo to react to this, especially if Akuma cancels into Hyakki Shuu and jumps while Hugo is still in block stun. If Hugo ever does get close and scores a knockdown, Akuma can just teleport to the other side of the screen on wakeup, and Hugo must live with that.

The key for Hugo to win this match up is simple: parry. There is no other way to get around Akuma's Zarku Hadokens. If Akuma can jump in with a Zanku Hadoken ahead of him, he can land safely and start a ground attack pattern. You can't let Akuma do this. Parry this attack and don't let him have a free jump-in. Pay careful attention to Akuma canceling any ground attacks into a Hyakki Shuu. If he does, catch him with a Shootdown Backbreaker (you must react quickly!) during the upward part of his jump. Be patient and don't let Akuma pin down Hugo. Create openings with parries and capitalize with command grabs.

Ibuki

NORMAL MOVES

STANDING

LP is an incredible close range poke that comes out quickly and has a huge amount of frame advantage after it. It's possible to perform walk up LP, walk up LP repeatedly, then mix in walk up throw or walk up LP → MP → → + LK target combo for great close range mind games and pressure.

MP is a palm thrust with frame advantage after it. Possible to verify and link a Yami-Shigure off this move. Good at close ranges when mixed in with walk up LP and throws. If opponents think you might throw and try to tech, hit MP, then land a super art.

LP		Jab
START UP	2	CS
+6	+6	+6	SC
		SA
GUARD	H/L
PARRY	H/L

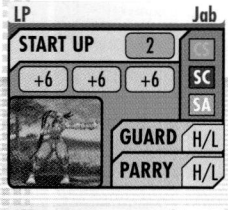

MP		Strong
START UP	6	CS
+6	+7	+8	SC
		SA
GUARD	H/L
PARRY	H/L

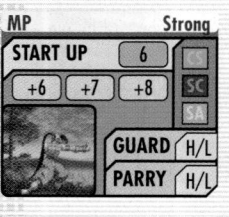

HP		Fierce
START UP	9	CS
-1	+1	+3	SC
		SA
GUARD	H/L
PARRY	H

LK		Short
START UP	4	CS
+1	+1	+1	SC
		SA
GUARD	H/L
PARRY	H/L

MK		Forward
START UP	6	CS
+1	+2	+3	SC
		SA
GUARD	H/L
PARRY	H

HK		Roundhouse
START UP	9	CS
-2	-1	+1	SC
		SA
GUARD	H/L
PARRY	H

STANDING CLOSE

LP		Close Jab
START UP	2	CS
+5	+5	+5	SC
		SA
GUARD	H/L
PARRY	H/L

MP		Close Strong
START UP	6	CS
+6	+7	+8	SC
		SA
GUARD	H/L
PARRY	H/L

P		Close Fierce
START UP	9	CS
-3	-1	+1	SC
		SA
GUARD	H/L
PARRY	H

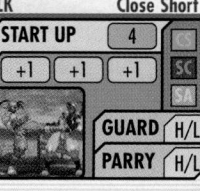

LK		Close Short
START UP	4	CS
+1	+1	+1	SC
		SA
GUARD	H/L
PARRY	H/L

MK		Close Forward
START UP	5	CS
+1	+2	+3	SC
		SA
GUARD	H/L
PARRY	H

HK		Close Roundhouse
START UP	5	CS
-11	0	0	SC
		SA
GUARD	H/L
PARRY	H

COSTUMES

 LP
 MP
 HP
 LK
 MK
 HK

 Start + LP
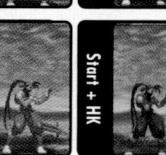 Start + MP
Start + HP
Start + LK
Start + MK
Start + HK

 LP + MK + HP

SPECIAL NORMALS

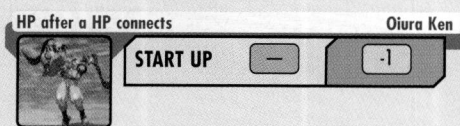

HP after a HP connects — Oiura Ken

START UP	—	-1

More flash than substance, it's cool to see, but not to use.

→ + MK — Koube Kudaki

START UP	27	+9

Slow leaping overhead with a huge frame advantage after it. For the most part, this move cannot be parried and punished very easily, plus it links into Yami-Shigure. Very few normal or special moves can hit Ibuki after a parry. The only option for many characters is to parry and go strait into a super art with a four frame or less start up. Some characters don't have any way to really punish Ibuki from doing this move over and over. If you want to get back in after any blocked string or failed attack, this is the move to use.

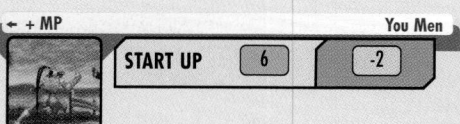

← + MP — You Men

START UP	6	-2

This two hit uppercut is used to initiate to some of Ibuki's chains. Unless you plan on using a chain, it's uses are extremely limited.

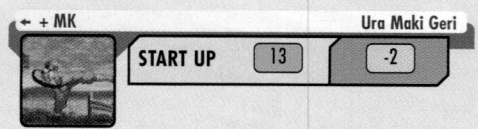

← + MK — Ura Maki Geri

START UP	13	-2

A slow spin kick that can cancel into Koube Kudaki.

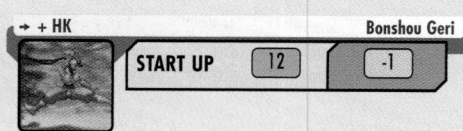

→ + HK — Bonshou Geri

START UP	12	-1

Remarkably fast with great priority; goes over low attacks

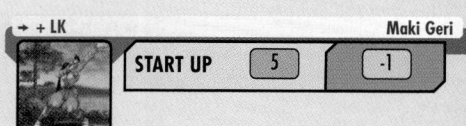

→ + LK — Maki Geri

START UP	5	-1

A shin kick with decent range. However, LP is a better option.

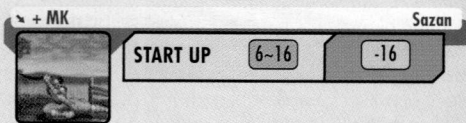

↘ + MK — Sazan

START UP	6~16	-16

A slide kick with decent range. It's safe if it hits late from the right distance, plus it's hard to avoid during foot games.

CROUCHING

↓ + MP is an okay poke, and it's possible to cancel into a super art somewhat late into the recovery of the move. It's a passable way to combo Yami-Shigure on reaction to hit, although it's not easy to do so.

Although difficult, ↓ + LK, ↓ + LP is Ibuki's most flexible opening to land damage off low attacks. Cancel into an EX Tsumuji or Yami-Shigure for decent damage. ↓ + MK is an overall decent poke, fairly fast, and it has a good recovery.

↓ + HK → HK chain is the opening to some of Ibuki's most damaging juggles. Use it in punishment situations or when you're willing to kill flexibility for damage in wake up situations. If opponents block the sweep, chain into HK and cancel into a backwards super jump to get away from harm.

↓ + LP — Low Jab

START UP	3		
+5	+5	+5	SC SA
GUARD	H/L		
PARRY	H/L		

↓ + LK — Low Short

START UP	5		CS
+3	+3	+3	SC SA
GUARD	L		
PARRY	L		

↓ + MP — Low Strong

START UP	9		
+2	+3	+4	SC SA
GUARD	H/L		
PARRY	H/L		

↓ + MK — Low Forward

START UP	6		
-2	-1	0	SA
GUARD	L		
PARRY	L		

↓ + HP — Low Fierce

START UP	8		
-3	-1	+1	SC SA
GUARD	H/L		
PARRY	H		

↓ + HK — Low Roundhouse

START UP	10		
-8	0	0	SC SA
GUARD	H/L		
PARRY	L		

JUMPING

Jumping forward or backward HK has a startup of eleven frames, instead of the ten from jumping straight up.

↖/↗ + MP — Jumping Strong

START UP	6	CS SC SA
GUARD	H	
PARRY	H	

↑ + MK — Vertical Forward

START UP	5	SC SA
GUARD	H	
PARRY	H	

↑ + LP — Vertical Jab

START UP	3	SC SA
GUARD	H	
PARRY	H	

↑ + HP — Jumping Fierce

START UP	11	SC SA
GUARD	H	
PARRY	H	

↖/↗ + MK — Jumping Forward

START UP	7	SC SA
GUARD	H	
PARRY	H	

↖/↗ + LP — Jumping Jab

START UP	3	SC SA
GUARD	H	
PARRY	H	

↑ + LK — Vertical Short

START UP	4	SC
GUARD	H	
PARRY	H	

↑ + HK — Jumping Roundhouse

START UP	10	SC
GUARD	H	
PARRY	H	

↑ + MP — Vertical Strong

START UP	5	SC SA
GUARD	H	
PARRY	H	

↖/↗ + LK — Jumping Short

START UP	3	CS SC SA
GUARD	H	
PARRY	H	

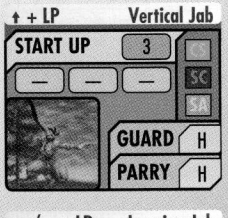
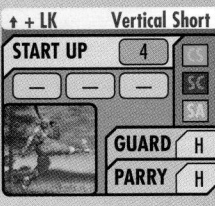

THROWS

LP + LK — Yamitsudzura

In air, LP + LK — Tobizaru

→ ↘ ↓ ↙ ← + P — Raida

4	—
5	—
6	—
—	—

Exploding close range chi blast. Great for Ibuki's most basic and important combos.

← ↙ ↓ ↘ → + P — Kubi Ori

14	-16
15	-16
17	-19
15	-15

Comes out quickly and does good damage, but isn't safe. Use during foot games to catch opponents while they are standing up, trying to move out of Ibuku's poke range. The EX versions of this attack comes out much faster and does more damage. However, it remains a risky attack in general.

In air, ↓ ↘ → + P — Kunai

9	—
10	—
11	—
8	—

Air based projectile that is thrown at varying angles depending on the button strength used. Mostly good when used in a defensive manner to push opponents away after some of Ibuki's offensive patterns and special attacks. The EX version throws two blades, comes out faster, and has an unusually long hit stun. Use it as an early jump-in that allows for combos afterward.

→ ↓ ↘ + P — Tsuji Goe

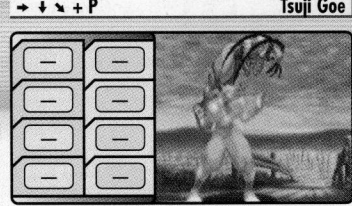

Tsuji Goe is an overhead flip that can be canceled into a Kunai. Not the most useful move, but can be valuable for escapting corners. Also works as a passable set up to make opponents block a Kasumi-Suzaku barrage for block damage.

↓ ↘ → + K — Kasumi Gake

Cancel into this command dash behind some of Ibuki's chains to get close after failed attacks, most often LK → MK. Kasumi Gake can be risky if opponents are expecting it. If Ibuki is hit during this move, she takes more damage than normal. Still, not bad option to help stay close.

→ ↘ ↓ + K — Kazekiri

4	-17
6	-15
8	-17
4	-21

Kazekiri has some use in juggle combos, but otherwise is limited. The EX version comes out faster and doesn't knock down, allowing Ibuki to come down with an air attack as she descends, provided it hits. It's also Ibuki's only good reversal, which is important to keep in mind if you need to stop an attack.

↓ ↘ ← + K — Tsumuji

11	-4
13	-2
14	-8
7	-11

For the MK version, press MK again to add an extra hit. Press ↓ during the LK / HK versions, or ↓ + MK after the second hit of the MK version, to kick low instead of high. The MK version remains safe if blocked, and can be used as a decent poke. The EX version comes out faster and hits more times; good for Ibuki's best low hitting non super art combo: ↓ + LK, ↓ + LP → EX Tsumuji.

← ↓ ↙ + K — Hien

22	-31
25	-38
29	-35
26	-30

Can be canceled into a Kunai or Kasumi-Suzaku during its recovery. Although slow as an overhead, use Hien as a set up to make opponents block a Kasumi-Suzaku for block damage. The EX version has homing properties and does more damage. Decent way to instantly get into range to make opponents block a Kasumi-Suzaku or to go over projectiles and land a super art.

IBUKI

SUPER ARTS

SUPER ART I

↓ ↘ → ↓ ↘ → + P   **Kasumi-Suzaku**

Great for punishing ground attacks with heavy recovery such as projectiles. Kasumi-Suzaku also does a great deal of chip damage. Use it to finish off opponents who are one or two moves away from a knockout. Ibuki can combo into Kasumi-Suzaku behind many of her ground

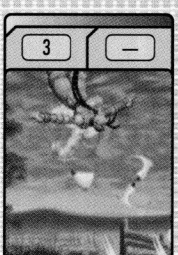

chains, canceled into Kazakiri → Kasumi-Suzaku. It also combos after a Hien. Trick an opponent by doing the first two hits of LK, MK, HK chain, then cancel into Hien on the second hit. If you catch an opponent blocking low, immediately Kasumi-Suzaku for good damage.

Kasumi-Suzaku has three super meter stocks, so it is the ideal super art to use in tandem with EX moves. An EX Kazekiri canceled into Kasumi-Suzaku is a solid wake up maneuver.

SUPER ART II

↓ ↘ → ↓ ↘ → + P   **Yoroi-Doushi**

Yoroi-Doushi is like an option select super art. If an opponent is within throw range, Ibuki hits instantly with a super version of Raida. It comes out in a single frame, so an opponent cannot jump out of it. However, if an opponent is not in range for Raida, the super art changes up and sends out a multi-hitting projectile. The start up time is much greater on this variation of the super art, and it is hard to get all the hits. Yoroi-Doushi is much better as a grab super art than a projectile super art. Also, it's difficult to land, so if you miss, you must resort to other means to inflict damage. Yoroi-Doushi only has one super meter stock, so Ibuki is limited in her EX capability.

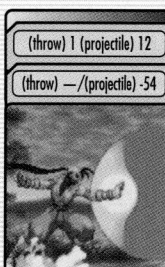

| (throw) 1 (projectile) 12 |
| (throw) —/(projectile) -54 |

SUPER ART III

↓ ↘ → ↓ → + P   **Yami-Shigure**

If any of the kunai thrown during this super art connect, Ibuki slashes back and forth. The button used determines how far Ibuki throws the kunai. Also, the farther she throws them, the slower they travel. Yami-Shigure is a an excellent punisher of whiffed moves. It forces shotos to think twice before trying ↓ + HK against Ibuki. Yami-Shigure also makes Ibuki's over-heads more useful. It's possible to link Yami-Shigure off Koube Kudaki, UOH, or after a properly timed Kunai. It combos easily from many of her ground chains, and links after MP as well as LP → MP target combo.

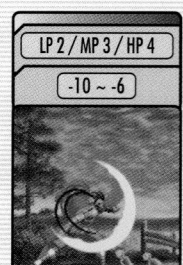

| LP 2 / MP 3 / HP 4 |
| -10 ~ -6 |

Yami-Shigure only stocks one super meter, so performing any EX moves prevents Ibuki from using this super art. Reduction costs Yami-Shigure in overall damage inflicted. For the best results, combo off her over-head attacks, MP link, or from ↓ + LK, ↓ + LP → Yami-Shigure.

Recommended Super Art:
Kasumi-Suzaku

Kasumi-Suzaku provides Ibuki with the most meter. She has many good EX moves that are safe and keep her playing aggressively. EX Kunai are great ways to jump in, while EX Tsumuji is an excellent and safe ground attack, and EX Kazekiri is one of the best wakeup moves in the game. To use another super art and be without these great EX moves really slows down Ibuki. Additionally, toward the end of many matches, it's possible to utilize the huge chip damage that Kasumi-Suzaku inflicts to finish off opponents in an efficient, if cheap, manner.

COMBOS YOU NEED TO KNOW

3 HITS

TOTAL DAMAGE: 32

Close LK → MK → Raida

Verifiable. Does okay damage.

4 HITS

TOTAL DAMAGE: 38

Close LP → MP → HP → Raida

Good for punishment situations. Knocks down.

6 HITS

TOTAL DAMAGE: 30

↓ + LK, ↓ + LP → EX Tsumuji

Flexible, verifiable combo that hits low. ↓ + LK, ↓ + LP is tough to link. EX Tsumuji is fairly safe, so no worries off a missed ↓ + LK, ↓ + LP. Knocks down.

5 HITS

TOTAL DAMAGE: 44

↓ + HK → close HK, super jump cancel straight up, → + HP → MK

Damaging juggle starting off a low attack. Does decent stun damage as well. If it's blocked, super jump cancel the close HK to jump away to safety.

6 HITS

TOTAL DAMAGE: 40

↓ + HK → close HK, juggle with late ← + MP (1 hit) → HP → Kazakiri (LK)

Damaging juggle starting off a low attack. If it's blocked, super jump cancel the close HK to jump away to safety. Although it does less damage than super jumping canceling the close HK, then juggling with HP → MK, it knocks down instead of pushing away, then resets the match, leaving Ibuki in a position to attack while the opponent is waking up.

9 HITS

TOTAL DAMAGE: 54

↓ + LK → ↓ + LP → Yami-Shigure

Verifiable way to land Yami-Shigure off a low attack. Good damage. Knocks down.

7 HITS

TOTAL DAMAGE: 47

Koube Kudaki linked into Yami-Shigure

Another verifiable way to land Yami-Shigure. Knocks down.

TARGET COMBOS

JUMPING HP → → + MK

| 11 |
| — |

Ibuki's most damaging air chain. Comes out slower and pushes opponents back the furthest after it hits, making it the least flexible of her air chains. Good in air juggles after ↓ + HK → HK.

JUMPING LK → → + MK

| 3 |
| — |

Low damage two hit air chain. Fast, and doesn't push Ibuki too far back after it hits, meaning it's easy to combo after when she lands. Her best overall jump in chain.

LP → MP → → + LK

| 2 |
| +2 |

Decent when used in combination with walk up LP pressure tactics. If opponents anticipate a walk up throw from that range, walk up and initiate this combo instead to foil tech throw attempts.

CLOSE LK → CLOSE MK → HK

| 4 |
| -2 |

The close MK in this chain is cancelable. Don't execute the entire chain, but LK → MK by itself is a decent, safe, and verifiable chain that is good for comboing into Raida.

CLOSE LP → CLOSE MP (1 HIT) → HP

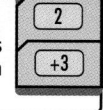

| 2 |
| +3 |

High damage three hit chain that's good for various combos in punishment situations. The HP in this chain whiffs versus most crouching opponents.

10 HITS

TOTAL DAMAGE: 53

Close LP → MP → HP → Yami-Shigure

Good in punishment situations. Knocks down.

8 HITS

TOTAL DAMAGE: 51

MP linked into Yami-Shigure

Easy and verifiable. Always look for a hit every time MP is used. Knocks down.

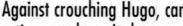

← + MP (1 HIT) → HP

| 6 |
| — |

Against crouching Hugo, can be used for some interesting combos. It has a small amount of frame advantage after it, and HK juggles behind it. Juggle with both hits to reset opponent, then cancel into a command dash for an ambiguous ground cross up.

JUMPING LP → → + HP

| 11 |
| — |

Two hit jump chain with good range. Can be done from further away than most air chains.

CLOSE HP (2 HITS) → ↓ + HK → HK

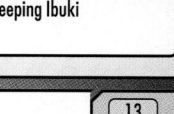

| 9 |
| -2 |

Damaging four hit chain that starts off of a mid level attack. Although much less damaging than some of Ibuki's other combo options, the super jump cancelable ending can help with momentum, keeping Ibuki on top of opponents after she combos.

← + MK → → + MK

| 13 |
| +9 |

Doesn't combo, but it's a passable way to get closer behind some frame advantage after a blocked ← + MK.

CLOSE LP → CLOSE MP (2 HITS) → ↓ + HK → HK

| 2 |
| -2 |

More damaging variant of Ibuki's ↓ + HK → HK chain. Slightly less useful as the second hit of MP tends to miss crouching opponents, but decent for punishment situations. It's possible super jump cancel the last HK if it connects.

← + MP (2 HITS) → ↓ + HK → HK

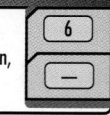

| 6 |
| — |

Another variant of Ibuki's ↓ + HK → far HK chain, but lacks any real use.

STRATEGY

Souken

Ibuki plays very well as a total rush down character. She has multiple attack strings that cancel into other attacks that allow her to keep pressure on constantly. She also plays well in a more careful style of poking from a distance, only attacking when it's safe. At mid-rage, ↓ + MK is a great poke. Although it doesn't cancel into anything, use it to punish whiffs and stop dashes from a distance. ↓ + MP is another decent poke that goes over some low attacks and is cancelable on reaction to combo into Yami-Shigure. Against opponents large enough to be hit by Bonshou Geri, it allows you to keep them pinned down from far away. It goes over any ground attacks, and is safe if blocked. In closer, opponents might try to throw after blocking this move. Jump and hit with an instant air Kasumi-Suzaku. When just outside of its range, opponents usually dance back and forth and poke. If you are quick enough, catch opponents with an EX Kubi Ori while they are standing. This move comes out quickly, but it is not safe if it misses.

Ibuki is more enjoyable when played with an aggressive mindset. Her close attack strings allow for constant pressure and a variety of mix ups. Koube Kudaki is the perfect attack to move her in close and start attacking. This move caries a huge frame advantage, and is almost always safe, even if parried. Hop over ground attacks to get in close with little fear. From this move, start attacking however you want. She is usually able to jump and cross up opponents, especially in the corner. Dash through your opponent for a tricky ground cross up, or start an attack string or tick into a throw. After any blocked attack string that moves Ibuki out of range, a quick Koube Kudaki is always a good, safe way to get back in close again.

LP is Ibuki's fastest move with a two frame startup. It also carries an amazing frame advantage blocked or hit. Against characters that get hit by this move low, LP is a great pressure tactic. Poke with jab, walk up, poke, and walk up and throw or ↓ + LK, ↓ + LP etc. If you think an opponent will stand up to either tech a throw or attempt to parry, do ↓ + HK, HK and juggle. Mix it up even by jabbing a few times, then dashing through them and hitting them from the other side.

Jumping MK is an excellent cross up. After a few ground attacks, Ibuki is usually pushed far enough away to be in range to cross up an opponent. Her jumping MK is especially good in the corner where it typically crosses up. A great trick is to cross up opponents in the corner, then immediately dash through them when Ibuki lands. This has the dual effect of being deceptive, and repositioning opponents back into the corner.

When opponents jump in at Ibuki, she has an advantage of height, or lack thereof. Opponents must perform jumping attacks late in order to hit her, so it is relatively easy to parry jump-ins. Parry and launch with HK, then juggle. Another good anti-air attack is to jump at opponents, then option parry air throw. It is hard to beat this tactic. Ibuki scores a knock down, which should be capitalized on wake up with a jumping cross up or any other offensive pattern.

Ibuki has many air chains that work great as jump-ins. Properly timed Kunai is another move to get in from the air. Hit with the Kunai to keep opponents in block stun long enough for her to land safely, then start a ground chain. It's easier with an EX Kunai, but be careful since most anti-airs go right through Ibuki's Kunai.

WAKEUP GAME

Many of Ibuki's best pokes and ground chains can be parried low, so Ibuki is better off either crossing up opponents, or just hanging around a waking opponent to start an attack string after the wake up parry window. If you must attack, consider Koube Kudaki because of its relative safety, and frame advantage afterwards. It also hits as an overhead. Mix it up with ↓ + LK, ↓ + LP to ward off wake up parries. If a ↓ + LK, ↓ + LP combination is blocked, Ibuki is still in range to walk up and continue pressuring with LPs.

When Ibuki is the one getting off the ground, she has a great wake up move in EX Kazekiri. It comes out quickly and beats almost all ground attacks. On the way down, continue to attack with either an air chain or a Kunai. This is a good wakeup move to surprise opponents with because it shifts the momentum into Ibuki's favor. However, if opponents are quick to react, a Shouryuken or similar anti-air will strike Ibuki on the way down. If you just want to get a pressuring opponent away, cancel the EX Kazekiri into a Kasumi-Suzaku (HP). An EX Kazekiri is also good for trying to attack during openings in tick throw patterns.

ADVANCED TACTIC 1: SUPER JUMP CANCELING

Ibuki can super jump cancel her HKs to allow her to follow up close HK with air juggles, her HK with a jump-in, or cancel into a super art. Ibuki can super jump cancel HK and immediately link Kasumi-Suzaku in the air against a grounded opponent. She can also super jump cancel HK and cancel the very first frames of her jump animation into a super art to link Yami-Shigure on the ground.

ADVANCED TACTIC 2: INSTANT AIR SUPER ART

Kasumi-Suzaku is available to Ibuki close to the ground, almost immediately after she jumps. To do this instant air super art, input a super jump so that it doubles as the first QCF of a super art motion. It does not matter that you went to ↗ instead of stopping at →. Input the second QCF immediately after the super jump to initiate the super art. This is a great way to fake out opponents and punish whiffed throw attempts. This is especially good against characters that get hit by Ibuki's LP while they crouch. Tick with walk up LP two or three times, then go for the throw. The next time, tick with LP, then use an instant air super art. Anyone expecting a throw gets hit by the quick fake out maneuver. There's another great setup to use when Ibuki gets pushed away: do a MK, then cancel into Kasumi Gake (LK) and throw immediately after the dash finishes. The next time this situation presents itself, do an instant air super art the moment Ibuki recovers and catch opponents trying to tech the anticipated throw.

SETUPS

Ranges setups for UOH → super art

Against small and wide sized characters:

> (↓ + LK, MK), UOH → Yami-Shigure
> (LK → MK chain), UOH → Yami-Shigure

Against Oro:

> No setup is required. UOH → Yami-Shigure works in close on crouching Oro.

RESETS

If Ibuki connects with a ↓ + HK, HK chain she knocks opponents into the air. One possibility is to super jump cancel and air combo, or reset opponents on the ground and go for an ambiguous cross up. As an opponent comes down, juggle from the ground with either MK or ← + MP, HP target combo. Cancel the hit into Kasumi Gake. Mix-up the distances of the command dash to confuse opponents when they land. Hit with another ↓ + HK, HK chain to repeat this trick again and again.

PARRY SET UPS AND TACTICS

Ibuki has an air throw that can be used effectively as an air-to-air option with an option parry. Tap → before Ibuki is in throw range. If the opponent did an attack, Ibuki will parry, then air throw. Without the opponent's attack, it simply turns into a throw.

The last hit of LP → MP → HP target combo tends to whiff on smaller opponents. They may react to this and try to retailiate. Down parry that attack and counter.

GROUND CROSS UPS

Ibuki can cross up Chun-Li, Makoto, Twelve, Alex, Ryu, Ken, Sean, Elena, Dudley, Oro, Necro, Hugo, Urien, and Akuma in any corner.

Ibuki can cross up every character mid screen.

FAVORABLE MATCH UP: HUGO

When one of the fastest characters in the game matches up against one of the slowest, the faster character typically is able to run rampant, and Ibuki vs. Hugo is no exception. Keep attacking with multi-hit jump-ins (Hugo's size allows him to be crossed up easily) and ground chains to keep Hugo pinned down and unable to move. Attacking early in the air will beat any Shootdown Backbreaker attempts, and still permit Ibuki to connect with the second hit of an air chain to keep her momentum going as she lands.

Against Hugo, be on guard against random down parries. Many of Ibuki's offensive patterns start with mid attacks that can be parried low. If Hugo starts to threaten Ibuki with parries, back off a bit and annoy him with her air supremacy. Jump in with EX Kunai to create a safe opening to start a ground chain, and chip him as often as possible with Kasumi-Suzaku.

31 HITS

TOTAL DAMAGE: 72

WORKS ONLY ON CROUCHING HUGO

LP → MP → HP chain linked into MK → EX Kazekiri, and link LP → HP air chain on the way down; land and EX Kazekiri → Kasumi-Suzaku

UNFAVORABLE MATCH UP: CHUN-LI

Expect Chun-Li to out reach and out prioritize most of Ibuki's ground pokes. Fighting from a distance is hard against Chun-Li, but fighting from up close isn't any easier. Many of Ibuki's important normal attacks and ground chains whiff over a crouching Chun-Li. It is hard to keep pressure on her. She also has one of the few normal moves that can counter a parried Koube Kudaki. Worse yet, she can cancel that move into a Houyoukusen for a ton of damage on Ibuki. Chipping Chun-Li with Kasumi-Suzaku is also not an option as she hits Ibuki with Houyokusen during her recovery.

For Ibuki to win this match up, she must avoid being hit by Chun-Li's ↓ + MK → Houyokusen. Jump in with EX Kunai and stick with whatever safe offensive pattern you can from up close. As soon as Ibuki gets pushed a little bit away, it's not worth the risk to attempt an attack. As long as Ibuku remains in range of Chun-Li's ↓ + MK, it's too risky to poke at her. Get back to a safe distance, then jump in again with a lead in EX Kunai.

Ken

NORMAL MOVES

STANDING

MK comes out quickly, covers a large area and is useful against anticipated jumps at close range.

HK is a great poke that moves Ken forward slightly, has good range, and does heavy damage. From further away it goes over low attacks and beats them cleanly. Be careful though, it must hit because if it whiffs you're going to take damage.

LP	Jab	
START UP	5	CS
+4	+4	+4	SC
		SA
GUARD	H/L	
PARRY	H/L	

MP	Strong	
START UP	6	CS
+3	+4	+5	SC
		SA
GUARD	H/L	
PARRY	H/L	

HP	Fierce	
START UP	9	CS
0	+2	+4	SC
		SA
GUARD	H/L	
PARRY	H	

LK	Short	
START UP	4	CS
+2	+2	+2	SC
		SA
GUARD	H/L	
PARRY	H/L	

MK	Forward	
START UP	8	
-6	-2	0	SC
		SA
GUARD	H/L	
PARRY	H	

HK	Roundhouse	
START UP	11	CS
-4	-2	0	SC
		SA
GUARD	H/L	
PARRY	H	

STANDING CLOSE

Close MP is a good poke with frame advantage off of it, so it is good for tick throw setups and other mix-ups. For example, after a blocked MP, hesitate, then walk up and MP again (Or ↓ + LK (x2)). The trick is to make it look like a throw attempt, that will lead to an opening.

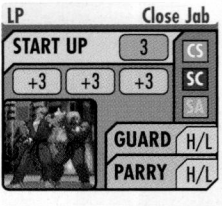
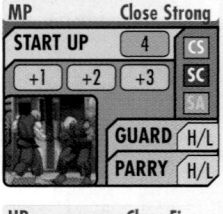

LP	Close Jab	
START UP	3	CS
+3	+3	+3	SC
		SA
GUARD	H/L	
PARRY	H/L	

MP	Close Strong	
START UP	4	CS
+1	+2	+3	SC
		SA
GUARD	H/L	
PARRY	H/L	

HP	Close Fierce	
START UP	6	CS
-2	0	+2	SC
		SA
GUARD	H/L	
PARRY	H	

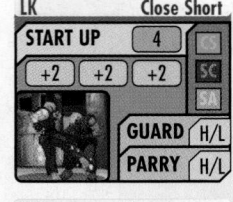

LK	Close Short	
START UP	4	CS
+2	+2	+2	SC
		SA
GUARD	H/L	
PARRY	H/L	

MK	Close Forward	
START UP	8	CS
-6	-2	0	SC
		SA
GUARD	H/L	
PARRY	H	

HK	Close Roundhouse	
START UP	11	CS
-4	-2	0	SC
		SA
GUARD	H/L	
PARRY	H	

COSTUMES

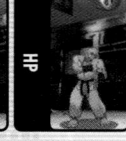

LP | MP | HP | LK | MK | HK
Start + LP | Start + MP | Start + HP | Start + LK | Start + MK | Start + HK
LP + MK + HP

SPECIAL NORMALS

← + MK, or hold MK — **Inazuma Kakato Wari**

START UP	18	+1

Two hit overhead with frame advantage. Fairly slow start up, but the ability to link a super art after it hits cannot be overlooked. Good in any mix-up situation, whether it's after a blocked cross up or done when the other player is waking up after a knock down.

← + HK, hold HK to cancel attack — **Shiden Kakato Otoshi**

START UP	30	-1

A lunging overhead kick that moves Ken forward. The overhead kick itself can be canceled, giving you the ability to mix up with a throw or ↓ + LK (x2) to keep opponents guessing. However, Ken goes into a small, noticeable recovery when you fake this move, which is open to attack from a player with fast reactions. The overhead itself is also not safe if blocked.

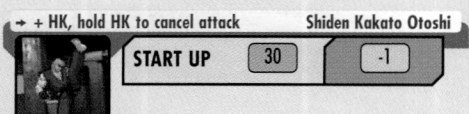

→ + MK — **Fumikomi Mae Geri**

START UP	16	-4

A lunge kick that moves Ken forward. Due to its long start up, it's easy to see coming, making it somewhat easy to parry. It also carries a slight disadvantage if blocked, leaving you in no position to start a real offense. Some players use this to their advantage as bait for option select parries or a "psychic" Shouryuken, but this is risky.

CROUCHING

↓ + LK has many uses. It is a quick poke that can be used for tick throw setups and mind games. After a blocked ↓ + LK, you have many options: throw, hesitate and ↓ + LK (x2) follow up, dash back and punish a reaction, etc. It chains into itself, so it's possible to combo ↓ + LK (x2) into any super art.

↓ + MK is Ken's best poke for mid range fighting. It combos into Shippu-Jinrai-Kyaku from long range to punish whiffs or to apply pressure.

Use ↓ + HK to punish whiffed normals when you lack super meter. It comes out fast and knocks down, but has terrible recovery. It's vulnerable to combos if blocked close, and some super arts from further away.

↓ + LP	Low Jab		
START UP		4	CS
+3	+3	+3	SC
			SA
GUARD		H/L	
PARRY		H/L	

↓ + LK	Low Short		
START UP		4	CS
+2	+2	+2	SC
			SA
GUARD		L	
PARRY		L	

↓ + MP	Low Strong		
START UP		4	CS
+3	+4	+5	SC
			SA
GUARD		H/L	
PARRY		H/L	

↓ + MK	Low Forward		
START UP		6	CS
-3	-2	-1	SC
			SA
GUARD		L	
PARRY		L	

↓ + HP	Low Fierce		
START UP		5	CS
-8	-6	-4	SC
			SA
GUARD		H/L	
PARRY		H	

↓ + HK	Low Roundhouse		
START UP		7	CS
-13	D	D	SC
			SA
GUARD		L	
PARRY		L	

JUMPING

Use jumping HP to get in safely. If opponents block, you have significant frame advantage to set up a throw or some mix-up into a super art. For instance, jumping HP, land and hesitate, making it look like a throw setup, then ↓ + LK (x2), super art. Jumping HP also has the property that if it's executed at the latest possible moment before hitting the ground, it is totally safe from any ground parry attempt.

Jumping MK is arguably the best cross up in *Street Fighter III: 3rd Strike*. Because its hit box is so large, it cannot be crouched under (unlike Ryu's cross up). When opponents are waking up, making them block a cross up gives you a fairly large frame advantage to work with, putting you into prime mix-up position.

↑ + LP	Jumping Jab	
START UP	4	
		SC
		SA
GUARD		H
PARRY		H

↑ / ↖ + HP	Jumping Fierce	
START UP	6	
		SC
		SA
GUARD		H
PARRY		H

↑ / ↖ + MK	Jumping	
START UP	For	
		SC
		SA
GUARD		war
PARRY		d

↑ + MP	Jumping Strong	
START UP	5	CS
		SC
		SA
GUARD		H
PARRY		H

↑ + LK	Jumping Short	
START UP	4	
		SC
		SA
GUARD		H
PARRY		H

↑ + HK	Vertical Roundhouse	
START UP	7	
		SC
		SA
GUARD		H
PARRY		H

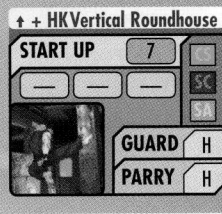

↑ + HP	Vertical Fierce	
START UP	7	CS
		SC
		SA
GUARD		H
PARRY		H

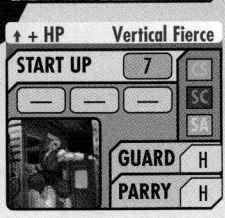

↑ + MK	Vertical Forward	
START UP	5	CS
		SC
		SA
GUARD		H
PARRY		H

↗ / ↘ + HK	Jumping Roundhouse	
START UP	6	
		SC
		SA
GUARD		H
PARRY		H

SPECIAL MOVES

↓ ↘ → + P	Hadouken

11	11	11	12
-11	-11	-11	-6

In some ways, this is Ken's ideal poke. Because of its limitless range and the speed at which it travels, characters trying to play a normal foot games cannot make this poke whiff, they must deal with it in some shape or form. Because of the semi-slow start up and its heavy recovery, Hadouken is a fairly risky move to do at mid range, the range you would normally want to perform it. Many characters, like Chun-Li, can hit Ken with a super art, hit or blocked, during the recovery of a normal Hadouken. Parrying also reduces the usefulness of this move since opponents no longer need to block or jump over the projectile. They can just tap forward to nullify it altogether. This makes throwing a Hadouken at the wrong time a game-losing decision. The EX version is only slightly better. Although it hits twice, knocks down, and travels faster, it is still unsafe versus some super arts if blocked at point blank range.

→ ↓ ↘ + P	Shouryuken

2	3	3	12
-17	-24	-31	-36

On start up, it has a small window of invulnerability, giving it the ability to consistently beat opponents' attacks. The HP version of Shouryuken is ideal as anti air with its large invulnerability window and multiple hits. The EX version hits 4 times, making it harder to parry if someone is jumping in on top of you. Shouryuken (LP) is useful for dealing damage. Many of his most flexible and damaging combo options use the Shouryuken (LP) because of its massive range, high damage, and the ability to juggle after it with another Shouryuken.

↓ ↙ ← + K	Tatsumaki Senpuu Kyaku

6	6	6	4
-5	-6	-7	-3

In air, ↓ ↙ ← + K	Tatsumaki Senpuu Kyaku

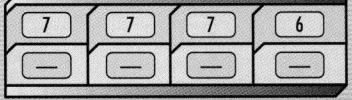

7	7	7	6

↓ + MK → Tatsumaki Senpuu Kyaku combos versus a crouching character, however if it's blocked, the Tatsumaki Senpuu Kyaku completely whiffs leaving you open to attack. The EX version has the same properties, but does more damage and hits more times. The jumping version of this move's value lies in its ability to change the arc of Ken's jump. This comes in handy when trying to get out of corners. The EX version of the jumping Tatsumaki Senpuu Kyaku is a different story altogether. If done during the downward arc of a jump that would normally land in the front of an opponent, the EX version carries Ken over, hitting from behind and crossing up. After it hits, opponents are immediately put into a juggle state, allowing follow ups for more damage.

THROWS

LP + LK	Hiza Geri

→ + LP + LK	Seoi Nage

← + LP + LK	Jigoku Guruma

SUPER ARTS

SUPER ART I

↓ ↘ → ↓ → + P	Shoryu-Reppa

Compared to Ken's other super arts, Shoryu-Reppa is not a good choice in high level play. Although it is easily comboed into and does more damage than Shippu-Jinrai-Kyaku, it is no where near as useful. The extra damage it inflicts does not make up for the greater length of the super meter. Shoryu-Reppa simply does not compare with Shippu-Jinrai-Kyaku when it comes to Ken's ground game, and Shinryu-Ken is superior as anti air.

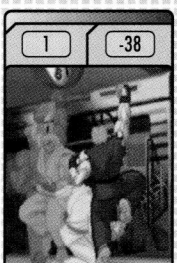

1	-38

Recommended Super Art:
Shippu-Jinrai-Kyaku

There is no question that Shippu-Jinrai-Kyaku is Ken's best super art. It provides the ability to control spacing from max range and in close. Any mistake from opponents can lead to a super art. It makes laying a methodical ground game without any guesswork possible. In addition to all its great features, it holds three stocks of super meter, allowing the freedom to use an assortment EX moves in addition to keeping the threat of Shippu-Jinrai-Kyaku. Shippu-Jinrai-Kyaku works with almost any style of play, from hyper-aggressive, to an all out turtle game.

SUPER ART II

↓ ↘ → ↓ ↘ → + K (tap K rapidly)	Shinryu-Ken

Shinryu-Ken is one of the best anti-air super arts. After it connects, mash the kick buttons for extra damage. You can vary the timing of the start the super art from early to late in a jump in to confuse parry attempts. Shinryu-Ken remains effective at all times, and is invincible on the way up. Use it to blow through air projectiles from characters like Akuma and Ibuki. Shinryu-Ken combos easily off of Ken's target combo or ↓ + LK (x2). If you are within a few ↓ + LK's distance, punish throw whiffs with ↓ + MK → Shinryu-Ken.

2	-80

The biggest drawback to Shinryu-Ken is that it must be used in close. Although it is excellent if used as anti-air, Ken doesn't really have the ability to pressure opponents into jumping at him. Outside of a few ↓ + LK's distance, Ken is never a real threat to do big damage. Most characters are free to poke from medium distance without fear of retaliation. Ken must play aggressively to get inside and create opportunities to land this super art, or he must be defensive and bait jumps so he can unleash an anti-air Shinryu-Ken.

TARGET CHAIN

CLOSE MP → CLOSE HP	4
Two hit command chain with a cancelable last hit. It is Ken's only verifiable way to land damage without a super art. Shouryuken (LP) and Shippu-Jinrai-Kyakuu both combo off of this chain for solid damage.	-2

SUPER ART III

↓ ↘ → ↓ ↘ → + K	Shippu-Jinrai-Kyaku

Shippu-Jinrai-Kyaku is one of the best super arts in the game. The bar is short and holds three stocks. It combos verifiably off of all of Ken's important moves. It comes out quick enough to punish moves and is deadly from all ranges. It's possible to hit confirm it off of ↓ + LKs, target combo, ↓ + MP, MP, his special normals, HP, and Straight. With all these options, Ken has high and low options as well as close and far options to land this super art. If you want to play it safe, you never need to get inside of an opponent's throw range because Ken can go into Shippu-Jinrai-Kyaku from ↓ + LK (x2) or ↓ + MP.

2	-11

Ken's up close options are incredible, but his ability to control space from just outside of his maximum range with ↓ + MK → Shippu-Jinrai-Kyaku make it a dominating super art. Keep people out of range with ↓ + MKs while buffering super art motions. When just outside of maximum range, if opponents dash in or try to poke at the same time, Ken's ↓ + MK hits and the super art automatically executes. A perfect time to try this is after a teched throw attempt. Ken is positioned at the perfect distance to buffer ↓ + MK → super art safely. Stay just outside of range with enough super meter and wait for an attmpted attack. If Ken is positioned just right, counter the whiffed attack as it retracts.

COMBOS YOU NEED TO KNOW

3 HITS
TOTAL DAMAGE: 27

↓ + MK → EX Hadouken

Safe low combo using an EX move. Knocks down.

3 HITS
TOTAL DAMAGE: 40

Close MP → close HP → Shouryuken (LP)

Ken's basic, verifiable combo. In the corner, juggle with a kara canceled Shouryuken (LP) for an extra 17 damage. Knocks down.

3 HITS
TOTAL DAMAGE: 53

Close MP → Shouryuken (LP), juggle with another early kara canceled Shouryuken (LP)

High damage non super combo. Good for punishment situations. Knocks down.

3 HITS
TOTAL DAMAGE: 52

Cross up jumping EX Tatsumaki Senpuu Kyaku, land, dash forward; as soon as possible, juggle with Shouryuken (LP), when Ken recovers, immediately juggle with a kara canceled Shoryuuken (LP).

11 HITS
TOTAL DAMAGE: 44

↓ + LK, ↓ + LK → Shippu-Jinrai-Kyaku

Flexible, verifiable way to land a super art. If ↓ + LK (x2) is blocked, Ken remains fairly close and has a slight frame advantage to work with to mount another offense. Walk up throw, short walk up ↓ + MP linked into Shippu-Jinrai-Kyaku, walk up close ↓ + LK (x2) → Shippu-Jinrai-Kyaku, or walk back a step, Universal Overhead linked into Shippu-Jinrai-Kyaku are all affective patterns in this situation.

10 HITS
TOTAL DAMAGE: 49

↓ + MK → Shippu-Jinrai-Kyaku

Good way to punish whiffed attacks for solid damage. Knocks down.

10 HITS
TOAL DAMAGE: 50

↓ + MP linked into Shippu-Jinrai-Kyaku

Verifiable way to land a super art. Useful in situations when you are too far away to land ↓ + LK (x2) → Shippu-Jinrai-Kyaku, specifically set ups after a blocked attack. Knocks down.

11 HITS
TOTAL DAMAGE: 54

Close MP → close HP → Shippu-Jinrai-Kyaku

Verifiable way to land a super. Knocks down.

11 HITS
TOTAL DAMAGE: 59

Inazuma Kakato Wari linked into Shippu-Jinrai-Kyaku

High damage combo starting off of Ken's command overhead. Verifiable. Knocks down.

11 HITS
TOTAL DAMAGE: 67

close HP → Shouryuken (MP) → Shippu-Jinrai-Kyaku

High damage super combo. Best way to deal damage with a super art if the combo is guaranteed. Good for punishment situations. Knocks down.

16 HITS
TOTAL DAMAGE: 76

Close MP → Close HP → Shinryu-Ken

Verifiable way to land a Shinryu-Ken off of a mid level hit. Knocks down.

17 HITS
TOTAL DAMAGE: 72

↓ + LK, ↓ + LK → Shinryu-Ken

Verifiable and flexible way to land a Shinryu-Ken off of a low attack.

STRATEGY

Straight

Ken's general strategy revolves around landing Shippu-Jinrai-Kyaku repeatedly. It's important to keep at least one stock of super memter ready to go. When you have less than one and a half stocks, don't use a super art even in a guaranteed combo situation. When Ken doesn't have enough meter for a super, he loses his ability to control space from mid to long distances. Also, from up close, Ken cannot do any significant damage starting low, so he is at risk for a high parry of his target combo.

When you lack sufficient meter for a super art, counter attack whiffed limbs with ↓ + HK, and pressure with HK. Don't miss here, or you are vulnerable to counter attack. Once you are able to get in close, via knockdown or a jump in, cycle between throw setups, the target combo, and overheads. Since you are at risk for high parries, mix it up with dash backs. For instance, ↓ + LK (a typical tick throw setup), then dash back instead of throwing. Look for movement from the character, such as a whiffed tech throw attempt, and punish it with a ↓ + HK. If they did nothing and continue to block low, dash back in and either throw or target combo.

Some good throw setups with Ken are:

↓ + LK, walk up throw
↓ + LK, crouch and hesitate, kara throw
↓ + LK, whiffed LP, walk up throw
LP, throw
MP, walk up throw

When Ken has enough meter for a super art, he becomes a dominating ground presence rivaled only by Chun-Li. Ken's ↓ + MK has the length and priority to beat out most ground attacks. Keep opponents from approaching on the ground by zoning with this move. It's possible to use ↓ + MK → super art against many actions on reaction, such as dashes and forward-moving special moves. The idea is to bait a low attack by moving just in and out of the opponent's maximum poke range. Make it appear as if you could be ht, then counter attack during the recovery of the whiffed move. This should instill fear in opponents on the ground, making it easier for Ken to get in, if that's your plan. Ken is so effective from maximum footsie range that you may decide to fight the entire match from that distance. This can frustrate opponents, especially those characters that must be in close to fight effectively.

With his ability to out range and zone opponents, many may resort to jumping to gain a favorable position. Ken has plenty of anti-air options to deal with airborne opponents. Shouryuken (LP) beats all jump ins, and has the ability to juggle with another Shouryuken (LP) for nice damage. The Shouryuken must be done late to achieve the damaging juggle. At only one hit, this move is parry bait. It's best to Shouryuken (LP) only when you see the jumping opponent throw out an attack first. Shouryuken (HP) on the other hand is 3 hits (4 on EX). Vary the timing to throw off parry attempts and you have a solid anti-air defense. Mix it up and dash under opponents from time to time. If they committed to an air attack, they cannot block when they land. Dash under and either ↓ + LK (x2) or target combo → super art.

Against airborne opponents, Ken has arguably the best air to air move in the game, jumping EX Tatsumaki Senpuu Kyaku. It hits multiple times and sets up a juggle state. It's possible to either combo with Shouryuken (LP), or set up a reset situation. Even if opponents manage to parry every hit, Ken is usually safe from any retaliation. It can be used effectively as anti-air as well. As soon as you see an opponent jump, super jump towards them and EX Tatsumaki Senpuu Kyaku immediately.

An aggressive Ken player should have no problem getting in from the air. Ken has a late jumping HP which is unpunishable from the ground if parried. If opponents block the punch, hesitate until they are out of block stun, then mix it up with throws, ↓ + LK (x2), and target combo. He also possesses one of the best cross ups in the game in jumping MK. If the cross up is blocked, go into any one of his numerous up close patterns similar to his wake up game. One trick that is sure to work a few times is to immediately do Inazuma Kakato Wari upon landing from the cross up. The natural reaction of defending players is typically to block low after a jump in, so they are open to an overhead attack.

WAKEUP GAME

After a knockdown, apply pressure with Ken's mix-ups. Turn any mistake from opponents into an opportunity to land a super art. Ken has sufficient low and high options, and overhead attacks, that lead into super arts. Change up your pattern often to discourage opponents from attempting to parry. Once you train them to block on wakeup, go ahead and throw. If opponents are worried about potential throws, they often try to tech them. Attempting to tech a throw at the wrong time will be an opening for you to land a super art. Start any tick throw pattern and change it into a super setup. For example:

↓ + LK, ↓ + MP → super art
↓ + LK, crouch and hesitate, ↓ + LK (x2) → super art
↓ + LK, whiffed LP, ↓ + LK (x2) → super art
↓ + LK, MP → super art
LK, target combo ' super art
MP, ↓ + MP → super art
↓ + LK, dash back ↓ + MK → super art
Ken has many quick fake out maneuvers used to trick people on wake up. For example, whiff a standing LP over an opponent's head right before they get up, then immediately throw. The missed move makes it look like you are going for something other than a throw, leaving opponents open for one. Next time on wake up, whiff the LP and they might anticipate the throw, so instead use ↓ + LK (x2) → super art. You can do the same sequence with a whiffed ↓ + LK into throw, then do a high attack that is verifiable into a super art. Ken's kara throw is also pretty good for fake outs. He can kara throw from one low short's distance away. After a kara throw in the corner, Ken is at his maximum range to kara throw again. The range is deceptive. Just stand there for a second and do nothing, then surprise opponents with another kara throw.

Ken's ↓ + MP link → super art must be mastered. ↓ + MP is fast and has high priority. It is safe enough to use often in close mix-ups. The key to playing Ken is to capitalize with a super art after any landed hit. Ken has the ability to link or cancel into super arts off of almost any poke. ↓ + MP his most important link. Learn it and use it often.

ADVANCED TACTIC: KARA SHOURYUKEN

It's possible to kara cancel ↓ + HK (or ↓ + MK) to increase the range of Shouryuken (LP). The extra range allows Ken to combo two Shouryuken (LP) in situations where he normally couldn't. The command input for this is: → ↓ + HK, ↘ + LP. It is difficult to do consistently, but if mastered, can really benefit your game. In many instances you create openings to land ↓ + MK → super art from close ranges. Instead, if you do ↓ + MK 'Shouryuken (LP), kara Shouryuken, not only will you do more damage, but you save super meter. In those instances where you are close and you bait a tech throw whiff, instead of ↓ + MK → super art, go for ↓ + MK → Shouryuken (LP), kara Shouryuken.

SETUPS

Ranges setups for UOH → super art

Against small and medium sized characters

(↓ + LK, ↓ + MP), UOH → Shippu-Jinrai-Kyaku
(HK), UOH → Shippu-Jinrai-Kyaku
(Target combo), kara UOH → Shippu-Jinrai-Kyaku
(Close MP, ↓ + MP), kara UOH → Shippu-Jinrai-Kyaku

Against medium sized characters

(Close MP, LK), UOH → Shippu-Jinrai-Kyaku
(↓ + LK, dash back), UOH → Shippu-Jinrai-Kyaku

Against wide characters:

(Close MP, ↓ + MP), UOH → Shippu-Jinrai-Kyaku
(↓ + LK (x3)), UOH → Shippu-Jinrai-Kyaku

Against Hugo, Elena:

(Target combo), UOH → Shippu-Jinrai-Kyaku

Against Oro:

No setup is required. UOH → Shippu-Jinrai-Kyaku works at close distance on crouching Oro.

AMBIGUOUS CROSS UP SET UP

Shippu-Jinrai-Kyaku leaves opponents at the perfect distance to set up an ambiguous cross up. After connecting with Shippu-Jinrai-Kyaku, hesitate a split second, then super jump towards your opponent, timing it so that you land at the exact moment they get up. Ken lands right on top of them, making it difficult to determine on which side he lands. Before jumping, move a tiny step forward or a tiny step backward to further confuse your opponent. When Ken lands, immediately start his target combo. This gives you enough time to determine what side Ken is on so you can verify a hit and combo into super art. If you have another super meter ready to go, repeat with another super jump. The idea is to force opponents to guess on what side Ken will land.

RESETS

Reset 1: After a jumping air to air EX Tatsumaki Senpuu Kyaku, stand LP to reset, then dash forward. Ken dashes up to opponents right as they recover on the ground. From there, you have the advantage to attack first from close range. You can throw, ↓ + LK (x2), target combo, or dash back and counter.

Reset 2: After a cross up air EX Tatsumaki Senpuu Kyaku, MK to reset, then dash forward. From there, Ken is at a perfect distance to super jump and cross up with another air EX Tatsumaki Senpuu Kyaku to repeat the process.

PARRY SETUPS AND TACTICS

In wakeup and up-close situations, you can option parry on any of the hesitation or tick throw setups. Start a tick throw setup with ↓ + LK, bring the controller back to neutral, then tap down. If the opponent stuck out a low poke, you will parry it. Take advantage of the situation and launch into ↓ + MK → super art. If the opponent did nothing, continue on attack pressure or throw.

GROUND CROSS UPS

Ken can cross up the following characters in any corner:

Twelve, Alex, Dudley, Necro, Hugo, Urien

Ken can cross up Chun-Li and Elena only in his own corner.

FAVORABLE MATCH UP: YANG

Ken can have an easy time against Yang if he is patient and has quick reflexes. Ken's ↓ + MK out ranges Yang, making it hard for Yang to get in close on the ground. Although you cannot just stick out ↓ + MKs randomly (Yang can retaliate during the recovery with EX Tourou Zan). Ken must patient and keep Yang from getting close. Yang cannot use EX Tourou Zan to get in on Ken because if blocked, Ken can unleash Shippu-Jinrai-Kyaku

Yang usually tries to get in close from the air. His dive kicks are his best jump in, although he is very vulnerable to anti-airs. Ken must be quick and use either jumping HP, or even better, jumping EX Tatsumaki Senpuu Kyaku any dive kick attempt. A Shouryuken is risky because Yang can be tricky with whiffed dive kicks. Whenever Yang does get close and tries MP/HP/EX Tourou Zan, punish the recovery with a super art.

UNFAVORABLE MATCH UP: CHUN-LI

Chun-Li is one of the few characters that can out range and out zone Ken on the ground. Her ↓ + MK is faster and harder to punish. If Ken whiffs any moves, Chun-Li can punish with ↓ + MK or standing HP. Getting in on the ground against Chun-Li is extremely difficult. She can keep Ken away with a barrage of ↓ + MKs. If Ken jumps, she can easily walk under his cross up attempt or air throw as a counter.

For Ken to win this match up, take advantage of the first round when Chun-Li has no super meter. Chun-Li without meter is not a threat. All of Chun-Li's dominance comes from the fear of her ↓ + MK → super art. Ken must be aggressive and win the first round before she builds super meter. After that, Ken must be extremely patient and careful. Chun-Li is similar to Ken in that any connected hit can lead to a super art. Ken must defensively, but cannot let Chun-Li pressure him into the corner. Jumping HP is a good way to get close to Chun-Li when she is controlling the ground. Get in close that way and try a mix-up pattern to land a super art. If you are able to get close to Chun-Li, know her maximum ranges. After ↓ + LK (x3) you are just outside of her ↓ + MK range. Bait her to stick out ↓ + MK and use HK to counter it. You can do the same after a blocked target combo. If you are quick enough, punish her ↓ + MK with a ↓ + MK → super art.

Makoto

NORMAL MOVES

STANDING

In close, MP is fantastic for wake up games, with a large amount of frame advantage after it, allowing Makoto to verify and link a super art or LK → Hayate (LP) after it. Also good for Karakusa ticks if blocked.

LP			Jab
START UP		4	CS
+2	+2	+2	SC
			SA
	GUARD	H/L	
	PARRY	H/L	

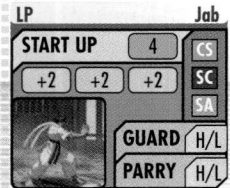

LK			Short
START UP		4	
-2	-2	-2	SC
			SA
	GUARD	H/L	
	PARRY	H/L	

MP			Strong
START UP		8	
+6	+7	+8	SC
			SA
	GUARD	H/L	
	PARRY		

MK			Forward
START UP		7	
-2	-1	0	SC
			SA
	GUARD	H/L	
	PARRY	H	

HP			Fierce
START UP		8	
-5	-3	-1	SC
			SA
	GUARD	H/L	
	PARRY	H	

HK			Roundhouse
START UP		11	CS
0	+2	+4	SC
			SA
	GUARD	H/L	
	PARRY	H	

COSTUMES

LP | MP | HP | LK | MK | HK | LP + MK + HP

Start + LP | Start + MP | Start + HP | Start + LK | Start + MK | Start + HK

SPECIAL NORMALS

→ + LP			Kazami
START UP		0	CS
0	0	0	SC
			SA
	GUARD	H/L	
	PARRY	H/L	

Cancelable, but no real uses.

→ + MP			Kaoruna
START UP		9	
+2	+3	+4	SC
			SA
	GUARD	H/L	
	PARRY	H	

Kaoruna has a slight amount of frame advantage after it and can be linked into a Seichusen-Godanzuki. Decent poke at close ranges.

→ + HP		Shimaki
START UP	16	
-4	-2	0	SC
		SA
GUARD	H/L	
PARRY	H	

A straight with exceptional range. Decent in foot games if used sparingly. Poor recovery and start up, so use with caution.

→ + LK			Shinbuki
START UP		6	CS
-5	-5	-5	SC
			SA
	GUARD	H/L	
	PARRY	H/L	

A toe kick that moves Makoto forward and serves as an okay poke up close. Use for starting resets after an EX Hayate.

→ + MK			Naruto
START UP		17	
-5	-3	-1	SC
			SA
	GUARD	H/L	
	PARRY	H	

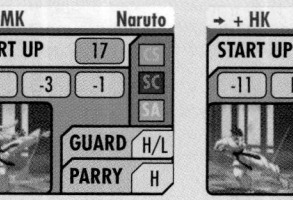

A turn kick with great range, plus it's hard to avoid during foot games.

→ + HK			Kurushio
START UP		22	
-11	D	D	
	GUARD	L	
	PARRY	L	

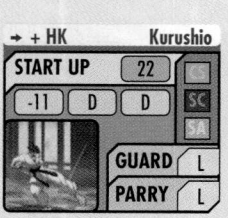

Turning sweep with good range. Hold HK to "fake" (cancel) the attack, allowing Makoto to mix in her command grab.

During Shimaki, tap HP — Yamase

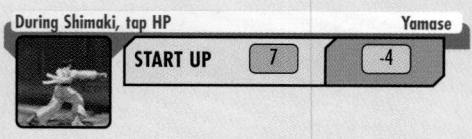

START UP	7	-4

Two hit punch extension at the end of the Shimaki. Passable damage for a move with such good range.

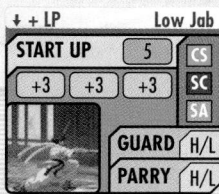

CROUCHING

↓ + MP is a decent, cancelable poke. Use it outside of an opponent's poke range while finishing the input for a Hayate. If the opponent dashes or hits a button, ↓ + MP hits and cancels into Hayate. ↓ + HP is an okay sweep with decent range and executes quickly. Not a safe move, it needs to hit. Use it to punish whiffed attacks.

↓ + MK has great priority, beating many random normals. It has a slight frame advantage after it, and links into Seichusen-Godanzuki. ↓ + HK has good range and covers a ridiculous amount of space. Safe to do if you correctly anticipate a jump after a comboed Hayate.

JUMPING

Jumping MK is a decent cross up and a good addition to Makoto's offense. Use the frame advantage after if it's blocked to set up opponents for a Karakusa mix up.

Jumping HK has fantastic priority, great range and executes quickly. It also serves as wonderful anti-air.

↓ + LP	Low Jab
START UP	5	CS
+3 +3 +3	SC
	SA
GUARD	H/L
PARRY	H/L

↓ + LK	Low Short
START UP	4	CS
-3 -3 -3	SC
	SA
GUARD	H/L
PARRY	L

↓ + MP	Low Strong
START UP	7	C
-1 0 +1	SC
	SA
GUARD	H/L
PARRY	H/L

↓ + MK	Low Forward
START UP	7	CS
+3 +4 +5	SC
	SA
GUARD	H/L
PARRY	H/L

↓ + HP	Low Fierce
START UP	10	C
-6 D D	SC
	SA
GUARD	L
PARRY	L

↓ + HK	Low Roundhouse
START UP	10	CS
+2 +4 +6	SC
	SA
GUARD	H/L
PARRY	H

↑ + LP	Vertical Jab
START UP	9	C
— — —	SC
	SA
GUARD	H
PARRY	H

↗ / ↖ + HP	Jumping Fierce
START UP	10	C
— — —	SC
	SA
GUARD	H
PARRY	H

↗ / ↖ + LP	Jumping Jab
START UP	4	C
— — —	SC
	SA
GUARD	H
PARRY	H

↑ + LK	Jumping Short
START UP	2	C
— — —	SC
	SA
GUARD	H
PARRY	H

↑ + MP	Vertical Strong
START UP	11	C
— — —	SC
	SA
GUARD	H
PARRY	H

↑ + MK	Jumping Forward
START UP	8	C
— — —	SC
	SA
GUARD	H
PARRY	H

↗ / ↖ + MP	Jumping Strong
START UP	11	C
— — —	SC
	SA
GUARD	H
PARRY	H

↑ + HK	Jumping Roundhouse
START UP	6	C
— — —	SC
	SA
GUARD	H
PARRY	H

↑ + HP	Vertical Fierce
START UP	13	C
— — —	SC
	SA
GUARD	H
PARRY	H

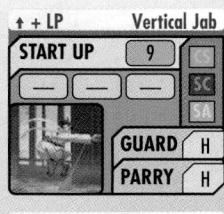

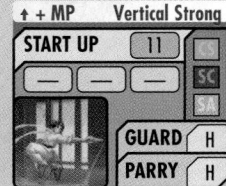

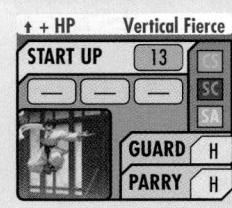

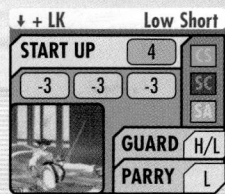

SPECIAL MOVES

↓ ↘ → + P	Hayate

6	9	11	17
-12	-12	-12	+2

Hayate is a quick dash punch with great range, but leaves Makoto vulnerable if it's blocked. The button strength determines how far the attack goes. The LP version can be added after any of Makoto's cancelable normals. After it hits, Makoto has a slight frame advantage, the perfect window to start a mix up game. Karakusa or ↓ + LK → Hayate again are both good in this situation. It's also possible to link a Seichusen-Godanzuki after the Hayate. The EX version has more range, knocks down, and is safe if blocked. It's possible to juggle after the EX version if it hits in the corner, although what you're able to do after it is very character specific. After pressing QCF + punch, hold punch and press a second punch button to cancel the Hayate. If you hold punch without canceling, Makoto yells out and poses before she executes Hayate. To do a special taunt, press HP + HK after hitting an opponent.

↓ ↙ ← + P	Oroshi

19	23	28	13
-4	-4	0	+4

Fairly slow overhead attack, but super art cancelable. The EX version knocks down and gets an unbelievable speed increase, making it easily the game's fastest overhead. A terrifying move to deal with in wake up situations.

→ ↓ ↘ + P	Fukiage

7	10	14	11
—	—	—	—

Awkward anti-air uppercut, but super jump cancelable if it hits. It's able to stop cross ups in a limited manner, and inflicts a remarkable amount of stun damage. Good for juggles after a connected Abare-Tosanami. The EX version moves forward slightly, making it easier to land as an anti-air.

→ ↘ ↓ ↙ ← + K	Karakusa

7	8	9	—
—	—	—	—

A command throw that allows moves to link after it. Her entire offense can revolve around landing this move. This is vital to Makoto's mix up game, and can lead to major damage with a super art or a number of resets after a normal Hayate hits.

↓ ↙ ← + K	Tsurugi

14	15	16	15
—	—	—	—

A jumping axe kick with slow start up. Fairly hard to parry as a jump in and can be used in juggles after landing a Abare-Tosanami. The EX version gets a major speed increase. Good if used the second Makoto leaves the ground for a jump, making it a fairly fast overhead that's safe.

THROWS

LP + LK	Tacchuu

← / → + LP + LK	Araiso

MAKOTO

SUPER ARTS

SUPER ART I

↓ ↘ → ↓ ↘ → + P | Seichusen-Godanzuki |

Seichusen-Godanzuki hits for big damage when linked off a normal attack. It's possible to verify Seichusen-Godanzuki from linking: MP, → + MP, ↓ + MK, close HK, and Hayate. Linking off of a Hayate gives Makoto the ability to land a super art from a full screen away with one hit. Punish whiffed pokes with Hayate linked into a super art. ↓ + MK is a high priority low poke, as is MP at mid level. These links are useful for landing Seichusen-Godanzuki. Makoto doesn't have any low attack to verify a hit to combo into Seichusen-Godanzuki. However, ↓ + LK links into Seichusen-Godanzuki up close, so use it to punish whiffs and throw attempts. Seichusen-Godanzuki is generally an all around good super for Makoto because of its numerous combo opportunities.

| 1 | -16 |

Seichusen-Godanzuki only stocks one super, so EX moves are generally out of the question if Makoto's goal is to land a super art. If this super art hits Yun or Yang in the corner, they recover in time to hit Makoto with Sourai Rengeki and Tenshin Senkyutai before she recovers from her last hit.

Recommended Super Art: Abare-Tosanami

While Seichusen-Godandzuki is a good super art and gives Makoto many chances to land damage off many of her best moves, it just doesn't carry the same raw intimidation factor that Abare-Tosanami does. With Abare-Tosanami stocked and ready to go, Makoto is just one Karakusa away from stunning opponents. The damage she can inflict with the combos and various resets is incredible. Makoto rushing down is a fearsome thing. When opponents try to avoid a Karakusa it leads to Makoto landing damage on opponents without using her super art. Hit them as they jump away from an anticipated Karakusa.

SUPER ART II

↓ ↘ → ↓ ↘ → + K | Abare-Tosanami |

The last punch can be canceled into either a dash or a super jump, setting up juggles and reset situations. The ability to combo after the super art is what makes Abare-Tosanami one of the game's most deadly super arts. Even the most basic combo starting from her Karakusa fills almost 90% of the stun gauge on most characters. It is a guaranteed stun on Akuma and Remy, which leads to easy "the match is over" combos. Against other characters, Makoto can reset and do 50/50 mix ups that can stun and lead to huge damage.

| 15 | -20 |

Abare-Tosanami combos off of Karakusa anywhere from the corner to mid screen. If an opponent is hit at least once before landing a Karakusa, a full Abare-Tosanami combo is almost certain to stun. Against crouching opponents, combo into Abare-Tosanami behind Oroshi (MP). Oroshi hits as an overhead and is hit confirmable.

The HK version of Abare can be used to go over projectiles and punish characters from a full screen away. Makoto is vulnerable as she jumps up to the wall before starting the super art. If she is hit before reaching the wall, she does not initiate a super art freeze, so no super meter is lost. Abare-Tosanami stocks two supers, ideal for EX use while keeping the threat of a super art.

TARGET COMBOS

| LK → MK | 4 |
| | -3 |

| → + MK → HK | 17 |
| | -3 |

An awkward chain that doesn't combo. However use it as a way to tick into Karakusa if opponents start anticipating the HK follow up to the target combo.

SUPER ART III

↓ ↘ → ↓ ↘ → + P | Tanden-Renki |

When Makoto activates Tanden-Renki, she glows red and powers up, resulting in all attacks inflicting 75% more damage until a timer expires. However, Makoto loses the ability to block during that time. This super art is meant for Makoto to go on an all-out offensive rush. Expect any smart opponent to go on an all-out offensive rush on Makoto during Tanden-Renki. If Makoto isn't the one doing the attacking, she must anticipate and parry any incoming attacks. Makoto must score hits, and quickly, or else she is going to be helpless versus random attacks. Comboing into Tanden-Renki for massive damage is only possible in very specific situations by canceling her Fukiage.

| — | — |

COMBOS YOU NEED TO KNOW

2 HITS

TOTAL DAMAGE: 18

↓ + LK → Hayate (LP)

Makoto's only low combo worth doing, but still not safe. If it hits, she has frame advantage to work with, allowing you to put opponents into a 50/50 situation with a throw/attack mix up.

3 HITS

TOTAL DAMAGE: 29

MP linked into LK → Hayate (LP)

Flexible, verifiable way to land a Hayate (LP). If MP is blocked, use the frame advantage to start another mix up. Going straight into a Karakusa or ↓ + LK → Hayate (LP) are both effective in this situation.

3 HITS

TOTAL DAMAGE: 30

Karakusa linked into an early HP → Hayate (HP)

Solid and very easy option off of Makoto's command throw.

3 HITS

TOTAL DAMAGE: 38

Karakusa linked into an early HP → EX Hayate

Slightly more damaging option off of Makoto's command throw. Knocks down.

6 HITS

TOTAL DAMAGE: 76

↓ + MK linked into Seichusen-Godanzuki

Safe, verifiable way to land Seichusen-Godanzuki.

8 HITS

TOTAL DAMAGE: 76

MP linked into LK → Hayate (LP) linked into an early Seichusen-Godanzuki

Flexible, verifiable way to land a Seichusen-Godanzuki. Knocks down.

8 HITS

TOTAL DAMAGE: 61

Karakusa linked into an early HP → Hayate (HP) linked into an early Seichusen-Godanzuki

High damage Seichusen-Godanzuki combo off of Makoto's command throw.

7 HITS

TOTAL DAMAGE: 82

MAKOTO GRABS OPPONENTS WHILE CORNERED OR NEAR THE EDGE OF THE SCREEN

Karakusa linked into an early HP → Abare-Tosanami, cancel the last hit into a forward dash, then juggle with Fukiage (HP) super jump canceled straight up into a jump HP

Massive damage and stun damage. Almost a guaranteed dizzy against most characters.

7 HITS

TOTAL DAMAGE: 74

Oroshi (LP) → Abare-Tosanami, cancel the last hit into a forward dash, then juggle with Fukiage (HP) super jump canceled straight up into a jump HP

Abare-Tosanami combo off of Oroshi. Very good damage.

12 HITS

TOTAL DAMAGE: 87

Karakusa linked into an early HP → Abare-Tosanami, cancel the last hit into a forward dash, then juggle with another Abare-Tosanami, super cancel the last hit into a forward jump, juggle with a short Tsurugi, land juggle again with a Hayate (HP), then finally juggle with another Hayate (HP)

Massive damage. Large amount of stun damage as well.

STRATEGY

Chigusa

Makoto's game plan revolves around landing Karakusa. Land one, and it's a combo for big damage and stun. Makoto must get close to do her damage; fortunately, she has the tools to get there. Her dash is incredibly fast and far reaching. Also, use it to sneak up on players during the recovery of any whiffed pokes. Use Hayate for the same purpose. These moves come out quickly, and are a good way to capitalize on openings. Connecting with a Hayate leaves Makoto in an advantageous position, where she can work Karakusa mind games.

The obvious option is to immediately Karakusa. Often, people expect the Karakusa and attempt to jump away. If this is the case, after the Hayate, immediately ⬇ + LK → Hayate (LP). If they try to do anything, she hits them and the fighters are back where they started. Another option is to skip the ⬇ + LK and just use Hayate (LP). If they try to jump, Makoto hits from close range and sets them up in a juggle state. Finish the combo with HP or Hayate.

A safer option after a Hayate is ⬇ + HK. This hits a jumping opponent and does not put Makoto at risk. However, it knocks away opponents and Makoto must work to get in close again. A more advanced tactic is an HP after a Hayate. Cancel the HP into a Hayate, immediately cancel out the move, then dash forward. If opponents jump, Makoto hits and recovers quickly enough to get back in their face when they land.

Makoto is a momentum character. Her rush down is fast and powerful. Anything you can do to stay near opponents and move forward is to your advantage because landing a Karakusa is the goal. However, expect opponents to continually jump back to escape any Karakusa attempts. Punish these jumps, keep mixing it up until catching them on the ground with a Karakusa.

Makoto inflicts damage quickly to opponents, however, her main weakness is the randomness of her offense. You want to go for the big damage off of the Karakusa, but you can't become predictable. Mix up Karakusa with knockdowns and random pokes to hit opponents as they try to jump away or counter.

Makoto seems to be a character of extremes, either dominant, or losing badly. To be fair, what Makoto lacks in consistency, she makes up for with her raw power and ability to do her damage off of one grab. She stuns opponents so quickly, and usually inflicts a tremendous amount of damage, even without landing a Karakusa, because opponents are constantly being hit while trying to avoid it. Rushing down a defensive player is a good tactic for Makoto. However, expect to run into wake up Shouryukens or super arts, simply because it's the nature of her game plan to be in close most of the time.

When an opponent jumps in, jump forward or backward and press HK as soon as Makoto leaves the ground. It comes out quickly and has great range. Use jumping HK to shut down Yun and Yang from ever getting a dive kick opportunity. If you are a bit braver, use LP as anti-air. If it hits, dash under opponents before they land in an attempt to confuse them.

WAKEUP GAME

Landing one Karakusa can lead to a big combo and a potential stun, so make landing a Karakusa your prime objective. Immediately attempting a Karakusa as an opponent gets off the ground is acceptable, but many players expect that attack. Instead, tick on wake up to prevent a jump, then Karakusa. Some really good tick setups into Karakusa are:

LP, Karakusa
MP, Karakusa
⬇ + LK, Karakusa
⬇ + MK, Karakusa

Don't rely solely on this move, however. A kara-canceled EX Oroshi works after a tick throw setup. It hits as an overhead if opponents block, and is fast enough to catch them trying to jump away. Performing EX Tsurugi as low to the ground as possible is another quick overhead attack that knocks down. The more variety of attacks used to punish opponents for trying to avoid a Karakusa, the greater the chance they block the next time on wake up, leaving the door open for it.

When Makoto is the one getting up, she doesn't have many fast normal moves to help her get an opponent away from her. ⬇ + LK → Hayate (LP) is pretty good if you think they are going for a throw. Also consider parrying on wake up; it's a complete guess, and shouldn't be done often, but Makoto has great damage and stun potential from one Karakusa that parrying shouldn't be completely ignored. If you make a habit of parrying on wake up with Makoto, opponents may be less willing to poke at her. If they hesitate and provide any breathing room, take the initiative and grab immediately with a Karakusa. This works surprisingly well and is embarrassing for them.

One way for Makoto to get out of a corner on wake up is to do a Abare-Tosanami (HK). She flies to the other end of the screen to safety. It's a waste of a full super meter, but sometimes it is the only way to escape a corner safely.

ADVANCED TACTIC 1: KARA KARAKUSA

Cancel a whiffed LK late into the move to kara cancel her Karakusa. Canceling the LK increases its range tremendously. Because LK involves Makoto sticking out her knee, it has a deceptive quality. If opponents react to that and decide to block, they are open for the Karakusa. Here are some good setups to get the proper range for a kara Karakusa on most characters:

MP (x2), LK → Karakusa

(→ + MP), LK → Karakusa

After a Araiso (→), dash back, LK → Karakusa

The LK must whiff in order for the Karakusa to connect. If LK lands, the Karakusa whiffs because the target goes into block stun, so the distancing must be precise. For one setup where the spacing isn't important, do a LK over a waking up opponent. Make it look like a meaty attack, but time it so it whiffs. If timed correctly, it's possible to kara cancel into the Karakusa to catch an opponent perfectly.

Another kara cancel for LK is into Oroshi. This works well with EX Oroshi, regardless if LK hits or whiffs.

ADVANCED TACTIC 2: INVULNERABILITY

Tacchuu has a unique property: Makoto is completely invulnerable immediately after finishing the head butt. Do not touch any controls after throwing for the invulnerability to take place. It lasts a brief time, but it is long enough to put to use. The throw knocks opponents just far enough away to where they can still usually reach her with their longest poke. Continue to stand after the throw, and allow them to try it. The move passes right through her, leaving a window of opportunity for a Hayate during the move's recovery. This works well against shotos since ⬇ + HK is their only move that can reach, and its recovery is long enough for her to punish it. Stand up to bait a low poke after the neutral throw, then Hayate counter or dash in and Karakusa.

Karakusa is also invulnerabile immediately after finishing. This shouldn't make any change since you should always start a combo after she lets go of her opponent.

SETUPS

Ranges setups for UOH → super

Against small, medium, and wide sized characters:

MP (x2), UOH → Seichusen-Godanzuki
MP, ⬇ + LK, UOH → Seichusen-Godanzuki
→ + MP, UOH → Seichusen-Godanzuki

Against small and medium sized characters:

⬇ + MK (x2), UOH → Seichusen-Godanzuki
⬇ + LP (x2), UOH → Seichusen-Godanzuki

RESETS AND OTHER ABARE-TOSANAMI SETUPS

Makoto has numerous resets and she can do after connecting with Abare-Tosanami. Resets enable Makoto to stun nearly any character off of a Karakusa.

Reset 1: Karakusa, HP → Abare-Tosanami, super jump cancel forward; Tsurugi, land and dash under; MP, Abare-Tosanami (HK), dash cancel forward under; Fukiage (HP), super jump cancel up and HK. This reset does 100% stun on most characters.

Setup 1a: Karakusa, HP → Abare-Tosanami, super jump cancel forward; Tsurugi, land and dash under; LP, then kara cancel an EX Fukiage (kara cancel with LK) to cross up as they land; super jump cancel up and HK. This reset does 100% stun on shotos. Mix it up after the LP by dashing under, then EX Fukiage to un-cross up at the last moment. There's also the option to land a Karakusa as they land.

Setup 2: Karakusa, HP → Abare-Tosanami, dash cancel forward under and Fukiage (HP), super jump towards and jump HK; land and dash under for either ⬇ + LK → Hayate or Karakusa for 100% stun on most characters.

Setup 3: After an EX Hayate in the corner, Shinbuki to knock opponents into flip recover to land on their feet. This sets up a perfect kara Karakusa. This is also an opportunity to dash under certain characters for a tricky ground cross up.

PARRY SETUPS AND TACTICS

After Makoto lands a Hayate, she is in prime position to attempt a Karakusa. Many players anticipate this and try to knock her out of it with a quick ⬇ + LP. Time the → motion of the Karakusa just as they recover from the hit stun of the Hayate. This way, if they do poke, Makoto parries, then grabs. If they block, she simply grabs them.

GROUND CROSS UPS

Makoto can cross up Twelve, Alex, Dudley, Necro, Hugo and Urien in any corner

Makoto can cross up Ibuki mid screen.

FAVORABLE MATCH UP: AKUMA

Concentrate on one thing against Akuma: land a Karakusa. Once that's done, it's all over for Akuma. Makoto stuns Akuma off a Karakusa with her most basic follow up. If she has enough meter, she can finish him off for a 100% combo.

Expect Akuma to make it difficult to get in close. Take advantage of Makoto's quick dash to get under air fireballs. When Akuma is close, take risks and attempt a parry. The risk/reward ratio is in Makoto's favor. All she needs is one Karakusa to win the match. One parry may give her the necessary opening.

UNFAVORABLE MATCH UP: CHUN-LI

It won't be easy to get in close with Chun-Li. Hakkei beats all of Makoto's pokes and keeps her from dashing in. Even if Makoto manages to get in close, she can't pressure Chun-Li with Karakusa mind games like she can other opponents. Chun-Li's low jab stops all Karakusa attempts along with Makoto's other pokes. Chun-Li just needs mash on ⬇ + LP whenever Makoto is close to prevent her from doing her thing. Even if Makoto parries, Chun-Li can always cancel into an EX Spinning Bird Kick on reaction. Tough break for Makoto.

For Makoto to win this match up, she must get in and trick Chun-Li. Take advantage of Makoto's quick dash to get in on Chun-Li after she whiffs one of her high priority pokes such as Hakkei. If she isn't in the recovery of one of her moves, do not dash in. A low forward → Houyokusen could come out at any time. Play patiently and carefully, with the goal of not getting hit by Chun-Li's low forward. Makoto only needs to land one or two Karakusas to turn this match around in her favor.

MAKOTO

Necro

NORMAL MOVES

STANDING

MP has good range, is super cancelable and goes over a variety of low normals. Decent against whiffed attacks and completely shuts down certain character types, like shots. Stay just outside an opponent's best poke range and whiff MP while inputting the command for Electric Snake. If opponents hit a button, they get hit and eat a super art.

MK is a good mid-range poke that goes over some low attacks. Can be parried high or low, so its use is limited. HK has great range with an upward angle. Use from far away early in anticipation of a jump.

LP		Jab	
START UP		5	CS
+2	+2	+2	SC
			SA
GUARD		H/L	
PARRY		H/L	

LK		Short	
START UP		4	CS
+1	+1	+1	SC
			SA
GUARD		H/L	
PARRY		H/L	

MP		Strong	
START UP		8	CS
-13	-11	-9	SC
			SA
GUARD		H/L	
PARRY		H/L	

MK		Forward	
START UP		9	CS
-1	0	+1	SC
			SA
GUARD		H/L	
PARRY		H	

HP		Fierce	
START UP		15	CS
-13	-11	-9	SC
			SA
GUARD		H/L	
PARRY		H	

HK		Roundhouse	
START UP		18	CS
-8	-6	-4	SC
			SA
GUARD		H/L	
PARRY		H	

COSTUMES

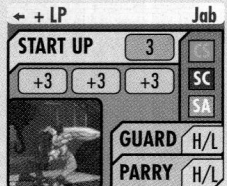

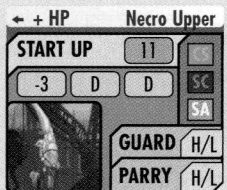

SPECIAL NORMALS

← + LP		Jab	
START UP		3	CS
+3	+3	+3	SC
			SA
GUARD		H/L	
PARRY		H/L	

← + MP		Elbow	
START UP		4	CS
+1	+2	+3	SC
			SA
GUARD		H/L	
PARRY		L	

A quick poke that's useful up close. Cancels into a super art on reaction to a hit. This is Necro's best move to get people off of him.

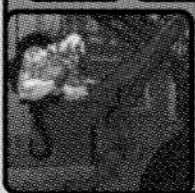

← + HP		Necro Upper	
START UP		11	CS
-3	D	D	SC
			SA
GUARD		H/L	
PARRY		H/L	

A stretching uppercut that is susceptible to parries. It serves to set up juggles, and is a passable anti-air.

← + LK		Knee Dagger	
START UP		3	SC
+3	+3	+3	SC
			SA
GUARD		H/L	
PARRY		H/L	

Use in Necro's target combo (← + LK → MP), and it's a decent way to land super arts.

← + MK		Knee Attack	
START UP		5	
+3	+4	+5	SC
			SA
GUARD		H/L	
PARRY		H	

Good for combos. Necro's only other decent mid level attack.

← + HK		Knee Missile	
START UP		12	
+10	+12	+14	SC
			SA
GUARD		H/L	
PARRY		H	

Stretching upward knee attack that carries a huge amount of frame advantage after it. Good as anti-air or in damaging combos used for punishment situations.

↙ + HP			Elbow Cannon
	START UP	9	+2

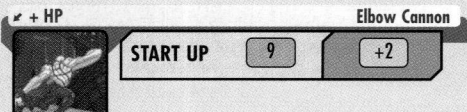

Great for combos. It's fast, does good damage, and puts opponents into a juggle state after it hits. Although the juggles off of it are fairly limited, against Alex and Hugo Necro can juggle with this move six times in a row for massive damage.

While jumping, ↓ + K			Drill Kick
	START UP	9	—

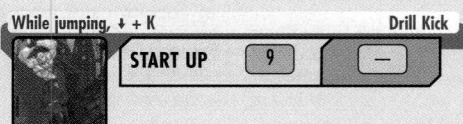

Button strength determines the angle of descent. Extremely important to Necro's offense as it's the main way he gets close. Use to keep opponents locked down in the corner.

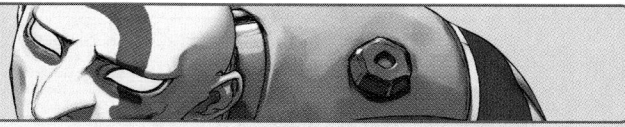

CROUCHING

↓ + MK has extremely good range for a low attack. During foot games, try to catch opponents with this move while they are dancing around.

↓ + LP	Low Jab	
START UP	6	CS
+3	+3	+3	SC
			SA
GUARD	H/L
PARRY	H/L

↓ + LK	Low Short	
START UP	6	CS
+2	+2	+2	SC
			SA
GUARD	L
PARRY	L

↓ + MP	Low Strong	
START UP	8	CS
0	+1	+2	SC
			SA
GUARD	H/L
PARRY	H/L

↓ + MK	Low Forward	
START UP	12	CS
-5	-4	-3	SC
			SA
GUARD	L
PARRY	L

↓ + HP	Low Fierce	
START UP	16	CS
-7	-5	-3	SC
			SA
GUARD	H/L
PARRY	H/L

↓ + HK	Low Roundhouse	
START UP	13	CS
-12	D	D	SC
			SA
GUARD	H/L
PARRY	H/L

JUMPING

↑ + LP	Vertical Jab	
START UP	5	CS
—	—	—	SC
			SA
GUARD	H
PARRY	H

↖/↗ + MP	Jumping Strong	
START UP	9	CS
—	—	—	SC
			SA
GUARD	H
PARRY	H

↑ + MK	Jumping Forward	
START UP	10	CS
—	—	—	SC
			SA
GUARD	H
PARRY	H

↖/↗ + LP	Jumping Jab	
START UP	4	CS
—	—	—	SC
			SA
GUARD	H
PARRY	H

↑ + HP	Jumping Fierce	
START UP	13	CS
—	—	—	SC
			SA
GUARD	H
PARRY	H

↑ + HK	Jumping Roundhouse	
START UP	15	CS
—	—	—	SC
			SA
GUARD	H
PARRY	H

↑ + MP	Vertical Strong	
START UP	8	CS
—	—	—	SC
			SA
GUARD	H
PARRY	H

↑ + LK	Jumping Short	
START UP	2	CS
—	—	—	SC
			SA
GUARD	H
PARRY	H

THROWS

LP + LK | Shoulder Attack

← + LP + LK | Frankensteiner

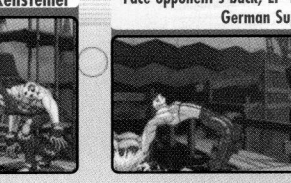

Face opponent's back, LP + LK
German Suplex

SPECIAL MOVES

→ ↓ ↘ + P (Push P rapidly)	Electric Blast

6	8	10	—
-10	-26	-24	—

Decent anti-air. If the LP version is used against jump attacks mid screen, it's possible to juggle with a far HP. If it's parried, tap punch to make Electric Blast hit again, making parry attempts hazardous. The LP version is also good for extended juggles after an Electric Snake. Electric Blast (HP) also has one use in a ground combo: Tornado Hook (HP) linked into a Electric Blast (HP), which does massive damage.

↓ ↙ ← + P	Flying Viper

26	26	28	24
-3	-2	-2	+2

It's easy to see this move as an overhead and this move doesn't really do anything else. The EX version is faster, hits twice, and has a slight frame advantage after it. Passable for pressure and to help move opponents towards a corner.

← ↙ ↓ ↘ → +K	Snake Fang

12	12	12	—
-15	-17	-19	—

Leg grab that hits low, and has great range. In the corner, it's possible to juggle after this move connects. This move carries a large frame disadvantage after it, meaning Necro will eat a super if it's blocked. There is also no reason to do this move over ↓ + MK, unless cornered and the plan is to land Magnetic Storm or try for minor juggles. Against crouching opponents, it's possible to combo into this attack behind Elbow (MP).

← ↙ ↓ ↘ → + P	Tornado Hook

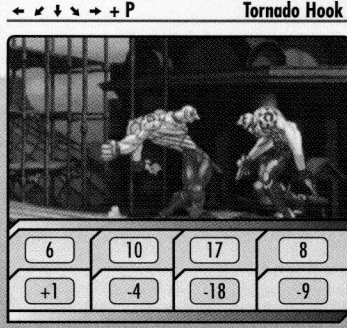

6	10	17	8
+1	-4	-18	-9

A juggle set up that's good for various combos. The LP version is safe if blocked. The HP version puts opponents into a long hit stun, allowing you to link after it. The EX version hits more times and does more damage.

↓ ↙ ← + K	Rising Cobra

23	25	27	25
-6	-6	-6	-3

Command overhead attack. Fairly slow, easy to anticipate. The EX version is slightly faster, does more damage and hits twice.

SUPER ARTS

SUPER ART I

| ↓ ↘ → ↓ ↘ → + P (push P rapidly) | Magnetic Storm |

A more powerful version of Electric Blast. It combos easily off of Necro's main pokes: MP, Elbow (MP), and his target chain. Juggle with Magnetic Storm after a Snake Fang in the corner, but the damage isn't that great. Magnetic Storm works well as an anti-air, although opponents tend to bounce up and miss some hits. It absorbs some projectiles, so it's useful against Akuma and Ibuki's air attack. Electric Storm has its uses, but the damage is not remarkable, and it only stocks one super meter.

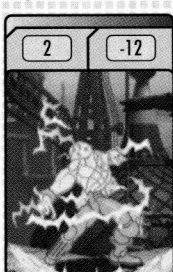

| 2 | -12 |

SUPER ART II

| ↓ ↘ → ↓ ↘ → + P | Slam Dance |

It's possible to combo into this after a Tornado Hook (HP) because of the turned around state that move leaves opponents. Unfortunately, if Necro doesn't combo into Slam Dance, he has no other guaranteed safe method to land it. It has a window of invulnerability at the beginning, which allows Necro to grab opponents through pokes, but this must be largely guess work. If opponents do nothing, they can also jump out of Slam Dance because of its slow start up time.

| 3 | — |

Drill Kick is a decent setup against opponents in the corner. When Necro lands, immediately use Slam Dance. If opponents jump to escape, hit with Necro Upper and juggle with Elbow Cannon. This works because Slam Dance recovers so quickly that most players are not prepared for Necro's anti-air attack. It is hard to actually land Slam Dance unless you parry or combo into it. Fishing for damage after Slam Dance misses might be the best you can hope for. In the corner, it's possible to catch Hugo in the air with a Slam Dance after Tornado Hook (LP) in the corner.

SUPER ART III

| ↓ ↘ → ↓ ↘ → + P | Electric Snake |

Electric Snake does fairly good damage and stun. It combos from max range off of Necro's most important pokes, namely MP and Elbow (MP). Cancel Elbow (MP) somewhat late to verify the super art. It is also possible to verify MP, but it is much faster and harder to do so. Cancel Tornado Hook (MP) on reaction to a hit to combo into Electric Snake. The last hit bounces opponents up into the air and sets up juggle opportunities in the corner.

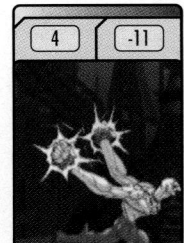

| 4 | -11 |

Electric Snake stocks two super meters, so it is ideal for EX use. Use Electric Snake to go under projectiles from full screen and punish opponents.

Recommended Super Art: Electric Snake

The high stun damage, two stocks of super meter, and the easy combo and zoning possibilities that Electric Snake brings to Necro's game makes it his super art of choice. Necro doesn't rely on his EX moves, but having access to them occasionally comes in handy.

TARGET COMBO

| COMMAND: ← + LK → MP | 3 |
| The MP ending whiffs vs. some small crouching characters, namely Elena, Yun, Yang, and Chun Li. However, it is cancelable and a decent way to land an Electric snake. | -3 |

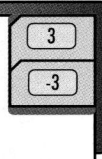

COMBOS YOU NEED TO KNOW

3 HITS

TOTAL DAMAGE: 21

↓ + LK → Tornado Hook (LP)

Necro's basic combo. Safe if blocked. In the corner, juggle again with Elbow Cannon for 14 extra damage.

2 HITS

TOTAL DAMAGE: 24

CORNER ONLY

Neutral throw, juggle with an early walk up MP

Decent damage off of a throw in the corner. Use it as an opening for a basic reset with either walk up a step, then universal overhead, or ↓ + MK as opponents hit the ground.

2 HITS

TOTAL DAMAGE: 36

Anti-air Necro Upper, juggle with early Elbow Cannon

Decent anti-air juggle that inflicts decent damage and knocks down.

7 HITS

TOTAL DAMAGE: 48

Tornado Hook (HP) linked into a Electric Blast (HP)

Damaging non-super art combo that knocks down.

6 HITS

TOTAL DAMAGE: 53

← + LK, ← + LK → MP → Electric Snake

Verifiable way to land an Electric Snake. Passable damage and knocks down. When near a corner, juggle afterward for extra damage.

11 HITS

TOTAL DAMAGE: 59

CORNER ONLY

Neutral throw, juggle after with a Magnetic Storm

Great damage off of a throw. Knocks down.

15 HITS

TOTAL DAMAGE: 75

Knee Missile linked into ↓ + LK→ Magnetic Storm

Easy, high damage Magnetic Storm combo. Good for punishment situations. Knocks down.

11 HITS

TOTAL DAMAGE: 58

Tornado Hook (HP) linked into early Knee Attack →Tornado Hook (MP) → Electric Snake; when Necro recovers, immediately juggle with early Electric Blast; when Necro recovers, juggle with early Elbow Cannon

High damage and stun damage off of a Tornado Hook (HP). Knocks down.

STRATEGY

Finger Attack

Necro has many long range moves, but he is surprisingly effective from close range. He is also good in a mid range footsie battle against characters that are large enough to get hit by MP while crouching. Use MP to pressure, and look for any movement. If you see it hit, cancel into Electric Snake. MP goes over low attacks and has good range. Keep characters out, and use it to punish whiffed attacks. This move is especially good for zoning against shots. When outside of their greatest poke range, whiff Elbows to build super meter. Mix it up with MK and ↓ + MK to do a good share of damage to opponents.

If you frustrate opponents on the ground, they might try to jump in. ↓ + MP comes out quickly and reaches far. If it is parried, Necro remains safe because he quickly retracts his arm. However, the move doesn't have the best priority. If opponents expect a ↓ + MP, they can do an early jumping attack to beat it. Use Necro Upper occasionally, too. It works as anti-air, and sets up a juggle. A Electric Blast (LP) is also good as anti-air. It sets up a juggle (follow up with HP).

Drill Kicks are great for getting in and playing aggressively. He can execute them low to the ground, making it hard to hit with an anti-air. Another good jump in is jumping HK. This hits from far away and links Electric Snake when Necro lands. Good for getting up close or applying pressure from far away.

When Necro gets close on the ground, use Tornado Hooks to keep on the forward pressure. After a Tornado Hook (LP), Necro has many options to mix it up. Go low with a ↓ + LK → Tornado Hook, attack from mid level with Knee Attack → Tornado Hook, throw, parry, or do another Tornado Hook (LP). Doing Tornado Hooks (LP) over and over can actually be effective, although this move is fairly easy to red parry on the second hit.

WAKEUP GAME

Necro doesn't have the best set of moves to scare a waking up opponent. His overhead attacks are slow and he doesn't have a jumping cross up. The best thing for Necro to do is to keep pressuring with mid and low attacks into various Tornado Hooks. Add in throws to keep opponents guessing.

Drill Kicks are a good way to keep pressure on waking opponents, and to play tricks on them. Walk up right next to them as they are getting up and jump over them and Drill Kick (HK) down. Change it up and land behind them, or land right on top of them. It is hard for them to tell where Necro is going to hit. Necro has another Drill Kick trick to use after landing an Electric Snake. Dash up once, then jump backwards and Drill Kick (MK). Necro lands right behind opponents right at the last second. It's tricky, and sets Necro up to combo ← + LK (x2) → MP and cancel into Electric Snake if it hits.

When Necro is the one getting off the ground, expect to have some trouble against aggressive opponents. Elbow (MP) is your best bet. It comes out quickly and it late cancels into Magnetic Storm or Electric Snake on reaction. If you can't find an opening for Elbow (MP), you may need to resort to a strategic parry to get out of a bad situation. Necro also has a hard time dealing with cross ups. Try to keep opponents away as best you can.

SETUPS

Ranged setups for UOH → super art

Against medium sized characters:

    (MP), UOH → Electric Snake
    (Knee Attack), UOH → Electric Snake
    (Knee Missile), UOH → Electric Snake

Against wide and large sized characters:
    (MP), UOH → Electric Snake

Against Oro:

    No setup is required. UOH → SA1 works at close distance on crouching Oro.

RESET

Reset 1: After a throw in the corner, hit with MP to knock opponents back on their feet. Take a small step forward to set up a perfectly distanced UOH that links into Electric Snake. Mix up by taking just a tiny a step forward, less than needed to connect, so that the UOH whiffs in front of opponents. Land and throw to start this pattern over again.

PARRY SET UPS AND TACTICS

Necro has a slight frame advantage after Tornado Hook (LP). At this range, most players go with a low attack against Necro. Parrying down in this situation often works. After a successful parry, combo Knee Attack → Tornado Hook (MP) → Electric Snake. If they do nothing and you crouch, immediately throw or do another Tornado Hook (LP) to set this situation up again.

If you use ↓ + MP for anti-air enough times, it's bound to get parried. Do it early enough, and Necro is safe from any counter attack. So after an opponent parries, tap → as soon as Necro recovers to counter parry jumping attacks.

GROUND CROSS UPS

Necro can cross up Hugo in any corner.

FAVORABLE MATCH UP: AKUMA

Necro's MP gives Akuma a hard time on the ground. It goes over all of Akuma's low pokes and hits while he's crouching. If Necro hits Akuma, cancel into Electric Snake on reaction. Electric Snake does a massive amount of stun to Akuma, on top of its regular damage. Keep Akuma at maximum MP distance and keep poking over his low attacks. If Akuma ever gets close, be patient, and hit him with Elbow (MP) → Electric Snake. Akuma's offense can be pretty hard to deal with sometimes, but Necro only needs to hit Akuma with one or two basic combos to stun him. Then it's all over for Akuma.

Necro has an easy 100% stun combo on Akuma. If Necro taunts first, the follow up combo does 100% life damage as well. In the corner, hit with Knee Missile, link MP → Electric Snake, juggle with Electric Blast (LP) → Electric Snake, then juggle with Elbow Cannon for the dizzy. When Akuma gets up, Tornado Hook (HP), and either do a Snake Fang (LK) or Electric Blast (HP).

UNFAVORABLE MATCH UP: CHUN LI

Chun-Li gives many characters problems, and Necro is one. Chun-Li ducks under Necro's MP, his main mid-range poke. Most of Necro's good pokes leave him open to be hit by Chun-Li's ↓ + MK → Houyokusen. Chun-Li's ← + HP and ↓ + HP tend to beat all of Necro's moves.

Necro has no choice other than to attack Chun-Li. From mid range, counterattack any whiffed HP Chun-Li does and poke with MK, but other than that, you must get close. Jumping HK is a good way to attack from long distance. Link Electric Snake behind a hit. Otherwise, rely on Drill Kicks to get in close. From there, play smart and don't get hit. Easier said than done, but it's possible. Because Necro has such a difficult time landing Electric Snake against Chun-Li, Slam Dance is also a viable option against her. Drill Kick, land, and Slam Dance is a decent tactic, but it might be a better idea to save it for wake up. With it, Necro has a way to bail himself out when he gets knocked down by Chun-Li.

Oro

NORMAL MOVES

STANDING

HP is a fast two hit overhead that does good health meter damage and stun damage. This move is an overall good option for mix up games.

A fast poke with good range, MK goes over low attacks and does decent stun damage and works well for punishing whiffed moves.

HK inflicts extremely high stun damage for a normal hit. Decent range and speed, but still good at close range when anticipating an attack. Use it in combination with Oro's back dash to avoid throws at close range, then punish the whiffed throw with HK.

LP		Jab
START UP	4	CS
0	0	0	SC
		SA
GUARD	H/L	
PARRY	H/L	

LK		Short
START UP	3	CS
+2	+2	+2	SC
		SA
GUARD	H/L	
PARRY	H/L	

MP		Strong
START UP	8	CS
-2	-1	0	SC
		SA
GUARD	H/L	
PARRY	H	

MK		Forward
START UP	8	CS
-5	-4	-3	SC
		SA
GUARD	H/L	
PARRY	H	

HP		Fierce
START UP	17	CS
-5	-3	-1	SC
		SA
GUARD	H	
PARRY	H	

HK		Roundhouse
START UP	7	CS
-5	-3	-1	SC
		SA
GUARD	H/L	
PARRY	H	

STANDING CLOSE

Close MP is a super jump cancelable two hit uppercut that sets up all of Oro's most important extended juggles. Also good as anti-air.

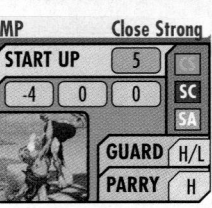

LP		Close Jab
START UP	2	CS
+5	+5	+5	SC
		SA
GUARD	H/L	
PARRY	H/L	

LK		Close Short
START UP	2	CS
+4	+4	+4	SC
		SA
GUARD	H/L	
PARRY	H	

MP		Close Strong
START UP	5	
-4	0	0	SC
		SA
GUARD	H/L	
PARRY	H	

MK		Close Forward
START UP	4	
-5	-4	-3	SC
		SA
GUARD	H/L	
PARRY	H	

HP		Close Fierce
START UP	17	CS
-5	-3	-1	SC
		SA
GUARD	H	
PARRY	H	

HK		Close Roundhouse
START UP	7	CS
-5	-3	-1	SC
		SA
GUARD	H/L	
PARRY	H	

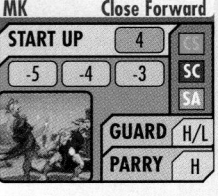

COSTUMES

SPECIAL NORMALS

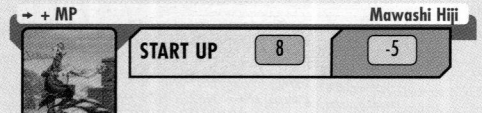

→ + MP — Mawashi Hiji

START UP	8	-5

Spinning back hand that moves Oro forward while attacking. Whiffs versus most crouching characters, limiting its usefulness.

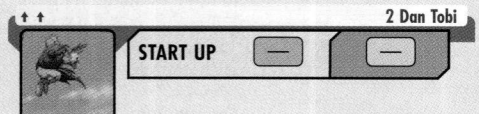

↑↑ — 2 Dan Tobi

START UP	—	—

A second jump while in mid air, used for multiple tricks. If you jump in and suspect opponents will try a ground based anti-air, perform the second jump towards (↗) to barely clear the anti-air and land an attack if the whiffed attack has sufficient recovery. The second jump can also be used for cross up tricks, like jump over opponents while they are getting up from a knock down, then double jumping backwards towards to set up a cross up MK. Depending on when you double jump during the first jump's arc, you can time the cross up MK to hit in front of or behind your opponent.

CROUCHING

↓ + LP			Low Jab	
START UP		4		CS
+1	+1	+1		SC
				SA
		GUARD	H/L	
		PARRY	H/L	

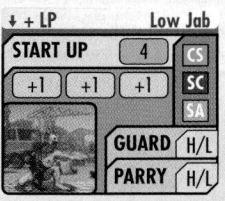

↓ + MP			Low Strong	
START UP		7		CS
-5	-4	-3		SC
				SA
		GUARD	H/L	
		PARRY	H/L	

↓ + HP			Low Fierce	
START UP		6		CS
-2	0	0		SC
				SA
		GUARD	H	
		PARRY	H	

↓ + LK			Low Short	
START UP		4		CS
+1	+1	+1		SC
				SA
		GUARD	L	
		PARRY	L	

↓ + MK			Low Forward	
START UP		6		CS
0	+1	+2		SC
				SA
		GUARD	L	
		PARRY	L	

↓ + HK			Low Roundhouse	
START UP		10		CS
-6	D	D		SC
				SA
		GUARD	L	
		PARRY	L	

JUMPING

Jumping MK is a decent cross up and helpful for setting up guessing games with some frame advantage. If it's blocked, walk up throw, HP, ↓ + MK → Niou Riki, or back dash to HK are all options in this situation.

↑ + LP		Vertical Jab	
START UP		3	CS
—	—	—	SC
			SA
	GUARD	H	
	PARRY	H	

↑ + HP		Vertical Fierce	
START UP		7	CS
—	—	—	SC
			SA
	GUARD	H	
	PARRY	H	

↑ + MK		Vertical Forward	
START UP		4	CS
—	—	—	SC
			SA
	GUARD	H	
	PARRY	H	

↗ / ↖ + LP		Jumping Jab	
START UP		7	CS
—	—	—	SC
			SA
	GUARD	H	
	PARRY	H	

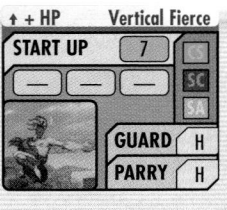

↗ / ↖ + HP		Jumping Fierce	
START UP		9	CS
—	—	—	SC
			SA
	GUARD	H	
	PARRY	H	

↗ / ↖ + MK		Jumping Forward	
START UP		3	CS
—	—	—	SC
			SA
	GUARD	H	
	PARRY	H	

↑ + MP		Vertical Strong	
START UP		5	CS
—	—	—	SC
			SA
	GUARD	H	
	PARRY	H	

↑ + LK		Vertical Short	
START UP		2	CS
—	—	—	SC
			SA
	GUARD	H	
	PARRY	H	

↑ + HK		Vertical Roundhouse	
START UP		5	CS
—	—	—	SC
			SA
	GUARD	H	
	PARRY	H	

↗ / ↖ + MP		Jumping Strong	
START UP		10	CS
—	—	—	SC
			SA
	GUARD	H	
	PARRY	H	

↗ / ↖ + LK		Jumping Short	
START UP		3	CS
—	—	—	SC
			SA
	GUARD	H	
	PARRY	H	

↗ / ↖ + HK		Jumping Roundhouse	
START UP		5	CS
—	—	—	SC
			SA
	GUARD	H	
	PARRY	H	

THROWS

LP + LK	Kubi-jime Kataguruma

← + LP + LK	Tomoe Nage

In air, LP + LK	Kuuchuu Jigoku Guruma

SPECIAL MOVES

Charge ← → + P	Nichiirin Shyou

15	15	13	15
-6	-4	-2	+1

Charge ↓ ↑ + P	Oni Yanma

6	6	7	5
-22	-30	-38	-48

Spiraling uppercut. Usable in some combos and as a wake up. EX version is faster and does more damage.

→ ↘ ↓ ↙ ← + P	Niou Riki

9	10	11	—
-15	-15	-15	

Three hit command grab. Blockable, but it cannot be parried. It's good for basic ground bombos, as it combos behind medium attacks.

While Jumping, ↓ ↘ → + K (tap K rapidly)	Hitobashira Nobori

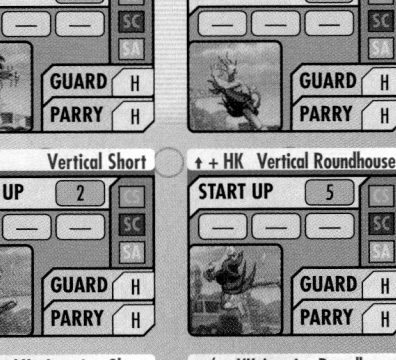

27	31	35	31
—	—	—	—

Great as an "instant" overhead. When opponents wake up from a knock down, jump forward and input the command as quickly as possible. The Hitobashira Nobori is performed close to the ground, making it a fairly fast overhead. It's also usable in other high/low mix ups. Example: After a successful knock down in the corner, jump towards your opponent, timing it so that you will land just as they stand up, then do ↓ + MK → Niou Riki. The next time in this situation, open with Hitobashira Nobori (HK) just before touching the ground, which hits as an overhead. Land, then juggle with MP → Jinchuu Watari for extra damage.

↓ ↘ → + K	Jinchuu Watari

27	31	35	31
—	—	—	—

Good for Oro's extended juggles off of close MP. Can be used for some cross up tactics, like blocked close MK → Jinchuu Watari (MK), which crosses up opponents, then doing close MK → Jinchuu Watari (LK), which hits opponents from the front. However, this move is very unsafe if blocked, making it risky for these applications. The EX version travels much faster and homes in on opponents.

ORO

SUPER ARTS

SUPER ART I

↓ ↘ → ↓ ↘ → + P, Approach opponent, P	Kishin-Riki

Oro has two ways to use this super art. Activate it with two punch buttons and Oro hops towards opponents and grabs with Kishin Tsui, jumps high into the sky, then crashes them down into the ground for decent damage. It's possible to combo into this grab with ↓ + HP, or try to bait opponents to throw out a move and hop right through it to grab them.

The other variation to this super art is to activate with only one punch button for Kishin Riki. The super meter turns into a timer that counts down. During this brief time, all of Oro's punches become multi hit versions of his command throw. However, during this time, those throws are unblockable. In the air, all of his punches become multi hit versions of his air throw. This version of the super art does not have much potential to deal much damage. Also, with only one stock of super meter, Oro doesn't have the luxury to do EX moves and still have a super art ready to go.

SUPER ART II

↓ ↘ → ↓ ↘ → + P	Yagyou-Dama

Oro sends out a large, slow moving projectile. The stronger the punch button used, the higher the arc that the projectile travels. Use Yagyou-Dama in Oro's juggle combos. It's also possible to use it as a safe way to get close to opponents. Send out a Yagyou-Dama, then follow behind it and attack safely. If Oro has all three stocks of super meter, activate the more powerful Yagyou-Oodama by pressing two buttons. Oro jumps up high and sends down out a monstrous projectile that hits many more times than a normal Yagyou-Dama. It can also be used in juggle combos with the ability to continue juggling after Yagyou-Oodama hits.

30	+27

With three super meter stocks, it is the ideal choice if accessibility to EX moves is something you desire. One of the most important uses of Yagyou-Dama is setting up unblockable situations. After knocking down opponents, send out a Yagyou-Dama, then jump over them and cross them up at the same time Yagyou-Dama hits them from the other side. It's not too difficult to set up an unblockable from Oro's juggle combos. Cancel a MP into the appropriate Yagyou-Dama, then dash up and jump over your opponent, and double jump straight up. Time it so Oro comes down with a jumping HK to hit from one side as the Yagyou-Dama hits from the other. Immediately start a new juggle combo with MP, and continue to juggle and end with another MP → Yagyou-Dama. Keep repeating this unblockable situation so long as you have enough super meter and are positioned properly mid-screen. This repeating sequence is usually easy to keep up because Oro builds meter during the juggles before the super art.

SUPER ART III

↓ ↘ → ↓ ↘ → + P	Tengu-Stone

There are two variations to Tengu-Stone. Activate it with one punch button, and three random floating items appear above Oro's head that attack with him, increasing the hits and damage. This lasts until Oro's super meter is exhausted. This variation is useful for pressuring cornered opponents. It is extremely risky for opponents to try to attack, so do not hesitate in yours. Even as they are blocking, they take chip damage from every hit. End with a hit before the timer runs, then link into a MP to start a juggle combo after the super meter expires.

The other variation is Tengu-Midareishi. The timer runs out much faster, but Oro gets the floating items and can juggle with each hit. Use Tengu-Midareishi to continue a juggle combo when normal and special moves no longer combo. At the end of a Tengu-Midareishi juggle, juggle with another MP to keep it going for a few more hits. The Tengu-Stone stocks a single super meter.

Recommended Super Art:
Yagyou-Dama or Tengu-Stone

Yagyou-Dama and Tengu-Stone both lead to punishing opponents off a MP, or by starting a juggle in some other way. Yagyou-Dama has the added benefit of setting up multiple unblockable situations, but Oro must land a hit to set these up. Use Tengu-Stone to corner opponents and land damage while they try to block the onslaught of high and low attacks. Both super arts are good, and both can give Oro opportunities to really hurt opponents.

TARGET COMBO

| COMMAND: CLOSE LK → MK | 2 |
| Quick and safe chain with limited uses. | -5 |

COMBOS YOU NEED TO KNOW

4 HITS

TOTAL DAMAGE: 34

↓ + MK → Niou Riki

Easy and damaging combo off of a low attack. Although it's not safe, there are some set ups that require a good low combo to be effective.

5 HITS

TOTAL DAMAGE: 43

Close MP (1 hit) →Jinchuu Watari (MK); land, then juggle again with a late close MP (1 hit) → Jinchuu Watari (MK); land, then juggle with Oni Yanma (MP)

Damaging juggle combo. Good for punishment situations and knocks down.

6 HITS

TOTAL DAMAGE: 45

Extremely late jumping Hitobashira Nobori (HK) (1 hit); land, then juggle with close MP (1 hit) → Jinhuu Watari (MK)

Damaging juggle combo off of an overhead attack. Use with Oro's basic jump in / empty jump in set up.

9 HITS

TOTAL DAMAGE: 45

Close MP (1 hit) →Jinchuu Watari (MK); land, then juggle again with late close MP (1 hit) → Jinchuu Watari (MK); land, then juggle with an early close MP (1 hit) → Kishin Riki activation, then immediately jump and hit punch to juggle

A safe way to activate Kishin Riki. After the combo hits, Oro still has about 70% of Kishin Riki timer left. Decent for punishment situations and knocks down.

2 HITS

TOTAL DAMAGE: 68

↓ + HP → Kishin Tsui

Easy, high-damage combo for punishment situations. Knocks down.

41 HITS

TOTAL DAMAGE: 91

Close MP (1 hit) →Jinchuu Watari (MK); land, then juggle with late close MP (1 hit) →Jinchuu Watari (MK); land, then juggle with early close MP (1 hit) → Tengu Midare Ishi, immediately juggle with a HK, juggle with Mawashi Hiji, HK, Mawashi Hiji, HK, Mawashi Hiji, Tengu Midare ishi ends; walk up a step to late close MP (1 hit) → Jinchuu Watari (MK); land, then juggle with late close MP (1 hit) → Jinchuu Watari (MK); land, then juggle with an immediate Oni Yanma (MP)

Basic Tengu-Stone combo. For consistency, skip the Jinchuu Watari juggles at the beginning and do the MP (2 hits) → Tengu-Stone to start it. In the corner, replace the Mawashi Hiji juggles with HK.

13 HITS

TOTAL DAMAGE: 74

MIDSCREEN ONLY

Close MP (2 hits) → Yagyuu-Oodama; recover, dash forward 3 times, juggle with close MP (1 hit) → Jinchuu Watari (MK); land, then juggle with late close MP (1 hit) → Jinchuu Watari (MK); land, then juggle with early Oni Yanma (MP)

Decent damage and knocks down.

STRATEGY

Tobi Hiza

Off of a single MP, Oro has the potential to deal an impressive amount of damage. If he has a few stocked super meters, Oro has the ability to win a round off of a MP, then a series of unblockable Yagyou-Dama set ups. The trick is landing the MP. Most opponents will be careful to avoid MP when Oro is close. The move has a recovery long enough that some characters can block and retaliate with a super art. Sometimes the risk is necessary due to the large reward. Oro must throw often when close. The goal is to get opponents to react in a way that leaves them open to MP connecting.

While patiently waiting for an opportunity to land MP, Oro has enough ways to possibly trick opponents into getting hit. Oro is fortunate to have many good ground pokes to frustrate and, more importantly, deal damage to opponents. HK and MK are both excellent for going over low pokes and keeping opponnets out of range. Both of these moves give most opponents enough trouble to where they will resort to jumping at Oro.

Oro has many good ways to deal with jump-ins. The obvious move is MP. If it connects, then a massive juggle combo and setup should follow. Unfortunately this move comes out somewhat slow and tends to get beat. However, if MP trades, it's still possible to set up a juggle. Many opponents are aware of the danger of MP, so use Oro's quick dash and small size to combat jumping opponents. Wait as long as possible and dash under opponents before they land. If you are quick enough, it's possible to catch them with an anti-air MP from the other side. If they land before Oro can connect with MP, try ↓ + MK → Niou Riki as they land, or go for a throw. If Oro is a good distance away, HK works surprisingly well as anti-air. If you're playing aggressivly, meet a jumping opponent in the air with an option parry air throw.

Oro's back dash is extremely fast and useful. Use it similarly to a shoto's back dash to bait out throw tech attempts. Whenever Oro is close, either back dash immediately or tick with ↓ + LK or another quick poke that looks like a throw setup, then dash back. If you see opponents flinch and do something, use HK. If you want to stay close, dash forward and throw. After a back dash, Oro is also at a good distance to jump in, which is a good option if an opponent did nothing for you to punish after the back dash.

Use Oro's double jump to invite anti-airs and jump out of the way. Jump towards opponents and either double jump back or upward to escape any possible anti air. This is a good way to land some hits and get close to opponents. After missing with one or two anti-airs because of this, opponents are likely to be more conservative with anti-air attempts. This provides the opening necessary to get in on opponents to land MP.

When Oro has a jump-in opportunity, an extremely late, close to the ground Hitobashira Nobori is an easy and deceptive way to land a MP. Jump and wait until Oro is almost at the ground, then execute a Hitobashira Nobori. Most characters will see Oro jump and do nothing, preparing to block low. You can hit them as they transition to blocking low, land, and juggle with MP and proceed to do any of Oro's many high damaging options. This trick works extremely well in training opponents into blocking low as Oro get close to the ground, provided you have previously done nothing in the air, then immediately used a ↓ + MK upon landing. Set this up after a backward throw. If opponents don't quick recover, Oro is at a great distance to super jump in and use Hitobashira Nobori right before the opponent lands.

WAKEUP GAME

Depending on how Oro scores a knockdown, his wakeup tactics change. Super art selection plays a role as well. With Yagyou-Dama, go for an unblockable setup if it's possible. Otherwise, trick opponents with double jump cross ups, or a Hitobashira Nobori. It's available both very early and very late in Oro's jump. Get right next to opponents and do it as an instant overhead. It is too fast for players to react to, most likely catching them as they block low. This is good for quick damage, and it knocks down, setting up another wakeup pressure situation. If you're having difficulty getting close, wait for a knockdown that an opponent quick recovers. Send out a Yagyou-Dama and follow behind it; while they are blocking the Yagyou-Dama, mix up overheads, low attacks, and cross ups from either jumping MK or Jinchuu Watari. Landing a hit while Yagyou-Dama is out usually leads to MP to start a juggle.

With Tengu-Stone, use any knockdown as an opportunity to activate Tengu Ishi and get close to apply pressureand inflict as much damage possible. With Tengu-Stone activated, there's no need to worry about being hit on wakeup, except by high priority super arts.

When Oro is getting up off the ground, he has a few decent attacks to push away opponents. EX Oni Yanma is a great wakeup move. Cancel it into Yagyou-Dama to potentially set up an unblockable situation if it hits, or it provides a nice opening to either dash up or jump in on opponents. Oro's LK comes out quickly, so it is useful in wakeup situations. Wait for an opponent to tick or do some sort of hesitation move, then retaliate with LK at the first opening. LK usually comes out quicker than a poke or throw attempt. If you want to get out of a corner, cancel LK into a Jinchuu Watari to escape, and possibly cross up at the same time.

Oro's back dash is good for getting him out of trouble, except when in the corner. Back dash on wake up and HK to punish attackers. Back dash out of tick throw setups and any hesitation moves. Don't become predictable by back dashing too often on wake up, Oro is vulnerable during it.

ADVANCED TACTIC: UNBLOCKABLE YAGYOU-DAMA

The easiest way to set this off is after repeated MP → Jinchuu Watari combo. Cancel the first hit of the last MP into a Yagyou-Dama. Yagyou-Dama should juggle opponents and knock them to the ground. This is important because they can't quick recover from a super art. Position Oro to double jump over the fallen body and come down to hit from one side as the Yagyou-Dama hits from the other side. The Yagyou-Dama is unblockable, and it's possible to link another MP to start a new juggle combo. Repeat this setup until the super meter is depleted. The meter builds throughout this combo, so you may keep this pattern going long enough to knock out opponents. The specific Yagyou-Dama variations and setups vary between certain characters. Here are some basic setups that work on a large percentage of the cast.

SETUPS

Setup 1: Against characters that only bounce off of the Yagyou-Dama once, such as shotos. At the end of the juggle combo, cancel MP into a Yagyou-Dama (MP). Wait just a second, then dash forward twice. It's important to wait so you don't end up dashing under them. You want to dash so that you push the opponent's body into position for the unblockable Yagyou-Dama to connect on wakeup. After the dash, jump over their body, then double jump again in the same direction. As Oro comes down, hit with a HK before landing. By timing it to hit at the same time as Yagyou-Dama, it is unblockable. The Yagyou-Dama continues to hit, and you are free to launch a new juggle with MP.

Setup 2: Against characters, such as Alex, Twelve, and Urien, that bounce off of the Yagyou-Dama twice. At the end of the juggle combo, cancel the MP into a Yagyou-Dama (HP). As soon as you recover, super jump towards the opponent to position properly. When Oro lands, jump over the fallen body, then double jump again in the same direction. As Oro comes down, hit with HK before landing.

Setup 3: Against smaller characters, such as Yun and Yang where you can't do the repeated MP → Jinchuu Watari combo, you must cancel into a Yagyou-Dama (MP) directly from the second hit of MP. Dash under opponents as they are juggled by the Yagyou-Dama. Jump straight up, and time it so you can come down and HK before landing, hitting at the same time as the Yagyou-Dama hits from the other side.

Setup 4: Oro is on the ground and the opponent is right next to him. If you manage to land a wakeup EX Oni Yanma, cancel immediately into a Yagyou-Dama, then do one of the previous setups that is appropriate for the character type faced. This is a great way to setup an unblockable against an aggressive opponent.

Setup 5: Use EX Nichirin Shou to confuse an opponent's ability to block. If you land a MP, immediately perform an EX Nichirin Shou. Next, input a Jinchuu Watari (MK) to cross up right as they land. Oro hits them at the same time as the EX Nichirin Shou, which can set up a MP to launch the opponent again. This setup is less usable because opponents can quick recover after the MP hit to roll away to safety.

RESETS

Reset 1: At the end of one of Oro's juggle combos, reset for a tricky ground cross up setup. For instance, at the end of this combo: MP → Jinchuu Watari, MP → Junchuu Watari, instead of finishing the juggle, hit with LP. This resets opponents to recover back to their feet. Quickly dash under before they land to cross up. Start a new juggle combo if they don't react in time to block properly. Mix this up by hesitating and dashing just a split second later so Oro doesn't make it under their falling body.

Reset 2: At the end of Oro's repeated MP → Jinchuu Watari combo, reset opponents with ↓ + HP. Cancel it into the Tengu Midareishi variation of Tengu-Stone and begin a new juggle. This may not do any more damage than canceling directly into Tengu-Stone for the full combo, but it does reset the stun damage of the new combo.

PARRY SETUPS AND TACTICS

Oro has an air throw that can be used with an option parry to be an effective air to air option. Simply tap → slightly before Oro enters throw range. If your opponent attempts an attack, Oro parries, then air throws them. Otherwise, the throw just comes out.

GROUND CROSS UPS

Oro can cross up Alex, Twelve, Hugo, Dudley, Necro, and Urien in any corner.

FAVORABLE MATCH UP: AKUMA

Akuma can teleport out of unblockable and Tengu-Stone setups on the ground. However, Akuma has other weaknesses that give Oro a slight edge against him. First and foremost, Akuma has a small stun bar, and Oro's HK deals a ton of stun damage. Play footsie games with Akuma and try to land HK over one of his low pokes. It only takes a few to dizzy him. Oro's small size also helps him out against Akuma, allowing him to duck under Tatsumaki Senpuu Kyakus, and dash under Zanku Hadouken pretty easily. There are many chances for Oro to land big hits on Akuma. If you can dizzy Akuma, then one big combo should seal the deal.

UNFAVORABLE MATCH UP: KEN

Oro actually does quite well against Ken from medium range on the ground. Oro even defends against Ken's offense fairly well. The reason Oro has trouble with this match up is because he can't be aggressive against Ken. Oro can beat many of Ken's pokes from a distance, but expect trouble in getting past Ken's low forward danger zone.

The air is no better. Oro's double jump tricks don't work on Ken because Ken can just do random EX Tatsumaki Senpuu Kyakus in the air to keep Oro grounded. Attacking is risky against Ken. If you ever manage to get close, it is too risky to go for MP because if Ken blocks it, he has the chance to land Shippu-Jinrai-Kyaku.

To win this matchup, play defensively. Be annoying and make Ken be the aggressor. Beat him at poking games with MK and HK from a safe distance. Maintain distance and don't let him rush you down. Dash back whenever he gets close and force him to jump, then dash under him. Play keep away and slowly land your hits. Keep this up long enough generally leads to an anxious Ken player who might do something that leaves him vulnerable. You must capitalize on any mistakes, but don't rely on this. Just play safe and don't allow Ken to get in close.

Q

NORMAL MOVES

STANDING

MK is good against some low attacks. It comes out fast and has decent recovery.

HK has ridiculous range and is very good against low attacks. However, it has absolutely terrible recovery. Don't bother with it against a Chun-Li with a stocked super meter; hit or miss with it, and Q is open to a super art.

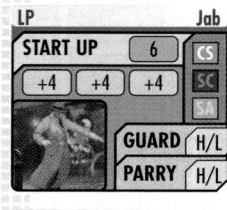

LP	Jab
START UP	6	CS
+4 +4 +4	SC
	SA
GUARD	H/L
PARRY	H/L

LK	Short
START UP	4	CS
+2 +2 +2	SC
	SA
GUARD	H/L
PARRY	H/L

MP	Strong
START UP	12	CS
-2 0 +2	SC
	SA
GUARD	H/L
PARRY	H

MK	Forward
START UP	8	CS
-1 +1 +3	SC
	SA
GUARD	H/L
PARRY	H

HP	Fierce
START UP	18	CS
-23 D D	SC
	SA
GUARD	H/L
PARRY	H

HK	Roundhouse
START UP	20	CS
-12 -10 -8	SC
	SA
GUARD	H/L
PARRY	H

STANDING CLOSE

LP	Close Jab
START UP	4	CS
+2 +2 +2	SC
	SA
GUARD	H/L
PARRY	H/L

LK	Close Short
START UP	4	CS
+2 +2 +2	SC
	SA
GUARD	H/L
PARRY	H/L

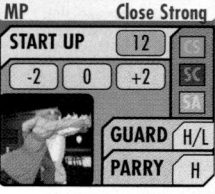

MP	Close Strong
START UP	12	
-2 0 +2	SC
	SA
GUARD	H/L
PARRY	H

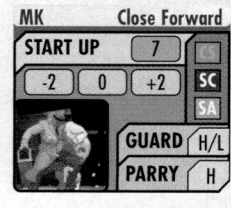

MK	Close Forward
START UP	7	CS
-2 0 +2	SC
	SA
GUARD	H/L
PARRY	H

HP	Close Fierce
START UP	18	CS
-22 D D	SC
	SA
GUARD	H/L
PARRY	H

HK	Close Roundhouse
START UP	20	CS
-12 -10 -8	SC
	SA
GUARD	H/L
PARRY	H

COSTUMES

LP MP HP LK MK HK
Start + LP   Start + MP   Start + HP   Start + LK   Start + MK   Start + HK   LP + MK + HP

SPECIAL NORMALS

← + MP	Toubu ni yoru Jouhou Kougeki (Kari)
START UP	8	-2

A swift uppercut that serves as a passable anti air. It's susceptible to parries.

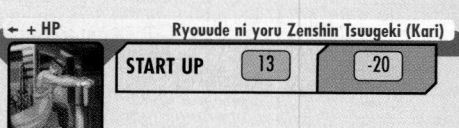

← + HP	Ryouude ni yoru Zenshin Tsuugeki (Kari)
START UP	13	-20

Lunging punch similar to HP. Faster start up and recovery, but doesn't knock down. Whiffs versus most crouching characters. Use in juggles with Capture & Deadly Blow, otherwise avoid it.

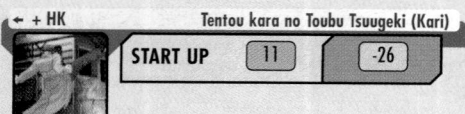

← + HK	Tentou kara no Toubu Tsuugeki (Kari)
START UP	11	-26

A strange kick that ends with Q falling down. Terrible recovery, but it's cancelable, providing an opportunity to eliminate the recovery with one of Q's safer special attacks. Could be used as an awkward anti-air. If it connects, it's a safe way to land a taunt.

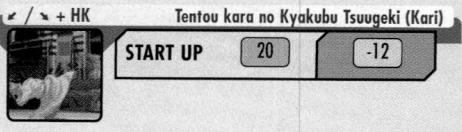

↙ / ↘ + HK	Tentou kara no Kyakubu Tsuugeki (Kari)
START UP	20	-12

Moving version of ↓ + HK. Exact same properties as ↓ + HK, except that it can be moved forward or remain stationary.

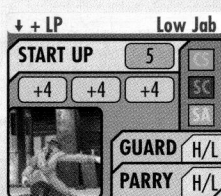

CROUCHING

↓ + HK has a heavy start up and recovery. It's a risky move, but does have strange priority to it. It often trades with reversals.

↓ + LP		Low Jab	
START UP	5		CS
+4	+4	+4	SC
			SA
GUARD			H/L
PARRY			H/L

↓ + LK		Low Short	
START UP	6		CS
-2	-2	-2	SC
			SA
GUARD			L
PARRY			L

↓ + MP		Low Strong	
START UP	8		CS
-2	-1	0	SC
			SA
GUARD			H/L
PARRY			H/L

↓ + MK		Low Forward	
START UP	7		CS
-3	-2	-1	SC
			SA
GUARD			L
PARRY			L

↓ + HP		Low Fierce	
START UP	14		CS
-3	-1	+1	SC
			SA
GUARD			L
PARRY			L

↓ + HK		Low Roundhouse	
START UP	12		CS
-25	D	D	SC
			SA
GUARD			L
PARRY			L

JUMPING

Jumping LP (a.k.a. THE CLAW) comes out quickly and stays out the entire arc of Q's jump. Good for throw set ups when blocked.

Jumping HP is a great jump in that executes fairly fast and does heavy damage.

↑ + LP		Vertical Jab	
START UP	2		CS
—	—	—	SC
			SA
GUARD			H
PARRY			H

↑ + LK		Jumping Short	
START UP	4		CS
—	—	—	SC
			SA
GUARD			H
PARRY			H

↗ / ↖ + LP		Jumping Jab	
START UP	2		CS
—	—	—	SC
			SA
GUARD			H
PARRY			H

↑ + MK		Jumping Forward	
START UP	9		CS
—	—	—	SC
			SA
GUARD			H
PARRY			H

↑ + MP		Jumping Strong	
START UP	7		CS
—	—	—	SC
			SA
GUARD			H
PARRY			H

↑ + HK	Jumping Roundhouse	
START UP	17	CS
— — —		SC
		SA
GUARD		H
PARRY		H

↑ + HP		Jumping Fierce	
START UP	10		CS
—	—	—	SC
			SA
GUARD			H
PARRY			H

THROWS

LP + LK	Hokaku Oyobi Shippu o Mochi ta Tsuuda (Kari)

→/← + LP + LK	Hokaku Oyobi Touteki ni yoru Daraku Shougeki

SPECIAL MOVES

↓ ↙ ← + P	High Speed Barrage

9	8	9	6
-6	-9	-8	-23

Button strength determines the angle at which Q attacks. Use as an early anti-air against players that parry often. The EX version hits multiple times for more damage and knocks down. Good for a combo (MK → EX High Speed Barrage) to deal damage in situations when Q doesn't have a charge for a Dashing Head Attack.

Charge ← → + P	Dashing Head Attack

13	15	19	14
-2	-2	-3	-21

Press and hold any punch button for a overhead punch variation of the same move. Fast start up and good recovery. Makes this a large part of Q's offense. Good for various combos and lets Q get into his preferred range safely. The overhead variations can be tricky to deal with when combined with Dashing Leg Attack. The EX version sacrifices the good recovery for more damage and a juggle opportunity after it hits.

Charge ← → + K	Dashing Leg Attack

25	28	31	27
-13	-14	-15	-18

Low hitting version of Dash Head Attack, keeping the fast start up, but it has bad recovery. Can be tricky to deal with when used in combination with the overhead variation of Dashing Head Attack. EX version does more damage and hits twice. It's possible to super cancel off of the first hit.

Charge ← → + P (hold P)	Dashing Head Attack

25	29	33	—
-10	-11	-12	—

→ ↘ ↓ ↙ ← + K	Capture & Deadly Blow

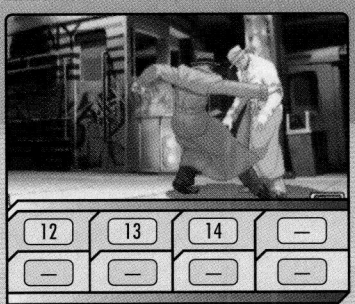

12	13	14	—
—	—	—	—

A slow command throw with incredible range. Can be juggled after for major damage. Great addition to Q's offense when combined with Dashing attack combos in mix up situations.

SUPER ARTS

SUPER ART I

↓ ↘ → ↓ ↘ → + P   **Critical Combo Attack**

Five Dash attacks, comprised of four mid level attacks and one low attack. Critical Combo Attack has an invincibility window at startup that can be used to blow through attacks and projectiles. It has a fairly slow start up, but it is still quick enough to punish certain moves, such as a

| 5 | -19 |

blocked shoto ↓ + HK. Close MK is Q's only useful normal attack that cancels into super arts. Use that to cancel into Critical Combo Attack when you have an opening. It also super cancels from Dash attacks. It's possible to verify a hit on the Dash attack before canceling into Critical Combo Attack. Use Dash attacks to constantly apply pressure and make landing a super art a possibility from a full screen away.

Critical Combo Attack stocks two levels of super meter. This gives Q the ability to use EX moves for combos and still have access to a super art.

SUPER ART II

↓ ↘ → ↓ ↘ → + P   **Deadly Double Combination**

Q's most damaging super art; it combos similarly to Critical Combo Attack. It can also be linked behind an overhead Dash attack on crouching characters. It is effective as anti-air even though it is only one parry. The downside to Deadly Double Combination is that is stocks a single super meter.

| 2 | -25 |

SUPER ART III

↓ ↘ → ↓ ↘ → + P, then ↓ ↘ → + P / K   **Total Destruction**

During Total Destruction, there is a limited amount of time where Q has two moves that blow up himself and causes damage to opponents. The punch varation is a normal hit, while the kick version is a grab. The grab does more damage, but is much slower. Q glows brightly during the duration of Total Destruction.

| — | — |

Total Destruction stocks only one super meter, so Q is limited on EX moves. Also, after activating Total Destruction, there is no guarantee on landing a hit before the timer expires. Both variations have extremely slow start up and can be escaped easily.

Recommended Super Art: Critical Combo Attack

Critical Combo Attack and Deadly Double Combination can both be used in similar manners. However, Critical Combo Attack gives Q the most options with the availability of two stocks of super meter. In addition, its ability to pass through projectiles and other ground attacks should help Q get in on some characters.

COMBOS YOU NEED TO KNOW

2 HITS

TOTAL DAMAGE: 30

Close MK → Dashing Head Attack

Basic, safe Q combo.

4 HITS

TOTAL DAMAGE: 67

Jump in HP, land, close MK → EX Dashing Head Attack, juggle with early HK.

Good in punishment situations; for example, after a dizzy, or parrying an anti-air while jumping in. Knocks down.

7 HITS

TOTAL DAMAGE: 67

Close MK → Dashing Head Attack (MP) → Critical Combo Attack.

Verifiable ground combo for heavy damage. Knocks down.

3 HITS

TOTAL DAMAGE: 50

CORNER ONLY

Capture & Deadly Blow, juggle with early Dashing Head Attack (MP), juggle again with early Ryouude ni yoru Zenshin Tsuugeki (Kari)

High damage off of his command throw near a corner.

3 HITS

TOTAL DAMAGE: 57

Capture & Deadly Blow, juggle with semi early EX Dashing Head Attack, juggle again with early HK

High damage option off of a command throw that works mid screen. Knocks down.

8 HITS

TOTAL DAMAGE: 43

Close MK → EX High Speed Barrage

Good for punishment situations when you don't have a charge for a Dash attack. Knocks down.

6 HITS

TOTAL DAMAGE: 101

Jump in fierce, land, Close MK → Dashing Head Attack (MP) → Double Deadly Combination; wait about a second after Q recovers, then juggle with Dashing Head Attack (MP)

Round winner. Deals heavy damage and is verifiable during MK → Dashing Head Attack. Good in punishment situations. Knocks down.

4 HITS

TOTAL DAMAGE: 72

Capture & Deadly Blow, juggle with a semi late Dashing Head Attack (MP) → Double Deadly Combination

Good way to land damage off of a command throw. Knocks down.

3 HITS

TOTAL DAMAGE: 64

CORNER ONLY

Capture & Deadly Blow, juggle with a semi late Dashing Head Attack (MP) → Total Destruction, immediately juggle with QCF + P Total Destruction follow up

Safe way to activate and land Total Destruction's QCF + P follow up. Knocks down.

2 HITS TOTAL DAMAGE: 62

Activate Total Destruction, then do a close MK → QCF + P Total Destruction follow up

Not so safe way to land Total Destruction's QCF + P follow up. Knocks down.

STRATEGY

Shippu ni yoru Ko-Chouyaku Kougeki (Kari)

Q is big and slow, but makes up for it with stamina and defense. Q's taunts increase his defense rating. Q with three taunts (the max) has the highest defense rating in the game. It should be your goal to get in taunts whenever safely possible. Q doesn't have the best offensive arsenal and he is a big, slow target for many characters. Q must raise his defense as much as possible to withstand enough attacks until he can score a knock down. Good opportunities to taunt are after:

- a super art
- any anti air that knocks down
- an air to air jump fierce mid screen
- any Capture & Deadly Blow combo

The goal is get opponents into the corner (Q has a hard time fighting mid screen) to start Capture & Deadly Blow mind games. Stay a safe distance and attack with long range Dash attacks. If one connects, cancel into super art. Keep up the pressure with Dash attacks, move opponents into corners and don't let them jump away. Toubu ni Yoru Jouhou Kougeki (Kari) is a good way to stop someone from jumping over Q to get out of the corner. Q is tall, and the move covers more area above his head. From far enough away, it's possible to meet airborne opponents with an early jumping MP or jumping LP to send them back to the ground. Jumping LP may seem like a silly move, but it is great for jumping on opponents whether on the ground or beginning to jump. It stays out for the entire length of Q's jump, so use it the moment he gets off the ground to control space.

If Q manages to get an opponent into the corner, he becomes scary. A successful Capture & Deadly Blow can lead to combos and setups that do massive damage and stun meter damage. Dash attack to juggle, then HP to reset. As opponents flip back to recover, they have the unfortunate fate of having to deal with Capture & Deadly Blow mind games similar to his wake up game. If opponents block upon landing, use Capture & Deadly Blow again to repeat the process.

WAKEUP GAME

Q's wake up pressure game revolves around Capture & Deadly Blow. Use Capture & Deadly Blow on wake up to keep opponents guessing. Blocking becomes the least safe option for waking up opponents. Opponents will be so worried about being grabbed that they most likely try to jump away or do some sort of wake up move. If you anticipate this, use either EX High Speed Barrage to hit jumpers, or ↓ + HK to beat similar jump attempts and trade with many wake up moves. Be careful here because many players will use wake up super arts or a Shouryuken to counter Capture & Deadly Blow. Keep the pressure on, but don't get reckless. Get a feel for how often opponents take risks on wake up moves, then gauge how often it is safe to attempt Capture & Deadly Blow.

Against large enough characters, ticking with LP is a good tactic on a waking up opponent, because it cancels into Capture & Deadly Blow. This move is slow enough that it grabs after opponents are out of block stun. It is hard for opponents to hit Q between the LP and Capture & Deadly Blow tick. The easiest way to escape this is to jump, and the best way to counter this is to fake a Capture & Deadly Blow setup with LP, but then use EX High Speed Barrage.

While Q is intimidating against someone in the corner, he is essentially helpless when he is the one knocked down. He has no fast, high priority wake up moves to get someone off of him. His pokes are generally slow, with only LK somewhat useful in this situation. Unfortunately, Q's only safe wake up option is to block and wait it out. If it looks hopeless, parrying or doing a wake up super art are his only high risk options worth trying.

SETUPS

Ranges setups for UOH → super art

Against small and medium sized characters:

> (Close MK, LK), UOH → Critical Combo Attack / Deadly Double Combination
> (↓ + LP (x2)), kara UOH → Deadly Double Combination
> (After a blocked Dash attack), UOH → Deadly Double Combination

Against Oro:

> No setup is required. UOH → Deadly Double Combination works at close distance on crouching Oro.

RESETS

Reset 1: LP as anti-air to knock over opponents, then dash forward and Deadly Double Combination before they land. After this lands a few times, and becomes expected, mix it up by throwing as soon as they land. Most players will concentrate on landing that air parry and not react in time.

PARRY SETUPS AND TACTICS

After a Dashing attack, Q is a bit out of range for throws and many pokes. In order to reach Q at this distance, many characters will attempt to go low. Down parry, then proceed to Capture & Deadly Blow.

GROUND CROSS UPS:

Q can cross up Necro in any corner.

At first look, this match up doesn't seem like it would go in Q's favor. Twelve is highly mobile, and much faster than Q. However, Twelve is limited in terms of dealing damage, basically flying around and using pokes. Because of this, Q is free to taunt three times early in the round, and there's not much Twelve can do about it.

Use jumping HP to combat Twelve's air dashes. Q only needs one good knock down to turn the momentum of the round his way. Twelve does not have a solid wake up move when he is playing defensively. Q should be able to finish off a cornered Twelve fairly quickly. In order to score a knockdown, take some risks and attempt to parry Twelve strategically. When Twelve is air dashing in, he almost always goes for an attack (after landing) that is parriable low. Red parry the low ground attack and grab him. Q's defense is good, so it is worth the risk to score that knock down.

UNFAVORABLE MATCH UP: KEN

Q must get close to start Capture & Deadly Blow patterns to deal damage, but Ken has the attacks needed to keep Q away. Ken's low forward can go under Dash attacks and shut down Q's rush. Ken is also much faster than Q. Ken has no problems jumping all over Q and pressuring him. Ken also can land a big damage combo on Q anywhere on the screen without using any meter (MP, HP → Shouryuken (LP), Shouryuken (LP)).

To win this match up, get Ken into the corner. Ken cannot just mindlessly stick out low forwards. Use either Dashing attacks or Critical Combo Attack to punish Ken on reaction. Use these to keep Ken from zoning. If Q can land a Dashing attack, either blocked or hit, he is in prime range to attempt a kara throw. Start some Capture & Deadly Blow patterns on him, but at the same time beware of a Shouryuken. The last thing a Q player wants is to be knocked back to mid screen.

Remy

NORMAL MOVES

STANDING

A good anti-air, MP comes out and recovers quickly. Great to throw out inbetween Light of Virtue patterns from mid range. If it's parried at maximum range, Remy often recovers fast enough to parry again or block. If opponents hit Remy's recovering limb early, he recovers before they hit the ground, allowing you to throw them for free.

MK is a great poke that comes out fast and has good recovery. It beats a plethora of crouching attacks.

LP		Jab
START UP	4	CS
+4	+4	+4	SC
			SA
GUARD		H/L
PARRY		H/L

LK		Short
START UP	3	CS
+2	+2	+2	SC
			SA
GUARD		H/L
PARRY		H/L

MP		Strong
START UP	7	
+1	+2	+3	SC
			SA
GUARD		H/L
PARRY		H

MK		Forward
START UP	8	
-3	-2	-1	SC
			SA
GUARD		H/L
PARRY		H

HP		Fierce
START UP	10	
-2	0	+2	SC
			SA
GUARD		H/L
PARRY		H

HK		Roundhouse
START UP	10	
-9	-7	-5	SC
			SA
GUARD		H/L
PARRY		H

STANDING CLOSE

Close MP is a good normal to use when opponents are waking up. It carries a significant amount frame advantage, allowing you to verify and link ↓ + LK or a Supreme Rising Rage Flash. When blocked, use the frame advantage to mount another offense. However, MP whiffs against some crouching characters (Chun-Li, Ibuki, Oro and Elena). Against those characters, completely refrain from using close MP.

Close LK is a great defensive move and good for beating throw attempts during guessing games.

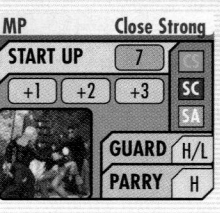

LP		Close Jab
START UP	4	CS
+3	+3	+3	SC
			SA
GUARD		H/L
PARRY		H/L

LK		Close Short
START UP	2	
0	0	0	SC
			SA
GUARD		H/L
PARRY		H/L

MP		Close Strong
START UP	7	
+1	+2	+3	SC
			SA
GUARD		H/L
PARRY		H

MK		Close Forward
START UP	4	
+1	+3	+5	SC
			SA
GUARD		H/L
PARRY		H

HP		Close Fierce
START UP	6	
+1	+3	+5	SC
GUARD		H/L
PARRY		H

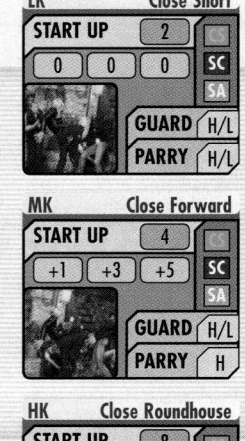

HK		Close Roundhouse
START UP	8	
+3	+5	+7	SC
			SA
GUARD		H/L
PARRY		H

COSTUMES

 LP
 MP
 HP
 LK
 MK
 HK

 LP + MK + HP

Start + LP · Start + MP · Start + HP · Start + LK · Start + MK · Start + HK

SPECIAL NORMALS

→ + MK		Amari ni Muku na Aiguille
START UP	18	-7

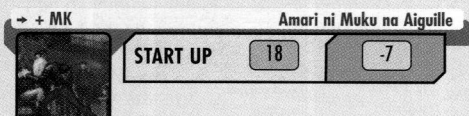

Semi slow overhead with good range and has the added bonus of not looking like an overhead. However, it has a huge frame disadvantage after it, which can be countered hit or miss. Use sparingly and from as far away as possible.

THROWS

LP + LK   Valse no you ni Kuruoshiku

→/← + LP + LK Nemuri wo Midasu Contour

CROUCHING

Remy's most used mid range attack, ↓ + MP is good for combos and Light of Virtue pressure patterns up close.

↓ + MK has extremely good range. Important for scoring hits after parried Light of Virtues followed by a dash. It has a significant frame disadvantage. Always do it from maximum range, and never against Ken with super meter stocked.

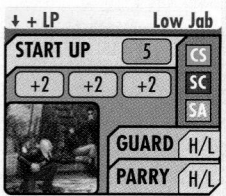
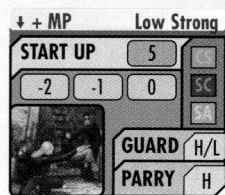
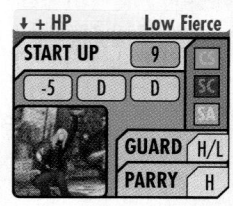

↓ + LP		Low Jab
START UP	5	CS
+2	+2	+2	SC
			SA
GUARD		H/L
PARRY		H/L

↓ + LK		Low Short
START UP	3	
0	0	0	SC
			SA
GUARD		L
PARRY		L

↓ + MP		Low Strong
START UP	5	
-2	-1	0	SC
			SA
GUARD		H/L
PARRY		H

↓ + MK		Low Forward
START UP	8	
-9	-8	-7	SC
			SA
GUARD		L
PARRY		L

↓ + HP		Low Fierce
START UP	9	
-5	D	D	SC
			SA
GUARD		H/L
PARRY		H

↓ + HK		Low Roundhouse
START UP	9	
-11	D	D	SC
			SA
GUARD		L
PARRY		L

JUMPING

Jumping HP is a great anti-air. It comes out fairly fast and puts opponents into a juggle set up if they are jumping. It's a solid way to score big damage if you anticipate a jump in and meet opponents in the air early.

Jumping HK is Remy's best jump in. Steep angle, can be done much earlier during a jump then his other jump attacks, making it hard to anti air.

↑ + LP	Jumping Jab
START UP	4

			C
—	—	—	SC
			SA

GUARD	H
PARRY	H

↑ + LK	Jumping Short
START UP	4

			C
—	—	—	SC
			SA

GUARD	H
PARRY	H

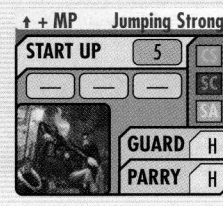

↑ + MP	Jumping Strong
START UP	5

			C
—	—	—	SC
			SA

GUARD	H
PARRY	H

↑ + MK	Jumping Forward
START UP	6

			C
—	—	—	SC
			SA

GUARD	H
PARRY	H

↑ + HP	Jumping Fierce
START UP	9

			C
—	—	—	SC
			SA

GUARD	H
PARRY	H

↑ + HK	Jumping Roundhouse
START UP	10

			C
—	—	—	SC
			SA

GUARD	H
PARRY	H

COMBOS YOU NEED TO KNOW

4 HITS

TOTAL DAMAGE: 38

Jump in early HK, land, ↓ + LP, ↓ + LP → Rising Rage Flash (HK)

Flexible, verifiable jump in combo. Knocks down.

2 HITS

TOTAL DAMAGE: 35

Close HP → Rising Rage Flash (HK)

Good for punishment situations. Knocks down.

4 HITS

TOTAL DAMAGE: 27

CORNER ONLY

Neutral throw, when Remy recovers, immediately juggle with a Rising Rage Flash (HK).

Remy's neutral throw near a corner can lead to extra damage. Does not work vs. small characters, like Yun and Yang.

2 HITS

TOTAL DAMAGE: 36

Late anti-air jump HP, land and immediately juggle with early Rising Rage Flash (HK)

Good anti air combo. Good after an air to air parry while jumping. Knocks down.

3 HITS

TOTAL DAMAGE: 50

CORNER ONLY

Near a corner, late anti-air jump HP; land and juggle with Cold Blue Kick (LK); when Remy recovers, juggle with early Rising Rage Flash (HK)

Higher damage variation of the above combo. Must be near a corner for it to work. Knocks down.

2 HIT TOTAL DAMAGE: 32

Anti-air ↓ + HP, when Remy recovers, immediately juggle with a Rising Rage Flash (HK)

Another damaging anti air combo. Knocks down.

3 HITS

TOTAL DAMAGE: 46

CORNER ONLY

Near a corner, anti air ↓ + HP, when Remy recovers, juggle with Cold Blue Kick (LK); when Remy recovers, juggle with early Rising Rage Flash (HK)

High Damage version of the above combo. Must be near a corner for it to work. Knocks down.

8 HITS

TOTAL DAMAGE: 60

CORNER ONLY

Near a corner, anti-air jump HP, land then juggle with immediate Cold Blue Kick (LK); when opponent recovers, walk up and juggle with ↓ + MP → Supreme Rising Rage Flash

High damage anti-air juggle. Knocks down.

11 HITS

TOTAL DAMAGE: 59

Close MK linked into Supreme Rising Rage Flash

Verifiable way to land Supreme Rising Rage Flash.

9 HITS

TOTAL DAMAGE: 47

↓ + LP, ↓ + LP → Light of Justice

Flexible, verifiable way to land a Light of Justice. If ↓ + LP (x2) is blocked, follow up with: walk up kara throw; low parry option select ↓ + MP → Light of Justice; or a UOH.

15 HITS

TOTAL DAMAGE: 71

CORNER ONLY

↓ + LK → Light of Justice, when Remy recovers, immediately link another Light of Justice

High damage option if you happen to land ↓ + LK → Light of Justice in the corner. Caution, the second Light of Justice whiffs against most crouching characters.

SPECIAL MOVES

Charge ← → + P			Light of Virtue

9	10	11	8
+5	+5	+5	+4

Slow moving projectile with a high altitude and great recovery. Use it to control space or in combination with dash to get in safely. Use this in combination with Low Light of Virtue by using charge partitioning to let loose a barrage of high and low projectiles. Great when opponents are cornered. The EX version comes out faster and throws two Light of Virtues at the same time. Extremely good for catching opponents before they leave the ground for a jump.

Charge ← → + K			Light of Virtue (Low)

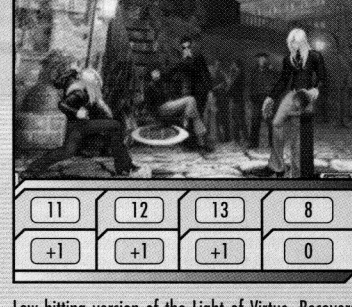

11	12	13	8
+1	+1	+1	0

Low hitting version of the Light of Virtue. Recovers slightly slower than the high version. It's a good poke and for dashing behind to get in close. The EX version comes out much faster and throws two Light of Virtues at once.

Charge ↓ ↑ + K			Rising Rage Flash

3	4	5	6
-17	-23	-26	-21

Good range, speed, and priority. Decent anti-air when used in combination with Light of Virtue. Good for combos as well. The EX version is faster, does more damage, and has slightly better priority. Works well as a reversal on wake up.

↓ ↙ ← + K			Cold Blue Kick

17	18	19	18
-4	-4	-6	-2

Button strength determines how far the kick travels. A decent poke that goes over low attacks and is fairly safe against everything but fast super arts. It also has deceptive block stun. The later and further away it hits, the safer it is. Do it directly after a Light of Virtue (LP / LK) to keep opponents from doing anything aggressive after parrying a Light of Virtue. EX version is faster, safer, and hits twice.

SUPER ARTS

SUPER ART I

| ↓ ↘ → ↓ ↘ → + P | Light of Justice |

Remy has many ways to combo into Light of Justice, although many of the setups off of mid attacks either whiff or hit inconsistently on medium and small sized characters. ↓ + LP (x2) → Light of Justice is his only useful verifiable combo that works on everyone. ↓ + LPs can be

| 2 | +3 |

parried high or low, so it is not useful for his wakeup game. Remy does have high and low options to combo into super arts that are safe, but they cannot be verified. You must guess with either close HP or ↓ + LK → super art. Light of Justice has a +3 frame advantage in addition to pushing away opponents, so it is safe to guess in these situations. It is also possible to link after the super art hits in the corner.

Light of Justice stocks two meters to give Remy enough flexibility to use EX moves along with a super art. Although if you only plan on using EX moves, Supreme Rising Rage Flash is a better choice because of the longer bar. However, Remy can set up many multi-hit juggles by mixing EX moves and Light of Justice.

SUPER ART II

| ↓ ↘ → ↓ ↘ → + K | Supreme Rising Rage Flash |

It's possible to verify this super art from various mid attacks to beat out low parries. Learn how to link into Supreme Rising Rage Flash on crouching opponents from close MK → Supreme Rising Rage Flash and close HP, link ↓ + MP (or ↓ + LK) →

| 1 | -29 |

Supreme Rising Rage Flash. It can also link after close HK and close HP, although these links aren't as useful. Another basic way to hit confirm this super art is off of ↓ + LP (x3). Regrettably, Remy has no safe combos that start low that he can use to land Supreme Rising Rage Flash. It is, however, useful as an anti-air.

Supreme Rising Rage Flash has two long super meter stocks, making it ideal for heavy EX use.

SUPER ART III

| ↓ ↘ → ↓ ↘ → + K | Blue Nocturne |

If he is attacked during Blue Nocturne, Remy takes the hit, then automatically counterattacks with a pre-set combo that does plenty of damage. However, it is hard to hit someone with Blue Nocturne. Remy starts his pose after the screen freezes for the super animation. Therefore, the

| 1 | — |

opposing player has been warned sufficiently to avoid attacking Remy. You must anticipate a move before executing it and hope you guess right. If opponents stick out a move before the super art flash, then Blue Nocturne will hit. That is the only situation where Blue Nocturne works. If Blue Nocturne does not connect, Remy is vulnerable to counterattack during its recovery. Since Remy always has access to parries, there is little reason, if ever, to pick Blue Nocturne.

It is possible to use Blue Nocturne as an anti-air if you see an attack coming. However, the majority of the hits whiff, and opponents actually recover before Remy. Furthermore, Blue Nocturne is only meant to counter normal moves. Many super arts continue to hit Remy even as he tries to counter.

Recommended Super Art: Supreme Rising Rage Flash

Supreme Rising Rage Flash gives Remy a lot of meter to work with for EX moves. He can combo the super off of some of his most important mid level attacks and verify before doing so. It gives him an additional anti air to his arsenal. Remy just has to be weary of high parries because of his inability to verify a combo into super off of a low hit.

TARGET COMBO

| CLOSE MK → HK | 4 |
| Second hit whiffs against crouching characters, making it very risky to do. | -9 |

STRATEGY

Izanai no Vague

Remy is the only character in *Street Fighter III: 3rd Strike* that can effectively control space at almost all times. He has the ability to make it difficult for opponents to get close while at the same time getting into his preferred offensive position. Remy is always a threat at long range, throwing high and low Light of Virtues from a distance while storing Rising Rage Flash charges in between and whiffing MPs periodically to keep opponents from getting in easily. While opponents are trying to get close, constantly force them into a corner, throwing Light of Virtues (LP / LK) and dashing behind them, scoring a hit with a overhead, low attack, or throw, then holding that position to secure another step towards the corner. When cornered, the options for escape from Remy's range game become limited.

Remy has a multitude of long range options. The most famous of which is the Light of Virtue, a slow moving charge based projectile that can be thrown high or low. The most basic use of the Light of Virtue is as a poke. Throw Light of Virtues (HP and HK) in a methodical manner, watching to see how opponents react to it. If opponents do anything brash, like jump over them, fake a Light of Virtue, whiff a LP or LK, or use one of Remy's many anti-air options accordingly:

Early MP
Early option select jump HP, juggle with a Rising Rage Flash (HK) when Remy lands
↓ + HP, juggle with Rising Rage flash when Remy recovers
Early Light of Virtue (LP) (parried), HK or EX Rising Rage Flash
When opponents don't take the bait and stay grounded, parrying or blocking Light of Virtues, advance on them. Throw a Light of Virtue (LP / LK) and dash behind it. This provides a wall to dash behind, making it harder to counter Remy's ground movement. Most opponents react in one of three different ways in this situation:

1. Jump straight up. Countered at the end of a dash and hitting HP or ↓ + HP depending on how close they are.

2. Block the Light of Virtue. This pushes opponents backward and allows Remy to come out of a dash with ↓ + MK, kara UOH or a charge partitioned EX High Light of Virtue to push them back further.

3. They parry. Create a guessing game consisting of ether throw, close LK, kara UOH, or hit ↓ + LK / ↓ + MK depending on distance.

No matter how opponents deal with the Light of Virtue, you have a distinct advantage when trying to get close. Although some characters can use specific attacks to get over and under a high or low Light of Virtue, counter this by baiting attacks behind the Light of Virtue by dashing one less time (or not at all), then waiting for a whiffed attack and punishing it. Once close, Remy's best pokes are far MK, Cold Blue Kick, and Low and High EX Light of Virtue. Low EX Light of Virtue is vital during foot games. It's extremely fast and it hits low, making it hard to avoid if opponents are dancing, trying to bait whiffed normals. Use Cold Blue Kick to go over baited low attacks. Use a High Light of Virtue early against anticipated jumps and far MK just outside of their best low attack range. If you manage to bait a whiffed attack, ↓ + HK is a passable whiff punisher.

However, its terrible recovery and easy-to-parry second hit makes it risky to do in general, if you're going to do it, make sure it hits.

WAKEUP GAME

One of Remy's biggest weaknesses is a complete lack of a safe combo starting off of a low attack. ↓ + LK → Light of Justice is all he has to work with and it can't be verified. This means you must work in many throws to get opponents to open up to high attacks. Thankfully, Remy has a great kara throw. Since Remy's damage dealing options in wake up games are so limited, it's best to attack with a Supreme Rising Rage Flash or a Light of Justice if you have super meter stocked. However, because Remy's EX specials are so vital to his mid range game, you won't have stocked super meter often. Ration your bar usage so that you have the means to mount an offense if you manage to get a knock down. Remy's options to work with in wake up situations include:

1. Meaty close MP, verify if it hits; if it does, link into Supreme Rising Rage Flash, if it doesn't, walk up kara throw, walk up close MK linked into Supreme Rising Rage Flash, or universal overhead linked into Supreme Rising Rage Flash.
2. Step back just out of their throw range, block as they wake up in case of a reversal attempt, then kara throw.
3. Step back, meaty ↓ + LK, then ether walk up kara throw, walk up close LK, or option select low parry ↓ + MP, if you get a parry, cancel into Supreme Rising Rage Flash.
4. Meaty ↓ + LP (x2), if it hits, cancel the second jab into Supreme Rising Rage Flash or Light of Justice. If it doesn't hit, ↓ + MP → Light of Virtue (LK), walk up kara throw, universal overhead linked into Supreme Rising Rage Flash, or walk up ↓ + LP (x2) → Supreme Rising Rage Flash or Light of Justice again.
5. Remy also has another trick on wake up that uses charge partitioning. As opponents are getting up from a knock down, dash on top of them, then jump straight up, start holding back to charge, then come down with a early blocked jump HK. When Remy lands, either kara throw or dash back and look for a throw whiff. If you see one, at the end of Remy's dash press → + KK (Low EX Light of Virtue) to punish the whiffed throw. Apply this same idea to other patterns to punish throw whiffs. On wake up, do an early whiffed HP while charging back, timed so that it looks like it may hit (but doesn't) recovering just before an opponent stands up. After Remy recovers, immediately throw, or do a quick close LK to beat tech throw attempts, then ether walk up kara throw or dash back, Low EX Light of Virtue. This pattern has two throw attempts and counters thrown into one.

When Remy is the one knocked down, use reversal EX Rising Rage Flash to beat most meaty attacks. Wake up throw, reversal super art, parrying or blocking are also available. Use close LK in a defensive manner in wake up situations. As Remy gets up, hold ↙ up to a split second after he stands, then let the controller return to neutral, hit LK, then press ↑ and LK to cancel the LK into a Rising Rage Flash. This blocks meaty attacks, while close LK → Rising Rage Flash (LK) should come out just in time to beat a throw attempt. This is extremely valuable to Remy. Although not fail safe, it's one of his safer wakeup options.

ADVANCED TACTIC 1: OVERLAPPING CHARGE TIMES

Overlap the charge times of special moves to allow the execution of multiple charge moves in succession. The execution for this is fairly simple. For consecutive Light of Virtues, charge ←, press →, then press ← for just a split second before pressing punch. Even though you pressed punch after pressing →, Street Fighter III: 3rd Strike's game engine gives you plenty of leeway with the timing of button presses with controller inputs for special moves.

ADVANCED APPLICATION 1: LIGHT OF VIRTUE TRAP

Take the idea of overlapping the charge times of Remy's Light of Virtues one step further by pipelining the charges, allowing for an unlimited number of alternating high and low Light of Virtues. The execution is fairly easy, although the timing takes some practice. Charge and throw one

low Light of Virtue with the advanced method, and as soon as you have a charge again, throw a high Light of Virtue, then continue to overlap the charges. If you set it up properly, you now have started to pipeline charges in advance that will continue on until you decide to stop. Use this to trap opponents in the corner. Use this trick with High EX Light of Virtues and low Light of Virtues, and opponents will not be able to move. You can set this up perfectly by using charge partitioning. Throw one low Light of Virtue with the advanced method, then dash once to follow it up and immediately throw a high Light of Virtue. If you used the charging trick, you are now all set to start throwing rapid fire Light of Virtues without any charge time to slow you down. This is a great way to pressure opponents from mid screen to push them into the corner.

ADVANCED APPLICATION 2: INSTANT RISING RAGE FLASH AFTER A LIGHT OF VIRTUE

It's possible to overlap the charge times of Rising Rage Flash during a Light of Virtue to make a Rising Rage Flash available directly after a Light of Virtue. Tap ← for just a split second, then start charging ↙. After charging enough for a Light of Virtue, throw it by pressing →, then → + P. Keep pressing ↙ until Remy finishes the Light of Virtue, then execute a Rising Rage Flash. Holding ↙ charges for both a Light of Virtue as well as a Rising Rage Flash. Throwing the Light of Virtue exhausts the backwards charge, but the downward charge continues, allowing a Rising Rage Flash to be charged while charging the Light of Virtue. You must have charge times down perfectly to get this to work. When you hold ↙ too long, you allow the ↙ direction to fully charge a Light of Virtue. When this happens, the game sees the initial backward charge as unnecessary and negates it. It is important to know the minimum amount of charge necessary to pull off this trick. This advanced technique should amaze and confuse opponents. Throw a high Light of Virtue, then catch a jump with Rising Rage Flash. No one expects it.

ADVANCED TACTIC 2: CHARGE PARTITIONING

To be an effective Remy player, you must learn charge partitioning, It's one of the few things Remy has going for him. It is important that the charge is not finished if you plan to continue moving. Once the charge is completed, you cannot break it up any further. Here are some examples of how to incorporate charge partitioning into your game:

1. Throw a Light of Virtue and dash in behind it. Charge for a second Light of Virtue while throwing the first one. Finish the charge during the dash and immediately throw another Light of Virtue after the dash.
2. Do a jump in attack and start charging back. When Remy lands, dash back and finish the charge and execute an EX Light of Virtue. This also works if you jump straight up and do an early jump HK, then dash back and do an EX Light of Virtue.
3. At mid to far range, stand up and walk back and forth, crouching every other step. Opponents assume Remy does not have a charge, and try to jump in. Mix it up by hiding charges in whiffed moves. Make it impossible for opponents to ever tell if you have a charge ready to go.

SETUPS

Ranged setups for UOH → super art

Against small and medium sized characters:

(↓ + LP (x2)), UOH → Supreme Rising Rage Flash
(↓ + LP (x3)), kara UOH → Supreme Rising Rage Flash
(Close HP, ↓ + LK), kara UOH → Supreme Rising Rage Flash

Against wide characters:

(Close HP, ↓ + MP), kara UOH → Supreme Rising Rage Flash

Against Oro:

No setup is required. UOH → Supreme Rising Rage Flash works at close distance on crouching Oro.

RESETS

Reset 1: LP → LK chain has the weird property of being able to juggle for both hits as anti-air. If an anti-air ↓ + HP lands, walk up, juggle with an early LP → LK chain, then dash under opponents as they flip out for an ambiguous cross up. This is a good way to land ↓ + LP (x3) → Rising Rage Flash (HK) or MK linked into Supreme Rising Rage Flash if you have a super meter stocked.

PARRY SETUPS AND TACTICS

After a blocked ↓ + LP (x2), tap and hold ↓, then press MP shortly afterwards. If you see a parry flash, do the motion for a super art to cancel ↓ + MP and combo a super art. If opponents don't parry, you're out of their throw range and ↓ + MP is blocked, pushing them away.

GROUND CROSS UPS

Remy can cross up Alex, Hugo, Elena, Dudley, Oro, Necro, Twelve and Urien in any corner.

Remy can cross up Chun-Li only in his own corner.

FAVORABLE MATCH UP: HUGO

Remy has the ability launch a barrage of high and low Light of Virtues, back to back. This tactic against a large character like Hugo, who cannot duck under Remy's high Light of Virtue, is devastating. Remy can completely shut down Hugo's movements, forcing him to resort to parrying in attempt to get around the moving wall. Defend against Hugo's attempts to jump and parry Light of Virtues by storing EX Rising Rage Flash charges after Light of Virtues (LP), allowing you to attack and air counter Hugo again if he manages to jump over or parry a Light of Virtue while jumping. There's no need to get close. Keep your barrage of projectiles coming in a methodical manner. Anticipate jumps and use anti-airs accordingly. Whiff occasional MPs in between Light of Virtues to cover the space in front of Remy and build super meter. Slowly move Hugo towards a corner by throwing a Light of Virtue (LK), dashing once behind it, then immediately coming out of the dash with the Light of Virtue partitioning trap. If you manage to get Hugo cornered, keep him there.

UNFAVORABLE MATCH UP: CHUN-LI

Light of Virtues are almost completely useless vs. Chun-Li, which eliminates half of Remy's offense. Without a stocked super meter, Chun-Li can use roundhouse to get over Low Light of Virtues and ↓ + MK under high Light of Virtues, making it hard or Remy to follow one to get close. With Houyokusen stocked and ready to go, Chun-Li can go through a Light of Virtue on reaction to its release. This limits the use of Light of Virtues, which makes adveancing against a character like Chun-Li, who completely controls the ground, extremely difficult. Remy must get close since he has no normals that compete with Chun-Li's ground game. If you manage to get close, Remy's most effective normal on wake up, close MP, completely whiffs against a crouching Chun-Li. This leaves only the less flexible ↓ + LP (x2) or close MK to land super arts.

To win this match up, jump the gun at Round 1 and get close to Chun-Li before she gets stocks any super meter. Throw Light of Virtues (LP / LK) and bait Chun-Li to try to get under or over them by dashing just outside of HK or ↓ + MK range, then punish the whiffs. Get close and deal as much damage as possible with throw and counter throw set ups. Save super meter for EX moves, and end the round before Chun-Li stocks up a meter of her own. When Chun-Li gets super meter (and she will), play patiently. Build up your own super meter from a range by whiffing crouching and standing MPs, then get back into footsie range and land as many low EX Light of Virtues as possible, punishing whiffs and nailing her while she is dancing back and forth.

Ryu

NORMAL MOVES

STANDING

MK is Ryu's best poke just out side of ↓ + LK range. His foot extends out and goes over most low attacks, yet has a wide enough hitbox to catch most characters as they attempt to stick out something. Use this to beat other character's pokes.

HK covers a wide hit area. Use it from far range to catch large characters at the beginning of jump attempts, or use it as a universal anti-air. It's possible to stick this out at almost any time to be effective and to confuse parry attempts.

LP	Jab
START UP	4	CS
+4	+4	+4	SC
			SA
GUARD	H/L
PARRY	H/L

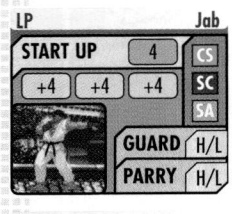

LK	Short
START UP	4	CS
+2	+2	+2	SC
			SA
GUARD	H/L
PARRY	H/L

MP	Strong
START UP	5	CS
+4	+5	+6	SC
			SA
GUARD	H/L
PARRY	H

MK	Forward
START UP	6	CS
-5	-4	-3	SC
			SA
GUARD	H/L
PARRY	H

HP	Fierce
START UP	11	CS
-3	-1	+1	SC
			SA
GUARD	H/L
PARRY	H

HK	Roundhouse
START UP	8	CS
-5	-3	-1	SC
			SA
GUARD	H/L
PARRY	H

STANDING CLOSE

Close MP is a good poke that provides frame advantage, so it is good for tick throw setups and other mix-ups. For example, after a blocked MP, hesitate, then walk up and use MP again (Or ↓ + LK (x2)). The trick is to make it look like a throw attempt which should lead to an opening. MP links into Shin-Shoryu-Ken, and is the only verifiable high attack into Shin-Shoryu-Ken that does so on all characters.

Close MK hits high, so it is useful against would-be low parriers. It links into Shinkuu-Hadou-Ken on all crouching characters. It links into Shin-Shoryu-Ken (universally on Alex and Dudley, on standing Elena, Necro and Twelve, and on crouching Urien, Makoto and Ibuki).

LP	Close Jab
START UP	3	
+3	+3	+3	SC
			SA
GUARD	H/L
PARRY	H/L

LK	Close Short
START UP	4	C
+2	+2	+2	SC
			SA
GUARD	H/L
PARRY	H/L

MP	Close Strong
START UP	5	C
+1	+2	+3	SC
			SA
GUARD	H/L
PARRY	H

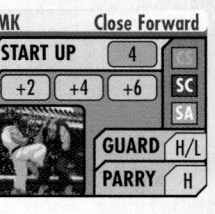

MK	Close Forward
START UP	4	CS
+2	+4	+6	SC
			SA
GUARD	H/L
PARRY	H

HP	Close Fierce
START UP	4	
-4	-2	0	SC
GUARD	H/L
PARRY	H

HK	Close Roundhouse
START UP	8	CS
-5	-3	-1	SC
			SA
GUARD	H/L
PARRY	H

COSTUMES

LP · MP · HP · LK · MK · HK

Start + LP · Start + MP · Start + HP · Start + LK · Start + MK · Start + HK

LP + MK + HP

THROWS

LP + LK	Seoi Nage

← + LP + LK	Tomoe Nage

SPECIAL NORMALS

→ + MP		Sakotsu Wari
START UP	14	-1

Basic overhead. Comes out fairly fast and does ok stun damage. An ok option to add to your mix up game. If done extremely early/meaty vs a character waking up from a knock down you can link after it with a ↓ + MK canceled into a EX Hadouken or Shinkuu-Hadou-Ken. However, because it has to be done so early to link after it, it's much easier to see and react to as a overhead.

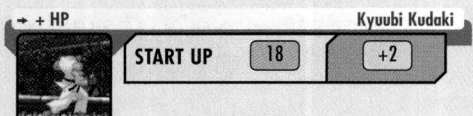

→ + HP		Kyuubi Kudaki
START UP	18	+2

Command attack with slow start up that hits twice and leaves Ryu at a slight frame advantage when blocked, giving you the ability to start a mix up game. If it hits, it's possible to link a EX Shouryuken or a Shin-Shoryu-Ken after it. Becuase if it's heavy start up however, it's fairly easy to parry and counter on reaction.

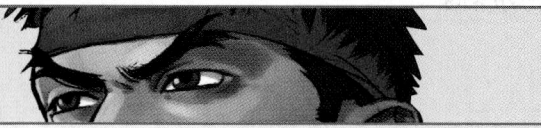

CROUCHING

↓ + LK has many uses. It is a quick poke that hits low that can be used for tick throw setups and mind games. After a blocked ↓ + LK, you have a lot of options: throw, hesitate and ↓ + LK x2 follow up, dash back and punish a reaction etc. It chains into itself, so you can combo ↓ + LK x2 into either Shinkuu-Hadou-Ken or Shin-Shoryu-Ken.

↓ + MK is Ryu's best poke for mid range fighting. It combos into EX Hadoukens or Shinkuu-Hadou-Ken from long range, punishing whiffs or to apply pressure. While good from a distance, up close it can be countered by a few super arts because of its blocked frame disadvantage.

↓ + HK is good for punishing whiffed normals when you don't have a stocked super meter. It comes out quickly and knocks down, but has terrible recovery. Vulnerable to combos if blocked close, and some super arts from further away. If you use this attack, make sure it hits.

↓ + LP — Low Jab

START UP		4	CS
+3	+3	+3	SC
			SA
GUARD			H/L
PARRY			H/L

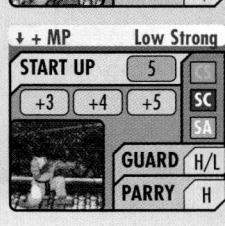

↓ + LK — Low Short

START UP		5	CS
+1	+1	+1	SC
			SA
GUARD			L
PARRY			L

↓ + MP — Low Strong

START UP		5	CS
+3	+4	+5	SC
			SA
GUARD			H/L
PARRY			H

↓ + MK — Low Forward

START UP		7	CS
-3	-2	-1	SC
			SA
GUARD			L
PARRY			H

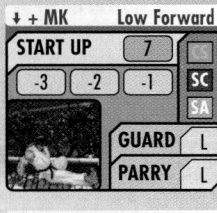

↓ + HP — Low Fierce

START UP		5	CS
-8	-6	-4	SC
			SA
GUARD			H/L
PARRY			H/L

↓ + HK — Low Roundhouse

START UP		7	CS
-13	D	D	SC
			SA
GUARD			L
PARRY			L

JUMPING

Jumping HP is Ryu's best jump in. Use it to get in safely. If opponents block, you have significant frame advantage to setup a throw or some mixup into super art. For instance, jump HP, land and hesitate (to make it look like a throw setup) then LK, LK super art. Jump HP also has the property that if it is executed at the latest possible moment (just before hitting the ground while still connecting) it is safe from ground parry attempts. The parry may happen, but Ryu lands in time to block any ground move and tech any throw attempt.

↓ + LP — Jumping Jab

START UP		4	CS
—	—	—	SC
			SA
GUARD			H
PARRY			H

↓ + MP — Vertical Strong

START UP		5	CS
—	—	—	SC
			SA
GUARD			H
PARRY			H

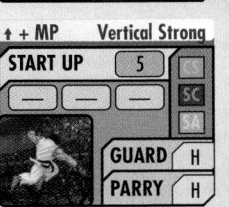

↗/↖ + MP — Jumping Strong

START UP		4	CS
—	—	—	SC
			SA
GUARD			H
PARRY			H

↑ + HP — Vertical Fierce

START UP		6	CS
—	—	—	SC
			SA
GUARD			H
PARRY			H

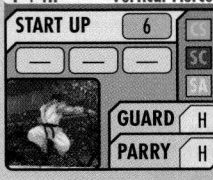

↗ or ↖ + HP — Jumping Fierce

START UP		6	CS
—	—	—	SC
			SA
GUARD			H
PARRY			H

↑ + LK — Jumping Short

START UP		4	CS
—	—	—	SC
			SA
GUARD			H
PARRY			H

↑ + MK — Vertical Forward

START UP		5	CS
—	—	—	SC
			SA
GUARD			H
PARRY			H

↗/↖ + MK — Jumping Forward

START UP		5	CS
—	—	—	SC
			SA
GUARD			H
PARRY			H

↑ + HK — Vertical Roundhouse

START UP		6	CS
—	—	—	SC
			SA
GUARD			H
PARRY			H

↗/↖ + HK — Jumping Roundhouse

START UP		6	CS
—	—	—	SC
			SA
GUARD			H
PARRY			H

SPECIAL MOVES

↓ ↘ → + P — Hadouken

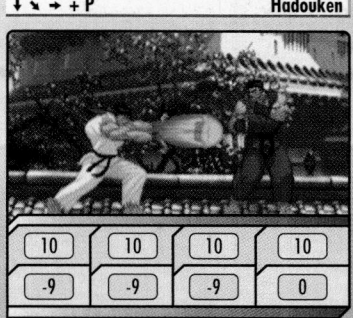

10	10	10	10
-9	-9	-9	0

Button strength determines the speed at which the projectile travels. In some ways, this is Ryu's ideal poke. Becuase of its limitless range and the speed at which it travels, characters trying to play a normal foot game cannot make this poke miss, they must deal with it in some other way. However, because of the semi slow start up and its heavy recovery, it's a fairly risky move at mid range, the range you would normally want to do it at. Many characters can super art (hit or blocked) Ryu during the recovery of a normal Hadouken. The EX version has none of the original Hadouken's weaknesses. It's completely safe if blocked, hits twice, giving opponents more to parry if they try, does more damage, and knocks down when it hits. Because of these positives, the EX Hadouken gives Ryu a fairly dominant poke at mid range, making the EX Hadouken a must.

→ ↓ ↘ + P — Shouryuken

3	3	3	2
-24	-32	-38	-37

On start up, it has a small window of invulnerability, meaning in wake up or anti-air situations, it has the ability to consistently beat an opponent's attack. The EX version hits twice and carries a longer invulnerability window, meaning more hits to parry if used as anti-air. Additionally, it consistently beats attacks more often than a normal Shouryuken. Due to the heavy recovery time, missing with this move means you're going to take a large amount of damage. Use carefully at unexpected times in situations where you need to stop an opponent's offense, scoring a knock down and reversing the flow of the match in your favor.

↓ ↙ ← + K — Tatsumaki Senpukyaku

10	11	11	10
-12	-8	-11	-4

In air, ↓ ↙ ← + K — Tatsumaki Senpukyaku

7	7	7	6

Use for combos, specifically punishment situations where you're guaranteed the damage. Because this move whiffs against crouching characters, it's completely punishable, hit or blocked. Only use in situations where opponents are standing like after a dizzy, or when recovering from a move. The EX version hits multiple times for heavy damage, and hits crouching characters. It is still unsafe if blocked. There is little reason to use it over a EX Joudan Sokutou Geri.

← ↙ ↓ ↘ → + K — Joudan Sokutou Geri

10	13	16	13
-12	-11	-10	-12

Largely used for combos. This move does good damage and stun damage, but it has a heavy recovery. Hits crouching characters, unlike Tatsumaki Senpukyaku. Use only in punishment situations. EX version puts opponents into a juggle state on impact. After bouncing off the wall, you are free to juggle for extra damage, preferably Shouryuken (HP). From far away, Hadouken (LP), dash once behind it. If the Hadouken was parried, cancel the dash recovery into Joudan Sokutou Geri (change button used depending on the range).

RYU

SUPER ARTS

SUPER ART I

↓ ↘ → ↘ → + P	Shinkuu-Hadou-Ken

Ryu's most versatile super art. With two stocks of super meter, it gives Ryu the ability to land super arts and use EX moves. Without super meter, Ryu doesn't have very many safe offensive options from mid to long range. Having EX moves available allows Ryu to overcome his difficulty getting in close and scoring knockdowns. EX Hadoukens are Ryu's best weapon, so this super art can be used to stock meter solely for the purpose of EX Hadoukens. Ryu also has many high damaging combos with the use of one or two EX moves.

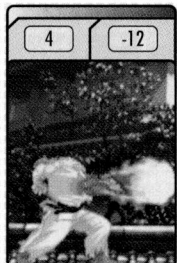

4	-12

Shinkuu-Hadou-Ken is useful if you manage to fill super meter without using EX Hadoukens. It combos easily from close range (↓ + LK (x2) → Shinkuu-Hadou-Ken; MK link Shinkuu-Hadou-Ken). It can also be used to from long range (↓ + MK -> Shinkuu-Hadou-Ken) to punish whiffs and provide a nice range game. It can also be used as a safe anti-air (Shoryuken → Shinkuu-Hadou-Ken). If opponents attempt to parry, Ryu recovers from the super art while they are still parrying it, so it is safe to continue attacking or block safely.

Recommended Super Art:
Shinkuu-Hadou-Ken

With two stocks of super meter providing access to EX moves and super art, Shinkuu-Hadou-Ken gives Ryu enough weapons to attack safely from all ranges. Getting in close is key to Ryu's game plan. His kara throw and knockdown mixups are good, but you must get in close to start his mix up game. EX Hadouken gives Ryu the help he needs to score a knockdown and get in safely.

SUPER ART II

↓ ↘ → ↓ ↘ → + P	Shin-Shoryu-Ken

Shin-Shoryu-Ken is Ryu's most damaging super art. With only one super meter to stock, avoid the use of EX moves. Your goal should be to land the super art. If you can get in close, there are many ways to safely combo into Shin-Shoryu-Ken (↓ + LK (x2) → Shin-Shoryu-Ken or MP link Shin-Shoryu-Ken). Getting in close to land this super art is difficult. Without the use of EX moves, it is hard for Ryu to attack safely and score a knockdown. You must be patient and wait for an opening to knock down opponents. With Shin-Shoryu-Ken stocked, opponents must become cautious. If they make any mistakes, you can punish them with a big combo into a super art. The fear that Shin-Shoryu-Ken instills in opponents gives you opportunities to stay on top of them. Use this fear to land kara throws and overheads until you eventually land the super art. Meter management and patience is crucial to making Shin-Shoryu-Ken effective.

1	-25

TARGET COMBOS

HP → HK

11
-9

Akward command chain that does decent damage. Becuase of the positioning needed to even connect a HP close enough for the HK to hit, this chain is difficult to land. Its only use is as anti-air, if the HP is parried, chain into the roundhouse and hope they don't parry that as well.

SUPER ART III

↓ ↘ → ↓ ↘ → + P (hold to charge)	Denjin-Hadou-Ken

Denjin-Hadou-Ken is an unblockable projectile that does massive stun damage. The longer you charge (by holding punch), the more stun damage it does. A fully charged Denjin stuns any character. You can speed up the charge time by jiggling the controller while holding punch. Once it is fully charged, it releases automatically.

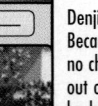

4	—

Denjin-Hadou-Ken has a scary potential. Because it is unblockable, opponents have no choice but to attempt to parry it, or get out of the way. The most common setup is back throw opponents into the corner, then start charging the super art while they are on the ground. With this setup, Ryu is so close to that it is extremely difficult to parry it on reaction, so they must guess when it is coming. Mix-up the timing of the release to frustrate many opponents.

The downside to Denjin-Hadou-Ken is that it is inherently random. You don't combo Denjin-Hadou-Ken, you release it and hope oppnents are unprepared for it. It is hard to hit someone with a fully charged Denjin-Hadou-Ken. Gain some extra time by throwing Hadouken (LP) and canceling into Denjin-Hadou-Ken. Hadouken keeps opponents grounded in blockstun while you charge.

COMBOS YOU NEED TO KNOW

3 HITS
TOTAL DAMAGE: 26

↓ + MK → EX Hadouken

Ryu's only safe combo without a full super meter. Knocks down.

2 HITS
TOTAL DAMAGE: 41

Close HP → Shouryuken (HP)

Most damaging combo to do without a stocked super meter in a punishment situation. Knocks down.

3 HITS
TOTAL DAMAGE: 55

Close HP → EX Joudan Sokutou Geri, late Shouryuken (HP)

Most damaging combo to do in a punishment situation with sufficient super meter. Knocks down.

6 HITS
TOTAL DAMAGE: 73

Jump in HP, land, close HP → EX Joudan Sokutou Geri, juggle with a late close LP → EX Shouryuken

High damage jump in. Use in punishment situation or after a successful parry while jumping in. Knocks down.

6 HITS
TOTAL DAMAGE: 77
CORNER ONLY

Jump in HP, land, close HP → EX Joudan Sokutou Geri, juggle with a early EX Shinkuu Tatsumaki Sempuu Kyaku, juggle again with a early Shouryuken (HP)

High damage jump in. Use against a dizzy opponent in the corner, or after a successful parry during a jump in near the corner. Knocks down.

8 HITS
TOTAL DAMAGE: 63
CORNER ONLY

↓ + LK, ↓ + LK → Shinkuu-Hadou-Ken, juggle with a early Joudan Sokutou Geri (LK)

At midscreen, the same is possible but without the extra juggle at the end. Knockdown. Verifiable. If ↓ + LK (x2) is blocked, Ryu remains fairly close. In range for low parry option select ↓ + MK, walk up kara throw or UOH.

13 HITS
TOTAL DAMAGE: 79

↓ + LK, ↓ + LK → Shinkuu-Hadou-Ken, juggle with another semi late Shinkuu-Hadou-Ken, juggle with an early Joudan Sokutou Geri.

Most damaging and flexible option using maximum super meter. Knockdown. Verifiable. If ↓ + LK (x2) is blocked, Ryu remains close and has a +1 frame advantage to work with to mount another attack.

7 HITS
TOTAL DAMAGE: 90

↓ + LK, ↓ + LK → Shin-Shoryu-Ken, juggle with Joudan Sokutou Geri (HK)

Flexible, high damage option to land a Shin-Shoryu-Ken. Verifiable. Knocks down.

7 HITS
TOTAL DAMAGE: 98

Close HP →Shouryuken (HP) → Shin-Shoryu-Ken, juggle with Joudan Sokutou Geri (HK)

STRATEGY

Straight

Ryu's game plan is highly dependant on super art selection. At long range, Ryu is a threat only if you're willing to burn meter on EX Hadoukens. As long as the opponent is on the ground, Ryu is completely safe after an EX Hadouken. Throw out EX Hadoukens from time to time to catch random pokes and dashes. A perfect time to just throw an EX Hadouken is after a teched throw.

↓ + MK and ↓ + HK are Ryu's best pokes for foot games. When at a distance, stay just outside of opponents' longest low poke, and bait them to stick out something. Punish the whiffed move with ↓ + MK, Hadouken, or ↓ + HK. After you knock them down, dash in close and try to stay as close as possible.

Ryu is deadly at close range. Ryu has an exceptionally long kara throw., so work to stay within its range. The kara throw range is from just inside two ↓ + LK's distance, close MK's distance. Some good throw setups are:

↓ + LK, throw.
↓ + LK (x2), throw.
LK, throw.
Close MK, throw.
↓ + LK, whiffed LP, throw.

When opponents expect throws, that leaves them open to super arts. For example, ↓ + LK, hesitate, ↓ + LK (x2) → Shinkuu-Hadou-Ken; ↓ + LK, whiffed LP, ↓ + LK (x2) → Shinkuu-Hadou-Ken; LK, walkup close MP link Shin-Shoryu-Ken; ↓ + LK, dash back, ↓ + MK, Tatsumaki Senpuu Kyaku; ↓ + LK, ↓ + HP, EX Hadouken. The key is to throw often to get opponents to expect a throw, which is the time to capitalize with a big combo.

Ryu's air options are rather limited. Jump HP is his best jump in because of its safe properties. Jump MK cross up is not very good on already standing opponents. Most characters can easily walk or dash under it. Always stay in front of opponents if they jump in. It is usually a better idea to stay on the ground and score a knock down via EX Hadoukens, or countering a whiffed attack with ↓ + HK.

Against airborne opponents, jumping MP is Ryu's best option. With two hits, it is a fairly safe move. An option select air parrier takes a hit, leaving Ryu at the advantage. It is also a good alternative to use for jump in attempts. Many players forget that it is two hits and tend to only block the first hit. Even if the move is parried, it is hard to counter attack Ryu when he lands.

When Ryu is on the ground and someone jumps in, a quick reacting jumping MP to counter works really well as anti-air. Vertical HP is good as well because of its range. For a more traditional and safe anti-air, use Shouryuken → Shinkuu-Hadou-Ken. In order for Shinkuu-Hadou-Ken to combo, it must be a Shouryuken (LP). The safest anti-air tactic, and the most unexpected, is to dash under opponents as they jump at you. If they commit to an attack, or attempt to parry, they will not be blocking when they land. You are free to use the combo of your choice.

Some characters are simply better at longer range than Ryu and will out footsie him all day. Against these characters, Ryu's only options are to burn meter on EX Hadoukens and hope to score a knockdown, or jump in with HP or attempt to parry. Getting in close is the hard part, but staying close is the key to success with Ryu.

WAKEUP GAME

With super art I and II, Ryu has both high and low options to verify into a super art. This is important in thwarting parry attempts. Sakotsu Wari is fast and does stun damage, ideal for Denjin-Hadou-Ken users. Super art I and II can both be comboed off of a meaty UOH on wake up. It's also possible to combo normal attacks into a big EX combo after a meaty UOH, although the timing is very precise.

Ryu has many quick fake out maneuvers to trick people on wake up. For example, whiff an LP over their head right before they get up then immediately throw. This makes it look like you are going for something other than a throw and they tend to block. Next time on wake up, whiff the LP and they might anticipate the throw, so perform a ↓ + LK (x2) → super art. You can do the same sequence with whiffed ↓ + LK into throw, then next time do a high move that is verifiable into a super art. Another good tactic is to option parry into throw as opponents are getting up. Do this right in their face. Many players expect Ryu to throw from his maximum kara throw range. Surprise them with an in-your-face throw. Finally, to totally fake them out, dash back on wake up to bait a throw attempt or wake up move, then ↓ + MK combo for big damage and another knockdown to repeat the process.

When Ryu is the one knocked down, he has the traditional wake up options such as psychic Shouryuken, wake up super art, parrying or blocking. If opponents tick or do any hesitation move, a good counter is a quick ↓ + LP, ↓ + LK combination. If they block, they are pushed away to a safer distance. If it hits, finish with Shinkuu-Hadou-Ken, if available.

SETUPS

Ranges setups for UOH → super art

Against small and medium sized characters:

(↓ + LK, ↓ + MP), UOH → Shinkuu-Hadou-Ken
(Close MK, LK), UOH → Shinkuu-Hadou-Ken

Against wide characters:

(↓ + LK (x3)), UOH → Shinkuu-Hadou-Ken

Against Hugo, Elena:

(close MP, ↓ + MP), UOH → Shinkuu-Hadou-Ken

Against Oro:

No setup is required. UOH → Shin-Shoryu-Ken works at close distance on crouching Oro.

RESETS

Reset 1: LP as anti-air, dash forward and Shin-Shoryu-Ken before the opponent hits the ground. The LP causes a flip recovery and landing. Because of this, it's possible to use a super art the moment they fully recover in the air. Their only option is to attempt to parry. After doing this a few times, mix it up and dash forward and ↓ + LK (x2) → super art instead. This works if people are expecting the reset and attempt to parry. They must input the parry command so close to the ground that they will not have time to react and block low in time.

Reset 2: After an EX Joudan Sokutou Geri combo. instead of finishing with a Shouryuken (HP), dash up and LP, then reset with Shinkuu-Hadou-Ken for more damage. Opponents have no choice but to parry. If they do so, you recover while they are still parrying, so you can continue to attack them during the Shinkuu-Hadou-Ken to mess up their parry timing.

Reset 3: After a mid air jumping kick. By hitting air to air so that Ryu lands first, juggle with a Shinkuu-Hadou-Ken. With two full two super meters, juggle again with another Shinkuu-Hadou-Ken.

PARRY SETUPS AND TACTICS

If you're fishing for damage, and ↓ + LK (x2) is blocked, a good pattern is to either walk up a step and kara throw, walk up ↓ + LK (x2) again, or let the controller go to neutral, tap ↓, then hit ↓ + MK. If they hit a button to try to stop what they think is a throw, and it's a low attack, you parry the attack, ↓ + MK hits, then you can cancel ↓ + MK into a super art or special attack on reaction to the parry. If they don't press anything ↓ + MK comes out to push them away. The key is to avoid canceling into a super if you don't visually see the parry happen.

GROUND CROSS UPS

Ryu can cross up the following characters in any corner:

Twelve, Alex, Dudley, Necro, Hugo, Urien,

Ryu can cross up Elena only in his own corner.

FAVORABLE MATCH UP: DUDLEY

This is a good match up for Ryu mainly because of one move: HK. Ryu can zone Dudley and keep him away with this move all day. It covers ground and air and beats most all of Dudley's normals. Dudley has a wide ducking hit box, so this move even hits Dudley when he goes low. Dudley has a low jump, so it is hard for him to get over HK. Dudley must resort to parries to successfully jump in. Use this is to your advantage by mixing up the timing of attacks to prevent Dudley from parrying. Add HP and execute the target combo to mix it up further.

With Dudley into the corner, use mix ups off of throws to keep opponents confused about what to do. It's possible for Ryu to ground cross up Dudley off of a back throw if Dudley quick recovers. Do this enough times and Dudley will probably stop quick recovering. If he doesn't quick recover a neutral throw in the corner, combo on the ground Shin-Shoryu-Ken.

6 HITS

TOTAL DAMAGE: 88

CORNER ONLY (VS. DUDLEY)

Neutral throw, just as Ryu recovers, do a Shin-Shoryu-Ken, if timed correctly it hits while Dudley is on the ground. Juggle with a Joudan Sokutou Geri (HK) after the Shin-Shoryu-Ken finishes.

The timing to hit Dudley off the ground with the super art is extremely inflexible. If you miss the off the ground hit Ryu flies into the air and is completely open when Dudley gets up from the throw.

UNFAVORABLE MATCH UP: CHUN-LI

Ryu is most effective from close range, but Chun-Li can out range and out footsie Ryu to the point that he can't get in on the ground. Chun-Li's low forward keeps Ryu away. When Chun-Li doesn't have super meter, play Ryu's EX Hadouken game to score a knockdown and get close. As soon as Chun-Li has a stocked super meter, her ability to super art through Hadoukens renders this strategy useless.

Ryu's only option to get in is to jump. Late jumping HP often works against a defensive Chun-Li, but an active Chun-Li knows to stop any jump in attemps with a counter air throw, anti-air, or by walking under Ryu. For Ryu to win this match, start the match off strong, attacking while Chun-Li doesn't have any super meter. Once she does have a meter, be patient, and try to jump in safely.

Sean

NORMAL MOVES

STANDING

HP has okay range, a fast start up, and good recovery. A poke from close range.

MK moves Sean forward, and beats low pokes cleanly while keeping Sean close.

LP — Jab

START UP	3		CS
+5	+5	+5	SC
			SA
GUARD	H/L		
PARRY	H/L		

LK — Short

START UP	4		CS
+2	+2	+2	SC
			SA
GUARD	H/L		
PARRY	H/L		

MP — Strong

START UP	5		
0	+1	+2	SC
			SA
GUARD	H/L		
PARRY	H		

MK — Forward

START UP	6		
-2	-1	0	SC
			SA
GUARD	H/L		
PARRY	H/L		

HP — Fierce

START UP	9		
-7	-5	-3	SC
			SA
GUARD	H/L		
PARRY	H		

HK — Roundhouse

START UP	7		CS
-9	-7	-5	SC
			SA
GUARD	H/L		
PARRY	H/L		

STANDING CLOSE

Close MP has frame advantage off of it, so it is good for tick throw setups and other mix ups. For example, after a blocked MP, hesitate, then walk up and use MP again (Or ↓ + LK (x2)).

Close HK is a mid-level attack with a large amount of frame advantage if blocked. Good for verifying and linking into Hyper Tornado, or Hadou-Burst when close enough.

LP — Close Jab

START UP	3		CS
+5	+5	+5	SC
			SA
GUARD	H/L		
PARRY	H/L		

LK — Close Short

START UP	4		CS
+2	+2	+2	SC
			SA
GUARD	H/L		
PARRY	H/L		

MP — Close Strong

START UP	5		
0	+1	+2	SC
			SA
GUARD	H/L		
PARRY	H		

MK — Close Forward

START UP	6		
-2	-1	0	SC
			SA
GUARD	H/L		
PARRY	H/L		

HP — Close Fierce

START UP	5		
-4	-2	0	SC
			SA
GUARD	H/L		
PARRY	H		

HK — Close Roundhouse

START UP	5		
+2	+4	+6	SC
			SA
GUARD	H/L		
PARRY	H		

COSTUMES

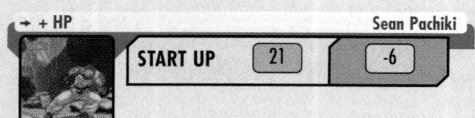

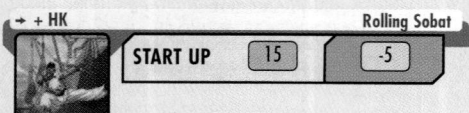

SPECIAL NORMALS

→ + HP — Sean Pachiki

START UP	21	-6

Slow two hit overhead attack with heavy recovery time. Hit or blocked, many characters can retaliate with a fast super. However, if they don't have any stocked super meter, use this move at point blank range in mix-up games. Use HP as cover before an attack pattern, HP → Sean Pachiki or HP → Sean Tackle, then ↓ + LK (x2) or throw for a three way mix-up.

→ + HK — Rolling Sobat

START UP	15	-5

Goes over many mid level attacks to score a hit. Extremely unsafe however, and whiffs against most crouching characters and low attacks.

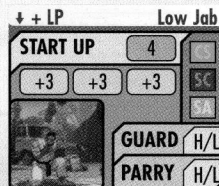

SPECIAL MOVES

CROUCHING

↓ + LK has many uses. It is a quick poke that can be used for tick throw setups and mind games. After a blocked ↓ + LK, you have many options: throw, hesitate and ↓ + LK (x2) follow up, dash back and punish a reaction and so on. It chains into itself, so you can combo ↓ + LK (x2) into any super art.

↓ + MK is Sean's best poke for mid range distance fighting. Combo into Hadou-Burst or Hyper Tornado from long range to punish whiffs or to apply pressure. Up close it can be countered by a few super arts because of its blocked frame disadvantage.

↓ + LP	Low Jab	
START UP	4	CS
+3 +3 +3		SC
		SA
GUARD	H/L	
PARRY	H/L	

↓ + LK	Low Short	
START UP	5	CS
+1 +1 +1		SC
		SA
GUARD	L	
PARRY	L	

↓ + MP	Low Strong	
START UP	5	CS
+3 +4 +5		SC
		SA
GUARD	H/L	
PARRY	H/L	

↓ + MK	Low Forward	
START UP	7	CS
-4 -3 -2		SC
		SA
GUARD	L	
PARRY	L	

↓ + HP	Low Fierce	
START UP	7	CS
-9 -7 -5		SC
		SA
GUARD	H/L	
PARRY	H/L	

↓ + HK	Low Roundhouse	
START UP	8	CS
-16 D D		SC
		SA
GUARD	L	
PARRY	L	

JUMPING

Jumping straight up LP, MP and LK add one frame to the start up times of those attacks compared to jumping forward or backward.

Use jumping HP to get in safely. If opponents block, you have significant frame advantage to setup a throw or some mix-up into a super art.

↑ + MP	Jumping Strong	
START UP	5	CS
— — —		SC
		SA
GUARD	H	
PARRY	H	

↑ + MK	Vertical Forward	
START UP	5	CS
— — —		SC
		SA
GUARD	H	
PARRY	H	

↑ + HP	Vertical Fierce	
START UP	7	CS
— — —		SC
		SA
GUARD	H	
PARRY	H	

↗/↖ + MK	Jumping Forward	
START UP	5	CS
— — —		SC
		SA
GUARD	H	
PARRY	H	

↗/↖ + HP	Jumping Fierce	
START UP	6	CS
— — —		SC
		SA
GUARD	H	
PARRY	H	

↑ + HK	Vertical Roundhouse	
START UP	7	CS
— — —		SC
		SA
GUARD	H	
PARRY	H	

↑ + LP	Jumping Jab	
START UP	4	CS
— — —		SC
		SA
GUARD	H	
PARRY	H	

↑ + LK	Jumping Short	
START UP	4	CS
— — —		SC
		SA
GUARD	H	
PARRY	H	

↗/↖ + HK	Jumping Roundhouse	
START UP	6	CS
— — —		SC
		SA
GUARD	H	
PARRY	H	

THROWS

LP + LK	Seoi Throw

← + LP + LK	Tomoe Throw

↓ ↙ ← + P		Zenten

—	—

Command roll. Button strength determines the distance rolled. Sean rolls through opponents and cannot be thrown out of, but he remains vulnerable to low attacks. Use it to create throw whiffs in wake up situations.

→ ↓ ↘ + P			Dragon Smash

5	7	9	8
-24	-30	-34	-37

Mostly good for knock down combos in punishment situations. The EX version is a decent reversal in wake up situations.

↓ ↙ ← + K			Tornado

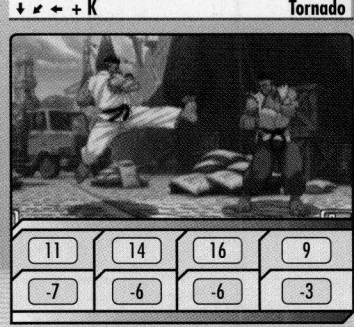

11	14	16	9
-7	-6	-6	-3

Hits crouching opponents, but it does not knock down and is not safe if blocked. Passable for use in punishment situations when the damage is guaranteed. The EX version has similar properties except that it's slightly safer, hits more times and does more damage.

← ↙ ↓ ↘ → + P (hold P)			Sean Tackle

18	22	26	28
-7	-6	-6	-3

Command dash with a low hitting follow up if you hold punch down after you input the command. Otherwise, Sean goes into a small recovery, canceling out the tackle at the end, leaving him free to attack with other moves.

Although the follow up cannot combo off of anything, the command dash itself is useful, allowing Sean to stay close after failed attacks. Canceling into this move from heavy attacks is one way to go for basic mix ups such as close HP → Sean Tackle, throw; close HP → Sean tackle, ↓ + LK (x2); or close HP → Sean Tackle (hold P to follow up). The tackle grab follow up variation is important when you anticipate opponents attempting to punish the recovery of a Sean Tackle.

↓ ↘ → + K			Ryuubi Kyaku

15	15	15	27
-3	-2	-3	-1

A leaping kick that arcs towards opponents. Very slow and carries a slight disadvantage if blocked, vulnerable to fast super arts. Does nothing for Sean offensively. The EX version is much safer, but it still doesn't do much for Sean's game.

SUPER ARTS

SUPER ART I

↓ ↘ → ↓ ↘ → + P	Hadou-Burst

Hadou-Burst is a one hit fireball. With three stocks of super meter and a short bar, it is ideal to use in every combo opportunity in tandem with EX moves. Hadou-Burst combos from ↓ + LK (x2) and close HK link, giving Sean high and low options. Hadou-Burst also combos nicely off of ↓ + MK from all ranges. ↓ + MK →

3	-39

Hadou-Burst is Sean's only threatening attack from long distances. Use it to zone out characters and punish whiffs.

The downside to Hadou-Burst is its long recovery. Hadou-Burst sends opponents flying across the screen while Sean is stuck in his projectile stance. He must quickly dash across the screen to regain a position near opponents.

SUPER ART II

↓ ↘ → ↓ ↘ → + P (push P rapidly)	Shoryu-Cannon

Shoryu-Cannon has a longer bar than Hadou-Burst and only two stocks, but does more damage and has more juggle potential. It hits multiple times so it works as anti-air. Combo into it low from ↓ + LK (x2), or high on a crouching opponent from close MP link. Unfortunately, Sean must be extremely close to land these combos.

1	-43

Sean isn't the most offensively oriented character, especially against characters that can keep out of range such as Chun Li and Akuma. It is hard for him to actually land Shoryu-Cannon from that distance, and it is unlikely that Sean will be able to pressure his opponent enough to bait them to jump and get caught with an anti-air Shoryu-Cannon.

SUPER ART III

↓ ↘ → ↓ ↘ → + P	Hyper Tornado

Hyper Tornado only stocks one super meter, but it does the most damage of any of Sean's super arts. It has the same combo possibilities as Hadou-Burst. With Hyper Tornado stocked and ready to go, Sean is a threat from far mid to long ranges. Punish any poke or rush down attempt with ↓ + MK → Hyper Tornado.

2	-31

Only having one stock of super meter for Hyper Tornado is a big disadvantage. After landing it, it takes Sean a long time to refill his meter to use it again. During that time Sean does not have any high damaging combos off of pokes to keep opponents from rushing in on him.

Recommended Super Art:
Hadou-Burst

Hadou-Burst is the best super to give Sean a fighting chance. The bar is short enough so he should always have at least one super stocked and ready to go. The ability to do EX Dragon Smashes without worry helps Sean get out of corners and turn the momentum in his favor. With Hadou-Burst, you can turn any opening into an opportunity to connect with a combo into super.

TARGET CHAIN

CLOSE MP → HK	4
	-2

Sean's only safe combo without a stocked super meter. Not so good damage off of a mid level attack. Safe in most situations, the roundhouse whiffs against Yun and Yang when they are crouching.

COMBOS YOU NEED TO KNOW

2 HITS

TOTAL DAMAGE: 30

Close MP → Dragon Smash

Damaging combo used for punishment situations. Knocks down.

5 HITS

TOTAL DAMAGE: 41

Close HK → EX Tornado

Heavy damage non super combo. Good in punishment situations.

3 HITS

TOTAL DAMAGE: 36

↓ + LK, ↓ + LK → Hadou-Burst

Flexible, verifiable way to land a Hadou-Burst. If ↓ + LK (x2) is blocked , Sean remains close and has a +1 frame advantage. Walk up ↓ + LK (x2) → Hadou-Burst, walk up throw, low parry option select ↓ + MK → Hadou-Burst, or walk back a step universal over head linked into Hadou-Burst are all good patterns in this situation. Knocks down.

14 HITS

TOTAL DAMAGE: 65

↓ + LK, ↓ + LK → Hyper Tornado

Flexible, verifiable way to land a Hyper Tornado. If ↓ + LK (x2) is blocked, Sean remains close and has a +1 frame advantage. Walk up ↓ + LK (x2) → Hyper Tornado, walk up throw, low parry option select ↓ + MK → Hyper Tornado, or walk back a step universal over head linked into Hyper Tornado are all good patterns in this situation. Knocks down.

13 HITS

TOTAL DAMAGE: 73

Close HK linked into Hyper Tornado.

Verifiable way to land a Hyper Tornado. Heavy damage. Knocks down.

15 HITS

TOTAL DAMAGE: 55

↓ + LK (x2) → Shoryu-Cannon

Flexible, verifiable way to land a Shoryu-Cannon. Knocks down.

3 HITS

TOTAL DAMAGE: 52

Close MP → Dragon Smash (HP) → Hadou-Burst

High damage combo using Hadou-Burst, good for punishment situations. Knocks down.

STRATEGY

Straight

Sean's offensive options are rather limited. He can't really score big damage outside of using a super art. To make up for this, concentrate on landing as many super arts as possible. Hadou-Burst is the best choice for giving Sean a decent offensive game. Without a stocked super meter, stick with ↓ + MK and ↓ + HK for poking to inflict damage and score a knockdown. When at a distance, stay just outside of the opponent's longest low poke, and bait an attack. Punish any whiffed move with ↓ + HK, then dash in after the knockdown.

At close range, use Sean Tackle to bait out an attack or tech throw attempt and punish accordingly. From mid range, use ↓ + MK → Sean Tackle (LP). Don't finish the tackle command (meaning don't hold the button). In essence, you use the Sean Tackle as a quick dash while opponents are in block stun from the previous move. When Sean recovers, throw or use (↓ + LK (x2) / close HK) → super art. Use Sean Tackle to apply constant pressure whenever pushed out of range. For example, if ↓ + LK (x2) is blocked, immediately ↓ + MK → tackle to get back in close.

After a jump in, hesitate a split second to make it appear like you might throw, then Zenten (LP) through opponents and attack from the other side. Expect to score a hit if you catch them in a throw whiff or they simply didn't react in time to block. Don't try this too often, but do it every once in a while to keep opponents on their toes.

When Sean gets close, throw often, especially without a stocked super meter. His kara throw has good range. If you can bait a tech throw attempt, punish with ↓ + MK → super art. Some good throw setups are:

↓ + LK, throw
↓ + LK (x2), kara throw
LK, throw
Close MK, throw
↓ + LK, whiffed LP, throw

Sean's air options are rather limited. He has a different jump arc than the other shotos, with a sort of lag which prevents him from jumping as far. Many characters out range and out zone Sean on the ground, leaving little choice but to jump in. Jumping HP is the best choice. Jumping MK cross up is not good on already standing opponents as most characters can easily walk or dash under it. Stay in front of opponents if you must jump in, unless the cross up is a sure thing.

Against airborne opponents, stick with option parry jumping HP or HK. As for anti-air, EX Dragon Smash is his only viable option other than using Shoryu-Cannon. EX Dragon Smash is only two hits, so it is easily parried. A better option is to take advantage of Sean's quick dash and dash under opponents as they jump. From this position, either throw or attempt (↓ + LK (x2) / ↓ + MK) → super art. Another effective option is jumping back HK in reaction to a jump in.

WAKEUP GAME

With all three super arts, Sean has both high and low options to verify combo into a super art, which is important to thwart parry attempts. Sean's target combo overhead is good every once in a while if opponents always block low on wake up. All three super arts can be used in a combo behind of a meaty UOH on wakeup.

Sean has many of the shoto fake out maneuvers used to trick opponents on wake up. For example, whiffing LP and LK as they are getting up, then switch it up and either throw, or ↓ + LK (x2) and look for a hit before doing a super art. A good mix-up is to tick with ↓ + LK, making it look like a throw setup, then use close HK, and link into Hyper Tornado if it hits. With Hadou-Burst, you must have quicker reflexes and cancel it on reaction if an opponent attempts anything. Tick with ↓ + LK, then dash back and use ↓ + MK, then cancel it into a super art if you see a move.

A neat little trick that is sure to work at least once after a throw is a Rolling Sobat over grounded opponents as soon as you throw them, and they don't quick recover. You cross them up just as they get up. Catch them while they are blocking the wrong way.

When Sean is the one knocked down, other than blocking or parrying, his only real safe wake up move is an EX Dragon Smash. After getting up, if an opponent is doing any tick throws or hesitation moves, use ↓ + LP, ↓ + LK combination. Combo that into Hadou-Burst or Hyper Tornado.

SETUPS

Ranges setups for UOH → super art

Against small characters:

(Close MP, MK), UOH → Hadou-Burst, Hyper Tornado

Against medium sized characters:

(Close HP), UOH → Hadou-Burst, Hyper Tornado
(Close MP, LK), UOH → Hadou-Burst, Hyper Tornado

Against wide characters:

(↓ + LK, close HP) UOH → Hadou-Burst, Hyper Tornado

Against Oro:

No setup is required. UOH → Hadou-Burst, Hyper Tornado works at close distance on crouching Oro.

RESETS

Reset 1: If you manage to land a Rolling Sobat, immediately throw a Hadou-Burst to hit opponents in their air recovery before they land. Although be wary about using this often because one parry nullifies this trick.

Reset 2: After any air-to-air jumping HP or MK, if Sean lands before an opponent does, Hadou-Burst the air recovery for an extra hit for decent damage. Although if done from close range and they parry, Sean is not safe.

PARRY SET UPS AND TACTICS

Sean can do the typical shoto parry setups such as ↓ + LK (x2) and option select down if blocked. He also can be tricky with close HP. He has significant frame advantage after the move. If it hits, link into a super art. If it is blocked, hesitate and bait a low poke, and parry down. From the range Sean is at after a blocked HK, the best moves to hit Sean are low pokes, so an option parry in this situation is generally without much risk.

GROUND CROSS UPS

Sean can cross up the following characters in any corner:

Twelve, Alex, Dudley, Necro, Hugo, Urien.

Sean can cross up Elena only in his own corner.

FAVORABLE MATCH UP: REMY

Sean is one of the underdog characters of *Street Fighter III: 3rd Strike*, but he can hold his own against Remy. Sean's ↓ + MK and ↓ + HK give Remy problems. Remy can't brainlessly throw out Light of Virtues at Sean. Hadou-Burst or Hyper Tornado through them if possible (it requires a quick reaction). Rolling Sobat goes the low Light of Virtue, and Sean Tackle early, or roll under the high Light of Virtue. At close ranges, punish Remy's low forward with Hadou-Burst or Shoryu-Cannon regardless if the move is blocked or hit. Remy's low roundhouse is also punishable. Take advantage of these weaknesses to knock Remy down and stay on him.

UNFAVORABLE MATCH UP: NECRO

Sean has a hard time dealing with Necro's MP. This move out ranges all of Sean's ground pokes and hits him even when he is crouching. Sean can't zone out Necro with ↓ + MK like he can other characters because Necro's MP always beats it. Furthermore, Necro can punish any whiffed limbs with it. Expect a tough time getting in close. Sean Tackle is unavailable for the same reason. Necro's HP stops Sean from advancing. The air isn't any easier for Sean because Necro has too many safe anti-air options. Sean's super jump is not as good as the other shotos for landing a safe cross up.

For Sean to win this match, resort to parrying. On the ground, parry Necro's MP from max range. If you successfully parry his attack, use ↓ + MK → super art, or ↓ + HK if you don't have enough super meter. Once you knock him down, dash up close or go for a cross up, and stay near him. If you choose to try jumping, an early jumping HK will beat his near perfect low MP anti-air. If Necro properly mixes up his anti airs, expect trouble. Parrying is not much help if Necro relies on low MP. Even after a parry, Necro recovers quickly enough to block or even parry attacks.

Twelve

NORMAL MOVES

STANDING

HP: Decent anti-air. Covers a lot of area at a good angle. Hard to parry.

MK: Upward knee that moves Twelve forward slightly. Super jump cancelable, meaning after doing it you can cancel it directly into a jump and then an air dash to pin your opponent down and start another attack. This is a must to help keep Twelve airborne after offensive patterns that start on the ground.

HK: Incredible range. Ok for hitting whiffed attacks with bad recovery from a distance. Very hard for a character to make this attack whiff as well. However, this attack has a slow start up and recovery.

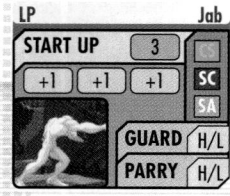

LP	Jab
START UP	3	CS
+1 +1 +1	SC
	SA
GUARD	H/L
PARRY	H/L

MP	Strong
START UP	9	CS
-2 -1 0	SC
	SA
GUARD	H/L
PARRY	H

HP	Fierce
START UP	12	CS
-3 -1 +1	SC
	SA
GUARD	H/L
PARRY	H

LK	Short
START UP	3	CS
-1 -1 -1	SC
	SA
GUARD	H/L
PARRY	H/L

MK	Forward
START UP	6	CS
-4 -1 0	SC
	SA
GUARD	H/L
PARRY	H/L

HK	Roundhouse
START UP	17	CS
-11 -1 +1	SC
	SA
GUARD	H/L
PARRY	H

STANDING CLOSE

LP	Close Jab
START UP	3	CS
+1 +1 +1	SC
	SA
GUARD	H/L
PARRY	H/L

MP	Close Strong
START UP	6	CS
-2 -1 0	SC
	SA
GUARD	H/L
PARRY	H

HP	Close Fierce
START UP	12	CS
-3 -1 +1	SC
	SA
GUARD	H/L
PARRY	H

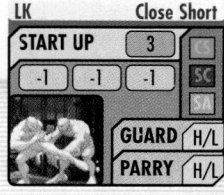

LK	Close Short
START UP	3	CS
-1 -1 -1	SC
	SA
GUARD	H/L
PARRY	H/L

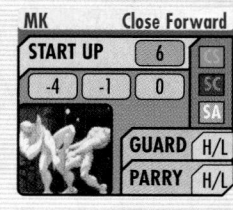

MK	Close Forward
START UP	6	CS
-4 -1 0	SC
	SA
GUARD	H/L
PARRY	H/L

HK	Close Roundhouse
START UP	17	CS
-11 -1 +1	SC
	SA
GUARD	H/L
PARRY	H

COSTUMES

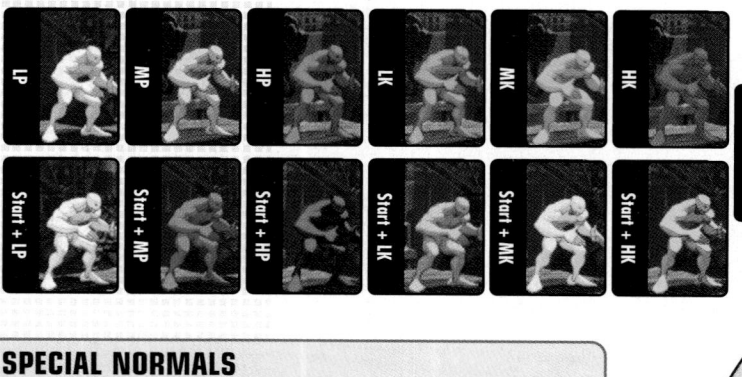

SPECIAL NORMALS

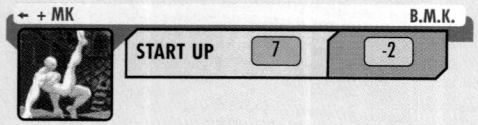

← + MK		B.M.K.
START UP	7	-2

An upward kick that's cancelable. If they parry it you can cancel into a A.X.E. (LP) to give them more to parry on the way down.

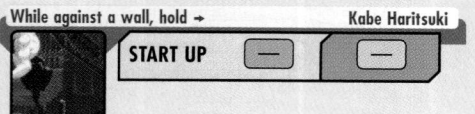

While against a wall, hold →		Kabe Haritsuki
START UP	—	—

While jumping, → → / ← ←		Kokkuu
START UP	—	—

Kokkuu: Flying air dash. Twelve's game revolves around his air dash, which gives him the ability to be able to fly in and out of attack range at will. When combined with Twelve's incredible jumping attacks, like jump HP and HK, Twelve can control a considerable amount of screen space at will. Use forward air dash to apply constant pressure with jump HP and HK. When close, you can whiff his air dash completely by doing a jump HK while the air dash is close to the ground, which whiffs, then when you land ether throw or ↓ + LK → A.X.E. to make blocking and parrying difficult.

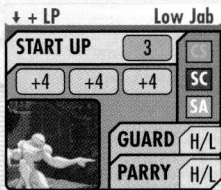

CROUCHING

↓ + MK: Overall decent safe poke. Comes out fast and has decent range. Good for punishing whiffed normals.

↓ + HK: Good range for a sweep. Hard to make it whiff during foot games. Will hit characters trying to walk backwards out of range if they are too close. This attack must be done from maximum range to keep it from being punished if blocked.

↓ + LP	Low Jab		↓ + LK	Low Short	
START UP	3		START UP	3	
+4	+4	+4	SC	+1	+1	+1	SC
		SA			SA
GUARD	H/L		GUARD	L
PARRY	H/L		PARRY	L

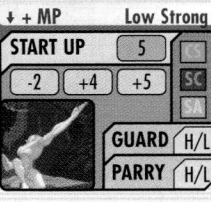

↓ + MP	Low Strong		↓ + MK	Low Forward	
START UP	5		START UP	8	
-2	+4	+5	SC	-2	-1	0	SC
		SA			SA
GUARD	H/L		GUARD	L
PARRY	H/L		PARRY	L

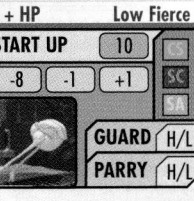

↓ + HP	Low Fierce		↓ + HK	Low Roundhouse	
START UP	10		START UP	13	
-8	-1	+1	SC	-11	D	D	SC
		SA			SA
GUARD	H/L		GUARD	L
PARRY	H/L		PARRY	L

JUMPING

↑ + LP	Jumping Jab		↑ + LK	Jumping Short	
START UP	3		START UP	2	
—	—	—	SC	—	—	—	SC
		SA			SA
GUARD	H		GUARD	H
PARRY	H		PARRY	H

↑ + MP	Jumping Strong		↑ + MK	Jumping Forward	
START UP	5		START UP	9	
—	—	—	SC	—	—	—	SC
		SA			SA
GUARD	H		GUARD	H
PARRY	H		PARRY	H

↑ + HP	Jumping Fierce		↑ + HK	Jumping Roundhouse	
START UP	12		START UP	14	
—	—	—	SC	—	—	—	SC
		SA			SA
GUARD	H		GUARD	H
PARRY	H		PARRY	H

THROWS

LP + LK	H.U.G.	→ + LP + LK	F.L.G.	← + LP + LK	T.R.W.

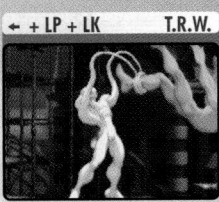

SPECIAL MOVES

↓ ↘ → +P	N.D.L	↓ ↙ ← + P (also in air)	A.X.E.

15	15	16	14		6	10	14	8
-5	-9	-13	0		-5	-6	-7	-4

Strange projectile attack that comes up from the ground at varying distances. Button strength determines where needles come up from. The EX version of this move comes out slightly faster, recovers slightly faster, and puts your opponent into a juggle set up. Although not extremely useful, when your opponent is waking up, it's actually possible to do an N.D.L. so meaty that the tail end of the needle hits and it's possible to get enough frame advantage after it to link a ↓ + LK. This can be helpful for point blank mix up situations, allowing Twelve to attack or tick throw behind a small frame advantage. The positioning for this is difficult, which is almost directly next to them on wake up with enough time to do a N.D.L. (LP) very early. This move is also vulnerable to quick recovers, which ruin the set up altogether. Easiest to set up after a successful X.N.D.L combo, which they can't quick recover from.

Multi-hit whip attack. Hits several times up close. Twelve's most damaging special attack. Can be comboed into after a ↓ + LK for minor damage. Twelve's only option outside of a throw for dealing damage when he gets an opening since he has very few combos to work with. If you get an opening, go straight into the move and mash on punch. The EX version of this move hits more times and does more damage. The aerial version of this move can be used to thwart anti-air parry attempts. Be careful, the ground version is vulnerable if blocked.

While jumping, ↓ ↙ ← + K	D.R.A.

14	14	14	6
—	—	—	—

Dive attack. Button strength determines the angle of the dive. Not very useful, although it can have a bit of a surprise factor to it. The EX version is extremely fast and knocks down, good for going over projectiles and punishing a whiffed attack while your jumping.

SUPER ARTS

SUPER ART I

↓ ↘ → ↓ ↘ → + P   **X.N.D.L.**

Super art 1 equips Twelve with 2 stocks of meter to do a super art version of his N.D.L. projectile. X.N.D.L. travels the length of the screen, although it does less damage the further it travels. You can verify it with

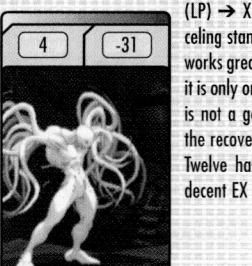

| 4 | -31 |

↓ + LK x2 → X.N.D.L., ↓ + LK → A.X.E. (LP) → X.N.D.L., and by super jump canceling stand close MK → X.N.D.L. X.N.D.L. works great as anti-air, although sometimes it is only one parry, so use with caution. This is not a good super to miss with, because the recovery is terrible. On a positive note, Twelve has a lot of meter to use for his decent EX moves.

SUPER ART II

While jumping, ↓ ↘ → ↓ ↘ → + K   **X.F.L.A.T.**

X.F.L.A.T. must be done from the air. Twelve does a repeating, quicker version of his D.R.A. move. It can hit an airborne opponent, although the damage is terrible. The only way to hit confirm this from the ground is to super jump cancel close stand forward kick and cancel into super immediately when in the air.

| 2 | -26 |

X.F.L.A.T. can OTG combo Hugo after Twelve's neutral throw if Hugo doesn't quick recover.

SUPER ART III

↓ ↘ → ↓ ↘ → + P   **X.C.O.P.Y.**

When Twelve activates X.C.O.P.Y., he morphs into his opponent for a limited amount of time. All of the morphed character's moves do 25% more damage than normal. Twelve also gains a 20% defensive boost as well. However, Twelve does not have access to their EX moves or super arts.

| — | — |

This is the reason not to use X.C.O.P.Y. Many characters are very dependant on their supers and EX moves. Although, it can be argued that almost any character has better offensive options than Twelve, so morphing actually helps Twelve in this way. When the timer runs out, Twelve morphs back into his original form. During his retransformation period, he takes an extremely high amount of damage if hit. Akuma for instance, can kill Twelve during this time with one move.

Recommended Super Art: X.N.D.L.

None of Twelve's super arts stand out as being terribly good. X.C.O.P.Y. can be OK against certain opponents. X.N.D.L. is Twelve's only super that actually helps him out in a reasonable way. X.N.D.L. can be comboed into for decent damage, considering Twelve doesn't really have very many combos to begin with. Twelve will probably get the most use out of his two stocks of meter by using it for EX moves. EX N.D.L. and EX D.R.A. are both good, and generally safe moves. Use both of these moves to help score a knock down. Then, get in close and score a hit, and try to verify a combo into X.N.D.L.

COMBOS YOU NEED TO KNOW

3 HITS

TOTAL DAMAGE: 13

↓ + LK → A.X.E.

Twelve's only low hitting non super art combo.

3 HITS

TOTAL DAMAGE: 22

CORNER ONLY

EX N.D.L from sweep-distance away, juggle with HK

Position specific juggle off of EX N.D.L.

8 HITS

TOTAL DAMAGE: 39

↓ + LK → A.X.E. → X.N.D.L.

Twelve's only low hitting super art combo

19 HITS

TOTAL DAMAGE: 69

MK SUPER JUMP CANCELED INTO VERY EARLY X.F.L.A.T.

Twelve's only option for comboing X.F.L.A.T. High Damage. Extremely difficult to do, not recommended.

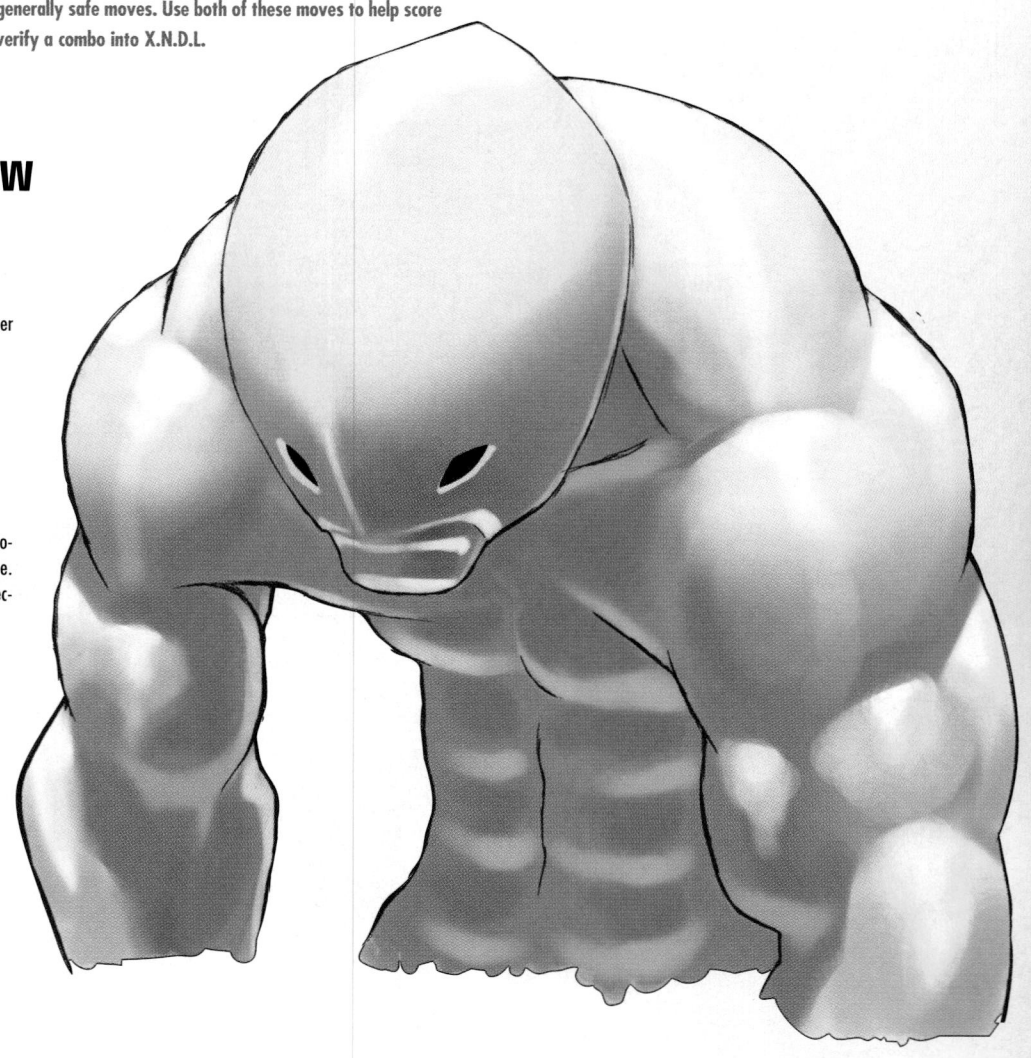

STRATEGY

S.J.A.

Twelve can only really do two things: poke and throw. Outside of a super art, he has virtually zero combo potential. Because of this, Twelve has no real way to punish anything significantly. This is really bad for Twelve, because opponents will have no fear of doing random Shouryukens, supers, or anything else that can hit for big damage and knock Twelve out of the air. What would normally be a big risk maneuver is actually in your interest against Twelve. His lack of punishment ability tips the risk/reward ratio into the favor of high risk paying off. Twelve is likely to be hit by random anti-airs and supers all the time, and there is not a whole lot Twelve can do about it.

Since Twelve can do nothing more than poke and throw, he doesn't have a very good close up game. Add to this the fact that his only verifiable ways to combo into super can both be parried low, why would he want to get close. When Twelve is on the ground, low forward is his best poke. Use it often. Against taller characters, use LP a lot to keep them grounded.

Twelve can take advantage of his air dash flight capabilities to form some sort of offensive game. Twelve's maneuverability is his strong point. He can fly in, poke or throw, do a little damage, then fly away, do a random N.D.L., fly back in, poke or throw, get any piece of damage he can, fly away, and repeat. Essentially, you want to fly around back and forth being annoying and scoring little bits of damage here and there. That is the best you can hope for.

There are some tricks Twelve can utilize to help him score those little hits. Twelve can air dash really low to the ground by inputting the first command of the air dash as you jump. From the ground, tap ↗, ↗, and as soon as Twelve gets in the air he will begin to fly. From this low height, you can cancel the dash into an air HK that will bring Twelve back to the ground really quickly. It is like performing a quick low jump. You can use this travel across the screen really quickly at a very low altitude. Use the speed of this trick to get in close and either throw immediately, or take advantage of the fact that they are probably still blocking high and do ↓ + LK → A.X.E. (LP) → X.N.D.L. This is one of the few good ways to land that combo.

If you are air dashing towards an opponent from far away, cancel into jumping HP to hit them at a distance. HP covers a lot of distance and can keep opponents away. Land then air dash back. If you do the low air dash trick to dash back, after you land immediately EX N.D.L. This will hit many characters who try to dash up and follow Twelve. Another good option when you land from an air dash is to HK. If you are near the opponent and they jump, use an HP them as they ascend. If you air dash in from medium range, cancel into jumping LP. The LP hits from high up and usually gives Twelve frame advantage when he lands. Use this opportunity to throw. If your opponent jumps while you are air dashing, cancel into jumping MP. This poke comes out fast and has great range.

At times when you air dash in pretty close, hit them with jumping HK, and when you land, do close stand forward kick and super jump cancel back into the air. From there you have many options. A tricky maneuver is to super jump cancel and jump backwards, then air dash forward again and cancel into HK immediately. The HK will whiff and you will land right back next to them really quickly. Use this opportunity to quickly throw, or do ↓ + LK → A.X.E. (LP) → X.N.D.L. This works really well against a cornered opponent.

Twelve's HP is great anti-air. You can hit opponents on the way up, at the height of their jump, or as they are coming down. Mix it up to discourage parries. Another good way to mess with parry attempts is to use LP as anti-air. If they parry, cancel into EX N.D.L. The parry timing for this is tricky, and if it hits, you can juggle with HK. Twelve's safest anti-air is to walk under his opponents and throw. His walking animation is so low to the ground that he almost never gets hit by cross ups. You can also use his walk to go under most projectiles.

WAKEUP GAME

If you score a knockdown, it is usually from a throw or EX N.D.L., so they will be sent flying across the screen. This is a good setup for a cross up. Super jump up and air dash towards them. Cancel into jumping HK to cross them up as they get up. Land and do ↓ + LK → A.X.E. (LP) → X.N.D.L.

When Twelve is the one getting up, his options are rather limited. ↓ + LP → A.X.E. (LP) comes out fast and pushes them away a bit. But if it is blocked you're in trouble. Twelve doesn't have any high priority moves to deal with this type of situation. Try not to get knocked down and cornered. If you do, you might have to resort to parrying.

SETUPS

Ranges setups for UOH → super art

Against small and medium sized characters:

(↓ + LK, ↓ + LK), UOH → X.N.D.L.

RESETS

Reset 1: In the corner if you hit your opponent with an EX N.D.L., juggle them with LP to reset them, then UOH. You can set up the distance perfectly to link X.N.D.L. after the UOH.

PARRY SETUPS AND TACTICS

When Twelve is air dashing in, he often does jump LP, lands, and throws. Before throwing, try to tap forward. This way, if they tried to poke you with a mid level attack, you will parry and then throw them. If they did nothing, you will throw them as well. This is a good option select tactic to help Twelve when he is close.

GROUND CROSS UPS

Twelve can cross up Hugo in any corner.

FAVORABLE MATCH UP: CHUN-LI

Chun-Li is one of the strongest characters in the game; one hit can lead to over 50% damage. Twelve is one of the weakest characters in the game, even his biggest combo only does around 35% damage, and it is hard to actually land. So how does Twelve beat Chun-Li? From the air. Twelve's unique (an arguably bad) style of poke and run away tactics actually are effective against Chun-Li. Twelve can attack Chun-Li repeatedly from the air because of her lack of any anti-air moves. And when Twelve is running away and flying across the screen, it is very hard for Chun-Li to catch him. The more time Twelve spends in the air, the less chance there is that he will ever get hit by Chun-Li's deadly low forward → Houyokusen.

This is by no means a free win for Twelve. Twelve always has to be careful. Chun-Li only needs to land two hits to essentially secure a win. Twelve on the other hand has to land numerous hits. If Chun-Li blocks or gets hit by Twelve's HK, she can super the recovery from half screen. If Twelve can avoid Chun-Li's low forward, and keep attacking safely from the air, then he can defeat one of the game's most deadly characters.

UNFAVORABLE MATCH UP: KEN

Twelve vs. Ken is one of the hardest match ups in the game. Twelve has pretty much no ground game against Ken. The best he can do is try to punish whiffed low forwards or roundhouses with his own low forward. The air isn't much better. Ken's Shouryukens can stop Twelve's air dash attack. Twelve also has to be weary of random jump EX Tatsumaki Senpuu Kyakus. Twelve has to get airborne to get his pokes in, but against Ken, this just isn't possible. Twelve is wide open every time he goes in the air. Twelve has no high damaging combos to punish whiffed high risk moves, so Ken is free to be as random as he wants with Shouryuken and Tatsumaki Senpuu Kyaku. This can be really hard for Twelve to deal with.

For Twelve to win this match up, he has to play perfectly. Attacking during air dashes is going to have to be kept to a minimum. Any poke can be beat by a Shouryuken. Low jump short air dashes and a lot of throws are going to be your main tools. Cancel an air dash and try to bait our Shouryukens that miss, and then do as much damage as you can. This win will not come easily.

Urien

NORMAL MOVES

STANDING

HP goes over some low attacks at the right range.

HK is a slow overhead kick that moves Urien's body back slightly. Can be used to avoid and punish throws at point blank range.

LP		Jab
START UP	4	CS
+3	+3	+3	SC
			SA
GUARD	H/L
PARRY	H/L

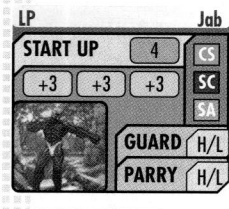

MP		Strong
START UP	5	CS
0	+1	+2	SC
			SA
GUARD	H/L
PARRY	H

HP		Fierce
START UP	10	CS
-3	-1	+1	SC
			SA
GUARD	H/L
PARRY	H

LK		Short
START UP	5	CS
+2	+2	+2	SC
			SA
GUARD	H/L
PARRY	H/L

MK		Forward
START UP	8	CS
-4	-3	-2	SC
			SA
GUARD	H/L
PARRY	H

HK		Roundhouse
START UP	17	CS
-7	-5	-3	SC
			SA
GUARD	H
PARRY	H

CROUCHING

↓ + HP as anti-air. Also Juggle set up, Urien's main opening for combos and big damage. Terrible recovery however, very unsafe if blocked. Use only when it's guaranteed.

↓ + MK has good range, speed, and recovery. Ok whiff punisher. Overall good poke in general.

↓ + HK is a sweep with amazing range. It can punish whiffed moves if it is done early.

↓ + LP		Low Jab
START UP	4	CS
+1	+1	+1	SC
			SA
GUARD	H/L
PARRY	H/L

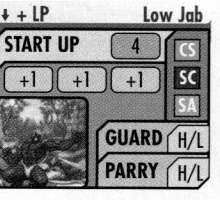

↓ + MP		Low Strong
START UP	11	CS
-2	-1	0	SC
			SA
GUARD	H/L
PARRY	H/L

↓ + HP		Low Fierce
START UP	9	CS
-10	D	D	SC
			SA
GUARD	H/L
PARRY	H/L

↓ + LK		Low Short
START UP	5	CS
+1	+1	+1	SC
			SA
GUARD	L
PARRY	L

↓ + MK		Low Forward
START UP	7	CS
0	+1	+2	SC
			SA
GUARD	H/L
PARRY	H/L

↓ + HK		Low Roundhouse
START UP	12	CS
-13	D	D	SC
			SA
GUARD	H/L
PARRY	H/L

THROWS

LP + LK	Destroy Claw

←/→ + LP + LK	Spartan Bomb

JUMPING

Jumping HK is an overall great jump in. Good damage, great range, average priority.

↑ + LP		Jumping Jab
START UP	4	CS
			SC
			SA
GUARD	H
PARRY	H

↑ + MP		Jumping Strong
START UP	6	CS
			SC
			SA
GUARD	H
PARRY	H

↑ + HP		Jumping Fierce
START UP	7	CS
			SC
			SA
GUARD	H
PARRY	H

↑ + LK		Jumping Short
START UP	4	CS
			SC
			SA
GUARD	H
PARRY	H

↑ + MK		Jumping Forward
START UP	6	CS
			SC
			SA
GUARD	H
PARRY	H

↑ + HK	Jumping Roundhouse
START UP	10	CS
			SC
			SA
GUARD	H
PARRY	H

SPECIAL NORMALS

→ + MP		Quarrel Punch
START UP	9	-3

Can be used as anti-air against frontal jump ins. Use it at the end of juggles to start a reset set up.

→ + HP		Terrible Smash
START UP	14	-6

Great overhead. Very fast. Extremely useful to land hits that lead to large combos while they are in block stun with an Aegis Reflector on top of them.

→ + MK		Quarrel Kick
START UP	16	-2

Lunging Kick with great range. Moves Urien very far forward while attacking. Use during foot games because it's hard for your opponent to make this attack whiff. Also important for Aegis Reflector unblockable setups.

COSTUMES

SPECIAL MOVES

↓ ↘ → + P — Metallic Sphere

14	14	14	15
-8	-4	+3	-16

Juggle set up if it hits as anti-air / projectile with slow recovery. Button strength determines what direction the projectile flies it. The MP and HP versions of this attack fly upward at an angle, can by used as anti-air if thrown early against anticipated jumps. If it hits as anti-air Urien can go into extended juggles for massive damage. The EX version travels slower and hits twice, but has even more recovery then the original.

Charge ↓ ↑ + P — Dangerous Headbutt

7	9	12	9
-2	-3	-6	+2

Juggle set up / leaping headbutt. Whiffs on crouching characters, however the recovery is still rather fast and hard to react to. Can sort of be useful for throw set ups. Helpful for setting up Aegis Reflector unblockable set ups. The EX version hits twice and puts your opponent into a juggle set up. Good for extended juggles.

Charge ← → + K — Chariot Tackle

7	10	13	6
-10	-11	-12	-9

Juggle set up if it hits as anti-air / Fast shoulder tackle with fast recovery. Great for extended juggle combos off of his ↓ + HP or anti-air Metallic Sphere. Also a good overall move for pressure and zoning. The EX version is faster, hits twice, and has a slight frame advantage after it that you can use to link after with a Tyrant Slaughter.

Charge ↓ ↑ + K — Violence Knee Drop

24	24	25	26
-18	-18	-18	-16

Flying knee drop. Helpful for initiating Aegis Reflector unblockable setups. The HK version can be helpful for getting out of a corner. The EX version hits twice and tracks your opponent, which can hit them from anywhere on screen.

COMBOS YOU NEED TO KNOW

3 HITS

TOTAL DAMAGE: 20

↓ + LP, ↓ + LP → Dangerous Headbutt (LP)

Urien's only safe and verifiable combo without a super. Whiffs on crouching characters however. Only do it if they are standing. Honestly not all that useful. Knocks down.

4 HITS

TOTAL DAMAGE: 26

↓ + LP, ↓ + LP → EX Chariot Tackle

Verifiable. Not so great damage, but it is safe.

7 HITS

TOTAL DMAAGE: 56

EX Chariot Tackle linked into an immediate Tyrant Slaughter

Ok combo if you happen to hit with a random EX Chariot Tackle

7 HITS

TOTAL DAMAGE: 62

↓ + LP, ↓ + LP → Tyrant Slaughter

Flexible and verifiable. Ok damage. Knocks down.

8 HITS

TOTAL DAMAGE: 61

LP, LP → MP → Tyrant Slaughter

Verifiable. Whiffs on most crouching characters. Knocks down.

5 HITS

TOTAL DAMAGE: 50

↓ + HP for 2 hits, juggle with an early EX Dangerous Headbutt, when Urien recovers, juggle again with Dangerous Headbutt (HP)

Good mid screen option for punishment situations. Knocks down

6 HITS

TOTAL DAMAGE: 64

MUST BE DONE MID SCREEN OR CLOSE TO A CORNER

↓ + HP for 2 hits, juggle with and early Chariot Tackle (MK), when able, juggle with an early EX Chariot Tackle, when Urien recovers immediately juggle with a Chariot Tackle (HK)

Damaging anti-air option. Also good in punishment situations. Knocks down.

10 HITS TOTAL DAMAGE: 61

↓ + HP for 2 hits, immediately juggle with an EX Dangerous Headbutt, then juggle with a early Chariot Tackle (HK) → Jupiter Thunder

Easy way to land Jupiter Thunder mid screen in punishment situations or as anti-air. Knocks down.

15 HITS

TOTAL DAMAGE: 85

↓ + HP for 1 hit → Chariot Tackle (HK) → Aegis Reflector (LP), immediately do a Chariot Tackle (HK) when Urien recovers, then while they are still being hit by Aegis Reflector, link a ↓ + HP, juggle with an early Chariot Tackle (MK), juggle with an immediate Metallic Sphere (MP), juggle again with a Charriot Tackle (MK), then finally juggle again with semi early HP.

Complicated Aegis Reflector combo. Does massive damage. Only works against Chun Li, Necro, Q, Elena, Makoto, and Twelve. Knocks down, allowing you to start an Aegis Reflector unblockable pattern again.

11 HITS

TOTAL DAMAGE: 76

MUST BE DONE MID SCREEN OR CLOSE TO A CORNER

MP → EX Dangerous Headbutt, juggle with a late EX Chariot Tackle, juggle again with an early Chariot Tackle (HK) → Jupiter Thunder

Does massive stun damage. Only good for punishment situations. Knocks down.

URIEN

SUPER ARTS

SUPER ART I

↓ ↘ → ↓ ↘ → + P　　　　　　　　　**Tyrant Punish**

Urien does 5 consecutive Chariot Tackles for good damage. A very basic super. Urien can cancel it easily from his LP, MP target chain, ↓ + LP x2, as well as from any Chariot Tackle. Use Chariot Tackles to attack from long distances and punish whiffs, and cancel into Tyrant Punish if one connects. Urien can also link into Tyrant

| 1 | -17 |

Punish after an EX Chariot Rush or Jumping HK. Jumping HK has really long reach and a long enough hit stun to allow Urien to attack from almost any height and still have time to link the super when he lands.

With 2 stocks of super meter, Urien is free to use EX moves for his big damage juggles. Tyrant Punish gives Urien big combo opportunities that his other super arts can't supply. An all around decent super.

SUPER ART II

↓ ↘ → ↓ ↘ → + P　　　　　　　　　**Jupiter Thunder**

Urien charges up to throw a giant projectile towards his opponent. It does good damage and has combo possibilities. It can be used to finish off many of Urien's long juggle combos. It does a lot of stun damage. Urien can easily stun Remy or Akuma with Jupiter Thunder at the end

| 1 | -36 |

of a juggle. Jupiter Thunder may be the super art of choice against Akuma because of his ability to teleport out of Aegis Reflector setups.

Recommended Super Art:
Aegis Reflector

All of Urien's super arts can lead to big damage if he has clean openings, but only Aegis Reflector can put immense pressure on opponents when they are blocking and lead to big damage without initially landing the super. With the addition of unblockable, and high/low mix-up setups, Aegis Reflector is clearly Urien's most useful super art. It can be used in almost any situation to inflict some damage on your opponent.

TARGET COMBOS

| **LP → MP** | 4 |
| Verifiable way to land a Tyrant Slaughter. Whiffs against most crouching characters though. Not very useful. | 0 |

| **QUARREL PUNCH → HP** | 9 |
| First hit whiffs against crouching characters, so it has limited usefulness. | -6 |

SUPER ART III

↓ ↘ → ↓ ↘ → + P　　　　　　　　　**Aegis Reflector**

Urien sends out a wall in front of him that can hit up to 6 times and reflect projectiles. The button pressed determines how far the reflector initially travels. After that, it has a homing feature, moving either forward or backwards from its initial position toward the opponent. Urien

| 12 / 24 / 32 / 1 |
| — |

can also press two punch buttons for a variation of the reflector that comes out almost instantly right in front of him, although higher than the normal reflectors. With this variation's frame start up, Urien can combo into this reflector after a UOH or after his neutral throw on some characters, and even after ↓ + LP x2 in the corner.

Aegis Reflector is a very complicated super. It doesn't do very much damage by itself, but it has the potential to be used in an almost unlimited number of ways to produce high damage combos, unblockable and ambiguous setups, and big damage off of overhead and low attacks. Urien can even use Aegis Reflector for the purpose of canceling his special moves to recover faster so he can add on a few more hits to the end of a juggle.

The most basic use of Aegis Reflector is to combo into it and allow the reflector to do some damage before starting a juggle with ↓ + HP. This can be easily done in the corner after a Chariot Tackle. Cancel into a Aegis Reflector (LP) , then simply launch them with ↓ + HP after the last hit of the reflector. In mid screen, if you can hit them into the reflector behind them, the reflector will bounce them back towards you. Continue to keep hitting them in to the reflector until Aegis Reflector runs out, then launch them with ↓ + HP and continue to combo them.

It usually is difficult for Urien to connect with ↓ + HP or a Chariot Tackle in order to combo into Aegis Reflector Directly. Urien usually has to resort to trying to do damage with Aegis Reflector indirectly. Chariot Tackle into your opponent, and even if they block, activate an Aegis Reflector. At this point, you can either do a low move, an overhead attack, or try to throw them. Hit them with any of these, and they will bounce into the Aegis Reflector. You may then possibly have the ability to hit them again while they are caught in the Aegis Reflector. This is especially useful in the corner. After an overhead or low attack, Urien has enough time to recover from his move and launch his opponent with ↓ + HP before the Aegis Reflector runs out. An overhead or low attack can lead to a big juggle for a lot of damage.

Aegis Reflector can be used to set up an unblockable scenario for Urien's opponent. Hit your opponent from the front while Aegis Reflector hits them from behind. If the hit boxes of the two moves overlap, then it creates a situation where your opponent cannot block. This makes Aegis Reflector extremely lethal. The only way to escape from an unblockable setup is to parry correctly, or execute a move with enough invulnerability to move out of the way of it. After landing an unblockable hit into Aegis Reflector, Urien usually has enough time to launch his opponent with ↓ + HP to continue with an air juggle for a ton of damage.

STRATEGY

Elbow

Urien has the potential to do a ton of damage and a lot of stun if he can land one of his long juggles. The problem is that it's hard to land his juggles straight up. ↓ + HP comes out slow, so it's only useful for punishment situations. Urien can't rely on ↓ + HP to get his damage. He has to use his Aegis Reflector to create openings to knock away at an opponents life bar and possibly trick them and land a juggle and possibly set up an unblockable Aegis Reflector. Urien is at such an advantage when he activates Aegis Reflector. The opponent usually can't attack while Urien is pressuring with Aegis Reflector. So Urien wants to fight with an Aegis Reflector on his opponent whenever possible.

Urien should play defensively when he doesn't have meter. He doesn't have a lot of high damaging offensive options that are safe. His Chariot Tackle is not safe if blocked, so it is hard to get in. It's better to stay back and charge your super meter. Whiff a lot of MPs to build your meter, and try to keep your opponent away from you as best you can. Poke with ↓ + MK, and keep charging your meter with MPs.

When you have enough meter for an Aegis Reflector, it is now safe to rush in and attack. Hit them with a Chariot Tackle to get in and cancel into Aegis Reflector. Canceling into this move gives Urien frame advantage when he recovers so it is safe to Chariot Tackle at any time if you have meter. If they block the Chariot Tackle, you have a lot of mix up options to try to land some damage. The most basic options are to either do an overhead attack, hit them low, or throw and bounce them into the Aegis Reflector to set up a juggle. At mid-screen the damage you can get off of a blocked Aegis Reflector setup is ok, but ideally you want to get them into the corner first. If they block and you activate a Aegis Reflector (LP) in the corner, any hit you connect with will allow you to launch them with ↓ + HP before the Aegis Reflector runs out. You can land a huge juggle and possibly set up an unblockable Aegis Reflector setup if you have enough meter. If your opponent blocks the Aegis Reflector and all of your mixups, simply dash back and start charging your meter again with MPs. Urien is a better character with an Aegis Reflector on screen to help him out. There is no reason to put yourself at risk when you can just run away for a little bit until you can activate it again.

↓ + HP is good as anti-air and sets Urien up for his big juggle combos and unblockable setups. It is a bit slow, so it tends to get beat by early jump attacks. Jumping back HK is another really good anti-air tactic.

WAKEUP GAME

Urien has many tricks he can do if he lands a knockdown while Aegis Reflector is out. Urien's dash is really good, and can dash through a lot of characters if they quick recover. He can use this to set up unblockable Aegis Reflector situations or to just confuse his opponents and hit them into it while they aren't blocking. Urien can also take advantage of charge partitioning to dash up quickly and do a Dangerous Headbutt over their fallen body to hit them from behind into the Aegis Reflector.

After knocking them down in the corner, there is no need to wait until they get up and Chariot Rush → Aegis Reflector. They could potentially parry this. Just activate a Aegis Reflector (LP) over their fallen body and let them wake up right into it. Try to hit them with an overhead or low attack and then launch them with ↓ + HP if it hits. If Urien doesn't have enough meter for an Aegis Reflector, he isn't going to be that much of a threat to a waking up opponent, so Urien is as risk to wakeup moves. Urien might want to back off and try to build up his meter before attacking again. Mid-screen jump HKs are good and fairly safe because of its long range. Urien just needs to annoy his opponent and keep them away for a little bit until he has his meter again, then he can charge in and active Aegis Reflector.

When Urien is the one getting up, he has a nice wakeup move in his Dangerous Headbutt. The LP version comes out fast and is generally safe. If it whiffs completely though Urien is vulnerable. ↓ + LP is also a pretty good poke up close. ↓ + LP → Dangerous Heatbutt (LP) is a fairly safe option to do as well to try to knock someone away from close range.

SETUPS

ADVANCED SETUPS: UNBLOCKABLE AEGIS REFLECTOR SETUPS

Setup 1: After a throw, immediately activate a Aegis Reflector (LP) . During the super freeze charge down, and do a Dangerous Heatbutt (HP) as soon as the action resumes to go over your grounded opponent's body. As soon as they get up, hit them with a Quarrel Kick to push them into the Aegis Reflector. The kick overlaps the Aegis Reflector and will be unblockable. As soon as you recover, launch them with ↓ + HP. This is a very basic setup. Your opponent can escape by quick recovering the initial throw.

Setup 2: Connect with ↓ + HP and juggle with a Chariot Tackle (LK) Cancel into a Aegis Reflector (HP) and charge during the super freeze. Immediately Chariot Tackle (HK) to juggle again. Charge down during the Chariot Tackle. Hesitate for a split second, then Violence Knee Drop (HK) to get to the other side of your opponent. Dash up twice to push your opponent towards the reflector while they are on the ground. Immediately hit them with a Quarrel Kick to push them into the Aegis Reflector and cause an unblockable situation. Hit them with ↓ + HP and juggle. If you have enough meter and are still positioned mid screen you can repeat the setup for another unblockable Aegis Reflector combo. This setup is really good because when the second Chariot Tackle hits, it pushes your opponent into the Aegis Reflector as the last juggle hit, thereby disallowing them to quick recover and escape this setup. The timing and spacing varies slightly on the characters this setup works on.

Setup 3: In the corner, juggle with a Chariot Tackle and cancel into Aegis Reflector (LP) . Walk backwards and charge, then do a Chariot Tackle (HK) to move your opponent back into the corner without hitting them. Charge down during the Chariot Tackle. Do a Violence Knee Drop (HK) to hit your opponent right as they wakeup. This will cause an unblockable situation and they will get hit by the Aegis Reflector. Land and launch them with ↓ + HP. Repeat from the start if you have enough meter. You can do multiple Chariot Tackles to increase the damage. You can set this up with a ↓ + HP or anti-air Metallic Sphere or any other means to juggle them. Another good way to set this up is after a blocked Aegies Reflector in the corner. Try to hit them with either a UOH or low attack, then ↓ +

HP to juggle and begin the setup from there.

Setup 4: Here is a setup that works on the smaller characters of the cast. Connect with a ↓ + HP, then juggle with a Chariot Tackle (LP) and cancel into a Aegis Reflector (HP). Dash back and do a whiffed ↓ + HP as a timing device. Then Violence Knee Drop (HK) to get close. Charge during the Knee Drop so you can immediately Dangerous Headbutt (HP) over their body. ↓ + LK when you land to set up an unblockable Aegis Reflector hit. Then ↓ + HP to launch them and finish them off with your favorite juggle.

ADVANCED TACTIC 1: OVERLAPPING CHARGE TIMES

Urien does a lot of damage off of his juggle combos. In the corner he can juggle with up to 4 Chariot Tackles in most situations. The timing is really strict to get 4 Chariot Tackles. You can give yourself some help by overlapping their charge times. The idea is simple: start charging for the next Chariot Tackle before you even execute the first one. Charge back for the first Chariot Tackle, and once you have a charge, press towards, then back and press kick. The 3rd Strike game engine gives you a lot of leeway to coordinate joystick motions and button presses, so you don't have to press the kick button exactly when you press toward. With this method, when you press kick after pressing back, you have already started charging for the next Chariot Tackle. This should give you sufficient time to full charge for your next Chariot Tackle so you can keep the juggle going. Do this for all your charges to cut down on the charge time.

ADVANCED TACTIC 2: CHARGE PARTITIONING

Urien has many charge moves that can take advantage of charge partitioning. The idea is pretty simple; split up the charge time of a charge move into pieces. In between the charges you are free to move around or do moves. Just make sure you don't wait too long before continuing the charge. As long as you haven't fully charged, you can keep partitioning the charge.

Urien can set up a lot of unblockable Aegis Reflector setups with the use of charge partitioning. Often times Urien will knock his opponent down while Aegis Reflector is out. He needs to get on the other side of his opponent so he can hit them into Aegis Reflector from the back. Usually the quickest way for Urien to move is by dashing. With charge partitioning, Urien can charge a little bit, then dash and complete the charge during the dash so by the time he gets next to his opponent he can quickly Dangerous Headbutt over their body and be all set to hit his opponent into an unblockable setup.

Urien doesn't have to wait until he has Aegis Reflector out there to make use of charge partitioning. Urien's dash is really fast, so dash up and throw is a really good tactic. You can trick opponents by dashing up next to them, and doing a Dangerous Headbutt immediately after the dash. If they tried to counter throw you, they will get hit by your tricky maneuver. Hide your charges in dashes and other moves and then surprise your opponent with a charge move when they least expect it.

RANGES SETUPS FOR UOH → SUPER ART

Against small, medium and wide sized characters:

(↓ + LP x2), UOH → Tyrant Punish
(↓ + MK), UOH → Tyrant Punish

RESETS

Reset 1: If you land a Chariot Tackle juggle in the corner, you can reset your opponent with a MP and immediately cancel into Jupiter Thunder. Jupiter Thunder comes out so quickly that it is extremely hard to react to and parry. It will start a new juggle combo and do massive stun damage. You can use this to set up an instant dizzy that leads to almost 100% life on shotos. If you land an EX Dangerous Headbutt against an opponent in the corner, juggle with 2 Chariot Tackle (LP)s, then hit them with MP → Jupiter Thunder. This will dizzy a shoto. Finish them off with a jump in HK, ↓ + HP, and juggle with Chariot Tackles and cancel into another Jupiter Thunder if you have enough meter.

PARRY SETUPS AND TACTICS

When Urien does a wakeup Dangerous Headbutt, it might whiff on some couching characters. The move comes out fast and is hard to react to. A down parry in this situation might just catch an opponent's attempt to punish your whiff. This could be the opening Urien needs to land his deadly ↓ + HP and start a juggle combo or unblockable Aegis setup.

GROUND CROSS UPS

Urien can cross up Twelve, Hugo, and Necro in any corner.

Urien can cross up Yun, Yang, Dudley Chun-Li mid screen after a juggle that ends with a Dangerous Headbutt.

FAVORABLE MATCH UP: HUGO

Hugo is really tall. Urien can use this to his advantage and really annoy and frustrate Hugo with high Metallic Spheres. Hugo cannot walk under them. Urien can keep Hugo away for a long time and build up his meter at the same time. Keep him away with Metallic Spheres, and only attack when you have meter. Charge in and activate Aegis Reflector and get as much damage as you can. After that, dash back, throw some more high Metallic Spheres, and build your super meter up again. Urien should have an easy time keeping Hugo away. Only get close to him when you are ready to activate Aegis Reflector. Play it safe against Hugo, and a victory should be easily within your reach.

UNFAVORABLE MATCH UP: KEN

Urien wants to keep characters away until he has meter for Aegis Reflector. Urien will have a hard time trying to keep Ken away. Urien cannot use his ↓ + MK at all against Ken. Ken's crouching MK will always beat Urien's. Ken can buffer supers safely from a half screen away with his low forward and connect with Shippu-Jinrai-Kyaku on any hit. Ken also has a great super jump cross up with his jumping forward and EX air hurricane kick. Urien just has to deal with the fact that Ken is going to get close and try to prevent him from charging his meter.

For Urien to win, he has to play smart. Don't ever ↓ + MK first. If you see Ken stick out a low foward, then it's ok to ↓ + MK him back. If you want to stick out pokes to try to keep Ken away, stick out standing MK. This will do a good job of stopping Ken from mindlessly zoning with low MK. When Ken crosses you up, just block and wait it out. If he does anything other than his MP, HP chain or ↓ + LK x2 immediately, then he is probably going for some sort of tick set up. Try to Dangerous Headbutt (LP) him between hits and knock him down. Get your meter, and activate Aegis Reflector, and just play Urien's game. This match will be tougher than most, but if Urien can keep getting meter for Aegis Reflector, he will chip away at Ken's lifebar bit by bit.

Yang

NORMAL MOVES

STANDING

HP has good range and deals decent damage. Use it to beat anticipated attacks early at close range.

MK is an upward kick with that covers quite a bit of area. Good in anticipation to jumps at a close range. Hits most crouching characters.

HK has ridiculous range, usually greater than any opponent's best poke range, and still hits most crouching opponents. Also good against anticipated jumps from further away, must be done early in this case, however.

LP		Jab
START UP		3
+4	+4	+4
GUARD		H/L
PARRY		H/L

LK		Short
START UP		3
+2	+2	+2
GUARD		H/L
PARRY		H/L

MP		Strong
START UP		5
-2	-1	0
GUARD		H/L
PARRY		

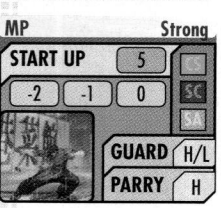

MK		Forward
START UP		9
-4	-3	-2
GUARD		H/L
PARRY		H

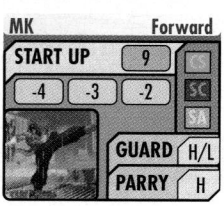

HP		Fierce
START UP		9
-5	-3	-1
GUARD		H/L
PARRY		H

HK		Roundhouse
START UP		14
-8	-6	-4
GUARD		H/L
PARRY		H

STANDING CLOSE

Close MP is Yang's best close mid-level attack. It has a decent amount of frame advantage after it, allowing Yang verify and combo with LK → EX Tourou Zan. If MP is blocked, walk up Zenpou Tenshin, ↓ + LK (x2) → EX Tourou Zan, or universal overhead linked into LK → EX Tourou Zan are all good patterns in this situation.

Close MK is a super jump cancelable kick that launches. Use it as anti-air or a safe mid-level attack on wake up. Whether or not it hits, you can cancel the attack into a super jump, allowing you to juggle after it. If it's blocked, follow up the failed attack with one of Yang's many Raigeki Shuu patterns.

LP		Close Jab
START UP		3
+4	+4	+4
GUARD		H/L
PARRY		H/L

LK		Close Short
START UP		3
+2	+2	+2
GUARD		H/L
PARRY		H/L

MP		Close Strong
START UP		4
+6	+7	+8
GUARD		H/L
PARRY		H

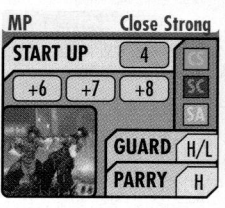

MK		Close Forward
START UP		7
-8	D	D
GUARD		H/L
PARRY		H

HP		Close Fierce
START UP		5
+2	+1	0
GUARD		H/L
PARRY		H

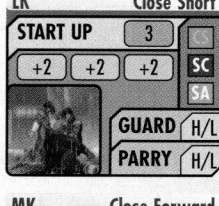

HK		Close Roundhouse
START UP		14
-8	-6	-4
GUARD		H/L
PARRY		H

COSTUMES

SPECIAL NORMALS

→ + MK		Sepnuu Kyaku
START UP	19	-1

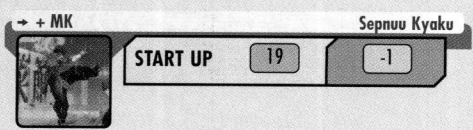

Fairly fast command overhead with good range. Can be done from rather unexpected ranges for passable damage.

While jumping, ↘ + K		Raigeki Shuu
START UP	6	—

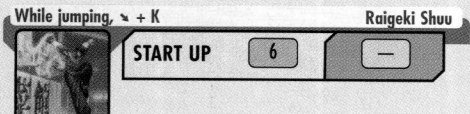

A diving kick with a steep angle. Button strength controls Yang's angle of descent. Yang's game revolves around this attack. Use it to get close quickly after a successful knock down. It can be used in an offensive manner to get close and stay on top of opponents. Depending on how close this move is done and how high up the move is blocked, the Raigeki Shuu can carry varying frame advantages or disadvantages. It's important to learn to pick the right kick strength so that this move hits late. Also, because of the varying angles, it's possible to use Raigeki Shuu to set up high/low/throw guessing games by whiffing a Raigeki Shuu, landing, throwing, or going straight into ↓ + LK (x2), or not whiffing it at all, making it hit extremely deep, which hits high. If a deep Raigeki Shuu is blocked, Yang has a slight frame advantage to work with to start a mix-up game.

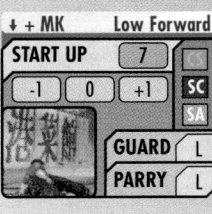

CROUCHING

↓ + LK (x2) is the opening to Yang's most useful combo: ↓ + LK (x2) → EX Tourou Zan. It is also one of the only safe ways to land super arts off of a low attack. Use it for set ups and guessing games like ↓ + LK, command throw, or ↓ + LK, MP, HP, ← + HP chain.

↓ + MK is Yang's only decent low poke. Although slow, use ↓ + MK → EX Tourou Zan to punish whiffs if done early. Also useful as anti-air because Yang's crouching hit box is so low.

↓ + HK is a sweep that moves Yang forward. Good for punishing whiffed attacks.

↓ + LP		Low Jab	
START UP		3	CS
+4	+4	+4	SC
			SA
GUARD			H/L
PARRY			H/L

↓ + LK		Low Short	
START UP		4	CS
+2	+2	+2	SC
			SA
GUARD			L
PARRY			L

↓ + MP		Low Strong	
START UP		5	CS
+2	+3	+4	SC
			SA
GUARD			L
PARRY			L

↓ + MK		Low Forward	
START UP		7	CS
-1	0	+1	SC
			SA
GUARD			L
PARRY			L

↓ + HP		Low Fierce	
START UP		8	CS
0	+1	+2	SC
			SA
GUARD			H/L
PARRY			H/L

↓ + HK		Low Roundhouse	
START UP		10	CS
-7	D	D	SC
			SA
GUARD			L
PARRY			L

JUMPING

↑ + LP		Jumping Jab	
START UP		2	CS
—	—	—	SC
			SA
GUARD			H
PARRY			H

↑ + LK		Jumping Short	
START UP		3	CS
—	—	—	SC
			SA
GUARD			H
PARRY			H

↑ + MP		Jumping Strong	
START UP		3	CS
—	—	—	SC
			SA
GUARD			H
PARRY			H

↑ + MK		Jumping Forward	
START UP		6	CS
—	—	—	SC
			SA
GUARD			H
PARRY			H

↑ + HP		Vertical Fierce	
START UP		8	CS
—	—	—	SC
			SA
GUARD			H
PARRY			H

↑ + HK		Jumping Roundhouse	
START UP		5	CS
—	—	—	SC
			SA
GUARD			H
PARRY			H

↗ / ↖ + HP		Jumping Fierce	
START UP		5	CS
—	—	—	SC
			SA
GUARD			H
PARRY			H

THROWS

LP + LK   Hiza Geri

→ + LP + LK   Youhon Shiun

← + LP + LK   Monkey Flip

SPECIAL MOVES

↓ ↘ → +P (up to 3 times; 5 for EX)   Tourou Zan

8	8	8	7
-1	-5	-9	-4

Yang's most important special attack at close ranges. Does good damage and knocks down. Each segment of the attack can be delayed slightly, meaning it's possible for Tourou Zan follow ups late after the previous Tourou Zan slash. This is good for tricking opponents into thinking you're going to retreat, stopping at one slash, allowing you to retaliate when opponents strike, thinking you're at a disadvantage. Because of the multiple hits, it's possible to verify a hit after ↓ + MK→Tourou Zan (LP) for 1 hit. The first hit of the LP version also has a slight frame advantage after it, allowing Yang stop at the first slash and mix-up with walk up throws. Because of the EX version's increased speed, it combos off ↓ + LK (x2), providing a flexible combo. The EX version is also a good whiff punisher. This attack alone makes Yang deadly at close ranges, an important move to his arsenal.

↓ ↙ ← + P   Byakko Soushouda

21	-3

Pressing two punches instead of one "fakes" the attack, cancelling just before the punch. Very slow start up, but extremely good priority because of its large hit box. Use from far away in anticipation against a jump in or an attack with range. Faking the move is useful in wake up or close range situations to bait a high parry, allowing you to land a ↓ + MK → Tourou Zan or walk up throw.

→ ↘ ↓ ↙ ← + K   Zenpou Tenshin

7	—

Command grab that switches sides with opponents and leaves them open for a combo, specifically ↓ + MK →Tourou Zan (HP / EX). This move can lead to major damage off of a throw. Has slightly more range than a normal throw.

↓ ↘ → + K   Senkyuutai

8	4	3	3
-25	-19	-16	-16

Button strength determines how far the roll travels before the kick segment. MK, HK and EX versions are a juggle set ups, (after MK or HK, use Tenshin-Senkyuutai, close MP, or LP). Use it to go under projectiles or close range combos. EX version travels further and faster while doing more damage.

→ ↓ ↘ + K   Kaihou

—	—

Kaihou travels varying distances depending on the button strength used. Although heavily open to attack on start up and recovery, this move is important when used in combination with Tourou Zan, as both the normal and EX versions of the Tourou Zan knock opponents fairly far away. Use LK or MK Kaihou to close distances and start another offensive pattern.

SUPER ARTS

SUPER ART I

↓ → ↓ → + P **Raishin-Mahhaken**

Raishin-Mahhaken is Yang's most damaging super art. It combos easily off of ↓ + MK, making it ideal for punishing whiffs. It provides a mid range poke that can lead to big damage. Raishin-Mahhaken is the only non-projectile super art in the game with frame advantage if blocked.

This allows Yang the freedom to be somewhat random with it if he chooses. As long as it makes contact, Yang cannot be hit back. Throwing out this super art randomly from time to time can make up for its limited combo ability. If opponents fear that Yang might use a super art on them at any moment, they might be more hesitant to throw out random pokes, or pressure Yang on wake up. Use this to your advantage to be more offensive and land more throws.

Raishin-Mahhaken only stocks one super meter, and the bar is very long. Be conservative with EX moves if you plan to have enough meter to land this move.

Recommended Super Art:
Tenshin-Senkyutai

Yang's EX Tourou Zan is too good to ignore. Tenshin-Senkyutai gives Yang the meter he needs to unleash an onslaught of EX slashes to keep on the offensive pressure. Tenshin-Senkyutai also gives Yang the option to verify a combo into super art from close range. With a short start up, it is able to punish many moves in their recovery as well. Tenshin-Senkyutai is an all around good super art for Yang.

TARGET COMBOS

LK → MK → HK	3
Quick three hit chain that does minor damage. It is easy and completely safe if blocked.	-4

MP → HP → ↓ + HP	5
Three hit chain with a super art cancelable last hit. Decent range and damage. Good way to land a Tenshin-Senkyutai off of a mid-level hit.	-5

JUMPING MK → ↘ + MK	6
Two hit air chain ending with Yang's Raigeki Shuu. This combo helps versus opponents that anti-air parry often.	—

SUPER ART II

↓ ↘ → ↓ ↘ → + K **Tenshin-Senkyutai**

Yang stocks of two super meter for Tenshin-Senkyutai. It combos nicely in a variety of situations because its homing properties. Yang rolls variable distances based on the location of opponents. It is good for rolling under projectiles from mid screen. Tenshin-Senkyutai easily combos behind MP, HP, ← + HP target chain, as well as ↓ + MK → Tenshin-Senkyutai, ↓ + LK (x2) → Tenshin-Senkyutai, ↓ + LP (x3) → Tenshin-Senkyutai, and links off of ↓ + MP.

Work to manage super meter to allow an assortment of EX moves along with Tenshin-Senkyutai. Selecting this super art could be used solely for the purpose of storing meter for EX moves.

COMBOS YOU NEED TO KNOW

4 HITS
TOTAL DAMAGE: 26

↓ + MK →Tourou Zan (LP)

Flexible low combo. The first slash of the Tourou Zan (LP) has a slight frame advantage after it. Verify a hit off of ↓ + MK → Tourou Zan. If it hits, finish the Tourou Zan command and combo the other two slashes. If it doesn't hit, either hesitate the follow up slashes to make it look like you're stopping the attack, then either execute delayed follow-ups or stop after the first slash, then ether walk up throw or ↓ + MK →Tourou Zan (MP).

7 HITS
TOTAL DAMAGE: 35

↓ + LK (x2) → EX Tourou Zan

Flexible, verifiable low combo. Very good damage. Knocks down. If ↓ + LK (x2) is blocked, Yang remains close, walk up throw, walk up ↓ + LK (x2) → EX Tourou Zan again, or immediately hit MP → HP.

7 HITS
TOTAL DAMAGE: 39

Close MP linked into LK → EX Tourou Zan

Flexible, verifiable combo of a mid level attack. Does good damage, knocks down.

4 HITS TOTAL DAMAGE: 31

EX Senkuutai, juggle with early close MP

Good for going under projectiles. It's possible to cancel MP into a Kaihou (LK) to teleport right directly next to opponents as they are flipping out of the LP, putting Yang into prime position to attack. ↓ + LK (x2) → EX Tourou Zan or Zenpou Tenshin linked into ↓ + MK → Tourou Zan are good in this situation.

4 HITS
TOTAL DAMAGE: 31

Close MK, juggle with immediate Senkyutai (MK), juggle again with LP

Okay as an early anti-air or after an anti-air parry.

2 HITS
TOTAL DAMAGE: 37
CORNER ONLY

Byakko Soushouda, juggle with an early HP

Simple high damage corner juggle. Not very useful, but the only decent option if Byakko Soushouda happens to hit while an opponent is cornered.

SUPER ART III

↓ ↘ → ↓ ↘ → + P **Seiei-Enbu**

Yang gains two shadows that mimic his moves with a slight delay. This allows Yang to recover while his shadows are attacking, allowing links to other attacks, meaning the combo can continue for the duration of Seiei-Enbu. As the Seiei-Enbu time runs out, it's possible to link one more combo that extends after the super art runs out.

Seiei-Enbu cannot be comboed into, so there are no guaranteed setups to land a Seiei-Enbu combo. The best way to use Seiei-Enbu is to activate it after scoring a knockdown. As opponents get up, mix up overhead, low, and cross up attacks to find an opening. Once you land that first hit, continue to combo until the super meter runs out. You must combo many Tourou Zans in order to keep Yang moving forward to stay in range. The inability to combo into Seiei-Enbu is its biggest limitation. If an opponent is able to react to all of the overhead attacks and cross ups, and blocks everything else low, Yang will not be able to initiate a combo. Yang's only other option is to grab them with Zenpou Tenshin in order to start the custom combo.

If you're able to land a cross up Raigeki Shuu while in Seiei-Enbu, go into a high/low pattern to make it difficult for opponents to block. After the Raigeki Shuu, land and use ↓ + MP, ↓ + HK. Yang hits them with ↓ + MP while his shadow is still hitting with a Raigeki Shuu up high. If you are able to knock down with ↓ + HK, Yang is in perfect position to super jump and cross up Raigeki Shuu again and repeat the sequence. Each knockdown resets the damage, so the damage potential of this confusion pattern is very high.

5 ~ 7 HITS
TOTAL DAMAGE: 26 ~ 30

Zenpou Tenshin linked into ↓ + MK → Tourou Zan (HP / EX)

Yang's most damaging options off Zenpou Tenshin. Use EX with sufficient super meter, or HP when there isn't.

9 HITS
TOTAL DAMAGE: 49

↓ + LK, ↓ + LK → Tenshin-Senkyutai

Flexible, verifiable way to land Tenshin-Senkyutai. Knocks down.

10 HITS
TOTAL DAMAGE: 47

MP → HP → ← + HP → Tenshin-Senkyutai

Verifiable way to land a Tenshin-Senkyutai. Knocks down.

9 HITS
TOTAL DAMAGE: 69

↓ + LK, ↓ + LK → Raishin Maha Ken

Flexible, verifiable way to land Raishin Maha Ken. Knocks down.

9 HITS
TOTAL DAMAGE: 49

Zenpou Tenshin linked into ↓ + MK → Raishin Maha Ken

Damaging option off of Zenpou Tenshin. Good if it ends the match, otherwise not recommended.

9 HITS
TOTAL DAMAGE: 67

Close stand strong linked into far LK → Raishin-Mahhaken

Verifiable, flexible way to land a Raishin-Mahhaken off a mid level attack. Knocks down.

28 HITS
TOTAL DAMAGE: 42

Activate Seiei-Enbu, UOH, Tourou Zan (LP), Tourou Zan (LP), Tourou Zan (LP), Tourou Zan (LP), Tourou Zan (LP), Tourou Zan (LP), ↓ + MK → Tourou Zan (HP), → HP follow up → HP follow up.

Basic Seiei-Enbu combo that starts high off of an overhead.

41 HITS TOTAL DAMAGE: 53

Activate Seiei-Enbu, ↓ + MK → Tourou Zan (HP) → 1 Tourou Zan (LP) follow up, link a ↓ + LK → Tourou Zan (HP) → 1 Tourou Zan (LP) follow up, link another ↓ + LK → Tourou Zan (HP) → one Tourou Zan (LP) follow up, link another ↓ + LK → Tourou Zan (HP) → 1 Tourou Zan (LP) follow up, then finally, link link a ↓ + LK → Tourou Zan (HP).

Variation of the repeated slash Seiei-Enbu combo that starts low.

STRATEGY

Toukuu Koushu

Yang works as a rush down character, but he also has more options on the ground than his twin brother because of EX Tourou Zan. EX Tourou Zan advances Yang forward quickly and beats out most pokes. Use it to get in on characters in footsie games. If you ever bait out a low poke that has bad recovery, EX Tourou Zan on reaction to counter attack and score a knockdown. EX Tourou Zan has good range, use it to hit any movement you see. Yang's LK is a good poke from mid range. It is fast and beats many moves, and you can cancel it into EX Tourou Zan to punish ground pokes.

From up close, keep pressure on opponents by mixing up Tourou Zans, overhead attacks, and throws. ↓ + MK → Tourou Zan (LP) is a good pressure tactic. It is generally safe when blocked, and moves Yang forward to stay close. If it hits, it's possible to finish all the hits of the Tourou Zan to knock down and start a wake up pattern. If opponents block the first hit, there are numerous options such as walk up throw, standing punch chain, ↓ + LK (x2), ↓ + MK → Tourou Zan again, or jump up and Raigeki Shuu. Yang's overhead is also a good move to keep advancing and pressuring because of its speed and ability to go over some low attacks.

Raigeki Shuu is Yang's main weapon to attack from the air and move in on opponents. The three variations of the Raigeki Shuu provide the ability to mix it up against a character that likes to anti-air or parry Raigeki Shuu. Raigeki Shuu (LK) is especially useful in this situation. Jumping and doing a Raigeki Shuu (LK) in front of opponents may bait out an anti-air or a jump attack that misses. Against a defensive opponent, whiffing a Raigeki Shuu can lead to an opening on the ground. Opponents may expect the Raigeki Shuu to hit and block accordingly. By the time they realize it isn't going to hit, Yang is usually already on the ground in prime position to throw or go into ↓ + LK (x2), or punch target chain combo. Learn the distances well for all of his Raigeki Shuus so you can gain position in front of opponents from anywhere on the screen.

After a blocked Raigeki Shuu, Yang usually has enough frame advantage to land and safely start his punch target chain combo, close stand MK and Raigeki Shuu again, or hesitate and Zenpou Tenshin. After the Zenpou Tenshin grab, Yang not only gets a combo and knockdown, but it also sets up various jumping cross up opportunities upon wake up. Another option is to Kaihou immediately to get back in close range. Against certain characters, especially Chun-Li and Makoto, it's possible to connect with close MK after a Zenpou Tenshin. Super jump cancel and jump towards opponents and hit with Yang's air target chain. Time it so only the first hit of the chain connects, causing the second hit to whiff. Yang lands before his opponent and has the ability to cross them up on the ground. If Yang hesitates and doesn't walk as far, he can uncross them up, creating an ambiguous situation. You can easily confuse an opponent's ability to block and often land another close MK to launch back into the air to repeat this sequence. Against an opponent who is quick enough to react to this cross up, grab with Zenpou Tenshin and start over from the beginning.

Yang does not need to rely on Raigeki Shuus to get in as much as Yun. Take advantage of his dive against characters that can't stop his rush, but don't take unnecessary risks against characters that can punish him for it. Yang has the ability to advance in a cautious and safe manner with EX Tarou Zan. However, if the Yang player is willing to take risks, and is in ↓ + MK range, cancel ↓ + MK in a Kaihou to teleport next to your opponent. If you are lucky you can surprise your opponent by teleporting behind them. But use this sparingly and with caution because Yang is highly vulnerable during Kaihou.

Yang has an interesting and effective anti air in his ↓ + MK. Yang crouches really low and extends his leg forward as he kicks. Many characters have a hard time hitting Yang from the air when he is in his ↓ + MK animation. Simply walk back a bit and ↓ + MK jump in attempts right as they hit the ground. Cancel into Tarou Zan to combo them back from where they came.

WAKEUP GAME

Yang can continue to pressure opponents on wake up just like he normally can when he is close by. But after a knockdown, Yang has enough time to start up a Kobokushi. Mix it up by doing the fake version, then going low and proceed to do Tourou Zans, or walk up and throw, or hit them with his overhead.

Yang can do a similar tricky Raigeki Shuu that Yun can mid screen on a waking up opponent after a knock down. Jump over their head just as they are getting up, and Raigeki Shuu (LK) on top of them. Wait until Yang is past their center point before using it. At this point, Yang is considered on the other side of them, so in order to Raigeki Shuu, you have to input the command for the Raigeki Shuu as if you were originally jumping from the other direction. What will happen is Yang will Raigeki Shuu straight down on top of them and hit them in the back of their body. It looks like Yang is going to land on the side of the direction he was jumping towards, but instead he will pop back out in front at the last moment and land back on the side from which he came. It all happens very fast and is very confusing for the waking up opponent to block correctly.

Yang is much better equipped to deal with being in a wake up situation than his brother. If Yang has Raishin-Mahhaken, that is free on wake up, use it at will. Tenshin-Senkyutai is more of a risk because your opponent can dash up and hit you on the way down if they blocked. A safer option is to wait it out and look for any opening to strike. Yang has a lot of fast normals he can rely on to get himself out of a wake up pressure situation. ↓ + LP and LK both come out in 4 frames, and can be canceled into EX Tourou Zan to get a pressuring opponent off of you. His punch target chain is also very helpful to get out of bad situations when up close.

SETUPS

Ranges setups for UOH → super

Against medium sized characters:

    (Zenpou Tenshin), UOH, ↓ + LK → Tenshin-Senkyutai
    (↓ + MP, ↓ + LK), UOH → Tenshin-Senkyutai

Against wide characters:

    (Zenpou Tenshin), UOH → Tenshin-Senkyutai

Against Oro:

    No setup is required. UOH → Tenshin-Senkyutai works at close
    distance on crouching Oro.

RESETS

Reset 1: It's possible to reset the damage of Seiei-Enbu every time a new combo starts. Use a cross up pattern that hits high and low at the same time, making it difficult to block. After a knock down (easiest to setup in the corner), activate Seiei-Enbu, jumping MK and Raigeki Shuu (HK) to cross up, land and ↓ + MP, ↓ + HK. After ↓ + HK knocks down, super jump forward and begin the sequence again with another Raigeki Shuu (HK). Repeat until super meter runs out. You can end the last sequence with a Zenpou Tenshin to get extra hits after Seiei-Enbu runs out.

PARRY SETUPS AND TACTICS

Yang is generally safe after a blocked Tourou Zan (LP). However, a lot of opponents will try to attack Yang before he can do another ↓ + MK → Tourou Zan. This is a great chance to try to parry their incoming attack low, and then counter with ↓ + MK → Tourou Zan.

Another blocked sequence that tends to bait low attacks is after a blocked ↓ + LK (x2). Try to parry your opponents attack down and counter with ↓ + MK → Tourou Zan.

GROUND CROSS UPS

Yang can cross up Twelve, Alex, Dudley, Necro, Hugo, Elena, Chun-Li and he can cross up Oro in any corner.

FAVORABLE MATCH UP: CHUN-LI

Yang can cause Chun-Li all sorts of problems. Yang can assault Chun-Li from the air with Raigeki Shuus. Chun-Li doesn't have any solid anti air moves, so Yang only needs to be careful of parries and an occasional stand roundhouse. Mix up the Raigeki Shuus, sometimes hitting, sometimes whiffing a Raigeki Shuu (LK) in front of her face. Yang should have no trouble getting in on Chun-Li.

He can also fight at a distance against Chun-Li, using her own fighting style against her. Try to stay just out side of her ↓ + MK range. If you see her poke, try to counter on reaction with EX Tourou Zan. Yang crouches pretty low down, so if you can bait out a standing HP, you can ↓ + MK → Tourou Zan underneath it. Yang's LK is another good poke to use when approaching Chun-Li. Cancel into EX Tourou Zan to be safe.

If Yang is able to launch Chun-Li into the corner with a close standing MK, he can juggle her with all 3 hits of his Tourou Zan (HP). For an even flashier combo, Connect with a Kobokushi in the corner, then proceed immediately juggle with Tourou Zan (HP) slash → LP slash follow up very quickly, wait, HP slash → LP slash follow up again, then juggle with one LP slash, then hit HP.

UNFAVORABLE MATCH UP: KEN

Yang doesn't have very many safe offensive options against Ken. Using Raigeki Shuu leaves Yang wide open to anti air Shouryukens, jumping attacks, and random EX Tatsumaki Senpuu Kyakus. Yang's ground game is not any safer. Ken already out distances Yang with his ↓ + MK. But it is Ken's super art 3 that shuts Yang down. Yang can not advance on Ken with his Tourou Zan because Ken can punish the recovery of the MP, HP, and EX versions. It is really hard for Yang to ever get close to Ken.

For Yang to win this match up, he has to rely his pokes more than ever. Be patient and try to counter the recovery of one of Ken's ↓ + MKs with an EX Tourou Zan. If you can score a knock down, Yang has a chance to get in close and mix it up with throws and ↓ + MK → short Tourou Zan. But once Yang gets pushed away again, it will be hard to get back in.

Yun

NORMAL MOVES

STANDING

HP is a decent poke with good range. From the right range, it beats low attacks clean.

MK travels upward and covers a significant area. Good against anticipated jumps at a close range. Hits most crouching characters and is usually safe if blocked.

Use HK to anticipate some whiffed attacks just outside of an opponent's max poke range. The slow start up can also bait an attack. If this move hits, it knocks down, but has terrible recovery.

LP		Jab
START UP	4	CS
+1	+1	+1	SC
		SA
GUARD	H/L
PARRY	H/L

LK		Short
START UP	3	
+2	+2	+2	SC
		SA
GUARD	H/L
PARRY	H/L

MP		Strong
START UP	5	CS
-3	-2	-1	SC
		SA
GUARD	H/L
PARRY	H

MK		Forward
START UP	9	CS
-4	-3	-2	SC
		SA
GUARD	H/L
PARRY	H

HP		Fierce
START UP	9	CS
-5	-3	-1	SC
		SA
GUARD	H/L
PARRY	H

HK		Roundhouse
START UP	14	CS
-5	D	D	SC
		SA
GUARD	H/L
PARRY	H

STANDING CLOSE

Close MP is Yun's best close mid-level attack. It has a decent amount of frame advantage after, allowing you to verify and combo after it with LK → Zeshou Houho (LP). If MP is blocked, walk up Zenpou Tenshin, ↓ + LK (x2) → Zeshou Houho (LP).

Close MK launches and is super jump cancelable. Can be used as anti-air or a safe mid-level attack on wake up. Whether it hits or not it's possible to cancel the attack after it connects into a super jump, allowing juggles after it, or if blocked, follow up the failed attack into a Raigeku Shuu pattern.

LP		Close Jab
START UP	3	
+4	+4	+4	SC
		SA
GUARD	H/L
PARRY	H/L

LK		Close Short
START UP	3	
+2	+2	+2	SC
		SA
GUARD	H/L
PARRY	H/L

MP		Close Strong
START UP	4	
+6	+7	+8	SC
		SA
GUARD	H/L
PARRY	H

MK		Close Forward
START UP	7	
-2	D	D	
		SA
GUARD	H/L
PARRY	H

HP		Close Fierce
START UP	6	CS
-2	-1	0	SC
		SA
GUARD	H/L
PARRY	H

HK		Close Roundhouse
START UP	14	CS
-5	D	D	SC
		SA
GUARD	H/L
PARRY	H

COSTUMES

LP · MP · HP · LK · MK · HK · LP + MK + HP

Start + LP · Start + MP · Start + HP · Start + LK · Start + MK · Start + HK

SPECIAL NORMALS

→ + HP		Dakai
START UP	17	-7

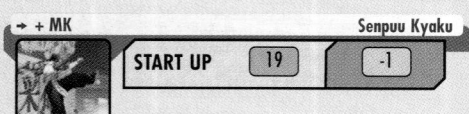

→ + MK		Senpuu Kyaku
START UP	19	-1

Command attack that moves Yun far forward with a Kobokushi. Very good range, slow start up. Has the added bonus of bieng able to beat jumping cross up attempts because of the hit box behind Yun. Very risky attack, heavy recovery, vulnerable to jumps. Use with caution.

Fairly good speed for an overhead with good range. Can be done from rather unexpected ranges.

While jumping, ↘ + K		Raigeku Shuu
START UP	6	—

Button strength controls the angle Yun dives at. Yun's game revolves around this attack. Use to get close quickly after a successful knock down. Can be used in an offensive manner to get close and stay on top of opponents. Depending on how close this move is done, and how high up the move is blocked, the Raigeki Shuu carries varrying frame advantages / disadvantages. It's important to learn to pick the right kick strength from different distances so that this move always hits late. Also, because of the varying angles, use Raigeku Shuu to set up high/low/throw guessing games by simply whiffing a Raigeku Shuu, landing, throwing.

CROUCHING

↓ + LK (x2) is one of Yun's only safe options to land super arts off of a low attack. Use it for set ups and guessing games, like ↓ + LK, command throw, or ↓ + LK, MP, HP, → + HP chain.

↓ + MK is Yun's only decent low poke. Although somewhat slow, ↓ + MK → EX Tetsuzankou or Sourai-Rengeki can be used to punish whiffs if done early.

↓ + LP			Low Jab
START UP	4		CS
+4	+4	+4	SC
			SA
GUARD			H/L
PARRY			H/L

↓ + LK			Low Short
START UP	4		CS
+2	+2	+2	SC
			SA
GUARD			L
PARRY			L

↓ + MP			Low Strong
START UP	4		
+5	+6	+7	SC
			SA
GUARD			H/L
PARRY			H/L

↓ + MK			Low Forward
START UP	6		
-1	0	+1	SC
			SA
GUARD			L
PARRY			L

↓ + HP			Low Fierce
START UP	5		CS
+1	+3	+5	SC
			SA
GUARD			H/L
PARRY			H

↓ + HK			Low Roundhouse
START UP	13		CS
-5	D	D	SC
			SA
GUARD			L
PARRY			L

JUMPING

↑ + LP			Jumping Jab
START UP	2		
—	—	—	SC
			SA
GUARD			H
PARRY			H

↑ + LK			Jumping Short
START UP	3		
—	—	—	SC
			SA
GUARD			H
PARRY			H

↑ + MP			Jumping Strong
START UP	3		
—	—	—	SC
			SA
GUARD			H
PARRY			H

↑ + MK			Jumping Forward
START UP	6		
—	—	—	SC
			SA
GUARD			H
PARRY			H

↑ + HP			Vertical Fierce
START UP	8		
—	—	—	SC
			SA
GUARD			H
PARRY			H

↑ + HK			Jumping Roundhouse
START UP	7		
—	—	—	SC
			SA
GUARD			H
PARRY			H

↗ / ↖ + HP			Jumping Fierce
START UP	5		
—	—	—	SC
			SA
GUARD			H
PARRY			H

THROWS

LP + LK	Hiza Geri

←/→ + LP + LK	Monkey Flip

SPECIAL MOVES

↓ ↘ → +P			Zeshou Houho

7	10	13	13
-11	-11	-11	-2

Button strength determines the speed and distance it travels. Very fast on start up, heavy recovery. Good for ground combos and some juggles. Use the LP version to punish some whiffed attacks.

↓ ↙ ← + P			Kobokushi

24	24	24	—
0	0	0	—

Pressing two punches instead of one fakes the attack, cancelling it just before the punch. Very slow start up. Extremely good priority because of its large hit box. Can be used from far away in anticipation to beat a jump in or an attack with range. Although risky, Kobokushi can be canceled into from LP → LK → MP target chain. Fake in the same situation to keep players from parrying the palm thrust, allowing you to mix up with a walk up throw or ↓ + LK (x2).

→ ↘ ↓ + P			Tetsuzankou

14	18	22	10
-1	-3	-5	-7

The MP, HP and EX versions of this attack are a juggle set up. Button strength determines how far the move travels. Can be used to travel under fireballs in a limited manner. The LP version is especially useful in combos with super arts. The EX version gets a HUGE speed and distance increase. Very good for punishing whiffed attacks from far away and going under projectiles. Safe from most everything but a handful of super arts if blocked.

→ ↓ ↘ + K			Nishou Kyaku

4	6	8	4
-25	-26	-28	-28

Yun's most damaging, comboable special. The normal version has some use in combos versus standing characters and some juggles. The EX version gets a speed increase and allows for juggles after it hits. Good as anti-air, and somewhat useful as a reversal, but whiffs versus some crouching attacks.

→ ↘ ↓ ↙ ← + K			Zenpou Tenshin

7	7	7	—
—	—	—	—

Command grab that switches sides with opponents and leaves them open for a combo. Incredibly useful as it can lead to major damage off of a throw. Has slightly more range than a normal throw.

SUPER ARTS

SUPER ART I

↓ ↘ → ↓ ↘ → +P   **You-Hou**

You-Hou is only three hits, but those hits do an incredible amount of damage. The last hit sets up a juggle state to continue a combo. A basic finish is Tetsuzankou (MP), Zeshou Houho (LP). You-Hou conveniently combos off both of Yun's LP, LK, MP and MP, HP, ← + HP target chains.

It's also possible to juggle an opponent with You-Hou after Yun's neutral throw before they hit the ground. You-Hou has a solid window of invulnerability at start up. Use it to blow through certain attacks, or as a solid anti-air. You-Hou is so strong that it has 100% combo possibilities on Akuma and on a morphing X.C.O.P.Y. Twelve.

You-Hou's main flaw is the length of the bar. It takes a fairly long time to build up enough super meter to use You-Hou. When Yun doesn't have any super meter, he cannot do any damaging combos. At those times he's not intimidating enough to discourage wake up moves and random attacks because of the low risk/reward ratio.

Recommended Super Art: Genei-Jin

Genei-Jin is so good that there is no need to ever pick You-Hou or Sourai-Rengeki. The damage potential is great and the super meter is short. Expect to refill super meter in no time after a Genei-Jin combo. Genei-Jin is deadly when comboed, and always scary whenever and wherever activated.

TARGET COMBOS

JUMPING LP → HP   [2] [—]

Decent two hit jumping attack versus players who anti-air parry often. Can be used in juggles.

↓ + MP → ↓ + HP   [3] [0]

Not so good, safe three hit chain. Does mediocre damage, but able to be parried high or low.

↓ + HK → HK   [14] [-11]

Two hit chain starting off a sweep. Decent damage. Second hit has terrible recovery however.

MP → HP → ← + HP   [5] [-4]

Three hit chain with a super art cancelable last hit. Third hit knocks down. Decent range and damage. Good way to land a You-Hou off of a mid-level hit. Verifiable through the first two hits. Slight frame advantage after the second hit.

CLOSE LP → LK → MP   [3] [-5]

Flexible three hit chain with a cancelable last hit. Yun's main opening for combos. The last hit of the chain carries a small disadvantage that is punishable with a fast super art or Ken's Shouryuken (LP). However the chain is perfectly verifiable off of the first two hits, so you never need to chain into the third hit if it's blocked.

SUPER ART II

↓ ↘ → ↓ ↘ → +P   **Sourai-Rengeki**

Sourai-Rengeki is the perfect super art for a rush down style Yun player. Sourai-Rengeki provides three medium sized super meters, which frees up the use of EX moves without worrying about super meter management. Sourai-Rengeki combos verifiably off of Yun's LP, LK, MP target chain, as well as ↓ + LK (x2). Use ↓ + MK → Sourai-Rengeki to punish whiffed pokes or throw attempts, as well as stopping dashes. Buffer super art motions into the move when out of range for an automatic super art if it hits something. When Sourai-Rengeki connects, it knocks down and sets up a cross up Raigeku Shuu opportunity on wake up. Constantly keep on the pressure with Sourai-Rengeki, landing super art after super art if super meter permits.

The only downside to this super art is that it is geared towards an aggressive style of play. Against certain characters, especially Ken, Yun is prone to get hit by random jumping attacks and anti-airs.

SUPER ART III

↓ ↘ → ↓ ↘ → +P   **Genei-Jin**

Genei-Jin is arguably the best super art in the game. It has the shortest super meter and has the highest damage potential of any super art. With Genei-Jin activated, any hit can lead to a juggle state and a big combo. There are many ways to combo into Genei-Jin. The most often used setup is to activate after canceling a LP, LK, MP target chain and linking Genei-Jin hits afterwards. When juggling opponents, after the Genei-Jin timer runs out it's possible to continue to juggle a few more times for added hits of extra damage. Yun also starts to build up super meter with those last few hits. An average full Genei-Jin combo can replenish around 15%-20% of the super meter.

COMBOS YOU NEED TO KNOW

2 HITS

TOTAL DAMAGE: 20

↓ + LK, ↓ + LK → Zeshou Houho (LP)

4 HITS

TOTAL DAMAGE: 25

Close LP → LK → MP → Zeshou Houho (HP)

5 HITS

TOTAL DAMAGE: 28

Close LP → LK → MP → Nishou Kyaku (HK)

3 HITS

TOTAL DAMAGE: 25

Close MP linked into a far LK → Zeshou Houho (LP)

3 HITS

TOTAL DAMAGE: 22

Zenpou Tenshin linked into ↓ + MP → Zeshou Houho (MP)

8 HITS

TOTAL DAMAGE: 36

Zenpou Tenshin linked into ↓ + MP → Sourai-Rengeki

6 HITS

TOTAL DAMAGE: 52

Zenpou Tenshin linked straight into You-Hou, when able, immediately juggle with Tetsuzan Kou (MP), when you recover juggle again with Zeshou Houho (MP)

6 HITS

TOTAL DAMAGE: 40

Close LP → LK → MP → EX Tetsuzan Kou, juggle with an early Zeshou Houho (LP)

5 HITS

TOTAL DAMAGE: 50

Anti-air ↓ + MP → EX Nishou Kyaku, juggle with a semi late Nishou Kyaku (HK).

3 HITS

TOTAL DAMAGE: 28

Close MK, super jump cancel, juggle with a semi late LP → HP chain.

10 HITS

TOTAL DAMAGE: 55

Close LP → LK → MP → Tetsuzan Kou (LP) → Sourai-Rengeki

8 HITS

TOTAL DAMAGE: 67

MP → HP → ← + HP → You-Hou, juggle with an early Tetsuzan Kou (MP), juggle again with a Zeshou Houho (MP)

7 HITS

TOTAL DAMAGE: 78

↓ + LK, ↓ + LK → You-Hou, juggle with an early Tetsuzan Kou (MP), juggle again with a Zeshou Houho (MP).

8 HITS

TOTAL DAMAGE: 50

↓ + LK, ↓ + LK → Sourai-Rengeki

15 HITS

TOTAL DAMAGE: 92

LP, LK, MP target chain → Genei-Jin, ↓ + MP → Dakai, hop kick, hop kick, HP, hop kick, hop kick, fierce → Tetsuzankou (MP), Tetsuzankou (MP), Dakai, Zeshou Houho (LP).

Basic corner Genei-Jin combo.

18 HITS

TOTAL DAMAGE: 75

LP, LK, MP target combo → Genei-Jin, ↓ + MP, HP → Tetsuzankou (HP), Zeshou Houho (MP), MP, hop kick, hop kick, Dakai, Zeshou Houho (MP), close MK, Dakai, Zeshou Houho (LP).

Basic full screen Genei-Jin combo. Has the option for a reset opportunity to achieve more meter after the combo, or to land a Zenpou Tenshin.

13 HITS

TOTAL DAMAGE: 94

↓ + MK → Genei-Jin, ↓ + LP → Dakai, hop kick, hop kick, Kobokushi, hop kick, hop kick, Kobokushi, Nishou Kyaku (HK), Tetsuzankou (LP), Dakai, Zeshou Houho (LP).

Very good damage off of a low attack in the corner. Cannot be parried high. Good for mix-ups against wake up parry attempts.

12 HITS

TOTAL DAMAGE: 104

CORNER ONLY

Close MK (super jump cancel) → Genei-Jin, Kobokushi, hop kick, MP, Kobokushi, hop kick, MP, Kobokushi, Nishou Kyaku (HK), Tetsuzankou (LP), Dakai, Zeshou Houho (LP).

MK must be super jump canceled to be able to super cancel into Genei-Jin. Most damaging basic combo that works on all characters in the corner. Stand forward is a mid attack that cannot be parried low. Good for mix-ups against wake up parry attempts.

STRATEGY

Gekihou Sui

Yun works well as a rush down character. His Raigeku Shuu is his main weapon to attack and move in on his opponent. The three variations of the Raigeku Shuu give Yun the ability to mix it up against a character that likes to anti-air or parry the Raigeku Shuus. The short Raigeku Shuu is especially useful in this situation. Jumping and doing a short Raigeku Shuu right in front of the opponent can bait out and anti-air or a jump attack that misses. Against a defensive opponent, whiffing a Raigeku Shuu out in front of them can lead to a free opening on the ground. They may expect the Raigeku Shuu to hit them, and block accordingly. By the time they realize it isn't going to hit, Yun is usually already on the ground in prime position to throw or start a target chain combo. Learn the distances well for all of his Raigeku Shuus so you can gain position in front of your opponent from anywhere on the screen.

Yun is very much a momentum character. When he starts Raigeku Shuuing and scores knockdown after knockdown, it is hard to get him off of you. But if he is constantly attacking, he is very open to be hit by a lot of random things, namely anti-airs, jump attacks, and parries. His Raigeku Shuu is his best attack, but also his most vulnerable move. Someone with quick reflexes can either parry, or immediately jump upon seeing a Raigeku Shuu. When this starts happening, it is very hard for Yun to continue attacking to keep his momentum going. Raigeku Shuuing from the air is Yun's best avenue of attack. His ground game is rather limited. Random Tetsuzankou (MP)s from time to time can help get Yun in, but they can be parry bait to someone who is looking out for them.

ADVANCED TACTIC: KARA KOBOKUSHI

With basic and easy to do Genei-Jin combos, Yun already has the highest damage potential in the game. But there is a technique he can use to further increase the damage of his Genei-Jin combos. Kobokushis are Yun's most damaging move. In most Genei-Jin combos it is ideal to do as many Kobokushis as possible. But Kobokushis move Yun away a significant distance to where he can't normally follow up with another Kobokushi without first doing a few moves that progress him forward a bit. Yun can get around this by kara canceling into a Kobokushi with moves that move him forward. By kara canceling, Yun can do repeated Kobokushi Genei-Jin combos for insane amounts of damage.

There are two methods to kara palm, and they are both equally hard. The first method is as follows: While in Genei-Jin, do a far MP and cancel it into LK and cancel into Kobokushi. You have to hesitate in canceling the MP in order to allow it to move Yun forward far enough. The LK needs to be cancelled immediately into a Kobokushi in order to give Yun enough time to juggle the opponent. A technique to help make this a little bit easier is to hold down strong. Then when you press short, hold that down to prevent yourself from negative edging a Zenpou Tenshin accidentally. Then as you go to press punch for the Kobokushi, first let go of strong to get the negative edge, then drum jab and fierce to help with the timing of it. If done properly, after the MP, you should only see the LK for a fraction of a second before the Kobokushi comes out.

The second method is: While in Genei-Jin, do a MP and cancel it into low roundhouse and cancel into Kobokushi. Like the previous method, make sure strong has enough time to move Yun forward before you cancel it. Try to hit roundhouse at the DB part of the Zenpou Tenshin input. Hold roundhouse to prevent any negative edge. Then drum all three punches to hit the Kobokushi at the right time. If done properly, you should hear Yun give his famous "Whoo" yell before being interrupted by the Kobokushi sound.

ADVANCED GENEI-JIN TACTICS

While Genei-Jin is absolutely lethal at point blank range, it also has the effect of allowing Yun the ability to get in on characters from a full screen away. Ken for example can counter all of Yun's rush-down tactics and keep him away from landing combos. When Yun activates Genei-Jin however, Yun has the advantage now because if Yun lands any hit, it can lead to a high damage juggle. All of Yun's pokes are super fast and have super priority during Genei-Jin. If Yun can't get in on a certain character, all he needs to do is activate Genei-Jin from a safe distance away, then he can start his offensive rush down for free. If the opponent is unwise and tries to attack, they will most likely get beat by Yun's high priority Genei-Jin moves. With Genei-Jin activated, Yun has the ability to control all the space around him for the few seconds it lasts. This should be sufficient to get close to the opponent and score some damage as well as a knock down. Then Yun can safely mount an offensive strike as the aggressor in a wake up situation. If Yun starts to get in trouble and loses his momentum, he can simply wait until he refills his meter and can activate Genei-Jin again before he tries to attack again.

Another way to score damage during Genei-Jin when the opponent is blocking is to go for lots of hop kick overhead attacks. Yun's overhead comes out fast and does good damage. You can "hide" the overhead by doing a MP first and canceling into the overhead. After you have trained them to look for overheads, you can start to mix it up with low attacks into either Dakai or a Kobokushi. If they anticipated wrong and blocked high thinking an overhead was coming, you will knock them over and initiate a Genei-Jin juggle combo opportunity.

WAKEUP GAME

When Yun knocks someone down, he has a huge bag of tricks he can rely on to continue to score damage and apply pressure. His Raigeku Shuu is his most useful weapon. In the corner, Yun can cross up nearly every character with a properly timed Raigeku Shuu on wake up. If the cross up hits, follow up with a combo. If they block, Yun has many options. Since Yun is in the corner at this point, he can Zenpou Tenshin and flip over them, and combo them back into the corner and repeat the whole process. Yun can also tick into Zenpou Tenshin to mix it up. Stand jab, ↓ + LK, and ↓ + MK are good tick throw setups. Another option is to immediately do close stand forward after a blocked Raigeku Shuu. You can super jump cancel the MK and Raigeku Shuu them again.

When Yun is the one knocked down, he has very few options to get a character off of him. His only decent move in this situation is an EX Nishou Kyaku. But it is very vulnerable if it misses. It will tend to miss if the opponent is crouching. A better option is to wait it out and block and look for a safe opportunity to attack. If you see your opponent stand up to either throw or gain position, immediately ↓ + LK → Sesshou Hohou. Other than these options, Yun isn't the best character at dealing with being cornered.

SETUPS

Ranges setups for UOH → super

Against medium sized characters:
(Zenpou Tenshin), UOH, ↓ + MK → Sourai-Rengeki

Against wide characters:
(Zenpou Tenshin), UOH, ↓ + MP → Sourai-Rengeki

Against Oro:
No setup is required. UOH → You-Hou or Sourai-Rengeki works at close distance on crouching Oro. Yun can even do UOH → jab, short, strong target chain → Genei-Jin on crouching Oro.

RESETS

Reset 1: If Yun is able to catch an air borne opponent with a jumping MK, and lands before they do, he can activate Genei-Jin before they land and Zeshou Houho to juggle them before they hit the ground. They are now in a juggle state for Yun to continue comboing them. The opponent can parry the Zesshou if they anticipate it, but it is 3 hits and comes out fast, so it is difficult to see and do.

Reset 2: During a mid to full screen Genei-Jin combo, Yun can reset the juggle, causing the opponent to flip back and recover. Yun can then hit them before they land on the ground to start a new Genei-Jin juggle state. You will know if you are successful if the combo counter restarts back at 0 hits. The reason you would want to reset the combo is because scaling of the super meter is also reset. When Genei-Jin ends, Yun can land a few extra normal juggle hits before the opponent hits the ground. Those hits give Yun back some of his super meter. The amount of meter he gets per hit is dependant on how many total hits the combo was. Refilling the super meter has hit scaling similar to damage scaling. But in a reset combo, all of this is reset as well. So each hit after the reset gives back a ton of meter because the combo is starting over and is only a few hits at that point.

PARRY SETUPS AND TACTICS

If you activate Genei-Jin while the opponent is blocking, do some overheads and then hesitate. Make it look like there is an opening in your pressure tactics to bait them to hit you. Most opponents will do a low move to try to hit Yun during or after an overhead. This is when you down parry. If you stuck out a low poke, you can then ↓ + MK → Dakai to launch them into the corner and initiate a juggle combo. If they do nothing and continue to block, simply continue on with your barrage of Genei-Jin attacks.

GROUND CROSS UPS

Yun can cross up Twelve, Alex, Dudley, Necro, Hugo, Elena, Chun-Li, and Oro in any corner.

Yun can cross up Ibuki, Yun, and Yang only in his own corner.

FAVORABLE MATCH UP: CHUN-LI

Chun-Li controls the ground, but Yun doesn't primarily attack from the ground. Yun can successfully attack Chun-Li from the air because she doesn't have any solid anti-air moves. Use Raigeku Shuu on her. Be careful about Raigeku Shuu being parried, but whiffed Raigeku Shuu (LK) can overcome this. Even if Chun-Li is successfully stopping Raigeku Shuu rushes, Yun always has the option to run away and build super meter.

Avoid having Raigeku Shuus parried or countered to be able to handle Chun-Li without many problems. One thing to be careful of is Chun-Li's low jab. It's the quickest normal move in the game and beatd out many Yun's attacks in Genei-Jin. Option down parry during blocked Genei-Jin sequences to neutralize this threat and land big combos on Chun-Li.

UNFAVORABLE MATCH UP: KEN

Ken is the reason Yun needs the run-away strategy in his bag of tricks. Yun has a hard time attacking Ken without Genei-Jin activated. Ken's Shouryuken (HP) covers plenty of ground, perfect for punishing whiffed Raigeku Shuu (LK). Yun must be careful every time he jumps. Ken's jumping HP and HK consistently stop Yun from jumping in and Raigeku Shuu attempts. Also, since Yun spends so much time in the air, he is at risk for random jump EX hurricane kicks. Getting in on the ground is not any easier. Ken keeps Yun away with low MK.

For Yun to win this match, he must run away. Only attack when it is safe, meaning with Genei-Jin activated. Keeping Ken away long enough to build up super meter is no easy task. Play carefully with patience, waiting for the right times to attack.

GILL

NORMAL MOVES
STANDING

LP — Jab
START UP	2		CS
+5	+5	+5	SC
			SA
GUARD		H/L	
PARRY		H/L	

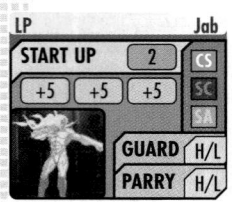

LK — Short
START UP	3		CS
+3	+3	+3	SC
			SA
GUARD		H/L	
PARRY		H/L	

MP — Strong
START UP	4		
0	+1	+2	SC
			SA
GUARD		H/L	
PARRY		H/L	

MK — Forward
START UP	6		CS
-4	-3	-3	SC
			SA
GUARD		H/L	
PARRY		H	

HP — Fierce
START UP	10		CS
-5	-3	-1	SC
			SA
GUARD		H/L	
PARRY		H/L	

HK — Roundhouse
START UP	16		CS
-10	-8	-6	SC
			SA
GUARD		H	
PARRY		H	

COSTUMES

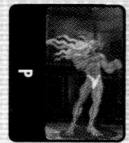

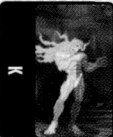

SPECIAL NORMALS

← + MP — Palm Upper
START UP	6	-5

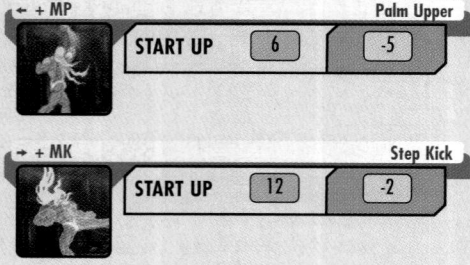

→ + MK — Step Kick
START UP	12	-2

SPECIAL MOVES

CROUCHING

↓ + LP — Low Jab

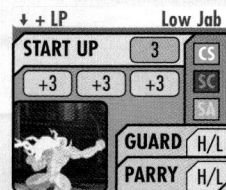

START UP	3		CS
+3	+3	+3	SC
			SA
GUARD	H/L		
PARRY	H/L		

↓ + LK — Low Short

START UP	3		CS
+4	+4	+4	SC
			SA
GUARD	L		
PARRY	L		

↓ + MP — Low Strong

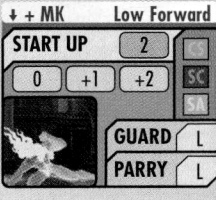

START UP	6		CS
-1	0	+1	SC
			SA
GUARD	H/L		
PARRY	H/L		

↓ + MK — Low Forward

START UP	2		CS
0	+1	+2	SC
			SA
GUARD	L		
PARRY	L		

↓ + HP — Low Fierce

START UP	5		CS
-3	D	D	SC
			SA
GUARD	H/L		
PARRY	H/L		

↓ + HK — Low Fierce

START UP	7		CS
-6	D	D	SC
			SA
GUARD	L		
PARRY	L		

JUMPING

↑ + LP — Jumping Jab

START UP	4		CS
—	—	—	SC
			SA
GUARD	H		
PARRY	H		

↑ + LK — Jumping Short

START UP	3		CS
—	—	—	SC
			SA
GUARD	H		
PARRY	H		

↑ + MP — Jumping Strong

START UP	5		CS
—	—	—	SC
			SA
GUARD	H		
PARRY	H		

↑ + MK — Jumping Forward

START UP	5		CS
—	—	—	SC
			SA
GUARD	H		
PARRY	H		

↑ + HP — Jumping Fierce

START UP	6		CS
—	—	—	SC
			SA
GUARD	H		
PARRY	H		

↑ + HK Jumping Roundhouse

START UP	9		CS
—	—	—	SC
			SA
GUARD	H		
PARRY	H		

THROWS

LP + LK — Impact Claw

←/→ + LP + LK — Guilty Bomb

SPECIAL MOVES

(facing right) ↓ ↘ → + P — Pyro-kinesis

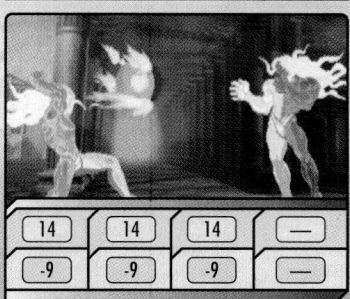

14	14	14	—
-9	-9	-9	—

A 2 hit projectile with fire elemental properties launches from Gill's fire side. Button strength used determines the angle of the projectile.

(facing left) ↓ ↘ → + P — Cryo-kinesis

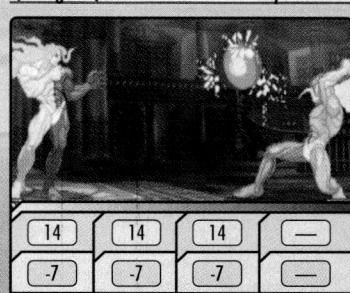

14	14	14	—
-7	-7	-7	—

A 2 hit projectile with ice elemental properties launches from Gill's ice side. Button strength used determines the angle of the projectile.

→ ↓ ↘ + P — Cyber Lariat

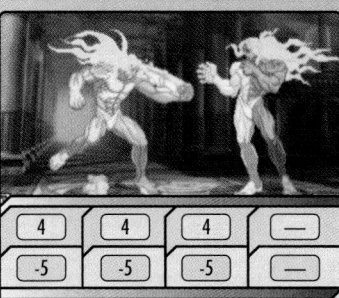

4	4	4	—
-5	-5	-5	—

(Fire elemental from left side. Ice elemental from right side.)

Cyber Lariat hits at two different points in the move, which cause different effects. Hitting early in the move knocks down. Hitting later in the move knocks down opponents in the air and causes a juggle state. It can also hit for twice if positioned right. Cyber Lariat can be done multiple times to continue to juggle an airborne opponent.

↓ ↙ ← + P — Psycho Headbutt

9	9	9	—
-2	-2	-2	—

Gill knocks opponents into the air with a flying heat-butt and puts them in a juggle state. Can be used as anti-air or to continue juggle combos.

→ ↘ ↓ ↙ ← + K — Moonsault Knee Drop

40	40	40	—
-19	-19	-19	—

Gill jumps and tracks opponents to land on them with a devastating knee drop.

GILL

SUPER ARTS

SUPER ART AVAILABILITY

Gill never needs to choose a super art, he always has access to all three.

SUPER ART

↓ ↘ → ↓ ↘ → + P	Meteor Strike

Gill summons a meteor shower from the heavens. If any meteor hits, it initiates a juggle state and allows the meteors that follow to combo for big damage. Gill is vulnerable during this super art.

7	-21

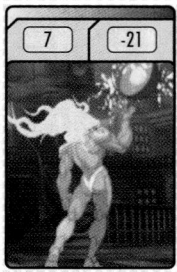

SUPER ART

↓ ↘ → ↓ ↘ → + K	Seraphic Wing

The ultimate super art because Gill is completely invulnerable. Seraphic Wing cannot be parried. It does massive damage on a hit, and even chip damage consumes around 25% of a lifebar.

50	-60

SUPER ART MAX

Super meter at MAX when Gill is KO'd	Resurrection

If Gill loses all of his lifebar, but has a full super meter, his Resurrection super art activates automatically to revive Gill and restore his health. It takes a few seconds for Gill to fully regain all of his health. He can be hit out of Resurrection before he gains all of his health back. However, he pushes opponents away with an invisible force that helps protect him while he recovers. After Resurrection, Gill cannot gain any more super meter for the rest of the round.

—	—

TARGET COMBOS

LP → MP	2
Whiffs against crouching characters. No real uses.	0

↓ + LK → ↓ + MK	3
Fast and flexible. You can tag on another ↓ + LK at the beginning for more damage. Very safe too.	0

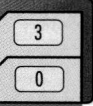

↓ + LK → PALM UPPER	3
Does not combo. Second hit is cancelable. Ok for guessing games: mix up ↓ + LK, walk up throw and ↓ + LK → Palm Upper → Fierce Cyber Lariat.	-5

COMBOS YOU NEED TO KNOW

3 HITS

↓ + LK, ↓ + LK → ↓ + MK

Easy low combo. Terrible damage but it's flexible and very safe.

6 HITS

↓ + HP (2 hits), juggle with an early Psycho Headbutt (HP), when Gill lands, juggle with another ↓ + HP (1 hit), juggle again with a late Cyber Lariat (HP)

Basic extended juggle. Can be used as anti-air or for punishment situations. Knocks down.

16-18 HITS

MIDSCREEN ONLY

Jump in with a semi early HK, land, link ↓ + HP (2 hits), immediately juggle with a Psycho Headbutt (HP), juggle again with an early HP; when Gill recovers, immediately juggle with an early Meteor Strike; when Gill recovers, juggle with ↓ + HP (2 hits), juggle again with a Psycho Headbutt (LP), then finally juggle with Psycho Lariat (HP).

Massive damage. Usually dizzies most characters. The Meteor Strike juggles rather inconsistently. Knocks down.

8 HITS

CORNER ONLY

Jump in with a semi early HK, land and link ↓ + HP (2 hits), juggle immediately with an early HP, juggle again with an immediate Cyber Lariat (LP); when Gill recovers, juggle with HP, then walk up and juggle again with a third HP

Instant dizzy combo. Very difficult against some characters like the shotos. The Cyber Lariat also misses one hit on some characters, though it doesn't affect the combo much. Knocks down.

STRATEGY

Elbow

In the age of the Gods, Gill rules over all. In *Street Fighter III: 3rd Strike*, Gill rules over the 19 normal characters as their supreme end boss. Gill is much more powerful than the normal cast of characters. He was not selectable in the arcade, however he is available as a secret character on the console version as a bonus feature. With his high priority attacks, huge damage off of ludicrous juggle combos, and 3 devastating super arts, most characters do not stand a chance against him.

Gill's body is split down the center to separate his two elemental abilities. His right side harnesses the element of fire. His left side harnesses the element of ice. Depending on which direction Gill is facing, many of his normal and special attacks will change based on what part of his body the move originates from. The move will either have the properties of fire, or ice.

Androids Shed No Tears.

Tokyo 2049. Three lifelike humanoid biological weapons enter into a continually shifting underground labyrinth to halt a major disaster affecting space and time. Utilizing their advanced weapons training, these three futuristic rebels must battle hordes of underground mutants. The battle for the future has begun.

PlayStation 2

CAPCOM
capcom.com

BRADYGAMES

TENTH ANNIVERSARY

BradyGAMES published its first strategy guide in November of 1993, and every year since then, we've made great efforts to give you the best guides possible. Now celebrating our 10th anniversary, we'd like to take this opportunity to say a few things and extend a special invitation to you—our readers.

First of all, THANK YOU! Whether you're a long-time customer, or this is your first BradyGAMES guide, we appreciate your support. We hope that our guides have enhanced your overall experience when playing games. These days, completing a game isn't just about how quickly you finish. It's about uncovering absolutely everything a game has to offer: side quests, mini-games, secret characters, and multiple endings just to name a few. That's what the **TAKE YOUR GAME FURTHER**® banner at the top of our guides is all about.

Many games deserve more than just a standard strategy guide, and we recognize that. Our guides are produced with the highest quality standards and are tailored specifically for the games they cover. With the introduction of our Signature Series and Limited Edition guides, we raised the bar even higher.

Now for the "invitation" part. Although we constantly challenge ourselves to improve our guides, we'd like your help too. You're formally invited to tell us what you think about our guides. Like something we do? Let us know. Think something we've done is totally lame? *Please* let us know. We want your feedback no matter if it's good, bad, or just plain ugly. You can write or e-mail us at the addresses below, and we *will* read what you send. Your opinions are important to us, and may influence the direction for our guides in the future.

Write to:
BradyGAMES
800 E. 96th Street, 3rd Floor
Indianapolis, IN 46240

Send e-mail to:
feedback@bradygames.com

For now, we hope you enjoy this guide. Thanks again for choosing BradyGAMES.

STREET FIGHTER™
ANNIVERSARY COLLECTION
OFFICIAL FIGHTER'S GUIDE

©2005 Pearson Education

BradyGAMES® is a registered trademark of Pearson Education, Inc.

BradyGAMES® Publishing

An Imprint of Pearson Education
800 East 96th Street, Third Floor
Indianapolis, Indiana 46240

ISBN: 0-7440-0394-6

LIBRARY OF CONGRESS CATALOG NO.: 20049374

Printing Code: The rightmost double-digit number is the year of the book's printing; the rightmost single-digit number is the number of the book's printing. For example, 05-1 shows that the first printing of the book occurred in 2005.

08   07   06   05   4   3   2   1

Manufactured in the United States of America.

BRADYGAMES STAFF

PUBLISHER
David Waybright

EDITOR-IN-CHIEF
H. Leigh Davis

MARKETING MANAGER
Janet Eshenour

CREATIVE DIRECTOR
Robin Lasek

LICENSING MANAGER
Mike Degler

ASSISTANT MARKETING MANAGER
Susie Nieman

TEAM COORDINATOR
Stacey Beheler

CREDITS

TITLE MANAGER
Tim Cox

DEVELOPMENT EDITOR
Chris Hausermann

SCREENSHOT EDITOR
Michael Owen

BOOK DESIGNER
Dan Caparo

PRODUCTION DESIGNERS
Bob Klunder
Tracy Wehmeyer

HYPER STREET FIGHTER™ II: THE ANNIVERSARY EDITION

JOEY CUELLAR - STRATEGY AND COMBOS
Thanks to:

Alex Valle – Ryu/Ken, Mike Watson – Balrog/Ken, David Sirlin – Dhalsim/M. Bison/Vega, Chris Li – E. Honda/ DeeJay/Sagat, Mike Creque – Cammy/Fei Long, Derek Daniels – Zangief/Balrog, Seth Killian – Chun Li/Blanka, David Wright – T. Hawk, Artavan Mkhikian – Guile, and John Choi – Sagat.

Special thanks to Alex Valle, John Choi, Mike Watson, Seth Killian, Derek Daniels, Tom Cannon, Tony Cannon, David Sirlin for being members of team Old School, and for keeping the Street Fighter community alive. Thanks to Shoryuken.com for being the best Street Fighter website out there and for letting me be a part of it. Finally, thanks to Southern Hills Golfland (now defunct) for creating the best competition in the country.

CHRIS HAUSERMANN - MOVE LISTS AND SCREENSHOTS
I want to thank my lovely wife Sara for all of her help and support. Marco Amitrano, Rob Ocampo, Bob Weber, and all of my friends who played videogames with me back in the day. Dave Blue for his music influences and his competitive nature. My Japanese friends Toshi Kosuge, Mr. Miura, Mr. Wada, and Shinya Kuze for their friendship and countless rounds of fighting games. Special thanks to Taki, and everyone at Capcom for their continued support.

STREET FIGHTER™ III 3RD STRIKE: FIGHT FOR THE FUTURE

ADAM DEATS - STRATEGY AND COMBOS
I want to thank Forrest Glen Walker for his help with the glossary and other technical matters. I also want to thank the Texas Street Fighter community for keeping competition alive for as long as they have.

MARK ROGOYSKI - STRATEGY AND COMBOS
I want to thank Hsien Chang for inspiring me to always improve my game, and to all the Austin 3rd Strike players for keeping the competitive spirit alive.

KEN SCHMIDT - MOVE LISTS AND SCREENSHOTS
I want to thank the little arcade next to the pizza place near Indiana University where I first encountered Street Fighter II and its amazing ability to consume quarters. Thanks to my brother, Rick, for helping me feed quarters into that machine and keeping my interest in Street Fighter II and its sequels for many years.